DATE DUE

JAN 2 7 1992	APR 0 1 1997
FEB 4 1992	MAR 3 0 1998
FEB 1 4 1992	MAR 1 3 2002
MAR 5 1992	FEB 1 1 2003
MAR 2 7 1992	
FEB 1 5 1993	
MAR 0 2 1993	
MAR 1 7 1993	
NOV - 7 1993	
NOV 2 6 1993	
JAN 2 7 1994	
FEB 1 5 1994	
MAR 2 9 1994	
MAR 2 4 1995	
APR 1 3 1995	
OCT 2 4 1996	
DEC - 7 1996	
FEB 2 6 1997	

Signals of War

by Lawrence Freedman

Atlas of Global Strategy

The Evolution of Nuclear Strategy

Britain and Nuclear Weapons

US Intelligence and the Soviet Strategic Threat

The Price of Peace:
Living with the Nuclear Dilemma

Britain and the Falklands War

by Virginia Gamba-Stonehouse

El Peon de la Reina

Estrategia, Intervencion y Crisis

The Falklands/Malvinas War:
A Model for North–South Crisis Prevention

Strategy in the Southern Oceans: A South American View

SIGNALS OF WAR

The Falklands Conflict of 1982

Lawrence Freedman and
Virginia Gamba-Stonehouse

PRINCETON UNIVERSITY PRESS

PRINCETON, NEW JERSEY

Library of Congress Cataloging-in-Publication Data
Freedman, Lawrence.
Signals of war : the Falklands conflict of 1982 / Lawrence Freedman
and Virginia Gamba-Stonehouse.
p.   cm.
Includes bibliographical references and index.
ISBN 0-691-07890-4 : ISBN 0-691-02344-1 (pbk.)
1. Falkland Islands War, 1982.   2. Argentina—Foreign relations—
Great Britain.   3. Great Britain—Foreign relations—
Argentina.   4. Mediation, International.   I. Gamba-Stonehouse,
Virginia, 1954–   .   II. Title.
F3031.5.F75   1991   997'.11—dc20   90-19610

Printed in the United States of America
by Princeton University Press,
Princeton, New Jersey

10   9   8   7   6   5   4   3   2   1

10   9   8   7   6   5   4   3   2   1
(Pbk.)

First published in Great Britain by Faber and Faber Limited

Maps reprinted with permission of Capricorn Design

For
Myra Freedman
and
Beatriz Gamba

CONTENTS

ACKNOWLEDGEMENTS

The authors wish to thank the Rockefeller Foundation for a grant which made their collaboration possible. Many individuals have helped us during the course of this study. As most would prefer not to be named, we offer them collectively our thanks. Special mention must be made of the expert advice from our colleague, Julian Thompson, the firm but patient guidance from our editor, Will Sulkin, as well as the tolerance and support of our families.

NOTE

Translations from Argentine material are by Virginia Gamba-Stonehouse. Except where the contents dictate otherwise we have used the English designations for place names. The Argentine names for some of the key locations are:

The Falkland Islands	Las Malvinas
East Falkland	Isla Soledad
West Falkland	Isla Gran Malvina
South Georgia	Georgias del Sur
South Sandwich Islands	Sandwich del Sur
Stanley	Puerto Argentino
Pebble Island	Isla Borbon
Fitzroy	Bahia Agradable

Time differences are a considerable problem in this analysis. The table below should help:

Greenwich Mean Time:	o
British Summer Time:	+1
Buenos Aires/Falklands:	−3
Washington DC	−4
Lima	−5

A further hour's time difference was added between Buenos Aires/Falklands and Greenwich during June because of summer time.

British forces were operating on Greenwich Mean Time throughout. There were time variations during the course of the conflict in the Rio Grande and Stanley areas but these do not affect the narrative.

DRAMATIS PERSONAE

Argentina

Allara, Rear Admiral Gualter: Commander of the Surface Fleet. From April 1982, Commander, Naval Forces, South Atlantic Theatre of Operations.

Anaya, Admiral Jorge: Commander-in-Chief of the Navy and member of the Junta.

Astiz, Alfredo: Marine Lieutenant in charge of landing party on South Georgia.

Bicain, Horacio: Captain of the *Santa Fé*.

Blanco, Ambassador Carlos Lucas: Director of the Malvinas and Antarctica Department at the Ministry of Foreign Affairs.

Büsser, Rear Admiral Carlos: Commander of the Marine Infantry.

Camilión, Dr Oscar: Foreign Minister in 1981.

Costa Mendez, Dr Nicanor: Foreign Minister.

Daher, General Américo: Commander 9th Infantry Brigade and Chief of Staff, Malvinas Joint Command.

Davidoff, Constantino: scrap-metal merchant.

Gaffoglio, Captain Adolfo: Naval representative in the Falkland Islands.

Galtieri, General Leopoldo: Commander-in-Chief of the Army and President.

García, General Osvaldo: Commander, Malvinas Theatre of Operations.

García Boll, Rear Admiral Carlos: Commander of Naval Aviation.

Girling, Rear Admiral Eduardo Morris: Chief of Naval Intelligence.

Hussey, Captain Barry Melbourne: naval officer, senior administrator in Stanley.

Iglesias, General Hector: Secretary-General of the Presidency and member of the Malvinas Working Group.

Jofre, General Oscar: Commander 10th Infantry Brigade, and of Puerto Argentino Group of Forces.

Lami Dozo, General Basilio: Commander-in-Chief of the Air Force and member of the Junta.

Lombardo, Vice-Admiral Juan José: Commander of Naval Operations. From April 1982, Commander South Atlantic Theatre of Operations.

Marchessi, Adrian: Argentine Bank employee.

Menendez, Brigadier General Mario Benjamín: Chief of Operations in the General Staff (to April 1982), Governor of the Malvinas (April–June 1982).

Miret, Brigadier: Head of the Planning Commission and member of the Malvinas Working Group.

Molteni, Atilio: Minister at Argentine Embassy in London.

Moya, Rear Admiral Roberto: Head of the Military Household and member of Malvinas Working Group.

Otero, Rear Admiral Edgardo: Chief of Naval Transport.

Padilla, Rear Admiral Alberto: Chief of Staff, South Atlantic Theatre of Operations.

Parada, General Omar: Commander 3rd Infantry Brigade, and of the Malvinas Group of Forces.

Piaggi, Lt-Col. I. A.: Army Commander, Darwin and Goose Green.

Pedrozo, Air Vice-Commodore Wilson, senior officer at Goose Green.

Pena, Oscar: Under Secretary, Ministry of Foreign Affairs.

Plessl, Brigadier General Sigfrido: Working Party on Intervention.

Rodriguez, Rear Admiral Angel: Lombardo's Chief of Staff.

Rouco, Jesús Iglesias : journalist on Argentine paper, *La Prensa*.

Roca, Eduardo: Ambassador to the United Nations.

Ros, Enrique: Deputy Minister, Ministry of Foreign Affairs.

Rozas, Ortiz de: Ambassador to Britain.

Ruiz, General Julio: Commander, Land Forces, South Atlantic Theatre of Operations.

Suarez del Cerro, Vice-Admiral Carlos: Chairman of the Joint Chiefs of Staff.

Trombetta, César: Captain of the *Almirante Irizar*.

Vigo, Vice-Admiral Alberto: Chief of Naval Staff.

Weber, Brigadier A.C.: Commander, Air Forces, South Atlantic Theatre of Operations.

Falkland Islands

Blake, Anthony: Member of the Falkland Islands' Legislative Council.

Cheek, Gerald: Member of the Falkland Islands' Legislative Council.

Dramatis Personae

Hunt, Sir Rex: Governor of the Falkland Islands.

France

Cheysson, Claude: Foreign Minister.

Hernu, Charles: Defence Minister.

Mitterrand, François: President.

South Georgia

Martin, Steve: Base Commander and Magistrate.

Peru

Belaunde Terry, Fernando: President.

Stella, Dr Arias: Foreign Minister.

Ulloa, Manuel: Prime Minister.

United Kingdom

Acland, Sir Antony: Permanent Under Secretary at the Foreign and Commonwealth Office (from April 1982).

Archer, Geoffrey: ITN's Defence Correspondent.

Armstrong, Sir Robert: Secretary to the Cabinet.

Atkins, Sir Humphrey: Lord Privy Seal (to April 1982).

Barker, Nicholas: Captain of HMS *Endurance*.

Bell, Robert: Captain, Royal Marines.

Dramatis Personae

Biffen, John: Secretary of State for Trade.

Bramall, General Sir Edwin: Chief of the General Staff.

Brittan, Leon: Chief Secretary to the Treasury.

Buxton, Lord: Peer.

Carrington, Lord (Peter): Foreign Secretary (until April 1982).

Clapp, Commodore Michael: Commander, Amphibious Warfare.

Cooper, Sir Frank: Permanent Under Secretary, Ministry of Defence.

Curtiss, Air Marshal Sir John: Air Deputy to Commander-in-Chief.

Fearn, Robin: Head of the South American Department in the Foreign Office.

Fieldhouse, Admiral Sir John: Commander-in-Chief, Fleet; Commander-in-Chief, Operation Corporate.

Foot, Michael: Leader of the Opposition.

Gurdon, Brigadier Adam: Chairman, Current Intelligence Group on Latin America in Joint Intelligence Organization.

Havers, Sir Michael: Attorney General.

Healey, Denis: Shadow Foreign Secretary.

Heath, Edward: Former Prime Minister.

Heathcote, Mark: Official, British Embassy in Buenos Aires.

Henderson, Sir Nicholas: Ambassador in Washington.

Herbert, Admiral Peter: Deputy to the Commander-in-Chief for Submarine Operations.

Ingham, Bernard: Prime Minister's Press Secretary.

Jones, Colonel 'H': Commander, 2 PARA.

Keeble, Major Chris: Second in Command, 2 PARA.

Dramatis Personae

Leach, Admiral Sir Henry: First Sea Lord.

Lewin, Admiral Sir Terence: Chief of Defence Staff.

Luce, Richard: Junior Foreign Office Minister (until April 1982).

Mills, Lt Keith: Commander of South Georgia garrison (April 1982).

Moore, General Jeremy: Land Deputy to Commander-in-Chief.

Norman, Major Mike: Commander, Falkland Islands garrison (April 1982).

Nott, John: Secretary of State for Defence.

O'Neill, Robin: Head of the Joint Intelligence Organization's Assessment Staff.

Palliser, Sir Michael: Permanent Under Secretary at the Foreign and Commonwealth Office (to April 1982); Adviser to War Cabinet (after April 1982).

Parkinson, Cecil: Paymaster-General and Chairman of the Conservative Party.

Parsons, Sir Anthony: Ambassador to the United Nations.

Pym, Francis: Secretary of State for the Foreign and Commonwealth Office (from April 1982).

Ridley, Nicholas: Junior Foreign Office Minister (until 1981).

Rose, Lt Colonel Michael: SAS.

Southby-Tailyour, Major Ewen: 3 Brigade.

Thatcher, Margaret: Prime Minister.

Thompson, Brigadier Julian: Commander, 3 Brigade.

Thomson, Sir John, Ambassador to the United Nations.

Ure, John: Under Secretary of State for the South American Department, Foreign Office.

Dramatis Personae

Wallace, Charles: Ambassador to Lima.

Whitelaw, William: Deputy Prime Minister and Lord President of the Council.

Williams, Sir Anthony: Ambassador to Buenos Aires.

Wilson, Brigadier Anthony: Commander, 5 Brigade.

Woodward, Admiral Sir John: Flag Officer First Flotilla.

Wreford Brown, Christopher: Captain of HMS *Conqueror*.

Wright, Patrick: Deputy Under Secretary of State in the Foreign and Commonwealth Office.

Young, Brian: Captain of HMS *Antrim*.

United Nations

Ahmed, Rafee: Under Secretary-General (Pakistan).

Cordovez, Diego: Under Secretary-General (Ecuador).

Perez de Cuellar, Xavier: Secretary-General (Peru).

Urquhart, Brian: Under Secretary-General (Britain).

United States

Biden, Joseph: Senator.

Bush, George: Vice-President.

Clark, William: President's National Security Adviser.

Eagleburger, Lawrence: Under Secretary of State for European Affairs.

Enders, Thomas: Under Secretary of State for Latin American Affairs.

Dramatis Personae

Helms, Jesse: Senator.

Haig, General Alexander: Secretary of State.

Inman, Robert: Deputy Director, Central Intelligence Agency.

Kirkpatrick, Jeane: Ambassador to the United Nations.

Kissinger, Dr Henry: Former Secretary of State.

Lichenstein, Charles: second in command at the UN delegation.

Moynihan, Daniel: Senator.

Reagan, Ronald: President.

Schlaudeman, Harold: Ambassador to Buenos Aires.

Stoessel, Walter: Deputy Secretary of State.

Streator, Edward: Minister at London Embassy.

Walters, General Vernon: special envoy.

Weinberger, Caspar: Secretary of Defence.

MAPS

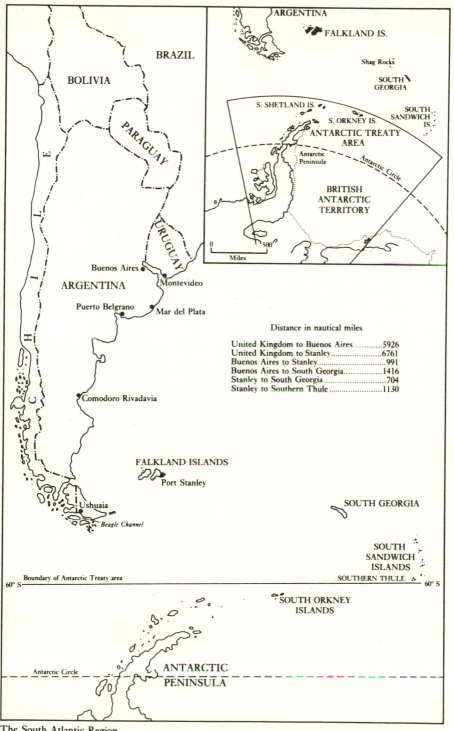

The South Atlantic Region

Distance in nautical miles
United Kingdom to Buenos Aires............5926
United Kingdom to Stanley.......................6761
Buenos Aires to Stanley.............................991
Buenos Aires to South Georgia................1416
Stanley to South Georgia 704
Stanley to Southern Thule 1130

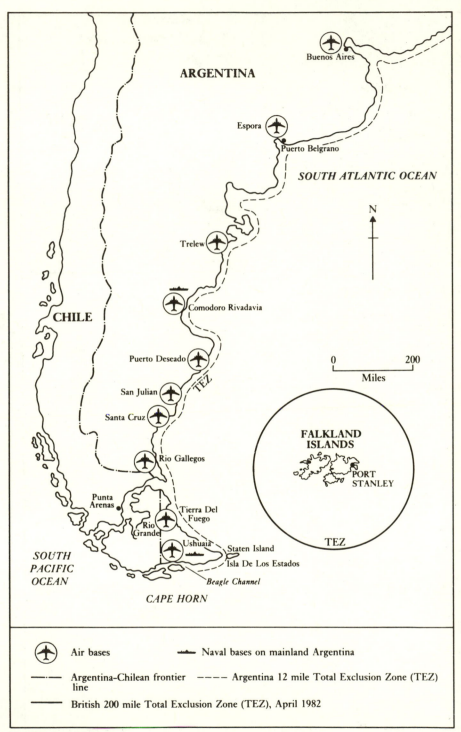

ARGENTINA

Buenos Aires

Espora

Puerto Belgrano

SOUTH ATLANTIC OCEAN

N

CHILE

Trelew

Comodoro Rivadavia

Puerto Deseado

TEZ

San Julian

Santa Cruz

Rio Gallegos

0   200
Miles

Punta
Arenas

Tierra Del
Fuego

Rio
Grande

Ushuaia

Staten Island

Isla De Los Estados

Beagle Channel

SOUTH
PACIFIC
OCEAN

CAPE HORN

FALKLAND
ISLANDS

PORT
STANLEY

TEZ

✈ Air bases   ⚓ Naval bases on mainland Argentina

—··—··— Argentina-Chilean frontier   ———— Argentina 12 mile Total Exclusion Zone (TEZ)
line

———— British 200 mile Total Exclusion Zone (TEZ), April 1982

The Islands and Mainland

xxiv

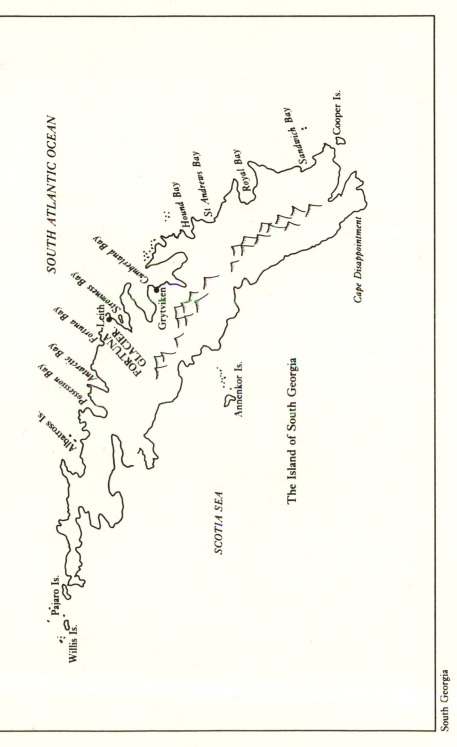

SOUTH ATLANTIC OCEAN

Willis Is.
Pájaro Is.
Albatross Is.
Possession Bay
Antarctic Bay
Fortuna Bay
FORTUNA GLACIER
Leith
Stromness Bay
Cumberland Bay
Grytviken
Hound Bay
St Andrews Bay
Royal Bay
Sandwich Bay
Cooper Is.
Cape Disappointment
Annenkor Is.

SCOTIA SEA

The Island of South Georgia

South Georgia

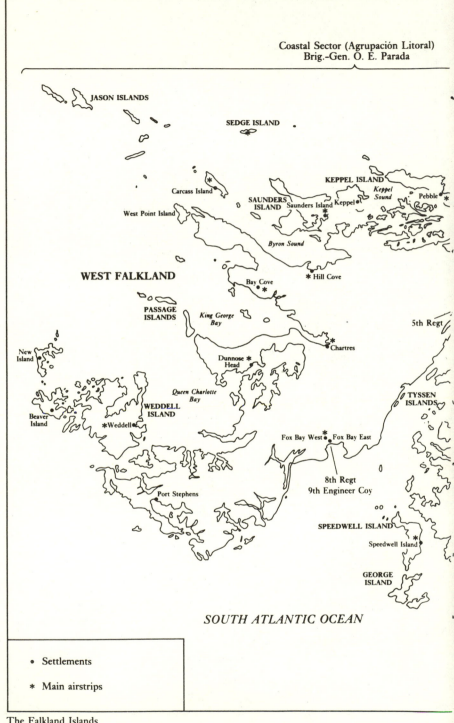

Coastal Sector (Agrupación Litoral)
Brig.-Gen. O. E. Parada

JASON ISLANDS

SEDGE ISLAND

KEPPEL ISLAND

Carcass Island

*Keppel
Sound*

Pebble

SAUNDERS
ISLAND Saunders Island Keppel

West Point Island

Byron Sound

WEST FALKLAND

Bay Cove

* Hill Cove

PASSAGE
ISLANDS

*King George
Bay*

5th Regt

New
Island

Chartres

Dunnose
Head

*Queen Charlotte
Bay*

TYSSEN
ISLANDS

WEDDELL
ISLAND

Beaver
Island

*Weddell

Fox Bay West Fox Bay East

8th Regt
9th Engineer Coy

Port Stephens

SPEEDWELL ISLAND

Speedwell Island

GEORGE
ISLAND

SOUTH ATLANTIC OCEAN

- Settlements

* Main airstrips

The Falkland Islands

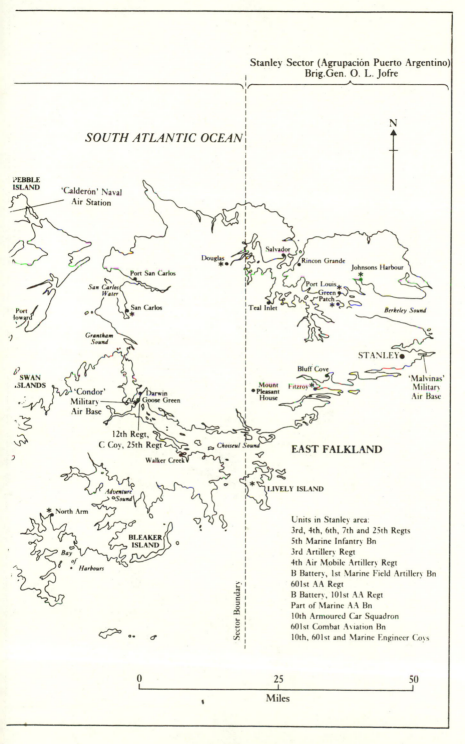

Stanley Sector (Agrupación Puerto Argentino)
Brig.Gen. O. L. Jofre

N

SOUTH ATLANTIC OCEAN

PEBBLE ISLAND

'Calderón' Naval Air Station

Douglas *●

Salvador

Rincon Grande ●

Johnsons Harbour *●

Port San Carlos ●

San Carlos Water

Port Louis ●*
Green Patch ●*

San Carlos *●

Teal Inlet ●

Berkeley Sound

Port Howard

Grantham Sound

STANLEY ●

Bluff Cove

'Malvinas' Military Air Base

SWAN ISLANDS

'Condor' Military Air Base

Darwin ●
Goose Green

Mount Pleasant House ●

Fitzroy *●

12th Regt, C Coy, 25th Regt

Choiseul Sound

EAST FALKLAND

Walker Creek

Adventure Sound

LIVELY ISLAND *

North Arm *●

Units in Stanley area:
3rd, 4th, 6th, 7th and 25th Regts
5th Marine Infantry Bn
3rd Artillery Regt
4th Air Mobile Artillery Regt
B Battery, 1st Marine Field Artillery Bn
601st AA Regt
B Battery, 101st AA Regt
Part of Marine AA Bn
10th Armoured Car Squadron
601st Combat Aviation Bn
10th, 601st and Marine Engineer Coys

BLEAKER ISLAND

Bay of Harbours

Sector Boundary

0   25   50
        Miles

xxvii

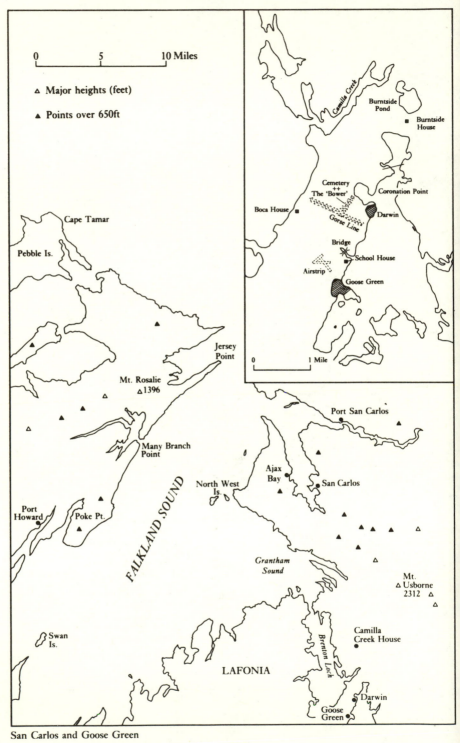

0   5   10 Miles

△ Major heights (feet)

▲ Points over 650ft

Cape Tamar

Pebble Is.

Jersey Point

Mt. Rosalie △1396

Many Branch Point

FALKLAND SOUND

Port Howard

Poke Pt.

North West Is.

Ajax Bay

San Carlos

Port San Carlos

Grantham Sound

Mt. Usborne 2312 △

Swan Is.

LAFONIA

Brenton Loch

Camilla Creek House

Goose Green

Darwin

Inset map (Goose Green / Darwin):

Camilla Creek

Burntside Pond

Burntside House

Cemetery ++ The 'Bower'

Coronation Point

Boca House

Goose Line

Darwin

Bridge

Airstrip

School House

Goose Green

0   1 Mile

San Carlos and Goose Green

xxviii

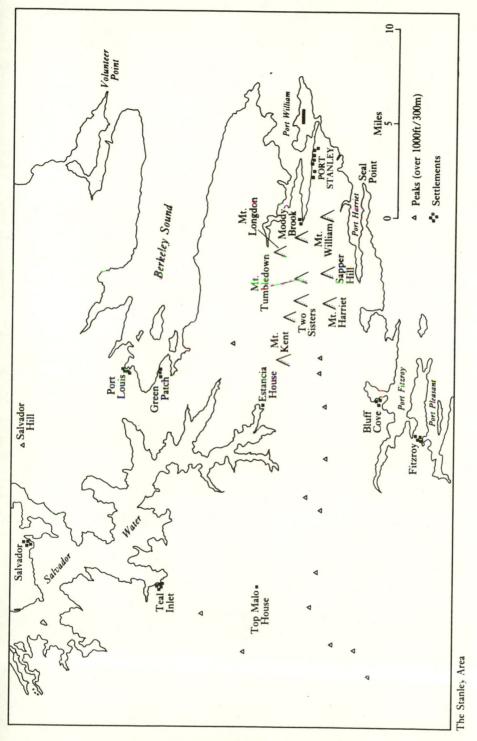

The Stanley Area

xxix

INTRODUCTION

The Argentine flag was first raised in the Falkland Islands on 6 November 1820 by the new Government of the United Provinces of the Rio de la Plata, as part of its effort to establish its right to the former possessions of Spain. On 3 January 1833 the flag was lowered by the crew of a British warship and replaced by the British flag. It was not raised again for another 149 years when Argentine forces occupied the Islands on 2 April 1982. British forces lowered it again on 14 June of that year.

When General Mario Benjamin Menendez arrived at Stanley on 7 April, following a few days after the occupying forces, he was to become the third Argentine Governor of the Islas Malvinas. The first such Governor had taken slightly longer to be appointed. A Frenchman, Louis Vernet, who had played a leading role in the attempt to establish a settlement on the Islands, did not take up his post until 1829. His period in office was almost as eventful as that of Menendez, for he also lost his position during the course of a major international crisis.

This time the protagonist was the United States. Vernet sought to enforce Argentine fishing regulations by seizing three American ships which were claimed by the US Government to be engaged in lawful trade. The American Consul in Buenos Aires protested and threatened reprisals, supporting this protest with a warship USS *Lexington*, which happened to be in the River Plate at the time. At the initiative of its captain, Silas Duncan, the USS *Lexington* sailed to the Islands, landed, destroyed all military installations, razed the buildings, seized sealskins, put most inhabitants under arrest and then left, declaring the Islands free of all government. As a result relations between Argentina and the USA were broken.

On 10 September 1832 Buenos Aires appointed a new interim military and political commander to the Malvinas and dispatched a gunboat, the ARA *Sarandi*, to repair the damage and reinstate law and order in the colony. The second Governor landed, but two months later, as the gunboat was cruising away from the Islands, the garrison revolted and killed him. The *Sarandi* returned and attempted to rout the mutineers.

As it was doing so the British sloop HMS *Clio* appeared in Puerto Soledad. Britain had established a fort at Port Eggmont, West Falkland, the previous century. It had almost gone to war with Spain after the latter had expelled British settlers in 1770. When Spain apologized the British returned in 1771, although there was a presence only for a few years. Sovereignty was still claimed and so Britain had protested not long after Vernet had been given his formal status.

Now the *Clio* had been sent by the Admiralty to reassert British sovereignty in the Islands, taking advantage of the dislocation created by the *Lexington* incident. Captain Onslow of the *Clio* informed Captain Pinedo of the *Sarandi* that the British flag would replace that of Argentina the next day, 3 January 1833. Pinedo protested but in the face of superior force he did not resist. No shots were fired and two days later the *Sarandi* left the Islands, taking with it the Argentine soldiers, convicts from the penal colony at San Carlos and some, but not all, of the Argentine settlers.

The Islands were formally established as a Crown Colony in 1840, and the first British Governor, Lieutenant Richard Moody, sailed from the United Kingdom in 1841. Thereafter, a small agricultural community was developed, and Britain remained in effective occupation until 2 April 1982. The inclement and inhospitable Islands themselves never became a jewel in the British imperial crown. The population in the 1980 census was 1,849 and slowly declining. The local economy was also in decline. In 1982 it was dependent on the export of wool, and was dominated by the Falkland Islands Company (FIC).

Introduction

Thus was established what was to become a permanent British presence on the Islands and the basis for an assertion of sovereignty. In the process a sense of grievance was created in the then fledgling Argentine state that thereafter became part of the national consciousness. Part of this consciousness, in 1982, was that this seizure of Argentine territory had taken place 149 years earlier. When questions of nationhood are at stake, notable anniversaries can gain a symbolic significance that they might not otherwise warrant.

At the start of 1982 the Argentine Government had made the recovery of the Malvinas, by the magic month of January 1983, a high priority. In London there was an awareness of this deadline, but largely among some academic specialists, those few officials with responsibility for the Falklands and relations with Argentina, and members of the slightly larger group, encouraged by the Falklands lobby, who feared a transfer of sovereignty of the Falklands to Argentina.

This reflected the basic asymmetry in the conflict up to April 1982. Britain was holding doggedly on to islands about which very few people cared, but those few who did cared strongly. In Argentina everybody cared.

Our objective in this book is to describe the consequences of this asymmetry as they unfolded during the first half of 1982. Our time-frame is deliberately limited. There are many complicated episodes in the Falkland Islands story, which have been pored over by scholars of various generations and nationalities in an effort to determine whether international law can provide a better guide to the true ownership of the Islands than armed force. Lord Shackleton has described the Falklands as islands 'surrounded by advice'. We might add that they are populated by history.

There are a number of histories of the Falkland Islands dispute available and we see no need to add to these.[1] For the same reason we make no attempt to come to a definitive conclusion on the true ownership of the Islands: we doubt if such a conclusion can be reached although many have tried. We have both addressed this question in earlier works[2] and there is an extensive literature arguing the point from both sides.[3] Neither case is watertight. In practice, ownership since the Islands were first discovered has been settled by force.

Introduction

There is also, of course, a substantial literature on the events of 1982 and so we must make a case for our addition. We believe that this account is distinctive in a number of respects from those that have gone before. First, we have been able to take advantage of the existing literature. There is much to be said for synthesizing the vast collection of first-hand and second-hand accounts that have accumulated over the past seven years. Second, we have been able to draw on original material, including Argentine records that have not yet reached the public domain, as well as interviews with key political and military figures in both Britain and Argentina. In both our countries we have been discussing the events of 1982 with many of those closely involved since the crisis began. A number of extra interviews were conducted specially for this book. However, these interviews were only part of a process of checking one source against another, seeking corroboration for interpretations and attempting to resolve conflicts of evidence. No potential source has been discounted in our effort to put together an account of the conflict.

Obviously a unique feature of this book is that it has been written jointly by two people from each of the belligerent countries. This has enabled us to knit together Argentine and British material to an extent that is extremely difficult when the material is approached from a particular national viewpoint. The result is a rare opportunity to see the development of a conflict from both sides, and also to examine the ways in which the statements and declarations of each side influenced the other.

We feel that the ease of our co-operation says something about the natural relationship between Britain and Argentina, but we are not trying to make a political point with this work. Nor is this in any way a compromise document: as it happens we were surprised by the extent to which agreement on the lines of our analysis was so readily achieved. We may have avoided the more controversial political issues by steering away from a judgement on the merits of the sovereignty dispute and any attempt to resolve the remaining differences between our two countries, but we have sought to confront directly the many controversial questions of historical interpretation contained in this study.

Introduction

This was important to us for we are both aware of how quickly a mythology can develop around wars, as heroes and martyrs are celebrated, failures chastised and even indicted, stirring stories retold and embarrassing episodes forgotten. A degree of myth-making may be unavoidable, some may even be healthy, but in excess it is dangerous. If truth is the first casualty of war, it can also be its most enduring victim. The pace and confusion of crisis and conflict create problems enough: records are not properly kept and even the most honest memories are fallible. Matters that seem critical now to our understanding seemed trivial then; pressing concerns of the moment which were not realized are neglected later. Hindsight renders reasonable decisions foolish and endows reckless gambles with great vision. If all that were not enough, when considerations of national pride and political reputation intrude, the separation of history from mythology becomes even more difficult.

By staying close to the evidence we hope to help protect history from the myth-makers. On a less elevated plane we also hope that those who have remained intrigued by the events of 1982 will find in these pages a version that is comprehensive in scope and convincing in its analyses of some of the more puzzling aspects of the conflict.

Limitations of space mean that this cannot be the whole story. It is largely told from the top looking down rather than the bottom looking up; that is, it examines the critical decisions and how they were made. There is much to be said for exploring the experiences of those caught up in the consequences of those decisions. It adds to the human drama and reminds us of all the reasons why wars are best avoided. Explanation, however, requires attention to the way political and military leaders came to define their objectives and choose among the options available for achieving them.

At times also the big picture can only be understood by looking at the smallest detail. For this reason we have examined some key engagements – such as the Argentine occupation of the Islands on 2 April, the sinking of the *Belgrano* and the battle for Goose Green – with great care simply because of what they reveal about the interplay between the political and military spheres. Thorough discussions of the attempts at mediation by US Secretary of State Alexander Haig,

Peruvian President Fernando Belaunde-Terry and UN Secretary-General Perez de Cuellar illustrate the relationship between negotiating styles and tactics and the substance of the issues under negotiation.

One drawback of our approach is that it can never do full justice to the strength of feelings involved on both sides and the passions generated during the course of the conflict. We urge our readers to remember this background to the decision-making, for it was a critical influence at all times.

The Falklands War provides a unique opportunity to analyse a major international conflict from a number of angles. It brings in the problems of crisis management and international mediation as well as the conduct of military operations. Although we have decided against drawing out the more general lessons that might be taken from this study, we hope that others will find our account useful in doing so.

One theme to emerge from this work is how the grander schemes of policy-makers are regularly frustrated by the simplest of confusions, the peculiarities of diplomatic behaviour and the sheer unpredictability of all military operations. Another, and closely related theme is that the most rational and careful of policy-makers is trapped not only by the passions generated as national interests clash, but also by the need to act on the basis of incomplete, contradictory and often hopelessly confusing information. The result is often misunderstanding not only between adversaries but also among those supposedly on the same side.

This is not simply another academic moan about the dangers of 'misperception'. The reader will find plenty of examples of that but also of people understanding each other perfectly well. At the heart of the major disputes and disagreements were not unfortunate misunderstandings but real conflicts of interest. None the less we gave this book its title because of our interest in the ways that states in dispute communicate both resolve and compromise. The answer that emerges from this case study is that, by and large, they do not do it very well and that the fault often lies with the recipients as much as the senders of the signals of war.

Part One
CONTEXT

Chapter One

ARGENTINE FRUSTRATION

On 5 January 1982 Argentina's new military Junta met at the Navy's Libertad building to review the state of the bilateral talks with the United Kingdom concerning the claim to the Falkland Islands, in the context of the Junta's broad approach to foreign policy.[1] This was the Junta's second meeting on the subject. The first had taken place on 18 December, ten days after the new Junta had come to power.

General Leopoldo Galtieri, the Army Commander, was now President, having been Commander-in-Chief of the Army since the previous March. He was to run the country with the head of the Navy, Jorge Anaya, and of the Air Force, Lami Dozo. Though the lineup in the new Junta made it likely that the Malvinas issue would be high on the agenda, this had not been the reason for the Navy and Air Force's support of Galtieri when he pushed General Viola aside from the Presidency. Rather, it was a disagreement on Viola's economic policies during 1980 and 1981. The new members of the Junta knew each other well, particularly Anaya and Galtieri, who had been schoolmates in the past.

One of the first appointments was Dr Nicanor Costa Mendez, who became Foreign Minister. He had long experience with the Falklands issue, having been closely involved in the early Anglo-Argentine talks of 1966–8. During this time he believed great progress to have been made towards a transfer of sovereignty, only for the effort to be thwarted by the emergence of an organized Falklands lobby in London. He now returned to his desk at the Foreign Ministry to find matters more or less as he had left them. This keen sense of the history of the negotiations, and in particular of Britain's lack of flexibility, was

3

to play a critical role in shaping Argentine strategy for the first months of 1982. He had briefed the Junta when it met on 18 December as to the dismal state of negotiations with Britain and the need to develop a policy prior to the resumption of talks in the coming February.

With or without Anaya running the Navy or Costa Mendez at the Foreign Office the issue would have come to the fore in 1982; 3 January 1983 would be the 150th anniversary of the visit of the *Clio* and the British occupation of the Islands. The symbolic importance of this anniversary meant that there would be pressure within Argentina demanding strong action by the government of the day in Buenos Aires. The demands often came from civilian politicians and academics who dared the Military Government to use force in support of valid national 'aspirations' related to 'territorial integrity' rather than in the name of internal politics and security.[2]

Lastly, there were powerful domestic and international reasons for action. The Junta's inheritance was uncomfortable. Its predecessors had made themselves unpopular through severe political repression combined with the steady deterioration of the economy, largely as a result of the policies of the first military Junta under General Videla, who had overthrown the Peronist Government in 1976. Internationally, widespread condemnation of human-rights abuses combined with unfavourable papal mediation over a long-standing dispute with Chile over islands south of the Beagle Channel. The Falklands issue was coming to be seen as central to Argentina's future position in the South Atlantic, as well as being the only major foreign policy issue upon which it could act in 1982.

The Geopolitical Perspective

The pre-eminent role of the military in Argentine political life reinforced the nationalistic tendencies that might have anyway bubbled to the surface at a time of economic and political turmoil. Nationalism, in turn, encouraged a focus on territorial disputes, with the particular twist provided by a geopolitical perspective popular in South America. This helped to give the Falklands issue an importance beyond the symbolic and linked it in with the development and modernization of the economy.[3]

Geopolitics relates control over critical parts of the earth's surface to security and prosperity. According to the Argentine geopolitical school, and indeed that of Brazil and Chile, control of the South Atlantic and a firm presence in the Antarctic region was bound up with the 'strategic triangle' of the Southern Cone: the Malvinas, Tierra del Fuego (The Drake Passage) and the periphery of the Antarctic Peninsula.[4]

Central to this geopolitical appreciation is Antarctica. In 1959 a number of territorial claimants to this region, including Argentina, Chile and Great Britain, signed the Antarctic Treaty. This froze the competing claims for as long as the Treaty remained in force and demilitarized the Antarctic. Once the competing claims could not be resolved within Antarctica itself, they tended to be projected over the surrounding waters.[5] This was encouraged by technological developments that make possible the exploration (and eventual exploitation) of resources in this inhospitable region. Thus future income and trade could well depend on the quality of the maritime presence maintained in the area. For military regimes this meant that if only internal order could be restored, access to maritime resources would permit rapid development.[6] With all eyes on the review of the Antarctic Treaty in 1991, the competition was hotting up. This was seen, for example, in the Brazilian and Uruguayan efforts to establish bases in the White Continent and their acquisition of polar vessels.

Within Argentina this perspective suggested an alteration in the relative value of national territory. The focus shifted from the Pampas and the northern territories, seen in the past to be central in terms of both economic potential and control of the insurgency movements, to Patagonia, the Sub-Antarctic and the South Atlantic.

This shift was reflected in improved relations with Argentina's northern neighbours. Since 1980 there had been a rapprochement within the military regimes in Brazil, Paraguay and Uruguay. The co-operative impulse was far less strong with Chile and the United Kingdom, for with each there was a territorial dispute with a long history and an intense symbolism. Bilateral relations were inadequate

5

to cope with these disputes. If they were to be handled peacefully it was necessary to opt for either mediation (Chile) or the use of fora such as the United Nations (Britain). In both cases, when the negotiations failed to yield satisfactory results, Argentina had in the past threatened military action.[7]

In 1978 the country had been on the verge of war with Chile as a result of a dispute over the territory south of the Beagle Channel. A timely offer of mediation from the Vatican had helped restore calm. In December 1980 the Vatican had made its first proposal which, following previous recommendations, favoured Chile. Argentina was unhappy with this and put in a counterclaim.

As the Junta met in January 1982 it awaited the second papal decision. In a move that was to deplete the Argentine representation in Britain during the March crisis, the Argentine Ambassador to Britain, Ortiz de Rozas, was put in charge of negotiations with the Vatican, though not relinquishing his post in London. However, the Junta had few grounds for optimism that the initial papal support for Chile's claims would be reversed. This threatened Argentina's overall position in the South Atlantic.

There was little diplomatically and militarily that could be done to improve this position except by taking a more forceful line on the Malvinas. The 1959 Treaty forbade any attempt to reinforce the Argentine presence in Antarctica itself; it would be difficult to challenge the papal position on the Beagle Channel. Only with the Falklands and its dependencies of South Georgia and the South Sandwich Islands was there much hope of a positive negotiation.

Here the Argentine claim had been put clearly and forcefully to the international and regional community and it had obtained a sympathetic response. Links with the Islands had been established since the Communications Agreement of 1971 and Britain had, at times, appeared prepared to negotiate seriously over the transfer of sovereignty.

Britain was far away from the South Atlantic. From the perspective of Buenos Aires it had no substantial strategic or economic interest in the Falklands, while the local population was small and declining. The Islands seemed to fall exactly into the category of old colonies that had been abandoned in the previous few decades. So, although Britain was still a major power, and militarily more capable than Chile, the issues at stake for London were far less vital than they were for Santiago.

A failure to settle the dispute with Britain satisfactorily over the coming year could, thereafter, see the Argentine position steadily worsen. Once Chile was confirmed in the Beagle Channel it could 'legally' offer logistics to the Falkland Islands should Argentina cut them off. Moreover, Chile could prove to be an attractive partner to Britain in maintaining a maritime presence in the South Atlantic, and this would come at the expense of Argentina. Thus, improved relations with Santiago could strengthen Britain's bargaining position.[8]

If, however, Britain did agree to Argentina's terms for the negotiations then Argentina's loss of territory to Chile would not impinge drastically on its future presence in the South Atlantic and Sub-Antarctic regions. In fact close co-operation with the United Kingdom in patrolling this region and undertaking joint ventures was highly desirable because of the standing this would give Argentina in the international community.

Every geopolitical consideration therefore seemed to push the Argentine Government to make the resolution of the Falklands dispute its top priority for 1982.

Understanding British Procrastination

Unfortunately, Argentina had been trying to resolve this dispute since the mid-1960s without success. How could the British be persuaded to move towards a settlement now? To answer this question the Junta made an attempt to identify a 'British behavioural pattern' in their dealings with Argentina over the Falklands. This analysis of British attitudes and behaviour was critical to the events of the next few months.

In 1964 the UN Committee on decolonization had included the Islands in its list of territories that ought to be decolonized; it also accepted the inclusion of the Argentine designation 'Malvinas' following 'Falkland' in the official denomination of the Islands. Soon afterwards the existence of the dispute was recognized and both parties were asked to search for a negotiated settlement.[9]

In September 1965, Argentina had invited Britain to negotiate; this had been accepted but with the exclusion of the issue of sovereignty. The question was then posed to the General Assembly of the UN who, with 45 votes in favour, none against and 14 abstentions approved Resolution 2065 on 16 December 1965. In this Resolution the Assembly recognized the existence of a dispute, invited the two governments to 'proceed without delay' with negotiations to find 'a peaceful solution to the problem, bearing in mind . . . the interests of the population of the Falkland Islands (Malvinas)'. In the semantics of the dispute the use of the word 'interests' rather than 'wishes' implied only a limited regard for whatever misgivings the islanders had about this idea. Although these resolutions were not binding, on 14 January 1966 Great Britain agreed to negotiate on those terms; sixteen years of bilateral talks followed.

From the Argentine perspective serious discussions, addressing the sovereignty issue, only took place for two short periods during these sixteen years: between 1966 and 1967, and from 1977 to 1980. For the rest of the time the Falkland Islands lobby undermined the flexibility of the Foreign Office in its conduct of the negotiations.

Initially there had been considerable progress. During the early stages of the negotiations a 'Memorandum of Understanding' was drafted which envisaged the eventual transfer of sovereignty to Argentina. However, this progress was cut short through effective lobbying by the Falkland Islands Committee in the Houses of Parliament in 1968. This resulted in Britain changing its negotiating position; now the 'wishes of the islanders' were to be critical.

Argentine governments had continued with the negotiations, ignoring demands by nationalists for immediate and drastic action. They were aware of the British Foreign Office's conviction that the development of the economic future of the Islands could not be carried out without the active assistance of Argentina. It was hoped to change the islanders' view of their position by making concessions designed to integrate the Islands with the continent. In 1969 the first steps were taken to open a line of communications with the Islands. The Communications Agreement of 1971 provided the introduction of a weekly air service with the mainland.

However, in 1975 it appeared that Britain was even going back on this integrative trend when an expedition was sent to determine the economic potential of the Islands (the Shackleton Mission).

There were also military incidents such as that involving the RSS *Shackleton* in February 1976.* Argentina had received the support of the Interamerican Juridical Committee, which had declared that the movements of British warships in the region 'constitute a threat to the peace and security of the continent'.[10]

After the 1976–7 crisis the British Government had appeared to be willing to negotiate seriously again. Argentina now understood that, whatever the private views of successive British governments with regard to the transfer of sovereignty, they were fearful of moving publicly because of the likely political reaction. The only possible approach that remained was that of a leaseback arrangement, by which Argentina would receive titular sovereignty but allow a British administration to continue. In 1977 bilateral negotiations resumed, a leaseback proposal was studied as well as possibilities for a joint Anglo-Argentine economic programme for the exploration, exploitation and development of the region.[11]

The Conservative Government of Margaret Thatcher continued with this approach through 1979 and 1980. But once again, as had been the case with the Memorandum of Understanding of 1968, fierce media and parliamentary opposition caused it to fail when Nicholas Ridley returned from the Islands in December 1980. The islanders obliged the Government to add their representatives to all future delegations discussing the Islands with Argentina and to freeze the sovereignty issue, thus channelling all bilateral (now trilateral) negotiations into exclusively peripheral matters.

This left the British Government 'talking for the sake of talking'. It was not difficult for Argentina to see through this approach. What was curious was that Britain was not backing it by providing for the development and defence of the Islands as demanded by the islanders.

---

* The *Shackleton*, a research ship, was intercepted in February 1976 by an Argentine destroyer some 78 miles south of the Falkland Islands and was commanded to stop because it was in Argentine waters. The Captain refused to stop, despite several shots across the bow from the destroyer.

Of particular significance was the decision to withdraw HMS *Endurance* from service by April 1982. The Defence White Paper of June 1981 suggested abandoning the British naval presence in the South Atlantic and in Antarctica.

So Buenos Aires had received mixed signals. On the one hand, three years of work on the possibility of leaseback had been abruptly abandoned and the islanders had become a third party to the negotiations with power to veto any progress on the sovereignty issue. On the other hand, the British showed no interest in building up their economic and military position as an alternative to serious negotiations with Buenos Aires.

It was judged in Buenos Aires that, despite the various shifts and turns in its negotiating position, the British Government was anxious to reduce its international commitments. It was suffering from the constraints of declining power. However, because there had been no countervailing pressure to that of the Falkland Islands lobby, the Foreign Office had not been obliged to address the problem head on and had taken refuge in procrastination. Here the fault in part lay with successive Argentine governments who had failed to convey a sufficient sense of threat and had thus encouraged this lack of seriousness in London.

Analysts in Buenos Aires saw evidence of collusion involving not only the Falkland Islands Committee and the Falkland Islands Company but also the British Antarctic Survey and some sections of the Navy who had seized on the *Endurance* issue and the South Atlantic question in general in an effort to reverse the June 1981 cuts.[12] In both Houses of Parliament it was argued not only that HMS *Endurance* should be spared but that the British presence in the South Atlantic needed to be reinforced.[13] It was therefore to be expected that this lobby would seek some opportunity to force the British Government to reverse the 1981 decisions. The issues had been raised in Parliament in mid-December and this had been noted by Costa Mendez when he first briefed the Junta on 18 December.

This analysis suggested to the Junta that the British Government should be encouraged to follow the logic of the position reflected in the *Endurance* decision by reactivating the negotiations. The Rhodesian settlement of 1981 had given hope, both that the Government could take a 'realistic' approach to these old colonial problems, and that it had an agenda for resolving them, even though the Falklands was probably low down on the list, coming only after Rhodesia, Belize, Hong Kong and Gibraltar.[14]

But any new diplomatic initiative should now be backed by the development of an alternative military option in case the Falkland Islands lobby prevailed and Britain refused to discuss sovereignty and concentrated instead on the provision of effective support for the Islands. So long as the June 1981 Defence White Paper was being implemented it seemed a good time to press Britain.

Options

The immediate Argentine objective was to return to the original negotiating framework of 1965–7. As this meant a return to a concern with the 'interests' of the islanders rather than their 'wishes' it would be necessary to offset:

> the pressure of the kelpers* and the interests of the Falkland Islands Company, that sought a permanent freeze of all bilateral negotiations on the sovereignty issue between Argentina and the United Kingdom.[15]

If Britain refused to negotiate seriously, Argentina could break diplomatic relations or cut the communications links to the Islands. The extra cost of defending and supplying the Falklands would impose a considerable burden on Britain just as it was trying to cut back on this sort of expenditure.

This option was, however, losing its attraction. The coincident Beagle Channel dispute with Chile created a risk of pushing the two countries into an alliance against Argentina which would frustrate any attempt to make Britain's position in the South Atlantic untenable.

* Kelpers refers to native-born Falkland Islanders.

Although the Labour Government had kept its distance from the Pinochet regime the Conservatives had moved to re-establish working relations with Chile. Thus, the anticipated attempt by the Falkland Islands lobby to harden the British posture was not the only reason why the Junta feared that its position might worsen during 1982.[16]

The Junta therefore decided at the meeting of 5 January 1982 to follow a double policy. It resolved to 'reactivate to the fullest extent all negotiations for the sovereignty of the Malvinas, South Georgia and South Sandwich Islands' and at the same time 'prepare a contingency plan for the employment of military power should the first alternative fail'.

To implement this it would propose reactivation of the sovereignty talks with the intention of returning to the more favourable conditions of at best 1966 or at least of 1979–80. Diplomatic pressure on Britain would increase; the issue would be brought to the notice of the international community whenever possible. If, as expected, the British 'behavioural pattern' persisted, possibly compounded by a reversal of the decision not to defend the Islands in the future, it was necessary to plan for a military confrontation.[17]

The double policy was implemented immediately. On 27 January 1982 the Argentine Foreign Ministry proposed a new negotiating agenda on a monthly basis and asked the British Government to have an answer ready by the time the two parties met in New York for their next scheduled round of talks.

On 5 January 1982 the special Joint Armed Forces study on the military contingency for the failure of negotiations started its planning phase.[18] A week later the Junta met again to refine its ideas on the military option. A group of senior officers from each of the services was established to analyse the possibility of using military force. To ensure secrecy the work of this group should be handwritten and its meeting points varied. Two weeks later the Junta approved National Strategy Directive 1/82:

The Military Committee, faced with the evident and repeated lack of progress in the negotiations with Great Britain to obtain recognition of our sovereignty over the Malvinas, Georgias and South

Sandwich Islands; convinced that the prolongation of this situation affects national honour, the full exercise of sovereignty and the exploration of resources; *has resolved* to analyse the possibility of the use of military power to obtain the political objective. This resolution must be kept in strict secrecy and should be circulated only to the heads of the respective military departments.

Preliminary plans for the military option were to be prepared by mid-March. The operation itself should be ready to be implemented by 15 May 1982. It should be bloodless, to limit the possibility of a British reaction and to help in creating a better atmosphere for negotiations. For this reason it depended on surprise; it would be fatally undermined if there were any British reinforcements.

Chapter Two

BRITISH APPREHENSION

This assessment of the state of play in the dispute at the start of 1982 accorded with that held by the Foreign and Commonwealth Office in London. Here it was recognized that matters were becoming more polarized between the Junta on the one hand and the islanders on the other. But ever since the previous initiative had been derailed at the end of 1980 there had been no long-term policy and, having seen what happened to Nicholas Ridley, ministers did not seem inclined to risk further controversy on an issue of, for them, peripheral interest. Over the previous year not only had Foreign Office ministers failed to agree on a course of action, but the British position had been severely compromised by policies adopted by other ministries.

Foreign Office Policy

Initially the Conservative Government had been decisive. The Foreign Secretary, Lord Carrington, took a view successive Foreign Secretaries had taken. He 'was entirely satisfied with the strength of our position in law'. But the islanders were wholly dependent on Argentina. Argentina was a 'country with, in other respects, a long tradition of friendship with Britain'. On the other hand,

> The Falklands represented no vital strategic or economic interest for Britain, and although nobody had questioned that the islanders'

views on their own future must carry proper weight it was clear that the only long-term solution to make sense must be one leading to peaceful co-existence with Argentina; while anybody could see that a protracted posture of defence against Argentina – if it were allowed to come to that – would be so intolerably expensive as to be an aberration of defence finance and priorities.

The problem had to be resolved through negotiation. 'They had the emotion. We had the interest. We had to try.'[1]

In the summer of 1980 it was agreed that the dispute with Argentina should be settled on the basis of leaseback, compromising with Argentina on sovereignty but allowing the islanders a continuity of administration and way of life. Later that year Nicholas Ridley, the Foreign Office Minister responsible for the Falklands, was dispatched to the Islands to ascertain the level of support.

The response was unenthusiastic. Ridley did not directly propose leaseback. An alternative was to freeze the question of sovereignty in future negotiations with Argentina. Ridley made it clear that he did not think that the status quo was an option. The Islands were suffering economic and demographic decline which could not be arrested unless the dispute with Argentina was resolved. Although there was clear hostility to any negotiations over sovereignty, some islanders were prepared to contemplate leaseback. Ridley thought the numbers sufficient to warrant pursuing the idea further.[2]

When he suggested all this on his return in December 1980 to both Parliament and the Cabinet's Defence and Oversea Policy Committee he was given a rough ride. In Parliament he seemed to equivocate on whether the principle of the paramountcy of the islanders' wishes still applied, and whether they would be backed if they opted for the status quo.[3] The reaction was a formidable demonstration of the strength of the Falkland Islands lobby and the instinctive distrust of manoeuvres apparently designed to force people who wanted to remain British into the hands of a regime widely regarded as repressive.* It was also a

* The Falkland Islands Emergency Committee was established during the course of a visit to Britain by four members of the Islands' Executive Council in 1968. It was re-formed in 1973 as the UK Falklands Islands Committee with the objective:

demonstration of the lack of sympathy for the Foreign Office's approach in Cabinet, a tendency that had constantly made it difficult to take on the lobby in Parliament.

Carrington had discovered in an early conversation with the Prime Minister that 'this might be one of those cases' when she 'suspected a defeatist Foreign Office of finding ways to appease a foreign Government'.[4] He found it difficult to get her – and the rest of the Cabinet – to focus on the issue. John Nott, at the Ministry of Trade and then (from 1981) Defence, has admitted that he did not spend 'a lot of time mugging up my brief on matters surrounding the Falklands. I did not consider it to be of any importance in my life.'[5] Nott's Ministry when asked by the Foreign Office in May 1981 for a 'short politico-military assessment of the UK's ability to respond to a range of possible Argentine actions', took five months to respond.[6]

The unwillingness among the political elites in London to be seen to be putting pressure on the islanders to join another country against their will meant that policy could move no faster than islander opinion. Given a choice, the islanders opted for the status quo. The Falkland Islands Joint Council* proposed in January 1981 that the British delegation at future talks with Argentina should 'seek an agreement to freeze the dispute over sovereignty for a specified period of time'.[7]

Although it had proved impossible this time round to persuade the islanders of the virtues of leaseback, the initial response by Carrington was to hope that over time, even in the absence of pressure from Britain, they would see the virtue of this scheme. Participation in the talks might even have an educative effect on the islanders. So that was another reason for keeping the negotiations going, in addition to keeping the lines of communication open to Buenos Aires.

The first talks under the new conditions took place in February

---

To assist the people of the Falkland Islands to decide their own future for themselves without being subject to pressure direct or indirect from any quarter.

It maintained good links with the press and members of all political parties.

* This was made up of the Executive and Legislative Councils. The Executive Council was composed of two elected members, two members nominated by the Governor, and the Chief Secretary and Financial Secretary of the Islands. The latter two were also *ex officio* members of the Legislative Council, along with six elected members.

1981. Not surprisingly, when Mr Ridley proposed a freeze to Argentina, this was rejected outright. Now that the islanders understood the position better, the Foreign Secretary decided that there was little point in having further talks until they had cleared their own minds. Accordingly he suggested to Argentina that further discussions should await the result of the October elections for the Legislative Council. Argentina accepted with reluctance, and not without a strong communiqué of protest from Dr Oscar Camilión, the Argentine Foreign Minister at the time.[8]

In a major review of policy in June, attended by the Ambassador to Argentina as well as the Governor of the Islands, John Ure, the Under Secretary of State for the South American Department, proposed that much more should be done to educate islander and British opinion as to the safeguards and positive measures that could accompany leaseback compared with the dangers of confrontation with Argentina if this was still rejected. This was what Mr Ridley then proposed to the Foreign Secretary, suggesting that the September meeting of the Cabinet's Defence Committee discuss a campaign of public education. However, Carrington took the view that such a campaign would be counter-productive. Senior officials doubted the wisdom of entering on a campaign of persuasion without a 'very firm government-approved policy'.[9]

The Head of the South American department explained to a disappointed British Ambassador in Buenos Aires: 'the domestic political constraints must at this stage continue to prevent us from taking any steps which might be interpreted either as putting pressure on the Islanders or as overruling their wishes'.[10] Effectively, as Carrington acknowledged, this meant conceding the initiative, in terms of suggesting that Argentina should come up with new proposals when the negotiations resumed, and preparing contingency plans in the event of physical pressures being put on the islanders.

The results of the October elections for the Islands Legislative Council demonstrated a hardening of attitudes. They were moving further away from the idea of leaseback.

Warnings from Buenos Aires

Before the major policy review in June 1981, Ure had visited Argentina and found Foreign Affairs ministers and officials reasonably 'relaxed', although military leaders were less 'patient'.[11]

Just after the policy review the Joint Intelligence Committee provided its own assessment of the Argentine position. There was no doubt that Argentina was as determined as before to extend its sovereignty over the Islands but it was assumed that it would prefer to achieve this objective by peaceful means. The key variable was therefore Argentina's perception of Britain's willingness to negotiate seriously about sovereignty. Here there was clear evidence of impatience, and if Argentina concluded that there was little hope of transferring sovereignty peacefully then 'there would be a high risk of its resorting to more forcible measures against British interests ... it might act swiftly and without warning.' However, it was more likely that the dispute would first escalate through more limited measures.

The assessment described a series of measures of increasing severity. In the first instance there would probably be diplomatic and economic measures, including the disruption of air and sea communications. A 'distinct possibility' was an occupation of one of the uninhabited dependencies, along the lines of the presence established on South Thule in 1976. It might even risk an attempt to establish such a presence on one of the Islands themselves, though remote from Stanley.[12]

Carrington decided in September not to take the matter to the Defence Committee. There was no 'immediate danger of hostile Argentine reactions', and in these circumstances he doubted that he could convince his colleagues to take the whole thing seriously. None the less in explaining the decision to carry on talking with Argentina without either new proposals or a campaign to educate the islanders, he recognized a risk of Argentina imposing pressure through a withdrawal of the air service and a significant part of the fuel supply, or even of a military confrontation.[13]

HMS *Endurance*

Exactly what weight to attach to the risk of confrontation was difficult to assess. There was, however, little doubt that the risk was growing rather than subsiding. In this context the most striking feature of British policy during 1981 was the decision to make it more difficult to cope with a confrontation should one arise, and to do so in a highly visible manner.

There was a general sense of hopelessness in all contingency planning for a sharp deterioration in the dispute. This, after all, was the main reason why the Government had hoped to resolve the dispute on the basis of leaseback. Analyses of an alternative air service during 1981 concluded that it would be impracticable. The sort of military capability that would need to be stationed in the South Atlantic to deter a military invasion would, according to the Chiefs of Staff, be 'very expensive and would engage a significant portion of the country's naval resources ... its despatch could precipitate the very action it was intended to deter'. To get such a force to the South Atlantic in response to a military threat to the Islands would take at least twenty days and probably longer, given the need to assemble and prepare. If it arrived after the Islands had been occupied there could be no certainty that they could be retaken.[14]

This sense of hopelessness should be borne in mind when considering the decision taken in June 1981 as part of a wide-ranging defence review to withdraw HMS *Endurance* at the end of her 1981–2 deployment. The ice-patrol vessel undertook hydrographic work and was the sum total of the British naval presence in the area. The proposal to scrap it had come from the Navy, which had never attached a high priority to *Endurance* and tended to deal with pressure for budgetary cuts by proposing sacrifices which it suspected might be politically unacceptable. The Royal Yacht *Britannia* also came into this category. That was too difficult for Secretary of Defence Nott. But *Endurance* was another matter. It was due for an expensive refit and this would have meant yet another frigate would have to be put on standby. 'Therefore one took the view that since *Endurance* had no defence requirement in terms of our *priorities* as a country, the *Nato* priority, it was better to scrap *Endurance* rather than go for another frigate.'[15]

An attempt to withdraw *Endurance* had been made as part of the last major defence review in 1975, when only the furore over the 1976 Shackleton Report led the Foreign Office to persuade the Ministry of Defence to continue with its patrols. When the Foreign Office heard of the new proposal Carrington pressed for a reconsideration on the grounds that it would be interpreted as a diminution in Britain's commitment to the Islands and to its claims to its Antarctic Territory. This was to no avail. When the decision became public at the end of June the Falkland Islands Councils held a joint meeting and wrote to Carrington deploring this move 'in the strongest terms'. Reports from Buenos Aires indicated that it was widely construed as the end of British protection of the Falkland Islands and understood diplomatically as a political gesture given that the £2 million per annum cost could not be critical to the defence budget.

The campaign to save *Endurance* gained considerable support in both Houses of Parliament. On 22 January 1982 Carrington tried again; at the start of February, Nott replied negatively. The military commitment would be sustained through the continued presence of a small Royal Marine detachment on the Islands and other Royal Navy ships could make periodic visits.[16]

The Assessment for 1982

All things considered, the Foreign Office assessment as 1982 began was remarkably similar to that of the Argentine Ministry of Foreign Affairs. There were the same doubts over Britain's long-term commitment to the Islands and the same sense of frustration that a settlement to the dispute had been thwarted through the intransigence of the islanders.

The Annual Review from the British Ambassador in Buenos Aires, submitted on 1 January 1982, noted that, while 1981 had passed without a 'bust-up', the Argentines and the islanders were 'more on each other's nerves'. The Head of the South American Department replied that it would be difficult to persuade Argentina of the virtues of negotiation unless the islanders modified their attitudes. The first draft had been even more blunt.

Meanwhile the Annual Review arrived from the Governor of the Falkland Islands. He noted how islander opinion had hardened against leaseback. There was growing suspicion of Government intentions because of the refusal to grant British citizenship to the islanders in the British Nationality Bill, the decision to withdraw *Endurance* and the threatened closure of the British Antarctic Survey Base at Grytviken in South Georgia.* Suspicion of Argentine intentions had grown too. The frequency of the air service with the mainland, which was operated by Argentina, had been cut without notice and there had been six overflights during the year by Argentine Air Force aircraft. The Governor saw little prospect for the talks with Argentina. If they did break down the most likely first step would be to stop the air service and he therefore suggested that contingency plans should be drawn up to cope with this sort of action.

In London this was received as evidence that the islanders were moving towards a 'Fortress Falklands' policy. The reply from the Foreign Office sought to warn them that if, as all those involved now seemed to agree, 'we are now perilously near the inevitable move from dialogue to confrontation', the pressure from Argentina could extend beyond the withdrawal of present services, which in themselves would be difficult to replicate. Britain would find it difficult to finance a Fortress Falklands let alone to provide the quality of defence that such an approach supposed. The Franks Report paraphrased the essential message as follows:

> While the Islanders should be in no doubt of the strength of the Government's commitment to act in accordance with their wishes, they should be under no illusion on the difficulties ahead or on the limits on their ability to mitigate the consequences. Unless there was

---

* Although at one point the British Antarctic Survey had warned that because of a shortage of funds it might need to close its base at Grytviken, extra funds were found in early 1982 to keep it going.

a negotiated settlement, the way forward for the Islanders could only be downhill.

This reply was sent on 4 March 1982. Within weeks the confrontation had begun.[17]

Chapter Three

DEADLOCK AGAIN

Later we shall examine the nature of the military planning undertaken in Argentina over the first months of 1982: for the moment all that is important to note is that very few people were involved in the planning process and very few knew that the work was being undertaken. For the Junta the threat of force was not to be used explicitly to extract concessions from the British. This would risk alerting London and giving it time to reinforce defences. The military option was to be developed while Britain was given a final opportunity to resolve the dispute in a peaceful manner. If anything, diplomacy would facilitate the eventual use of force. It would be legitimized through Argentina gaining the backing of international organizations as it demonstrated British intransigence.

Even Foreign Minister Costa Mendez was unaware of the planning exercise while he prepared his diplomatic initiative in January. He knew only that the Junta intended to increase tension if the British failed to offer serious concessions. His plan was to attempt to get the negotiating framework modified to add urgency to the discussions. This would be raised at the talks scheduled for New York in February 1982. Assuming little progress was made, the case would be presented to the United Nations Decolonization Committee in August, where a sympathetic hearing could be expected, and then on to the General Assembly meeting in November. This would help Argentina garner international support before 3 January 1983, the 150th anniversary of the British takeover of the Malvinas.[1]

When Costa Mendez was eventually informed in February of the military plans being drawn up to recover the Islands he responded cautiously. He suggested that a working group be set up to examine the scheme and explore alternatives. However, the President required total confidentiality. He wanted to see the outcome of the next round of talks.[2] Preparing a military plan did not preclude diplomatic action. Costa Mendez did not change his own approach. His ideas for a series of intensifying diplomatic measures culminating at the UN General Assembly were eventually presented to the Junta in mid-March, just before events pushed the military options to the fore.[3]

What he did request on hearing of the military policy was a say over any operations that individual institutions in Argentina were intending to mount in the South Atlantic area in the coming months. He sought to have a final say over exactly the sort of activity that triggered the confrontation in March.[4]

In January the first diplomatic step was a firm restatement of the Argentine position and proposals for new negotiating procedures. This took the form of a message to Britain on 27 January. It warned that unless sovereignty was transferred the dispute between the two countries could not end. It called for new negotiations towards this objective to be concluded 'within a reasonable period of time and without procrastination'. There should be no more 'delays or dilatory arguments'.

On the assumption that the question of sovereignty over the Falkland Islands, South Georgia and the South Sandwich Islands must be solved peacefully, finally and rapidly in the interests of the parties to the dispute and of all others concerned in its solution, the Argentine Government proposes, in order to expedite matters, the establishment of a permanent negotiating commission, which will meet during the first week of every month, alternately, in each capital and will be charged with maintaining continuity and impetus in the negotiations, not allowing them to be relegated to desultory meetings without clear objectives or concrete results . . .

The commission would have one year's duration. It could be discontinued at any time by either party, with prior notice.[5]

This proposal was sent with a specific request that the Foreign Office should assess its feasibility at both governmental and parliamentary levels before the next round of talks.[6]

Meanwhile, helping to convey the hardening Argentine stance, there was a series of newspaper articles in Buenos Aires. The most notable of these were by a well-informed journalist, Iglesias Rouco, writing in *La Prensa*. His first, on 24 January, anticipated the presentation of the new negotiating proposals to Britain, and in particular the precise time-limit that would be attached. After discussing the international context, in such a way as to suggest that a tough stand by Argentina might be supported by the United States and Europe, he warned that 'this year . . . a military attempt to resolve the dispute cannot be ruled out when sovereignty is at stake.'*

Sir Anthony Williams, the British Ambassador to Buenos Aires, had taken to reporting articles such as these back to London because he felt that they attracted more attention than repeating his own concerns with regard to the developing Argentine mood. He was also convinced, despite denials, that Sr Rouco was an instrument in a campaign of diplomatic pressure on Britain. It was still not clear how seriously these warnings were to be taken. At least it was recognized that the issue was hotting up sufficiently for it to be placed on the agenda of the next meeting of the Cabinet's Defence Committee in March.

Britain was able to make a more positive response than might have been expected to the Argentine message. Richard Luce had now taken over from Nicholas Ridley as the responsible Foreign Office Minister. He saw an opportunity to get talks under way without too many constraints. A year earlier Ridley had been hampered by the vote at the Falkland Islands Council insisting that the sovereignty issue be frozen. Although the new Council was even more hardline it had not yet met and so Luce had more freedom of manoeuvre than would be the case later on when it began to take formal decisions.[7] The Foreign Office therefore replied to Argentina reserving its position on sovereignty but expressing its readiness to negotiate and to discuss in detail the

---

* On 7 February he again stressed the importance of deadlines, the unwillingness of Buenos Aires to talk indefinitely and its readiness to use other action, including military means, to recover the Islands. A third article on 18 February developed the strategic rationale for a military initiative. Cited in *Franks*, paras 129–32.

proposal to establish working groups to look at various aspects of the dispute. Talks were arranged for New York on 26 and 27 February.

Not long before the talks began, Carrington circulated his view that this approach represented one means of preventing a breakdown in the negotiations. However, it would still have to be made clear to Buenos Aires that it would be extremely difficult to discuss sovereignty and that the proposed time-table was quite unrealistic. The Prime Minister's response was to ensure that it was made clear to the Argentines that the wishes of the islanders remained paramount.[8]

The Unilateral Communiqué

The head of the Argentine delegation to the talks was Enrique Ros, a career diplomat and now Deputy Minister for Foreign Affairs. His delegation included Ambassador Carlos Lucas Blanco, Director of the Malvinas and Antarctica Department at the Ministry, and from London Ambassador Ortiz de Rozas and his number two, Atilio Molteni. Luce was accompanied by Ambassador Williams, Robin Fearn, the Head of the South American Department in the Foreign Office, and two members of the Islands' Legislative Council, Messrs Gerald Cheek and Anthony Blake.

Luce has described his brief:

> I was to make it absolutely clear to them that, as far as sovereignty was concerned, there would be no change without the consent of the Islanders and of Parliament. Against that background I was given the broad brief to go into negotiations, to keep the dialogue going and, to be quite blunt about it, if things were getting difficult, we would just have to buy time.[9]

The main concession he was able to offer was to accept Argentina's proposal to establish a negotiating commission. The Argentine delegation were pleasantly surprised to have this proposal accepted. Luce was also prepared for regular meetings and for these to begin in May or June. The real difficulty was the Argentine proposal for a rigorous time-table, with a deadline, and for all the meetings to be conducted at a very high level. The British were prepared to have ministers drawn into the discussions when necessary and a review of progress after a year but *no* firm deadline: that would put exactly the wrong sort of pressure on the islanders and the House of Commons and so would probably be counter-productive.[10]

So much was agreed. An informal working paper outlined how a Commission would be presided over by ministers and would meet – how often was not said – over a period of one year, when progress would be reviewed. At any stage termination could be proposed.

Luce was relieved that Argentina accepted that the British delegation might include islanders, that the Commission's work would be conducted without prejudice to the sovereignty position of either side and that there was no absolute deadline. The result was satisfactory in that it allowed the talks to continue and gave more time for the islanders to see reason. By agreeing to this framework the Foreign Office recognized – indeed hoped – that pressure would be put on the islanders. The view of the British delegation was that they had 'bought three to six months'.[11]

As it had also been agreed that the details of the talks should be kept confidential, the joint communiqué was brief but, again from the British perspective, positive in tone:

> The meeting took place in a cordial and positive spirit. The two sides reaffirmed their resolve to find a solution to the sovereignty dispute and considered in detail an Argentine proposal for procedures to make better progress in this sense. They agreed to inform their Governments accordingly.

The Argentine delegation sent back an analysis of the British approach which suggested that there had been movement in the right direction, no doubt as a result of the diplomatic pressure that had been brought to bear and awareness of the problems that could result if negotiations broke down.

However, the delegation had not been let into the secret of the military planning or the critical importance of a strict time-table. So, believing that there had been *some* progress, unwittingly the delegation had exceeded its brief.

For the very same reason that the British delegation were satisfied with the results of the talks, Ros's superiors in Buenos Aires were furious. Here the assessment was that Britain was procrastinating once again. The aim of demonstrating British intransigence before the international community was not going to be helped by cryptic reports of cordial meetings. The key fact was that Britain had not formally accepted the Argentine proposal and had given no indication of when it intended to do so.

This created a problem for Costa Mendez. The tame communiqué did not even fit in with his strategy, never mind that of the Junta. This created a risk that his Ministry, and Costa Mendez himself, would acquire a poor reputation with the Junta and its influence be correspondingly reduced. As diplomacy was downgraded military options would be promoted.

To revive the pressure on Britain and to calm the Junta, Costa Mendez then drafted with some of his senior aides a unilateral statement which was issued two days after the end of the New York talks and before the delegation had arrived home. Contrary to what had been agreed, and to the intense embarrassment of Ros, the new communiqué disclosed the scope of the negotiations and stressed that the aim of the meetings should be to recognize Argentine sovereignty and that this result must be achieved 'within a time which at this advanced stage of the discussions will necessarily have to be short'.

Argentina wanted Britain to adopt the new 'system' for the negotiations which had been proposed *in toto*, 'as an effective step for the early solution of the dispute. However, should this not occur, Argentina reserves the right to terminate the working of this mechanism and to choose freely the procedure which best accords with her interests.'*[12]

This communiqué was accompanied by much press comment,

* The words 'the right' have been missed from the text reproduced in *Franks*. According to one account the first draft of this statement had the words 'as prescribed by the Charter of the United Nations' inserted after 'procedure'. Depending on how it was read this phrase could have either softened or toughened the message – the Charter of the United Nations is associated with the renunciation of force, but raising the issue at all could indicate that force was being considered. At this time Argentina did not want Britain to think that force was a serious option lest it improve its defences.

including another article by Sr Rouco in *La Prensa* which suggested that Britain had no more than three or four months to acknowledge Argentine sovereignty and agree a date for the return of the Islands. There was no flexibility over the time-table. He discussed the possibility of a direct seizure of the Islands, suggesting that this would be 'understood' by the United States, and that this might happen between the middle and end of the year.[13]

Although there was some discussion as to whether it was wise to fix a firm date for a British response, on 9 March the Junta decided to reconsider the issue on 1 April; if Britain had not produced a response by then, one would be demanded the following day. After another two weeks all the relevant documents would be published and the occasion of the UN's Special Session on Disarmament would be used to denounce Britain. The full Argentine case would be put to the General Assembly in October.

London Takes Notice

In London, the attempt by the intelligence community to make sense of all this over the next couple of weeks revolved around the question of whether there was any substance to these threats or whether they were simply a form of diplomatic pressure. Reports came back with a variety of interpretations gleaned from Argentine insiders. The initial consensus was that:

all elements of the Argentine Government apart from the Navy favoured diplomatic action to solve the dispute and that the military option was not under active consideration at that time. It saw no reason to believe that the Argentine Navy had any prospect of persuading the President or other Government members to adopt its proposed course of action or of going it alone.

This was in part a counter to a paper circulated by the British defence attaché in Buenos Aires who had visited the Islands. The Ministry of Defence had refused to authorize the journey so he went at his own expense. He concluded that the Argentine Navy might act independently even before the talks broke down, possibly by establishing a naval presence on an outlying island or landing marines for a brief period.

The majority view was that little would happen until the talks broke down and that then the most likely immediate consequence would be for Argentina to take the issue to the General Assembly of the United Nations to obtain a declaration recognizing its sovereignty over the Islands. Force could not be ruled out but it was still some way off. Costa Mendez at that time viewed the likely development of the dispute in similar terms.

By the middle of March intelligence was suggesting that the actual breakdown of talks might be imminent. The problem was said to be that Britain had not even agreed to a date that month for beginning the talks. Unless a date was forthcoming then retaliation could begin in the form of the withdrawal of air and sea services.

[T]here was a disposition in the Ministry of Foreign Affairs to take action to show all concerned that they were serious. Dr. Costa Mendez was also concerned to make up for the Argentine failure in the Beagle Channel dispute. An invasion was said not to have been seriously considered but in the last resort it could not be discounted in view of the unpredictability of the President and some senior members of the armed forces.[14]

The initial Argentine objective was now correctly seen to be to put pressure on the Foreign Office so that it would be obliged to review its position with some urgency and accept the Argentine proposal *in toto*. This sudden surge of pressure did help to concentrate the minds of Foreign Office ministers and officials but the result was not further concessions but the first tentative consideration of the implications of punitive action by Argentina.

As a first response Luce wrote to Ros expressing concern about the unilateral communiqué. This, together with the associated press comment, had created a 'difficult and unhelpful' climate for the talks. The threats were disturbing and progress could only be made through peaceful negotiation. Ros saw the British Ambassador Williams and accepted that the communiqué, for which he had no responsibility, was unfortunate. The Ambassador, also on 5 March, met Costa Mendez, who denied that threats were being made but also expressed his dissatisfaction with progress at the talks.[15]

The Foreign Office decided to attempt to get the talks back on the previously agreed lines by means of direct communications from Luce to Ros and from Carrington to Costa Mendez and also by indirect communications through the United States. Meanwhile the prospect of a breakdown in the talks had to be confronted; diplomatic contingency plans were needed should the issue now be taken to international organizations.

In part at the Prime Minister's urging, civil and military contingency plans were also to be reviewed. Mrs Thatcher's attention had been caught by Ambassador Williams's report from Buenos Aires on the unilateral communiqué. She had written on her copy 'we must make contingency plans'. The contingency planning would appear as annexes to the paper that the Foreign Office was now to prepare for a meeting of the Cabinet's Defence Committee. Unlike September, when Carrington had felt that there was nothing in Argentine behaviour that warranted putting the Falklands on the Committee's agenda, it was now at least felt that the issue had to be addressed 'fairly soon'.[16] Interestingly, the view of the Junta at this point was that it did not wish to cancel the Communications Agreement because of the loss of intelligence that would have resulted.

Gaining American Attention

Indirect communications through the United States achieved little because the Reagan Administration could not take the issue seriously. It had been part of the British plan even prior to this unexpected turn in the dispute to involve the Americans more closely. It was known that Thomas Enders, Under Secretary for Latin American Affairs at the State Department, was planning to visit Buenos Aires. Richard Luce went straight from the New York talks to see him. If the negotiations broke down he hoped Mr Enders would encourage the Argentines to 'keep things cool'.

When Enders arrived in Buenos Aires on 6 March the British Ambassador saw him and, with the added urgency induced by the unilateral communiqué, now asked him to stress to his Argentine hosts that Britain wished to find a solution to the dispute but could not do so against a background of threats. At the same time Carrington wrote to Secretary of State Haig warning him of the changing atmosphere in Argentina and seeking his help 'in ensuring that the issue was settled peacefully and in accordance with the democratically expressed wishes of the inhabitants of the Islands'.

From the start the British found it difficult to get the Americans to focus on the issue. In the State Department at the time 'the Falklands was not even a back-burner issue; it wasn't even on the stove'. It was not 'a full-time job even for those at the bottom of the bureaucratic ladder'.[17]

In his talks en route from New York, Luce found Enders resistant to the idea that the Falkland Islands were worth worrying about. The matter was a low priority in his discussions with Argentina. Far more important was fighting communism in the region, in which Argentine credentials were excellent, and avoiding war with Chile.

US relations with Argentina had been steadily improving under the Reagan Administration and Enders was going to Buenos Aires to see how much further this could be taken. The objective was to draw Argentina further into an anti-communist grouping. Argentina had become closely involved with US pressure against the Sandinistas in Nicaragua. Enders was interested in summoning a consultative meeting of the Inter-American Treaty of Reciprocal Aid (IATRA) against Nicaragua and possibly the creation of an inter-American force.

The Junta had its own ideological interests in getting involved in the campaign against the Sandinistas and left-wing insurgent groups in other Central American states, but this was also part of a wider policy of strengthening links with the United States. This was motivated by a desire to end the ban on arms sales to Argentina imposed during the Carter years as a response to human-rights abuses, to gain support in economic problems such as debt scheduling and, generally, to strengthen overall strategic links with the West.

The Argentine Government also shared Britain's interest in drawing the United States into the Falklands dispute, on the merits of which Washington had always been neutral. Costa Mendez had intended to bring up the issue himself when he met Enders.

When the two men met, the first possible use of force raised by Enders was with Chile over the Beagle Channel. Costa Mendez was able to reassure him that there would be no war with Chile. Later at dinner at the US Embassy Costa Mendez warned Enders that British delaying tactics in the negotiations were intolerable and that the military were getting restless. Enders told Costa Mendez that the US policy attitude was 'hands off'. According to Enders:

What I said to him was that we were 'hands off' *on the basic dispute*, but that we hoped they would get on with discussions with the British. That is what he was non-committal about, although . . . not negative. He said they were 'working on it' and they 'hoped to have something'.[18]

Costa Mendez confirms that he realized that the United States was not giving Argentina a 'green light' to do as it pleased in the affair. What he understood Enders to be saying was that 'his government considered the conflict alien to its interests, and that they did not wish to take any part in this conflict. In short, that the US would maintain on this issue its accustomed neutral stance.' He does not accept that Enders asked anything of Argentina on this matter.[19]

As to American perceptions of Argentine intentions, Enders and his team, as others, found it difficult to recognize the full significance of statements such as the 'patience of the Argentine people will not last forever', since these are the sorts of things diplomats hear regularly without much happening later on.[20] The Argentine version is that some comments communicating the British position were expected, because it was known that Enders had been asked to deliver them, but none were made.

Enders reported back to British diplomats that he had raised the matter with Costa Mendez and had not gained the impression that the

Argentines 'were about to do anything drastic'. The non-committal response he had received helped persuade him that Luce had been over-concerned. He had not even been asked for his views on an Argentine invasion.[21] When Haig wrote back to Carrington he also reported the non-committal responses Enders had received during his trip while promising to urge a constructive approach as opportunities presented themselves.[22]

Preparing for Breakdown

None of this made it any easier for the British to judge how serious the situation was becoming. Costa Mendez had said that no threats were being made but a more positive response was required from London to Argentine proposals, while other evidence pointed to the possible start of a campaign of pressure, opening with small-scale but extremely troublesome measures and then steadily escalating. Meanwhile negotiations had not actually broken down and the Americans clearly thought that the British were making a fuss about nothing.

The Government did not have any more room for diplomatic manoeuvre because of past commitments, of which the Prime Minister was keenly aware, to allow the wishes of the islanders to be paramount. While, over time, a serious and wide-ranging negotiating exercise might help to alter the wishes of the islanders, for the moment they were even more adamant than before that the sovereignty issue stay closed. The Argentine sense of urgency could simply not be matched. All that could be done was to attempt to get the negotiations back on course.

It was decided to concentrate on a letter from Carrington to Costa Mendez. The first draft expressed pleasure at the progress on procedures made at New York but disappointment with subsequent statements in Buenos Aires. Future progress could only be made if the negotiations were without prejudice to either side's position on sovereignty.

These talks must be genuine negotiations and cannot be based on any predetermined assumptions on what the outcome might be. Secondly, these negotiations cannot be pursued against a background of threats from either side of retaliatory action if they break down. We would welcome your assurance that the Argentine Government intends to further the negotiations on this basis.

The message gave nothing away. A joint meeting of the Falklands Islands Council considered that draft highly satisfactory, except that they would have liked to see it strengthened to emphasize that there could be no negotiations on the transfer of sovereignty.

Ministers and officials, however, began to have doubts. As they were preparing to send the message via a telegram for the British Ambassador in Buenos Aires they recognized that it would almost certainly produce a negative response. It was therefore unwise to send it before the Government had sorted out its contingency planning. In particular they hoped for agreement from the Ministry of Defence to keep *Endurance* on station for the time being and to prepare urgent plans for the replacement of services to the Islands. Carrington therefore decided to hold back his draft message. Instead, on 24 March, he circulated it to his Cabinet colleagues, warning that a positive response could not be expected and that the negotiations could be at an end, with other forms of pressure now being brought to bear. He hoped for an early meeting of the Defence Committee to consider the full implications of the situation and the actions it might be necessary to take.[23] By this time, however, the situation was already spinning out of control. A crisis had been precipitated by the landing on South Georgia of scrap-metal workers from Argentina.

What is noteworthy is that even then, when tension was rising, the rest of Whitehall was remarkably unresponsive to Carrington's requests. When he asked the Treasury for financial approval for further contingency planning on how best to replace air and sea services he was told by Leon Brittan, then Chief Secretary to the Treasury, that the cost could not be met from the Contingency Reserve administered by the Treasury.[24] Within the Foreign Office the unilateral communiqué had been recognized as a turning point but it was still unclear exactly where Argentina wished to take the dispute. There was a shift in gears as the Whitehall machine began to focus on the costs and consequences of a low-level confrontation, but the response was still sluggish.

Part Two

CRISIS

Chapter Four

DAVIDOFF'S VISITS

After the unilateral communiqué of the beginning of March all parties to the dispute recognized that it was moving into a new and more difficult stage, although none realized just how serious it was about to become. It cannot be said that there was any lack of understanding at this point. If anything everyone understood each other only too well. The dispute was intensifying because Argentina had decided that the time had come for a breakthrough, which Britain could not provide so long as the islanders' wishes remained paramount. The diplomats lacked any freedom of manoeuvre.

In Argentina a British response to the unilateral communiqué was awaited. If unsatisfactory, the ante would be upped in some way that had yet to be decided. Planning for a military intervention was continuing but the work was not yet complete. There was concern that the Falklands lobby might prove sufficiently powerful to get the decision on *Endurance* reversed, with the result that Britain would reinforce the overall military position in the South Atlantic and develop closer co-operation with Chile.

For their part the islanders were gloomy about the future as it became clear that the Argentine stance was toughening without a commensurate British response. And *Endurance*, it seemed, was still going to be withdrawn. In London it had now dawned on the Foreign Office that it would not be possible to prevaricate much longer, but the exact nature of the Argentine challenge remained uncertain.

This widespread feeling that matters were moving to a head was critical to the management of the scrap-metal merchants affair in March. In itself this was not an exceptional incident, but with both sides edgy it led to quicker and stronger reactions than before, working to confirm both sides' fears about the other's intentions.

Project Alpha

The scrap dealers in question were working for a private Argentine company, Georgias del Sur SA, run, since 1978, by Mr Constantino Davidoff. His contract had been awarded by a British firm in Edinburgh, Christian Salvesen Co., for the removal of what was left of the old whaling stations at Leith, Stromness and Husvik on the island of South Georgia. The British Embassy in Buenos Aires knew of the contract.

Davidoff was a free-wheeling entrepreneur and there is little doubt that his role in the affair was governed largely by a desire to make money out of his contract. Financial difficulties meant that he needed help to get to South Georgia and service his group. At one point he even inquired whether HMS *Endurance* might be able to provide passage; this was refused.[1] Accordingly in August 1981 he applied to the Ministry of Foreign Affairs and to the Argentine Navy for permission to use its Antarctic transport ships at a favourable rate. This would involve a place on the ship to get to the Islands and then subsequent logistic runs over the four-year span of the contract. It was quite standard for naval transports to be used in this way in the Sub-Antarctic.[2]

When they were approached by Davidoff the Argentine authorities were aware that the British Antarctic base at Grytviken could be removed in the near future, and that the decision had been made to withdraw *Endurance* from the South Atlantic. An Argentine presence for the next four years, with yearly runs by transports to the Islands, under a legal contract between a British and an Argentine company, offered a way of strengthening their position in the disputed territories while setting precedents for joint ventures in the South Atlantic. The Ministry of Foreign Affairs therefore recommended to the Navy that it agree to Davidoff's request.

This the Navy was happy to do. The advantages were obvious and could be achieved without having to do anything blatantly provocative. It had no alternative means of establishing a presence. The arrangement would allow for at least two stops a year for its ships on Antarctic duties to provide supplies. It seemed preferable to a covert attempt to establish a base on South Georgia, which might be precluded because of the fragile state of the negotiations with Britain.

However, there was also a scheme to take advantage of the Davidoff venture to establish a base covertly. This was Project Alpha. The aim was to replicate the successful venture in 1976 when, in one of the first Junta's earliest acts a presence had been established on South Thule in the South Sandwich Islands. During a routine visit by *Endurance* to the Island on 20 December 1976, Argentine personnel were discovered. They had been there since the previous month. On 5 January 1977 Britain asked Argentina for an explanation. This arrived on 14 January. Argentina described its objective as establishing a station on South Thule for future scientific investigation 'within the jurisdiction of Argentine sovereignty' and hinted that the presence would not be permanent. Britain formally protested the presence as a 'violation of British sovereignty', asserted an expectation of prior consultation and hoped that the scientific programme would be 'terminated', which it was not.

The precedent was enticing. Britain had not made a fuss either publicly or through international channels. It took until May 1978 before the news leaked. At first only an explanation was required, and the formal protest arrived a month after the landing. Moreover, it was followed almost immediately by a softening of the British position in the negotiations with a willingness to discuss sovereignty.[3]

The plan for South Georgia would allow a point to be made about sovereignty and a permanent presence established in the same way. Project Alpha had been formed in September 1981, just after the first request had come from Davidoff for passage on a naval transport, and under the previous regime. To the Argentine Navy here was an opportunity to exploit the British decision on *Endurance* and in such a way as to improve its reputation, which had been tarnished by its involvement in the 'dirty war' against the left.

South Georgia was politically more important than South Thule, and it already had the scientific base manned by the British Antarctic Survey. The plan was to infiltrate Davidoff's workforce wih military 'scientists' who would then be part of the 'legal' landing party on South Georgia. They would later be joined by a group of marines who would embark on a ship on the resupply route to Argentina's Antarctic bases and establish a more permanent military base of some fourteen men from April onwards. This would be just after *Endurance* had departed the South Atlantic for the last time. Over the southern winter, when no effective action could be taken to eject the base, *de facto* sovereignty would be asserted through broadcasting weather and navigational reports.[4]

The First Visit

Davidoff and his men were issued with the 'white cards' that served as bilateral documentation in the dealings of both countries in the South Atlantic region as per the 1971 Communication Accords.[5] On 16 December, two days before Galtieri replaced Viola as President, Davidoff left Buenos Aires aboard *Almirante Irizar*, a naval ice-breaker of the Antarctic Squadron, captained by Captain César Trombetta. They arrived on the 21st and Davidoff made his inspection of the whaling stations in Stromness Bay.

Although Davidoff had permission for the visit, the manner in which he was taken by the Argentine Navy was not calculated to ease British suspicions. He notified the British Embassy in Buenos Aires of his date of sailing, but the letter arrived after he had left and it was vague in detail and did not ask for diplomatic clearance for the *Almirante Irizar*. He also sent a telex to Salvesen, who relayed the message the next day, 17 December, to Governor Hunt in Stanley.[6] En route the *Almirante Irizar* maintained radio silence and did not notify the Magistrate (the designation given the commander of the British Antarctic Survey to indicate Crown authority) at King Edward Point, Grytviken, to notify him of the arrival. King Edward Point was the official point of entry where Customs and Immigration clearance was obtained.

By the time that the BAS discovered that the visit had been made the *Almirante Irizar* had gone. The Magistrate visited Leith on 23 December to find traces of the Argentine visit including a wall defaced with the slogan 'Las Malvinas son Argentinas', helpfully dated 20 December. The news of the visitation was passed to Governor Hunt, who in turn passed it to London on 31 December. This was almost two weeks after the landing. Hunt advised a strong protest and the institution of proceedings against Davidoff on the grounds that he was well aware of the requirement to obtain entry clearance at Grytviken.[7]

The Foreign Office was not sure what to make of this incident. If Davidoff reappeared Hunt was told to ensure that he respected the formalities. He was not, however, to institute proceedings as this 'would risk provoking a most serious incident which could escalate and have an unforeseeable outcome'.[8] After waiting to see if there was any further activity, on 4 January London instructed the British Ambassador to Buenos Aires to make a formal protest. When he approached the Argentine Ministry of Foreign Affairs two days later he was told that the Ministry had no knowledge of the incident and was investigating. He decided to wait.

When further information was obtained confirming that the visit had indeed taken place he was again – on 3 February – instructed to lodge a formal complaint. Six days later, and some fifty days after the offence had been committed, he did so. Ambassador Williams warned that this had been a violation of British sovereignty, and that if a further attempt were made to land without proper authority the British Government reserved the right to take whatever action necessary. After the passing of another nine days a rejection was received from the Argentine Ministry.[9]

Alpha Postponed

Although the British protest was rejected the Ministry of Foreign Affairs (now under new management) did make their own inquiries into the relations between Davidoff and the Navy. Enrique Ros, the Deputy Foreign Minister, discovered that there was a naval plan –

Project Alpha – to use the Davidoff venture to station a military detachment in South Georgia.

The new Junta had not been responsible for the first Davidoff visit but were sensitive from the start to its implications. It had been one of the matters discussed in its first meeting on 5 January. There was some concern that the issue could complicate the negotiating process with Britain and it was decided to postpone any further visits until after the next round of talks.

Doubts had also set in among the Navy as to whether it was wise to proceed with Alpha. Vice-Admiral Juan José Lombardo, the Commander of Naval Operations, had been a supporter of the Project, which he saw as a means of restoring morale following the decision to hold back from a confrontation with Chile. He, as with other proponents of the plan, had assumed that Britain would learn to tolerate an Argentine presence in South Georgia, as it had previously learned to tolerate that in South Thule, so long as all the communications agreements with the Falklands themselves continued to be observed.[10] But Lombardo was also one of the few officers closely involved in the preparation of military plans for a landing on the Falkland Islands themselves – the main prize. He realized that the surprise factor would be lost if Britain saw the South Thule example being repeated on South Georgia. Admiral Anaya agreed that it should not go ahead.[11]

The Ministry of Foreign Affairs was equally anxious for the Project to be at least postponed. Ros, who did not know of the plans for a military intervention, was concerned that it would interfere with the negotiating exercise upon which he was then about to embark. Costa Mendez, who did, was also concerned that such an operation could turn out to be a wild card and disrupt the orderly process of applied pressure planned for 1982. He was aware of renewed interest in Britain in the Thule affair and therefore possible sensitivity to an attempt at a repeat performance.

In addition, Costa Mendez was anxious that his Ministry's advice should be sought before any actions were taken in the South Atlantic over the coming months.[12] On 2 February 1982, the Junta considered Project Alpha. It was resolved that this was not a convenient time for its implementation. Whether or not it was to be executed in the future would depend, they agreed, on the advice of Costa Mendez. It was decided that Davidoff's proposed visit to South Georgia, which could be considered separately from Alpha, should not go ahead for the time being in order that it should not interfere with the bilateral negotiations that were to take place at the end of February in New York.[13] It would be unwise to alarm the British unduly when the negotiations were still at such a delicate stage. The operation was therefore held in reserve and not fully cancelled.[14]

The relationship between what was to happen in March and the original Project is not fully clear. The Junta's records show that it believed the Project to have been regularly postponed since it had been first conceived the previous September and that it was also something separate from the Davidoff contract. There was a decision to ensure that Alpha should not be considered except in the context of the Falklands campaign.

In early March the Junta received a proposal for the *Bahia Buen Suceso*, which was to deliver Davidoff's men to South Georgia, also to take six Air Force men to one of the South Sandwich Islands to do a reconnaissance to build a lighthouse in a less risky repetition of the South Thule episode. This idea was rejected. As late as 15 March the Minister of Foreign Affairs was asked again by the Chairman of the Joint Chiefs of Staff about the possibility of the Alpha project being set in motion. Costa Mendez recommended against it.

Although at the most senior levels of government Alpha was not authorized, it is likely from the number of times that the matter was raised that there was pressure for it to go ahead. In February a Panamanian-registered yacht, *Caiman*, with an Argentine crew had gone to Leith and had then been escorted to Grytviken. On board was an Argentine Bank employee, Adrian Marchessi, who told the BAS that he was doing some more reconnaissance for the Davidoff contract, although Davidoff subsequently claimed that he was a commercial competitor. Perhaps Marchessi is to be believed. The Junta had not authorized the trip, but Davidoff may have been trying to find out more at a time when his Government would not allow a naval transport to take him. Significantly no British protest was made.

It has been argued by a variety of investigators into this affair that

45

the main elements of Project Alpha were implemented. It has been suggested that the Navy personnel involved decided to go ahead anyway, perhaps with the authority of the two senior officers in charge – Rear Admiral Eduardo Morris Girling, Chief of Naval Intelligence, and Admiral Edgardo Otero, in charge of Naval Transport, and both hardliners. One source even argues that Anaya was still backing the Project despite having told Lombardo that it was cancelled.[15] We have found no evidence to support the key allegations made in support of this theory.[16]

The marines who eventually arrived at South Georgia had been at Thule, from where they had been taken by the *Almirante Irizar*, the ice-breaker involved in Davidoff's first visit, to the Islas Orcadas, where they were to help build a house. While the *Almirante Irizar* was in the Argentine port of Ushuaia, having returned from South Georgia and about to leave for Thule, during the period 24–28 December 1981 *Endurance* entered the port. Captain Barker received a frosty reception, and was given inaccurate information, since Captain Trombetta had no wish to tell him that he was going to Thule, where, according to the British, he had no right to be.[17]

For his part Davidoff wished to continue with his contract, having been convinced by his reconnaissance in December that there was plenty of material worth salvaging. He recruited his workmen and asked for naval transport. This was granted by the Navy provided the sailing date was postponed until after the talks due to be held with Britain in New York in late February 1982.

When it was decided to take Davidoff's salvage workers to South Georgia, this was not part of an effort to increase the pressure on Britain after the New York talks. Admiral Otero's office, in charge of transportation and logistics, gave the go-ahead to the trip without further consultation with the Ministry of Foreign Affairs.[18] This perhaps is the best indication that those involved in Project Alpha had not let the whole idea lapse and were still anxious, one way or another, to establish some sort of presence on South Georgia.

Davidoff was not held back while the New York talks were being assessed. He went to the British Embassy in Buenos Aires on 23 February, just five days after the Argentine rejection of the protest over his previous visit and four days before the start of the New York talks. He sought to smooth things over with the British, apologizing for causing so much trouble. He now wanted to return to South Georgia and asked for instructions on how to proceed. When news of the conversation was sent to London and to Stanley no objections were received. No substantive reply at all came from Governor Hunt in Stanley, apparently because he needed to consult with the Base Commander at Grytviken, who was en route to South Georgia at the time.

On 9 March Davidoff provided the Embassy with formal confirmation that forty-one of his men were about to sail with the Argentine Navy to South Georgia where they would stay for four months. Two days later his men sailed with the *Bahia Buen Suceso*. Just before they left Davidoff's lawyer rang to confirm that the boat was sailing; he was reminded of the need to report to King Edward Point, Grytviken, for entry purposes.[19]

The Second Visit

On 18 March the *Bahia Buen Suceso* arrived at Leith and began unloading supplies. While Davidoff may have been anxious to keep the British happy, the Argentine Navy was less concerned to do so. Once again the boat travelled in radio silence and did not stop at Grytviken, but went directly to Leith Harbour. Davidoff's original contract stressed the need to observe the legalities and this had been reaffirmed in the British protests following the December visit. It may be that Davidoff assumed that as he had done this time what he had failed to do before – notify the British Embassy in advance – there would be no problems.

The Argentine Navy certainly knew the rules for the Islands; these were part of the navigation code. Even if he was not intending to be deliberately provocative, the Captain might have disregarded this rule. He had a tight schedule – South Georgia was something of a detour and he still had to continue with his original itinerary. Just as likely, he found the idea of stopping officially at Grytviken when the territory was under dispute disagreeable. The Argentine Navy had not been to the Island prior to the first Davidoff visit so there were no precedents. The British protests following the previous visit had been late in coming, rejected by the Ministry of Foreign Affairs and without long-term consequences. Furthermore, Davidoff had ensured that the British were fully informed.

It may also have been hoped that the transport ship could reach its destination and unload the workmen and their stores before being discovered by the British. This had been achieved in December. Hence the radio silence.[20] It has to be said that if the Argentine Navy was seeking to establish a long-term presence on the Islands that behaviour was tactically foolish. There was no need to act as intruders and if the legalities had been observed Operation Alpha could have been implemented later. Instead the conduct of the second visit simply served to excite British suspicions.[21]

This time the ship was discovered while at anchor. On 19 March a party from the British Antarctic Survey arrived at Leith Harbour, where they found the *Bahia Buen Suceso* unloading and the Argentine flag flying ashore.[22] A warning notice against unauthorized landings had been defaced. There seemed to be around 100 people ashore. They were making themselves comfortable, having occupied the BAS refuge and shot some reindeer (although this was a protected species).* The observers went to explain to Captain Briatore of the *Bahia Buen Suceso* that his presence was illegal and that he should report to Grytviken. They were told that the landing had been authorized by the British Embassy in Buenos Aires. The four observers then reported all this back to King Edward Point from where, with some difficulty, the information was transmitted to Rex Hunt, the Governor of the Falkland Islands.[23]

---

* Similar problems were experienced at the same time with a French yacht which had inadvertently found its way to South Georgia at that time, the crew of which were also alleged to have carried firearms, shot reindeer and vandalized BAS depots.

Chapter Five

CRISIS OVER SOUTH GEORGIA

The View from Stanley

This time the British response came in hours rather than weeks. The failure to observe the rules was not now seen as a one-off incident; rather it was interpreted as consistent with an observable pattern. Hunt's immediate assessment of the Argentine landing was that it was part of a surreptitious attempt to establish a permanent presence on South Georgia. In this view he was supported by two other key figures – Nicholas Barker, Captain of HMS *Endurance*, and Lord Buxton, a peer with a longstanding interest in the South Atlantic who had been a leading figure in the campaign to save *Endurance* and was now visiting Stanley.

The second Davidoff visit to Leith demonstrated a complete disregard for the agreed procedures for arrivals at South Georgia, despite the strong protests that had been made after the December incident. He had been warned about unauthorized landings and yet here he was doing it again.

The pattern of activity noted in Stanley was not confined to the Davidoff visits. Also to be considered was the visit of the Panamanian-registered yacht, *Caiman*, to Leith with its Argentine crew and some link to the Davidoff contract. There had also been three overflights of South Georgia by Argentine Hercules aircraft in early 1982 – the last on 11 March. While such overflights were quite regular, those in 1982 seemed to indicate a disturbing amount of interest in South Georgia.

Lastly, the conduct of both the *Almirante Irizar* and the *Bahia Buen Suceso*, especially in maintaining radio silence, excited suspicions.

To Hunt, Barker and Buxton the evidence pointed to an Argentine attempt to repeat their success in establishing a presence in South Thule. The Argentine Navy had called the shots over South Thule and they seemed to be calling them again now.* The first Davidoff visit had taken place at the same time of the year as the South Thule landing and it had taken even longer to lodge an official protest. Perhaps the Argentine Government had drawn the conclusion from the weak response to the December landing that the Thule success might be repeated.

Buxton had gained the impression from talks with Costa Mendez while in Buenos Aires a few weeks earlier that while invasion was discounted as an option there might well be unopposed landings.[1] For his part Barker had been expecting such an attempt for some time. His experiences over recent months had rendered him suspicious of the Argentine Navy. Barker had met Captain Trombetta, Commander of the Antarctic Naval Squadron and then in charge of the *Almirante Irizar* not long before the first Davidoff visit to South Georgia and had been given a programme for the *Irizar* which contained no mention of South Georgia; in early January he had again met Trombetta and this time had been told that the *Irizar* was on its way to the Antarctic Belgrano base when in fact it was headed for South Thule. Later that month he had visited Ushuaia, where he received a cold reception and was told that he was in a war zone. This was said to be more a reflection of concern with Chile than with Britain, but the 'Malvinas' factor was not absent.[2]

According to one account: 'Hunt and Barker were agreed that the

* Intelligence in 1977 indicated that the Argentine presence was the result of a naval initiative. It had involved more personnel than admitted and was to have been made public in March 1977 if it had not been discovered. A stronger British reaction had been expected and the Navy had made contingency plans for this. *Franks*, para. 54. The initiative had in fact been taken by Admiral Massera, Commander-in-Chief of the Navy. Massera was later accused of unduly politicizing the Navy and of developing plans for the recovery of territories disputed with both Chile and Great Britain. He had political aspirations of his own and, although on good terms with the deposed President Isabel Perón, he became a member of the 1976 Junta.

landing by Davidoff's employees was nothing more than a cover for the establishment of an Argentine navy beachhead on South Georgia, leading later to assertions of sovereignty over the whole island. Their view was supported by Lord Buxton.'[3]

In discussing a response, in addition to a stiff protest, they felt that *Endurance* should be sent to South Georgia. The counter-argument was that if the affair turned into anything bigger it would be important to have *Endurance* at Stanley. But there were difficulties with expecting the British Antarctic Survey to carry responsibility for British policy. The Base Commander, though dignified by the title of Magistrate, was now being expected to organize surveillance and hand over diplomatic notes.[4]

This was the view sent by Hunt to London on 20 March. It was not until later that day that the first advice came from the Embassy in Buenos Aires on how to manage the issue. Then Ambassador Williams advised caution, as he was to do a number of times over the next few days. His suggestion was that 'great restraint should be used, at least until it was clear whether or not the incident was a deliberate challenge authorised at a higher level.'[5]

The View from London

In determining its response to the news of the second Davidoff visit, the Foreign Office had to decide whether it was sufficient to respond, as in December, with insistence that the rules be followed and a protest to Buenos Aires. Or should, as the Governor proposed, the Base Commander order the Argentine party to leave irrespective of whether the courtesy call to Grytviken was now made? The low-key approach after the first visit did not appear to have made the slightest impact on Argentine behaviour. If the British stance had to be toughened by refusing permission to Davidoff to continue with his contract, should the punishment be enforced by sending *Endurance* to South Georgia, as Hunt had recommended?

When Richard Luce, the responsible Foreign Office Minister, was contacted by telephone on the Saturday afternoon his concern was 'to smooth this one over'. He was told that the landing was a 'provocation'. However:

> The advice was that we should try and sort out the problem of Davidoff's papers and see whether we could legitimize his presence. It made sense to see if we could devise a formula which would allow him to do that. It was not, after all, a military invasion which would have been quite a different picture.

He also indicates, as does Franks, that this was the advice received from Ambassador Williams in Buenos Aires.[6]

None the less it was the advice from Stanley that was followed. Although the Franks Report suggests otherwise, that the decision-takers were 'Foreign and Commonwealth and Defence Ministers', it seems that this was the Prime Minister's decision. This is reported by Hastings and Jenkins, who say that it was taken 'with remarkable promptness' largely by the Prime Minister, together with Carrington. Given the political sensitivity surrounding anything to do with *Endurance* it would have been surprising if junior ministers had felt that this was the sort of decision that they could have taken on their own. Luce confirms this. The critical decision was Mrs Thatcher's – 'to demonstrate that we were concerned, that Britain *did* mind about it, and we could not allow this sort of thing to happen'.[7]

There was to be no delay: 'HMS *Endurance* should sail for South Georgia the next day, with additional marines, unless the Argentines obeyed the Governor's instructions.'[8] Not a lot of time was allowed to discover if the Argentines were interested in obeying the Governor's instructions. This expeditious departure may have been intended to demonstrate resolve, or indeed simply reflected the actual resolve of the Prime Minister, along with Governor Hunt and Captain Barker.

Yet in Whitehall there was still caution. Rather than the dispatch of *Endurance* being seen as the first step in a particular course of action, it appeared as the creation of a later option, should a tougher line become necessary. When, towards midnight on 20 March, the Commander-in-Chief, Fleet, sent instructions to *Endurance* to sail for South Georgia, the task was as much intelligence-gathering –

reporting any developments on the Island – as coercion. To avoid escalating the incident, Captain Barker was in fact instructed to keep his destination confidential. This would not enhance the demonstrative effect of the move.

None the less, demonstrative effect it did have, for, as we shall see, the Argentine representative at Stanley was aware of the sailing on the morning of 21 March, and the fact that *Endurance* contained a detachment of marines. This key move in the affair was thus taken with a degree of equivocation that was repeated every time the question of how to use *Endurance* and its marines was raised. The desire to take a tough line was continually qualified by an awareness that local military superiority belonged to Argentina.

The British Embassy in Buenos Aires was told to contact the Argentine Ministry of Foreign Affairs to explain how seriously this incident was viewed and to warn that, if the *Bahia Buen Suceso* did not leave, Britain would take whatever action was deemed necessary. It was suggested that at a time when the negotiations between the two sides were at such a delicate stage 'it would be hard to understand if the Argentine government endorsed the incident.' The same message was given to the Argentine Chargé d'Affaires in London, left alone to cope with the developing crisis with his Ambassador away dealing with the Beagle Channel dispute.[9]

The View from Buenos Aires

As it had not authorized the second Davidoff visit, the Ministry of Foreign Affairs was caught by surprise by the incident. When Costa Mendez received the news of the British protest he was in his summer house some miles from Buenos Aires – to where he now returned with the first objective of contacting Admiral Anaya to find out more information on the *Bahia Buen Suceso* before replying to Britain.

His decision was to play down the incident, rebutting the suggestion that there was an attempt to establish a military base on the Island, without admitting that there was any foundation to the British complaint over entry procedures. The formal Argentine response, handed over by Ambassador Blanco of the Ministry of Foreign Affairs to Ambassador Williams, therefore questioned the veracity of some of the information from the British Antarctic Survey, including the purported involvement of military personnel and firearms. It was explained that the *Bahia Buen Suceso* was a transport and not a warship, used on this occasion because there was no other way to get Davidoff to the Island. All this had been relayed to the British Government beforehand. However, Ambassador Blanco was able to promise that the *Bahia Buen Suceso* would be leaving the next day. He also insisted that South Georgia itself was not of great importance in the context of the Anglo-Argentine negotiations and that it was vital that the issue was not blown up out of proportion. According to the Argentine account of the meeting the two men agreed to 'collaborate to deflate the incident'.[10]

With the Embassy in Buenos Aires urging restraint and not casting doubt on the Argentine explanation, the Foreign Office adopted a more conciliatory stance. In London the next day, 21 March, a Foreign Office official, Mr Fearn, informed Mr Molteni (the Chargé d'Affaires) that Britain was satisfied with the explanations sent and that it trusted the *Bahia Buen Suceso* would depart by the next day with the landing party. He also hoped that this incident would not be repeated.

To the Foreign Office's relief the departure of the ship was soon confirmed on Monday 22 March, first by Argentina and then by the British Antarctic Survey. *Endurance* was instructed to resume her normal duties unless the Base Commander reported a continued Argentine presence at Leith.[11]

The relief was based on the assumption that all the Argentine party had left with the ship. It was reinforced by Monday's first contact with Argentina when the Chargé d'Affaires came to visit Fearn. Molteni reported that the *Bahia Buen Suceso* had departed from Leith, leaving behind equipment. According to the British account, he 'assumed' that all the personnel had left with the ship. In response he was told that the British Government had no wish to build up the incident.

This assumption was central to what followed, for part of the backlash against Buenos Aires was the belief that Britain had been misled on this score. Perhaps, it was thought, the second visit was comparable to the first and there never had been an Argentine intention to leave a presence on the Island. Alternatively the British diplomats may have judged that the quick and firm response had caught Buenos Aires wrong-footed and left it with little choice but to comply with British demands.

Argentine accounts confirm that when Ambassador Blanco spoke to Ambassador Williams on the Sunday he mentioned the ship leaving after material, but not personnel, had been taken ashore. They also note that in the Monday morning meeting in London Fearn expressed himself in conciliatory terms, thanked Molteni for the rapid Argentine reaction and insisted that his Government viewed the incident as finished. However, while the British account reports Molteni's *assumption* that the personnel had left with the ship, the Argentine account suggests that the Chargé d'Affaires had answered to the effect that he 'knew nothing about Davidoff's workers'.

If the affair was almost over then the press could be told. Of course, if it was not, the consequences of drawing in the media could aggravate matters. The proposed Foreign Office communiqué, which was later issued, reported simply that Argentine workers had landed without documentation in Leith but that the Argentine Government had given assurances to the effect that they would be evacuated.

According to the Argentine account of the Fearn–Molteni meeting, Molteni suggested that any communiqué should include a paragraph to the effect that the Argentine ship had already departed, that it was not a warship but a naval transport vessel, without service personnel or weapons on board, helping with a legitimate commercial enterprise. (It does not, however, indicate that he objected to the assurance that the workers would be evacuated.) Argentina also expected to be told when the communiqué was being issued.

However, the communiqué was released on the evening of 22 March without the extra paragraph. Argentine officials thought that the contents were still under negotiation, and had not been told that the communiqué was about to be issued. When this happened it was at first assumed that this was a press leak. The strong reaction in the British media the next day further excited Argentine suspicions. Costa

Mendez recalled a press leak in 1968 which had revealed the extent of Anglo-Argentine negotiations and led to such an outcry that the talks had been frozen.

The Argentine Ministry of Foreign Affairs therefore issued its own communiqué reporting that the *Bahia Buen Suceso* had left Leith after disembarking the workers and the material that belonged to a commercial enterprise in South Georgia under a valid contract.[12]

Thus Argentina argued that nothing untoward had happened and that there was no need to get agitated. It was pleased to point out that the boat had not intended to stay, and added that it had never accepted that Davidoff's expedition must now be aborted. The British had insisted that Davidoff had failed to play by the rules and could not expect his personnel to carry on in South Georgia as though nothing had happened. The apparent confirmation on the morning of the 22 March that this demand had been met raised hopes in London that the incident had been dealt with firmly and expeditiously. By the afternoon of that day these hopes had been dashed.

Left in Georgia

As soon as he heard of the arrival of the *Bahia Buen Suceso*, Hunt had sent the Base Commander a message to be taken to Captain Briatore informing him that his landing was without proper clearance and thus illegal. He should go to Grytviken. No military personnel were to land ashore nor firearms be taken on to the Island. The Argentine flag should be removed and there should be no more interference with the BAS depot. This was delivered early in the morning of 20 March. The Argentine flag was removed about a quarter of an hour after the Governor's message had been delivered, but none of the other directives was complied with.

The Governor also requested the BAS to establish an observation post overlooking Stromness Bay. One was established early on the morning of 21 March. Two men, in inclement conditions and equipped with powerful binoculars, occupied a spot five miles from Leith Harbour but with an excellent view. A Spanish-speaking member of the Survey monitored Argentine ship-to-shore and other radio signals.[13] This was not the BAS's natural function and the information was inevitably equivocal. The BAS still had to carry on with their normal scientific work and were not sure how seriously to take the arrival of the Argentine party.[14] It was not until *Endurance* arrived on 24 March that more professional surveillance could be arranged.

Thus, having been asked on the 21 March whether or not the Argentine party contained service personnel and was carrying military arms, the Base Commander could not be definite. Some of the party 'were dressed in what appeared to him to be military-style clothing and had behaved in a military way, but had not carried firearms. Between 50 and 60 Argentines had been seen, most of them in civilian clothing. Although no firearms had been seen, further shots had been heard and reindeer had been killed.'[15]

There were no signs that the party was preparing to leave. That evening radio communications were picked up to the effect that more drums of fuel were being unloaded, more reindeer were being shot and that Captain Briatore was planning to leave. Late that evening (19.00) they heard the siren of the *Bahia Buen Suceso* as she left. The next morning, the 22 March, the observers saw that the harbour was empty.[16] The Base Commander was able to report that the *Bahia Buen Suceso* had left Leith and that there was no sign of the shore party, although salvage equipment and many other items remained. This was the basis for Fearn's optimistic encounter with Molteni when he took the Chargé d'Affaires to have confirmed that the party had left with the ship.

Later that day it transpired that the first impressions had been incorrect. The BAS observation post reported again, this time informing London that some Argentines were still at Leith. At least ten men had been seen, though the actual number was much higher. Later it was determined that thirty-nine salvage workers were there, which was close to the forty-one workers that Davidoff had proposed to send to the Island when he discussed the matter with the British Embassy in February.[17] Throughout the crisis, however, the figure of 'ten men' was used by Britain and it is not contradicted in any of the Argentine accounts.

Confirmation came that evening from Buenos Aires that some men had been left behind at Leith. Williams had visited Blanco to check that all personnel had been evacuated. He was told that some salvage workers were still there. He said that the people should leave immediately; Ambassador Blanco informed him that evacuation would now be very difficult. In reporting this back to London Williams 'urged that no forceful action should be taken which would irritate public opinion in Argentina'.[18]

It was now becoming too late for moderation. Once again the Ambassador's plea for restraint (as before coupled with bad news) arrived after calls for stronger action from the triumvirate of Hunt, Barker and Buxton. All three had already been in contact with the Foreign Office. Lord Buxton had sent a personal message to Carrington reporting his recent conversations with Costa Mendez, warning that Davidoff was not a casual scrap-dealer and urging that his contract should be rescinded immediately. 'He judged that, if the British reaction was placatory, more illegal landings would follow, the next time probably on the Falkland Islands.' Captain Barker's signal reported 'indications of collusion between Sr. Davidoff and the Argentine Navy'. He had picked up a message from the naval headquarters in Buenos Aires congratulating the *Bahia Buen Suceso* on a successful operation, and directing her to return to Buenos Aires as soon as possible. The next day he sent a further signal outlining his earlier experiences with the Argentine Navy and the radio silence maintained by the *Bahia Buen Suceso* during its South Georgia excursion. To the BAS report, of the evening of 2 March, that the Argentines were still at Leith the Governor added his view that *Endurance* should now be instructed to proceed with their removal.[19]

On the morning of 23 March, the Foreign Office concluded that the Argentine expedition was not so innocent after all. Largely on the basis of the intelligence from Barker they accepted that 'the operation in South Georgia had been undertaken with the full knowledge and probable guidance of the Argentine Navy.' The Minister in charge, Richard Luce, was persuaded of this and agreed that *Endurance* and the Royal Marines aboard her should be used to remove the estimated ten Argentines left at Leith.[20] If it had been known then that there were four times as many men there a more cautious approach might have been taken.

Luce reported to the House of Commons what had been going on and the action taken:

We were informed on 20 March by the Commander of the British Antarctic Survey based at Grytviken on South Georgia that a party of Argentines had landed at Leith nearby. The Base Commander informed the Argentine party that its presence was illegal as it had not obtained his prior authority for the landing. We immediately took the matter up with the Argentine authorities in Buenos Aires and the Argentine Embassy in London and, following our approach, the ship and most of the personnel left on 21 March. However, the Base Commmander has reported that a small number of men and some equipment remain. We are therefore making arrangements to ensure their early departure.

Under questioning he reaffirmed that with regard to the Falklands 'The islanders' wishes are paramount' and that 'it is the duty of this Government and of any British Government to defend and support the islanders to the best of their ability.' With regard to this particular crisis he promised 'firm action' but he could be no more specific than to say that *Endurance* with a detachment of Royal Marines was 'in the area'.[21] The phrase 'to the best of our ability', which was used often by Luce and also by Lord Trefgarne in the Lords, indicated less than complete confidence that the islanders *could* be defended.

Ambassador Williams was informed of the decision to evict the remaining Argentines and was instructed to tell the Ministry of Foreign Affairs, that Britain had been left with no alternative but to take this action, which would be conducted correctly, peacefully and in as low a key as possible. *Endurance* would arrive the next day to evict the workers and take them to Stanley. The salvage workers' continued presence was contrary to previous assurances – although, as we have seen, there never had been unequivocal Argentine assurances that the workers would leave. The Ministry was also advised of the Commons debate that would take place that same day.

Search for a Compromise

Up to this point the Ministry of Foreign Affairs had been maintaining a consistent position with Britain. The question of the workers at Leith should not be exaggerated. They were only civilians doing their job and this had nothing to do with a military occupation. The incident should be reduced to more sensible proportions. The impression that they gained throughout from the British Ambassador was that he too wished to avoid exaggeration.

When first told that *Endurance* now had orders to evict the workers Molteni warned that the atmosphere in Buenos Aires was becoming as highly charged as in London. He repeated that the men in South Georgia were fulfilling a valid contract and were not part of an occupation force; evicting them would result in an incident of unknown consequences.

When Molteni reported this meeting to Buenos Aires, Ambassador Williams was summoned to talk to Costa Mendez while Molteni was instructed to seek a further interview with the Foreign Office. The message was that the Argentine Government wanted to continue to negotiate but that moderate elements were losing control. The British Government was urged not to proceed with the use of force. 'Harsh action would precipitate a harsh response.' Williams suggested that Costa Mendez explore the possibility of the *Bahia Buen Suceso* returning to South Georgia to take the men and so render the journey of *Endurance* unnecessary. Reporting back to London that Costa Mendez had agreed to do this he added his customary warning that great damage could result to Anglo-Argentine relations if Britain overreacted to Davidoff's 'trivial and low-level misbehaviour'.[22]

As before, Williams's advice made the Foreign Office hesitate before implementing a hardline policy already agreed. Responding to this initiative Carrington decided to modify the position taken earlier. When Molteni met Fearn at 20.30 that evening he was told that following the Costa Mendez–Williams meeting in Buenos Aires, the Foreign Secretary had decided to order *Endurance* to proceed to Grytviken instead of Leith and await further instructions. A compromise was available but an urgent decision from Argentina was necessary because of the intense pressure being faced by the Government.

Later a message from Lord Carrington to Costa Mendez was passed to the Chargé d'Affaires:

> In view of the high emotional tone that this incident has created in the United Kingdom (as your Chargé d'Affaires has witnessed today in the Houses of Parliament), it is now essential for the Argentine personnel that still remains in South Georgia to be evacuated promptly. If the Argentine Government can order the immediate return of the Bahia Buen Suceso to Leith Harbour to carry out this action, the use of HMS Endurance will not be necessary. If this is not done, we would have no alternative but to proceed. We hope that the Argentine Government will let us know as soon as possible when we can expect the Bahia Buen Suceso's return. Our principal objective now is to avoid that this issue should gain political momentum. It is essential for us not to lose the vital political climate for our mutual efforts regarding the peaceful resolution of the Falkland dispute through negotiations. For this end, we must proceed cautiously and with prudence on this incident.[23]

The initial response from Costa Mendez was positive; he thought that another Argentine ship might be able to remove the men and would ask the military. The next day, 24 March, he told Ambassador Williams that he was hopeful but this depended on decisions taken at the next meeting of the Commanders-in-Chief. By the evening the news was less optimistic; the Navy were reluctant to comply under the threat of force implied by the dispatch of *Endurance*. However, encouraged by the news that *Endurance* had not gone directly to Leith he said that he would discover whether Davidoff could arrange for a scientific ship in the area to remove the men, but he was not hopeful.

No Compromise

There was no compromise because the Junta was not interested in achieving one and because it had an alternative move to make to counter the military action proposed by Britain. The possibility for compromise had diminished between Costa Mendez's meeting with Williams on 23 March and the receipt of Carrington's message. By then the Junta had decided to harden rather than soften its own stance.

It was influenced at a basic level by underlying attitudes with regard to the disputed territories in the South Atlantic. There were also powerful political and military pressures not only against concessions to Britain but also to use this opportunity to take a strong stand. While the crisis had not been manufactured to deflect attention from the substantial economic and political discontent afflicting the country, publicly backing down to British demands would have further harmed the Junta's already shaky popular standing. As Molteni discussed with Fearn the emotional tone of the debates in Britain he warned that 'a similar atmosphere in Argentina cannot be discounted.'

The details of the crisis were also critical in shaping the Junta's attitude. Its members saw the Falklands lobby becoming active once more and concluded that the situation was being exaggerated by this lobby to compel a toughening of the British stance on the whole territorial dispute and, even worse, reinforcement of Britain's military presence in the area. If this took place it would thwart any later attempts by Argentina to use military means to support its renewed diplomatic offensive.

The Junta could assess the pressures correctly because it was well informed about the mood in both Stanley and London. From Stanley it was kept in touch by the Argentine naval representative in the Falkland Islands at the time. Since 1980 Captain Adolfo A. Gaffoglio had been in charge of the liaison between the Argentine ships that visited the Falklands under the Communication Accords of 1971.[24]

During the afternoon of March 20, we started getting the first rumours of an Argentine presence in South Georgia. The anti-Argentine committee was very active and held many meetings as of that time. I could almost say that they were in a state of alert even previous to this date. In the evening I went to the Town Hall where there was going to be a meeting . . . I immediately noticed that there were no marines in the Town Hall and this was strange because since March 18 they had been celebrating the fact that their period in the islands was now due to end . . .

At 0800 hours of March 21 (Sunday) the HMS Endurance left the harbour and hooted its farewell to Stanley. Rumours were rife that the ship was sailing to the South Georgia island and that the marines were on board with weapons and other elements . . .

Later that day Gaffoglio discovered that the LADE (Argentine Air Force airline) office had been broken into and a British flag had been placed over the Argentine one. (He had noted anti-Argentine activists outside the LADE office the night before.) A message was written on his desk which read: 'tit for tat, you buggers'. All this Gaffoglio reported back to Buenos Aires.

On 23 March, before responding to the British demands concerning the workers at Leith, the Ministry of Foreign Affairs complained about the incident at Stanley and 'sought an assurance that the matter would be investigated and any breach of the peace duly punished'.[25]

Reports from London warned that the media had now got hold of the story – the *Evening Standard*'s headline reported 'ARGENTINE INVASION OF SOUTH GEORGIA ISLANDS'. Further media comment stressed the landing at South Georgia but failed to comment on the incident at the LADE office at Stanley.[26] Most alarming of all was the debate in the House of Commons on 23 March.

Molteni's report of the debate, and of his conversations with the Foreign Office, suggested that the moderate elements within the Foreign Office faced a difficult situation and had failed to prevent the press and Parliament from exaggerating the incident. They felt let down by the failure to honour the agreement with regard to the removal of the whole party which they believed had been negotiated with Buenos Aires. As a result the British Government had no option but to order HMS *Endurance* to evacuate the workers to Stanley as their presence was now interpreted as an Argentine occupation force.

On that Tuesday, 23 March, the Junta met for the first time since the crisis had blown up. This was one of its regular, weekly meetings and had not been called specially. None the less, South Georgia dominated the agenda. (Thereafter, the Junta met almost daily.)

They met at 9.30 in the morning, without the presence of the Foreign Minister, who was then engaged in intense communications with London. He joined the meeting late in the morning and reported on the debate in the Commons which had just taken place and the news that *Endurance* had been ordered to evict the workers.

At the meeting Admiral Anaya moved, and the rest of the Junta agreed, that to counter HMS *Endurance* another ship should be sent. This was to protect rather than remove the workers, and would thus exacerbate rather than defuse the crisis. A naval auxiliary, the ARA *Bahia Paraiso*, had just delivered 250 fuel drums to the Argentine base off Laurie Island in the Islas Orcadas and not too far from South Georgia and was due to pick up personnel who had been constructing a house.[27] Captain Trombetta, now in charge of the *Bahia Paraiso* was ordered to take the fourteen marines left by the *Almirante Irizar* a month earlier to Leith and disembark them as rapidly as possible to protect the workers from eviction. Should it arrive too late, the order was not to attack or intercept the *Endurance*.

If *Endurance* had not been held back in the pursuit of a compromise then it would have arrived first and the eviction would have proceeded; as it was the ARA *Bahia Paraiso* arrived at 23.40 hours on 24 March off Stromness Bay and, soon afterwards, Lieutenant Alfredo Astiz and ten men landed unopposed. If the ARA *Bahia Paraiso* had not been available then the Junta might have been obliged to consider a compromise.

Anaya also sent a signal ordering two missile-carrying corvettes with the unlikely names, in the circumstances, of the *Gránville* and the *Drummond*, to position themselves between the Falkland Islands and South Georgia. However, Lombardo objected to this, saying that he needed the two ships for the main Falklands operation. Anaya agreed and the original order was withdrawn.[28]

Lastly those in charge of the planning and execution of the occupation of the Islands were told to bring the preparations forward.[29]

Chapter Six

THE DECISION TO INVADE

On the morning of 25 March the British Cabinet met for the first time since the crisis had broken. By now the Foreign Office had received news from *Endurance* that *Bahia Paraiso* had arrived at Leith. That evening three landing craft and a military helicopter had been seen, as had the pennant of the Argentine Navy's Senior Officer, Antarctic Squadron. But the full significance of its presence was not yet appreciated; the Foreign Office believed that it was an unarmed, scientific ship – which it normally would have been. More significant was intelligence to the effect that warships had been dispatched. It was assumed, incorrectly, that their orders were either to prevent *Endurance* evacuating the workers or else, if required, to intercept her en route to Stanley.[1]

Britain was in a bind. Because it did not yet know that Argentine marines had just disembarked at Leith it was assumed that the option remained to evacuate the workers. However, there was now a risk that *Endurance* would be intercepted or some counter-action taken against the Falklands. There seemed little option but to search for a compromise, which Carrington at the time still hoped would take the form of the voluntary evacuation of the workers by Argentina.

Even if some compromise could be found to the particular problem it was supposed that the Argentine attitude on the wider negotiations would harden even further. The previous day Carrington had circulated his draft letter to Costa Mendez on the need to get the negotiations back on course. It now had to be recognized that this was

65

unlikely to happen and that some action such as the cutting of the air service was possible.* If Argentina went further and took military action, defence of the Islands at such a long range seemed wellnigh impossible.

With the attention of senior ministers now engaged the possibility of confrontation was at last contemplated. The Cabinet agreed that when John Nott, the Secretary of Defence, returned from a NATO meeting in the United States the withdrawal of *Endurance* from service might need to be reconsidered. The Prime Minister later agreed that contingency planning for a sea service to the Islands should be taken forward with some urgency.

By the time Carrington had returned from Cabinet to his office it was apparent that the workers were not going to be evacuated by Argentina. If Britain attempted to remove them there was a risk of a military encounter in which Britain would probably fare worst. While the Argentine Government should be in no doubt that 'we are committed to the defence of sovereignty in South Georgia as elsewhere,' the Ambassador in Buenos Aires was instructed to attempt to find a way out of the impasse. Carrington offered to send a personal representative of his own to Buenos Aires or a personal message from Mrs Thatcher to President Galtieri.

The obvious compromise involved Britain backing down from its insistence that the workers should leave. This had been proposed by Costa Mendez on 24 March and now he raised it again. He had then said that it was impossible to remove Davidoff's men in apparent response to threats but he suggested that they could go to Grytviken to. get their 'white cards' (the document issued by Argentina for travel between Argentina and the Falkland Islands under the 1971 Communications Agreement). Williams had not considered this proposal feasible because the 1971 Communications Agreement did not apply to the dependencies, a point on which Costa Mendez disagreed. The Argentine Foreign Minister ruled out the obvious alternative – stamping passports – as unacceptable. In the absence of anything better, Williams recommended Costa Mendez's approach.

* Later that day it was decided not to send the letter for fear that it would exacerbate the situation. (See above p. 35.)

Governor Hunt, however, argued that, as the white-card arrangement applied only to the Falklands and not to the dependencies, the authorization should be based on stamping the Argentines' passports and not their white cards. The Government agreed to Hunt's crucial proviso.

In the evening of 25 March the Ambassador was instructed to tell Costa Mendez that 'as an ultimate act of goodwill' a visit by Davidoff's party to Grytviken would see the men furnished with the necessary documentation to enable a return to Leith and their continuing to work.[2] Costa Mendez said he would take the proposal with him to consult President Galtieri. On 26 March the Ambassador was told that the President was to discuss South Georgia with the Argentine Commanders-in-Chief and he might get a reply in the evening. No reply was ever received.

As we shall see, simple assent to the proposal by Costa Mendez might have averted further escalation. The proviso on passports appears to have made matters worse. However, it is probably the case that this compromise was now being mooted too late. It might have been possible to arrange a few days earlier but now the particular issue of the scrap-metal merchants was being swamped by the general concerns and anxieties over the Falklands issue. The two countries were moving towards a military confrontation.

The Decision

After first discussing the issue on 23 March the Junta met each day to consider the crisis. On the fourth day, Friday 26 March 1982, at 19.15 in the Libertador Building (Army) it was decided to order a military intervention. The Foreign Minister did not participate in the actual decision but was told afterwards.[3] Although it has been assumed that Anaya forced the pace here as elsewhere,[4] more recent evidence suggests that there was no great disagreement within the Junta.[5]

It is always difficult to appreciate the motives of those taking such decisions. There is rarely only one reason. In this account we stress the strategic logic behind the decision because we believe that this can explain both the timing of the intervention and the manner in which it was carried out. We do not doubt that this logic was infused with powerful passions. The Junta was led by men, especially Admiral Anaya, who had long taken seriously issues of national sovereignty.* The Malvinas issue had been preying on the minds of the Junta during its short period in office and it could convince itself that it had prepared the ground for this step more thoroughly than any previous government.

By 26 March the issue was all over the Argentine press and the military would certainly have lost prestige if it had appeared to back down to the British or let pass what might turn out to be the last opportunity to recover the Islands. The loss of prestige would make the governing of a disorderly country even more difficult. Part of the background to the crisis was the industrial action that had been called the previous week (before the crisis had blown up) for 30 March. While there is no evidence that the intervention was ordered to undermine the strikes and help bring the country into line, the Junta would have been keenly aware of the political consequences of being shown to be weak in precisely the area where it was supposed to be strong.

Our view is that it was the urgency of the dispute with Britain rather than the domestic situation which triggered the intervention. The Islands needed to be occupied before British military reinforcements, already believed to be on their way, arrived in the South Atlantic. The objective was not to hold on to the Islands indefinitely but to force Britain to engage in substantive negotiations on sovereignty, and to ensure that the United Nations and the United States took the issue seriously and helped bring the negotiations to a successful conclusion.

Although the actual decision was not taken until the Friday, it was based on the developing assessment of British strategy. The starting point was the 23 March debate in the House of Commons. From the London Embassy, Molteni wrote to Costa Mendez that in the debate 'not only the Opposition, but the Conservative benches too, severely questioned the official attitude, and enlarged the scope of the question,

---

* Anaya had gained some notoriety in 1978 when he had captured and brought to port Soviet and Polish fishing vessels that had been spotted breaching the 200-mile maritime zone.

linking it with the Falklands negotiations, with revelations after the meeting in New York, and with the British Government's defence policy.'[6]

This debate was analysed carefully in Buenos Aires, where it appeared significant because it fitted so well into the Junta's perception of the British 'behavioural pattern'. It had been expecting an attempt to harden the overall British position with regard to the Islands and the South Georgia incident appeared to have provided the Falkland Islands lobby with the occasion for which it had been waiting.

The conviction in Argentina was that Britain had blown up the South Georgia incident out of all proportion.[7] Whatever might have been suspected about the Navy's use of the Davidoff venture, it remained the case that the salvage workers were on the Island under a valid contract and with the full knowledge of the British Embassy in Buenos Aires. The *Bahia Buen Suceso* was a familiar ship in the area. There had been other incidents before without Britain making this sort of fuss. There seemed to have been a deliberate decision to magnify the importance of this particular incident.

The suspicion that the magnification was the responsibility of hardliners in Britain was reinforced by the fact that on Monday 22 March the Foreign Office had been conciliatory and had accepted that no military landing had taken place. Yet the next day there were threats to evict Argentine workers engaged on lawful business.

The proposal for a compromise that emerged out of the Costa Mendez–Williams meeting of 25 March seems if anything to have been counter-productive. Costa Mendez believed that the offer to have the white cards stamped, which was neither obligatory nor customary, was as far as he could go without damage to Argentine prestige.[8] When the reply came back from Carrington the Junta was irritated that passports had been substituted for the white cards. 'A series of progressive demands culminated in the imposition that the Argentine workers of the Davidoff company – who were in a land that we consider under a sovereignty dispute – should seal their passports at Grytviken, as if they were entering a foreign territory . . .'[9]

The apparent unwillingness to compromise suggested that once again Britain was playing for time by encouraging inconclusive diplomatic communications. As the Junta considered the diplomatic exchanges of 23–25 March it began to conclude that, voluntarily or under pressure from the Falklands lobby, the British Government had now given their answer to the Argentine demand of 1 March for a full response to its proposals for the Negotiating Commission. Luce's statement in the Commons on 23 March had repeated the standard British formula as to the wishes of the islanders and Parliament being paramount before the status of the Islands could be changed. In other circumstances this would have been unexceptionable. At a time when Buenos Aires was waiting for a positive sign of a shift in the standard British position the statement appeared as confirmation that there was to be no change. This interpretation was reinforced by the unncessarily close links that Britain had established between the South Georgia incident and the broader dispute.

The final element in what appeared to be the British orchestration of tension[10] was 'the evident intention of the British Government to reinforce the Falkland Islands'. This confirmed the worst fears that the affair was now being used as a pretext to boost Britain's military presence in the region in conjunction with a decision to take a hard line on the dispute.

It has to be remembered that Buenos Aires had anticipated for some time that the Falklands lobby would attempt to push for not only the reversal of the decision to withdraw *Endurance* but also a more general move towards a Fortress Falklands. A parliamentary motion signed by ninety-one MPs on 24 March argued for preparing to take a tough line with Argentina over the Falklands, including the retention of *Endurance* in the South Atlantic. This motion had no standing and was given scant attention in Britain; in Argentina it was seized on as a critical indicator of elite thinking.[11]

Now it seemed as if *Endurance* would remain and be joined by other forces in order to sustain an indefinite freeze on the sovereignty issue in the bilateral negotiations. It was assumed that provisions for alternative supply lines to the Islands would be sought from other South American countries, and in particular Chile.

Argentina's whole strategy for 1982 was starting to unravel. The British were regaining the initiative. The Junta became concerned that

it would soon face a *fait accompli* in the South Atlantic. The
from the London Embassy suggested that British di
sought to gain time through sterile negotiations to enable th
be reinforced so that future Argentine protests could be disregard

> All these facts, that today seem so superficial, carried with them a
> real danger of enormous consequences: by using the Georgias
> incident, London was in fact deciding on a non-negotiation with
> Argentina and on the sending off of a war fleet to the South Atlantic
> waters. This was evident on March 23 in the words of both Carring-
> ton and Luce in the Houses of Parliament. Georgias had been left
> behind, clearly the objective was now the Malvinas.[13]

All this not only imperilled the Argentine negotiating stance but also
undermined the feasibility of an eventual military option in the Islands
should this prove necessary to break the stalemate. It was judged that
British reinforcements could arrive as early as 4 April. Hence the need
for urgent action.

Misperception Again

Even allowing for a degree of *post hoc* rationalization by those responsible, there seems little doubt that this assessment of British strategy
influenced the decision to occupy the Falkland Islands in March 1982.
It was unfortunately wholly incorrect.

Although the Commons debate of 23 March had encouraged the
view that Britain saw the incident in terms of the Falklands dispute as a
whole, in practice the Government was trying to confine its hard line to
the South Georgia incident itself.

The growing Anglo-Argentine tension over the Islands that had
made itself felt during the first months of 1982 had created a greater
sensitivity on all sides to individual incidents as they sought clues to
each other's real intentions. It is the case that in previous years the
landing on South Georgia might not have led to such a strong response
and that the strength of the response this time was encouraged by

those with the closest connection to the Islands who were most suspicious, with reason, of Argentina's long-term objectives.

The general lack of sympathy in and out of government for the Argentine case had prevented the Foreign Office from being more conciliatory over the sovereignty issue. An unyielding response to the unilateral communiqué of 1 March had already been decided upon. The South Georgia incident had been seen not so much as a useful excuse by the Government to reverse its previous policy on a military presence in the Islands, but as an indication of the strength of Argentine feeling. It had therefore served to alert the Government to the likelihood of punitive action of one sort or another if the talks broke down. This is turn had encouraged the Foreign Office to withhold Carrington's letter to Costa Mendez – which was now recognized as likely to precipitate such a breakdown – until there had been serious contingency planning. The contingency upon which the Government was focusing, however, was not a full-scale military occupation but the cutting off of air and sea links to the Islands.

With regard to the South Georgia incident itself, Britain's limited intelligence on what was actually going on at Leith helped encourage an exaggerated view of its available military options. On 24 March marines had arrived at South Georgia on board *Endurance* and had assumed the task of manning the BAS observation spot overlooking Leith Harbour. On their second day of observation they spotted the *Bahia Paraiso*. But it was extremely difficult for the marines to get a clear view of what was happening on the ground. It was therefore decided on 26 March to get closer to the scene and a new post was established on Grass Island, inside Stromness Bay and under three miles south of Leith. It soon became apparent that the new ship was moving cargo on to South Georgia and that far from removing the salvage workers the Argentine presence was being reinforced. Still there was no direct line of sight into the area of buildings. Eventually on 27 March two marines decided to make a close-range reconnaissance and at last began to get a sense of the scale of the Argentine operation.[14] However, the actual role of the *Bahia Paraiso* only became apparent in a public statement by Costa Mendez on the evening of 26 March, to the effect that arrangements had been made to give the men on South Georgia adequate protection, and in reports in the Argentine press that the ship had taken marines to the Island.[15]

London's ignorance helps explain why there is no record in the Franks Report of ministers being appraised of the correct number of workers left by the *Bahia Buen Suceso*, and why the significance of the visit by the *Bahia Paraiso* was still not appreciated. On 26 March it was still assumed that there was no Argentine military capability on the Island. The real concern was with the Argentine vessels that it was believed were preparing to intercept *Endurance*. The way round this problem appeared to be to take the workers off the Island, which was the main objective of the exercise, and then, if challenged by an Argentine ship, hand them over to that ship. According to the Franks Report, Carrington, advised by Luce, decided on this course on the Friday. The eviction plan was then called off. No mention is made of this cancellation in the Franks Report, but the probable reason for it was the news from Buenos Aires that Argentine marines would need to be confronted in the attempt.[16]

While the Junta was concerned that British reinforcements were already on their way, in London the Ministry of Defence had only grudgingly agreed to allow the Royal Marine force on the Falklands to be doubled (by not bringing home the marines who were due to leave), and for *Endurance* to extend her patrol for the duration of this particular crisis. At the same time it was made clear that the Ministry of Defence was by no means convinced that it should pay for the retention of *Endurance* thereafter. The knowledge that it could do so little against potentially overwhelming Argentine force merely reinforced this view.[17]

What then was the basis of the Argentine Government's alarmist perception of an imminent threat? The intelligence is said to have come from both a reading of British and European publications and other 'information received by the Government'. When Costa Mendez was asked by the Rattenbach Commission (the official Argentine inquiry into the conduct of the war), he implied that the information was not very hard. 'The entire fleet is mobilized afterwards but there is a movement of warships that could well have meant the beginning of a "peaceful" (to give it a denomination) militarization of the Malvinas.'[18]

This belief that Britain was already mobilizing when Argentina decided to occupy the Islands was later reinforced by the degree and speed of mobilization that did eventually take place.[19]

Yet at the time of the actual decision on 26 March the only hard information received by the Junta, apart from that relating to *Endurance*, concerned the two supply ships which serviced the British Antarctic Survey – the RRS *John Biscoe* and the RRS *Bransfield.* Both were manned by civilians, unarmed and not under the Royal Navy. However, the *Biscoe* had very recently served as a troop carrier and this fuelled Argentine suspicions. A problem had arisen because the return of *Endurance* to South Georgia on 21 March meant that it was behind schedule. Forty marines were being flown to Montevideo, Uruguay, as the relief garrison for Stanley and *Endurance* had been due to take them to the Falklands. As the *Biscoe* was in Montevideo Harbour at the time it was proposed that it take the marines instead. The British Antarctic Survey agreed to this and on 23 March the ship left Uruguay for the Falklands. The Director of the BAS was on the *Bransfield* at this time – and was in radio contact with both the BAS base at South Georgia and the *Biscoe* – but at no point was it even close to becoming involved in the confrontation.[20] However, on 25 March it did leave Punta Arenas in Chile. These two departures were reported to Buenos Aires and given publicity in the Argentine press. When Argentine participants cite intelligence received on 25 March as critical to the decision to invade, it must be assumed that it was these two unarmed vessels to which they refer.[21]

The rest of the information now claimed for the Argentine threat assessment only arrived later and the bulk of it was based on press reporting from the London Embassy. It appears that these largely unofficial reports were not checked by the Junta.[22]

Speculation focused on two known naval deployments – HMS *Exeter* patrolling off Belize and a large group of destroyers and frigates engaged in exercises in the Mediterranean – and on nuclear submarines. In the media these units were identified as the basis of a South Atlantic task force.

HMS *Exeter* was patrolling off Belize (which had served as a greater source of concern than the Falklands over the preceding months).

However, it was not ordered to the South Atlantic until 5 May.[23]

A fleet of seven Royal Navy destroyers and frigates was exercising off Gibraltar. Ministers in London did discuss the possibility of sending this force to the South Atlantic, but only on 29 March. They then decided not to do so as it seemed an insufficiently substantial military presence, and would take up to a month to reach the area. The only decision was to ask the Flag Officer First Flotilla, Rear Admiral Sir John Woodward, to prepare to detach a group of these ships if required for the South Atlantic.

Two moves were agreed. The first was to send the Royal Fleet Auxiliary, *Fort Austin*, to the South Atlantic immediately to replenish *Endurance*. The second was to send a nuclear-powered submarine so as to reach the Falklands by 13 April. A second submarine would be prepared to join it,[24] and the next day it was agreed to send this as well. Carrington wanted to send a third, but the decision was deferred as the Ministry of Defence was concerned that this would result in severe operational penalties elsewhere. The Ministry was also reluctant to authorize the dispatch of any surface ships. Even the submarines were to go covertly; the objective was not to intimidate Argentina but 'to help counter any aggressive Argentine naval moves'.*[25]

In the Lords and the Commons on 30 March Carrington and Luce announced that 'a security review' was being undertaken, that in the circumstances it would be wrong to 'comment on the detail' but *Endurance* would 'remain on station for as long as necessary'. There was a hint that its long-term future might be reconsidered.[26]

How then were Argentine decision-makers able to turn all this into a major military reinforcement? The cryptic statements of Luce and Carrington sought to hide a lack of capability, but they could also be

---

* The model presumably was the late 1977 decision by the previous Government to send a submarine to the area, at a time when threatening noises were being made by Argentina, backed up by two frigates kept some distance away. This was a covert move, with the force available to respond to a 'limited act of aggression', though it would not be able to cope with anything substantial. It was withdrawn when the threat receded, and it is still unclear whether anyone in Argentina knew about it. Carrington had been told of this a few weeks earlier, on 5 March, in the context of growing Argentine pressure on the negotiating procedures, but no recommendation had been made then to repeat the action. *Franks*, paras 64–6, 148.

read as hiding a build-up. Argentine accounts of the British build-up[27] contain information that was at best premature and by and large wholly inaccurate. The actual evidence upon which the 26 March decision was based was an exaggerated assessment of the role of the two BAS ships. Thereafter, the steadily growing tide of speculation reported from London to Buenos Aires convinced the Junta that its initial assessment was wholly correct and that it dare not deviate from its original decision. Evidence that reinforcements had left on 25 March, even though wholly uncorroborated and actually erroneous, was given particular credence. It was assumed that leaks in the British press were not innocent (for they would not be in Buenos Aires) and that reference to ship movements would undoubtedly be dated by the time they appeared in the press. The Junta's assessment on the eve of the invasion concluded that the British task force had left as early as 25 March.

Information on the task force off Gibraltar may have come from Spain. Otherwise Argentina's basic source was press speculation in Britain. From the London Embassy, Molteni sent a regular digest of news which played a significant part in helping the Junta develop its threat assessment. Much of this reporting covered the tough stance demanded of the British Government by sections of the press and politicians from all parties, and the misrepresentation of the Argentine position. It was not until 30 March that Molteni suggested on the basis of the press reports the likely deployment of *Exeter* from the Caribbean. The next day he gathered that three destroyers and a frigate were leaving from Gibraltar and that a tanker had already sailed to provide logistic support to *Endurance*. The BBC also reported that lunchtime that the fleet was being prepared to sail to the South Atlantic.

The most critical piece of information, in that it bore some relation to the truth, that was picked up and relayed back to Buenos Aires related to nuclear submarines. The decision to send submarines had been taken on 29 March. The submarines involved were HMS *Spartan*, which sailed from Gibraltar on 1 April, and HMS *Splendid*, which left Faslane, Scotland, the same day.[28]

The next day this information was leaked by a minister to the

Westminster lobby, apparently to calm backbenchers who were becoming anxious at the apparent lack of response to Argentine provocation. Geoffrey Archer, ITN's Defence Correspondent, had seen the submarine HMS *Superb* leave the Gibraltar exercises the previous day and so put two and two together. ITN broadcast the story that evening.[29] According to its normal practice, the Ministry of Defence neither confirmed nor denied. In fact the detail was wrong and considerable embarrassment was caused to the press when *Superb* returned to base at Faslane on 16 April. Another reported detail was wrong: that *Superb* had left base on 25 March and would thus be 'well on its way'.[30]

However it came about, the Ministry of Defence regarded the leak as helpful. The Permanent Under Secretary, Sir Frank Cooper, observed afterwards to a parliamentary committee: 'I thought that was an extremely helpful thing because I am quite clear that the Argentinians thought that HMS *Superb* had gone to the Falkland Islands and therefore it must have had some impact on their naval operations.'[31]

The Foreign Office was less pleased. Luce has observed that when the news of the submarine leaked out 'it was very, very unhelpful indeed. We did not want it known, at that stage.' Rather than strengthen Britain's position the leak made Carrington more conciliatory, to counter the impression created that Britain was seeking a 'naval rather than a diplomatic solution'. Meanwhile it did harden the Argentine stance.[32]

Molteni reported the news about the submarines back to Buenos Aires on 31 March, drawing attention to the suggestion that one had left on 25 March, a date seized upon by the Junta. The nature of the Argentine interpretation of the haphazard evidence comes over clearly in Admiral Anaya's account: 'Some newspapers assure that they have received confirmation from the British Government that the *Superb* left finally on March 25 last. This news was neither confirmed nor denied by the Foreign Office.'[33] This news established that either Argentina should act now or it should accept that a military operation would be out of the question. Once the submarine arrived 'it would not be possible to execute the surface operations that would be required to place Argentine troops ashore at Port Stanley'.[34]

Diplomacy Backed by Force

Having persuaded itself that it was about to be pre-empted by Britain the Junta needed to act quickly. This did not leave much time for diplomatic action and the need for secrecy reduced its scope. However, even if there had been more time and more scope there was little confidence that diplomacy could achieve much in the current situation without recourse to a military intervention. As options were analysed, and their impact on the various parties assessed, it came to be assumed that an intervention could well tilt the political balance in Argentina's favour.

(i) Britain

There would have to be a diplomatic settlement with Britain at some point but negotiations under current conditions were pointless. The question was whether they might prosper in the aftermath of an occupation of the Islands.

As we saw earlier, it was assumed that the British Government's actual interest in the Falkland Islands was slight and that were it not for the islanders' lobby they would have been abandoned some time ago along with Britain's other former colonies. In addition, the Government had clearly not been willing to devote many resources to the welfare and security of the islanders. With sufficient countervailing pressure to the Falkland Islands lobby the Government could well be persuaded to relinquish sovereignty.

A dramatic crisis, which highlighted the Government's weakness in the area, might serve this purpose. Mrs Thatcher had shown herself capable of taking a conciliatory and rational diplomatic line over the Rhodesia question, despite her instincts. This confirmed a general pattern in British foreign policy of preferring negotiation to confrontation and respecting the strength of others. When it had adopted a more confrontational stance, as in Suez, it had been reined back by the United States. Perhaps the key model was India's takeover of the Portuguese colony of Goa in 1961. The international community had objected to the use of force, but in the end it had acquiesced.

All this analysis was based on the supposition that Britain would not attempt to end an Argentine occupation by means of force. As Argentina believed – albeit erroneously – that Britain was already sending a task force to the South Atlantic this confidence seems misplaced. However, it was one thing to attempt to prevent an intervention; quite another to mount a credible military response once the intervention had taken place. All Argentine leaders confirmed after the war that they simply did not expect a British attempt to regain the Islands.[35]

The military requirements to deter an Argentine occupation were far less than those required to retake the Islands after an occupation. The former seemed conceivable; the latter, with all the bloodshed and expense that would follow, seemed out of proportion to Britain's national interests. There would inevitably be some reaction but not sufficient to take from Argentina the upper hand it would gain simply by being in occupation of the Islands. Moreover, Britain would find Argentina taking a reasonable position in the negotiations. According to Costa Mendez:

> We did ... think that there would be a politico-military reaction from London: the sending of warships prior to 2 April made this evident. But the subsequent reaction that we could expect as of 2 April would be tempered by the characteristics of our planned intervention and by the Argentine will to negotiate the totality of the conflict without having to go to open war and without taking away from the islanders their liberties and freedom of movement.[36]

(ii) The United Nations

It had been hoped before the South Georgia incident for the diplomatic offensive of 1982 to reach a crescendo at the United Nations. There was now no time to frame a resolution for the General Assembly denouncing British intransigence in the sovereignty dispute; urgent matters had to be taken to the Security Council. Apart from the general lack of confidence in the efficiency of the UN in such matters, there was the technical problem that the UN could only be activated after an incident and not in anticipation – it is geared to cure rather

prevention. The Security Council option was not made any
by the fact that Britain was a permanent member with a veto
could be used to block any action it did not like.[37] The Organ-
on of American States would have been a more congenial forum,
but for that very reason it was recognized that Britain would not accept
its intervention.

Once an incident had taken place the Security Council would
become involved. Argentina might have a rough time because of the
recourse to force, but the likely requirement for a diplomatic settlement would see it in a much stronger position, as past UN resolutions
had always tended towards the Argentine line on sovereignty.

(iii) The United States

Much more promising prior to an intervention was the idea of mediation, with the United States taking up this role. This was set in motion
before the final go-ahead for the occupation forces was given. The
advantage of the US as a mediator was its professed neutrality in the
sovereignty dispute. It had always abstained in UN votes on the matter.
While American ties to Britain were appreciated, it would surely
recognize the need to prevent any major Anglo-Argentine flare-up
from getting out of hand. This would threaten its position in South
America and serve as a distraction from the main priority – East–West
relations. It was also assumed that the hard work that had already been
put into improving US–Argentine relations, including the co-
operation over Central America, would now yield dividends. If the US
began to address the sovereignty issue seriously then it would soon
realize the need to put pressure on Britain to modify its stance.

The question was how to turn the United States from passive to
active neutrality, when all the indications were that for Washington this
was a low-priority issue in a low-priority region. As with the United
Nations it did not seem likely that the necessary attention would be
gained until something dramatic happened. An intriguing case study,
which was examined with some care, was the Arab–Israeli war of
October 1973. Here President Sadat of Egypt had taken a military
initiative as much to gain international attention as to secure a victory.

In this he had succeeded. Crossing the Suez Canal turned the Arab–Israeli dispute into a top priority for the United States. This case, along with that of the 1956 Suez crisis, was also interesting for another reason. The Americans had not blindly supported their closest ally but, where necessary, had exerted considerable pressure to ensure a reasonable diplomatic posture.[38]

So, although the United States was approached with regard to mediation before the invasion took place, this did not appear as an alternative to military action. If it succeeded before the action took place then that would be welcome but such a success could not be assumed. It was suspected that the American interest would only be properly engaged in a crisis and that the occupation would be needed to gain its full attention.

According to Costa Mendez:

> in the diplomatic circumstances the peaceful and bloodless occupation of the islands would make the Argentine will to negotiate the solution of the underlying conflict evident. This occupation would make it possible for us to negotiate once and for all the underlying dispute. It would also induce the international community, the interested parties and even the United States of America to pay more attention to the reasons for the dispute, its character and the need for a rapid solution. The United Nations would not be able to procrastinate if faced with a military action and would have to discuss it at the highest possible levels.

The ultimate objective of the occupation was not to maintain the Islands by force but to serve as a catalyst in creating a favourable diplomatic atmosphere to resolve the dispute.[39] The military operation was thus 'conceived not as a bellicose provocation nor to break the bilateral negotiations, but on the contrary to make them prosper in a serious and in-depth manner'.[40]

Military Plans

All this, however, depended upon the occupation being carried out in a peaceful, bloodless and calm fashion so as not to raise the international temperature too high. In one sense this was easier to achieve with minimal notice than in action which might be expected to result in protracted warfare, with all that would imply in terms of logistics and tactical preparations. Such an operation also had to be undertaken quickly if it was to be virtually unopposed. One report suggests that Costa Mendez's first reaction on hearing of the decision to intervene was to urge that it be done quickly: 'There is no time to delay. Intelligence reports could filter out, ending any chance of a bloodless landing.'[41]

Furthermore, the military had kept the Malvinas case under study for some years, so some plans were already in existence. Of more significance was the military planning exercise that had begun in January 1982. Although this had been restricted to a very few people, those involved had just completed the first stage of their work.[42] The broad framework for a military takeover of the Islands had already been developed and there had been some specialist training undertaken and material prepared. As part of the Junta's initial response to the South Georgia incident the planning process was drastically changed and accelerated.[43]

On 24 March it was decided to ask the Commander of the Malvinas Operations Theatre whether the military option could be moved forward. The initial response was that it could be in place in two days (26 March) with forces ready to sail on 28 March and the landing on 1 April. It was then resolved to consider this possibility with the Military Directors of the Joint Chiefs of Staff.

There were a number of arguments against an immediate intervention. In March Army conscripts finished their term of service and it would take some time to recall them to active duty. The units who would be central to the action's success were not close to completing their training. The Navy had not yet received the full war material it had been buying abroad over the previous seven years; for example, the orders for Super-Etendard aircraft and Exocet anti-ship missiles from France were not yet completed. Those Super-Etendards that had arrived had not yet been modified to enable them to be launched from a carrier. The full complement of German submarines and frigates would not be in Argentina until 1983. In addition the Air Force had limited and very obsolete material which they were on the verge of replacing. Britain had not yet reduced its Navy in line with the 1981 Defence White Paper and it still had a military presence in the South Atlantic.

Nevertheless, when the Junta asked the opinion of the Chiefs of Staff of the three armed forces on 26 March whether or not they could mount an intervention immediately, the reply was in all cases affirmative. They were agreeing, however, to a brief intervention and not to a protracted fight for the Islands once they had been occupied. It was decided to execute the operation on the evening of 1 April. If that proved impossible then the date would be 2 or 3 April. It could be called off as late as 18.00 on 31 March. It was necessary to plan for only a small garrison in the Islands to stay until negotiations started.

On Friday 26 March the orders were given to sail from Puerto Belgrano on the Sunday and to move towards the Islands. A final order would need to be given before actual occupation would take place. It could still be called off.

Chapter Seven

DIPLOMATIC ENDGAME

To the extent that the Argentine plan depended on catching London by surprise it almost succeeded. As late as the morning of 31 March the Current Intelligence Group in Whitehall dealing with Latin America was still reporting that there was 'no intelligence suggesting that the Argentine Junta had taken the decision to invade the Falkland Islands', though it noted correctly that it now had the wherewithal to do so by 2 April. That afternoon, however, information was received in the Ministry of Defence which convinced the Government that an invasion was imminent. This was the day when, as the Prime Minister explained to Parliament, she received the 'first information' that an invasion was under way.[1] This was five days after the decision to invade had been taken.

Why Was Britain Caught by Surprise?

What were the capabilities of British intelligence with regard to the South Atlantic at the start of 1982?

The Foreign Office had the pre-eminent role in the assessment process. It provided not only an important input but also the key personnel in charge of running the Joint Intelligence system.* The

---

* The assessments prepared by the Joint Intelligence Organization, based in the Cabinet Office, were considered by the Joint Intelligence Committee, chaired by a Deputy Under Secretary of State in the Foreign and Commonwealth Office. The Chairman of

highest-priority targets for British intelligence collection are the countries of the Warsaw Pact. These are followed by countries with the power to inflict damage on Britain; and then countries in which Britain has substantial interests. Because of the Falklands, Argentina was in the second of these categories – as the Franks Report puts it 'a priority for intelligence collection but in a low category'.[2]

In Latin America only Guatemala (because of Belize) was also in this category. However, successive reviews had led to cutbacks. There had been two Secret Intelligence Service offices in Latin America – one for the Portuguese-speaking territories, the other for the Spanish-speaking – but the two had now been consolidated into one, run by Mark Heathcote, located in Buenos Aires. His office was 'massively overworked'.[3] Meanwhile the British Defence Attachés were encouraged as much to sell arms as to collect information.[4]

In October 1981, when the negotiations with Argentina were at a sensitive stage, the Joint Intelligence Committee had asked for more effort to be devoted to the collection of intelligence on Argentine intentions and plans but it had not allocated extra resources to this effort. One of the consequences of the lack of resources was that there was an increased reliance on signals intelligence (SIGINT) and a falling away of high-quality human intelligence (HUMINT). There was less money with which to acquire agents.[5]

There was little capacity for monitoring military movements within Argentina. Argentina is a long country with many key ports and air bases well away from the capital. The Defence Attaché's section in Buenos Aires 'had neither the remit nor the capacity to obtain detailed information' on what was going on in and around these bases and ports. Not having engaged in a study of normal military activity in the past, this section was in no position to identify with confidence an abnormal level of activity. As a result, much of the reporting from Buenos Aires, as that from the Argentine Embassy in London, was based on the local press.[6]

---

the Committee before the invasion was Sir Antony Acland, who moved on to be Permanent Under Secretary at the Foreign and Commonwealth Office. Patrick Wright then took over the chairmanship. The head of the Joint Intelligence Organization's Assessment Staff was Robin O'Neill, also of the FCO. The Current Intelligence Group on Latin America was chaired by Brigadier Adam Gurdon.

There could well have been some communications intelligence available throughout this period, allowing ships to be located when they used their radio communications. There would also have been some SIGINT. Throughout the conflict, material on the Argentine Navy was received from HMNZS *Irrangu Station* near Warren, New Zealand. There was a thirty-man SIGNIT base run by GCHQ* on Ascension Island and one run by the US at Galeta Island off Panama. These latter two listening posts were critical during the crisis. The Ascension Island facility would seem the most suited to the task.[7] *Endurance* was also listening to some Argentine communications.

Although two American satellites passed over key army, air and naval bases during the last days of March and on the day of the actual invasion, they had not been directed to gather signals from the area.[8] The Franks Report asserts categorically that 'No intelligence about the invasion was received from American sources, before it took place, by satellite or otherwise.'[9] There is certainly no evidence of US intelligence concluding that an invasion was being prepared. It had picked up signs of 'an unusual state of force readiness' in Argentina on 30 March, but it was not until information was received from Britain that it became convinced that an invasion was indeed under way.[10]

There were a number of reasonably high-level sources, but certainly not at a sufficiently high level to be privy to the innermost thoughts of the Junta. Intelligence from these sources consistently encouraged underestimation of the Argentine ambitions in the immediate crisis.

Because there was little doubt about the Argentine ability to seize the Islands should they wish to do so, the key question for the intelligence analysts was the nature of Argentine intentions. We have already noted the assumption that Argentine frustration with the course of the negotiations would be expressed through a series of graduated steps, with small-scale military actions possibly preceding any actual invasion. Visible Argentine preparations for war could be interpreted within this framework as no more than intimidation. Unless there was an agent with access to the critical decisions, for British intelligence to be persuaded that the preparations should be

---

* GCHQ, the Government's code-breaking centre at Cheltenham.

taken more seriously it would be necessary to pick up signs of activity that could not be explained by reference to a campaign of visible pressure.

With the negotiations entering a critical stage this question had become more acute, which is why it had already been decided to produce a new Joint Estimate on the subject in March. There was warning enough that *something* was going on, even if that 'something' only crystallized into an invasion late on. At any rate, no system had been established for securing early warning of Argentine military moves designed to force the issue, a point to which the Defence Attaché had drawn attention in early March: 'the chance of providing early warning from Argentina could be increased if some special arrangements could be made, but . . . as things were they could not realistically expect to be able to detect any Argentine military moves.'[11]

As the crisis opens we find the British aware of frustration in Buenos Aires over the slow pace of the negotiations. They thought that the belligerent press comment was probably inspired by the Navy and suspected that the Junta's first step would be to isolate the Islands by withdrawing air and sea outlets. Naval sources doubted that an invasion would take place.

As the crisis deepened, following the decision of 22 March to evict the intruders on South Georgia using *Endurance*, the Defence Attaché warned that the Argentine hawks who wanted action over the Falklands were prepared to use any such forcible eviction of nationals as an excuse. He suggested, but without effect, that before *Endurance* was committed to South Georgia the increase in the threat to Stanley should be taken into account.[12] Throughout this period, British diplomats were being warned by Costa Mendez and other Argentine officials that without British concessions it would be difficult to keep the hard men at bay.

A report came from the British Embassy on 26 March based on information from another embassy (probably the US) that all the submarines at the naval base of Mar del Plata had recently put to sea. The covering interpretation was that this was not necessarily sinister, but could be explained by exercises taking place with the Uruguayan Navy. It was no secret that units of the Argentine Navy had gone to sea on 23 March. On 27 March the Defence Attaché was still reporting press accounts of these exercises and suggesting that they were genuine.[13]

It has been reported that although exercises with Uruguay were normally conducted around this time of year, those for 1982 were not due for another month. None the less they were the best cover available.[14] However, these exercises were genuine and provide one of the main reasons why the Argentine surface fleet could get to sea so quickly.

Ironically the crucial piece of evidence that convinced those in London that matters were getting serious, and in particular that Argentina was prepared to prevent the forcible eviction of nationals from South Georgia, was incorrect. Anaya's signal of 25 March ordering the *Drummond* and *Gránville* to position themselves between the Falklands and South Georgia was picked up: the withdrawal of this order, at Lombardo's insistence, was not.

Other signals intelligence of 25 March picked up Argentine reports on the Royal Marines on the Falklands, the movements of *Endurance* and the overall disposition of the Royal Navy. Sources also reported an Argentine decision that the civilians should stay on South Georgia.[15] Signals intelligence may well have benefited at this stage from the Argentine Navy being forced to use their radios as a result of the two ships originally being sent to South Georgia and the delays and reroutings caused by bad weather.[16]

Throughout this period the reports of high-level Argentine views appear to have been based on meetings of at least two days earlier. In a developing situation this sort of dated intelligence can be quite misleading. By 29 March the perception, based on this sort of information, was still that Argentine actions would be short of full-scale invasion, while other sources, again probably SIGINT, reported that beaches on the Falkland Islands were being reconnoitred and that an amphibious task force was being prepared.[17] On the following day the Naval Attaché reported, on the basis of something other than press reports, that five Argentine warships, including a submarine, were sailing towards South Georgia, and that another force had left Puerto Belgrano. Travel restrictions had been imposed on personnel there.[18]

On this day – 30 March – assessments were made for both the Defence Operations Executive and Carrington, now in Israel. The Foreign Office understanding appeared to be that Argentina would take action immediately should any Argentine nationals be killed in the expulsion from the Islands. In any event some sort of military action was planned for April, possibly against an outlying island, but this would not be a full invasion.

In the Ministry of Defence there was also no sense of an imminent invasion. The position of Argentine ships was known, both close to South Georgia and in a separate task force exercising 800–900 miles north of the Falklands. This task force comprised the aircraft-carrier, four destroyers and an amphibious landings ship. Although this was unusual for the time of year, and so was suspicious, there had been no noticeable change in readiness and the air and sea services to Stanley were operating normally.[19]

This view, that there had been no irrevocable decision, was held by the Current Intelligence Group on Latin America, which met on the morning of Wednesday 31 March. Yet that afternoon the Government received the information that transformed expectations from an increase of pressure to an imminent invasion. The Franks Report does not explain what the information was, but it was sufficient to confirm the possibility of an invasion within forty-eight hours – 2 April – which is when it actually happened.[20] It would seem that SIGINT became available to the effect that elements of the task force had turned towards the Islands and would reach them in two days.[21] There was also a major increase in radio traffic among the various branches of the Argentine armed forces, with an amphibious task force serving as the focus.[22] It was on the basis of this information that the Government decided that an invasion was at least likely.

The next morning a paper circulated by the CIG found all this disturbing, though it still did not accept that an invasion was inevitable. The information that came in during the rest of the day was from the Defence Attaché in Buenos Aires quoting press reports of Air Force transports being prepared to lift troops to the south of the country and of a general mobilization. More secret information was obtained of a decision of late March to invade unless there was a constructive proposal from Britain.[23] Early next morning, again presumably from SIGINT, it became known that orders had been issued on 1 April for an invasion on 2 April. By this time the invasion was under way.

Argentina Fails to Threaten

Until 31 March, therefore, British policy was based on the assumption that a full confrontation could still be prevented, although it was recognized that the position had deteriorated markedly. Avoiding a confrontation depended on finding a compromise but this was becoming increasingly difficult.

Here the problem was that, because of the need for secrecy, Costa Mendez could not use the decision to intervene as a basis for his diplomatic efforts. When he had been told in February by Galtieri that military planning was under way he had said that so long as an intervention had not actually been decided upon he would not prepare for the accompanying diplomacy. Although the planners were working towards a political objective, in order to strengthen Argentina's negotiating position in time for the meeting of the UN General Assembly in October/November, the exact relationship between military and diplomatic pressure on Britain had not been thought through.

Costa Mendez assumed that should the military plans be activated he would be given due warning and would then be able to plan accordingly. As it was, he was caught out by the sudden developments of March 1982. Now he had little time to develop a diplomatic strategy while the success of the military operation had become the first priority. To exploit it diplomatically once executed, occupation had to be achieved without bloodshed and so with minimum resistance. This required absolute secrecy. It was therefore almost impossible to consult with and gain the support of friendly countries prior to the intervention.[24]

Nor was he able to exploit the threat in order to obtain concessions from Britain or to get American mediation efforts working in time to prevent the intervention taking place. So although Costa Mendez indicated what Britain had to do to prevent a confrontation he did not begin to describe the full character of the confrontation.

Even without giving away anything on the possible military action he needed to communicate the Junta's view that the South Georgia incident had now been superseded by the broader question of the Falkland Islands. Although it had been believed in Buenos Aires that the dispute had already been broadened in this way by London the actual proposals coming from London focused solely on South Georgia; there was no mention of the fundamental issue of sovereignty. This was the objection to Carrington's suggestion (noted below) that he send an emissary to deal with the South Georgia dispute.

This proposal was interpreted in terms of the prevailing analysis of British policy, which suggested that military reinforcements had already been ordered to the South Atlantic. The proposal was therefore seen as an attempt to use diplomacy to gain time for the fleet to arrive and so strengthen the negotiating position. The more Britain refused to discuss the underlying dispute, and sought to concentrate on the South Georgia crisis, the more Argentina became convinced that the diplomatic moves amounted to yet further procrastination.

Having promised to report back to Ambassador Williams on 26 March, Costa Mendez did not do so. Instead he made a public statement that the Argentine workers on South Georgia would be given all necessary protection.

This unyielding stance was confirmed in a letter to the British Government, received on 28 March. Costa Mendez blamed the current dispute on 'the persistent lack of recognition of the titles to sovereignty which my country has over the Malvinas, South Georgia and the South Sandwich Islands'. The Argentine Government had for fifteen years given 'adequate evidence of its wish to resolve the dispute by peaceful means'.

To resolve the present situation I consider it necessary that Your Excellency's Government should display, as does the Argentine Government, the political will to negotiate not only the current problem which concerns us but also the sovereignty dispute bearing in mind that so long as this continues our relations will be open to similar disturbances and crises.

Your Excellency can be sure of counting upon the co-operation and goodwill of my Government to achieve a satisfactory solution.[25]

Bearing in mind that this message was sent *after* the decision had been taken by the Junta to intervene, its content is remarkable. It communicated a tough line and made the sovereignty issue central, invited Britain to be more conciliatory but made no threats as to what might happen in the absence of compromise. It was not in the form of an ultimatum. It communicated neither a threat nor a deadline.

Britain Fails to Be Threatened

The British Ambassador to Argentina concluded that 'the Argentines intended no move in the dispute, but to let matters ride while they built up their naval strength in the area.' None the less, the message from Costa Mendez heightened the concern of the British Government (gaining the Prime Minister's attention) and encouraged it to draw the United States into the conflict as a mediator, maintain its limited military presence in the area and consider reinforcements. It did not convince the British Government to respond positively to Argentine proposals over the future negotiations on the status of the Islands, lest it be seen to be negotiating under duress.

On receipt of the message from Costa Mendez on 29 March, the Foreign Office took the view that the problem need not be broadened to include the Falklands sovereignty issue and indeed should not be broadened until the South Georgia dispute was resolved. It would be premature to do anything on the wider dispute. When Molteni repeated the suggestion he had made earlier in the crisis that the best way to calm everyone down was for Britain to agree to the procedural proposals put forward at New York, he was told that this would be difficult for Britain to accept.[26]

The next day, before flying to Tel Aviv on a prearranged visit (indicating that he then felt that the situation was sufficiently under control), Carrington had decided that as a response to Costa Mendez he should propose the visit of a senior diplomat to Buenos Aires as an emissary with the clear promise that once the South Georgia incident had been defused negotiations could be resumed on the Falklands. Failure to defuse the incident would prejudice the broader negotiating effort. This was seen as a conciliatory move. In fact Ambassador Williams was concerned that it might be deemed *too* conciliatory: 'it had so far been possible for him to maintain civil relations with the Argentines without conceding ground, and a conciliatory gesture and message at that time might serve to convince the Argentines that they had the British Government on the run, not only over South Georgia but over conceding sovereignty.' Carrington suggests that Williams was concerned that sending a more junior official might give the impression that he was being disowned, and he would thereby suffer a loss of credibility. The Foreign Secretary therefore agreed with Williams's advice to hold back the message while he waited to see how the American contacts with Buenos Aires developed.[27]

However, during 31 March Lord Carrington decided that the message should be sent. Interestingly this was not because of a greater sense of urgency over the Argentine threat but because of reports in the press that a British submarine was now en route to the South Atlantic. He did not want the Argentines to gain the 'impression that the British were seeking a naval rather than diplomatic solution'.[28] Unfortunately Argentina already had this impression. By the time the message was delivered later that day Whitehall was beginning to react to the stunning news of the Argentine invasion force. Costa Mendez replied that the message was not what he had been hoping for, while an intelligence assessment from Buenos Aires reported the Ministry of Foreign Affairs view that all that would now be accepted from London would be immediate negotiations on sovereignty and toleration of the Argentine presence in South Georgia. This assessment was confirmed the next day.

Carrington's proposal for an emissary was interpreted by the Junta as procrastination, especially given that he would be coming to settle the South Georgia dispute. A response to Carrington was agreed and communicated to Williams by Costa Mendez on 1 April. It was pointless, he explained, to send an emissary to negotiate on South Georgia since Argentina now considered this matter resolved: 'we would have accepted the despatch of the representative proposed by Great Britain if his task had been to negotiate the modalities of transferring sovereignty over the Malvinas and their dependencies to the Argentine Republic which is essentially the central cause of the present difficulties.'[29]

US Mediation: An Unpromising Start

We saw earlier how both Britain and Argentina had tried to interest the United States in the Falklands dispute during the first week of March but without success. Even as the South Georgia crisis developed, attempts to alert American diplomats to the danger signs fared little better.

On Sunday 28 March, following receipt of the reply from Costa Mendez, Carrington sent a message to Secretary of State Haig, a step that he had decided upon two days earlier. The mediation he had in mind was still confined to South Georgia. He explained to Haig that Britain wanted to solve the problem peacefully but could not 'acquiesce' in the continued infringement of sovereignty represented by the Argentine presence. To a prospective mediator his ideas for solving the problem would not have seemed encouraging – getting the workers to regularize their position by means of a visit to Grytviken, which Costa Mendez had just rejected, or having them taken away on a third country's ship, although Argentina was adamant that the workers would not leave even on an Argentine ship.[30]

The initial US response was not helpful. When Sir Nicholas Henderson, Britain's Ambassador in Washington, called next day on Walter Stoessel, the Deputy Secretary of State, at the latter's request, he was told that Haig was anxious for restraint on both sides and insisted that the US would remain neutral in the dispute. A similar message was being given to Argentina. The State Department appeared to be telling Britain along with Argentina not to be difficult and aggressive.

The Ambassador put a question that was to be repeated with even greater force a few days later. How could the United States be neutral in a case of illegal occupation of sovereign British territory? It was important to realize, he insisted, that Britain could not allow Argentina to assert a claim in this manner to a British possession.

When he heard of the reaction Carrington summoned Edward Streator, the American Chargé d'Affaires in London, to express his displeasure.

I ... told Streator that we had supported American policy in Sinai, had supported it in El Salvador; that this support had not been particularly willing, not wholly consistent with our own better judgement, but we had given it; and now we expected a better response than this not very friendly message, equating our case and position with that of Argentina.[31]

Henderson also went to see William Clark, the President's National Security Adviser, to express similar concern.

These remonstrances sufficed to get Stoessel to agree that, while there was still no desire to get involved in the broader Falklands dispute, the Americans would 'use their good offices to bring about a solution to the immediate problem on South Georgia'.[32]

Haig claims that when he first received Carrington's letter on the incident he 'saw at once it had the makings of a troublesome problem' and asked his Bureau of Inter-American Affairs to remain alert and report any unusual developments to him.[33] On 30 March US Ambassador Schlaudeman in Buenos Aires offered these 'good offices' to Costa Mendez to help solve the problem of South Georgia.

The Argentine Government was happy to accept mediation, except that it could not be confined to the South Georgia dispute. So long as the workmen there were left alone, there was no longer a problem. The British ideas for a compromise were unacceptable. Costa Mendez told the Ambassador that mediation must now address the underlying dispute, as that was where the confrontation had now reached. This was, however, exactly what the American Government at this stage wished to avoid. Nevertheless Schlaudeman agreed to see if Washington was prepared to do this. Costa Mendez was concerned that 'Washington did not ... understand the urgency and seriousness of the situation. It reacted too late.'[34] It took two days before Haig replied.

By the time he did so he had been appraised by Britain of the imminence of an Argentine invasion. The Prime Minister's first response to the intelligence she received on the evening of 31 March was to send an urgent message to President Reagan warning of what was about to happen, insisting that Britain would not acquiesce in an occupation, and asking the President to contact Galtieri immediately for an assurance that he would not authorize such a thing. For her part she promised that Britain would not escalate the dispute nor start any fighting.

To ensure a quick response Sir Nicholas Henderson went to see Haig first thing in the morning. Haig had not been alerted by US intelligence and was shocked at the news. Thomas Enders, who was also at the meeting, still refused to take the crisis seriously, reporting that he had been reassured by Costa Mendez that no invasion was contemplated and reminding Henderson of the importance of Argentina to US policy in El Salvador.

Haig, however, took the matter more seriously. Henderson was able to send news back later that the US would do all that it could to help and that the Ambassador in Buenos Aires would urge Costa Mendez not to do anything to aggravate the crisis. A message soon came from Reagan to the Prime Minister confirming that he shared her concern and would try to contact the Argentine Government.

The Americans also defined a position to which they held for most of April. Haig explained that 'he thought that the United States would have a greater chance of influencing Argentine behaviour if they appeared not to favour one side or the other.'[35]

Ambassador Schlaudeman asked for an urgent interview with Costa Mendez on the morning of 1 April to talk about the evidence that the Argentine fleet was moving towards the Islands. Costa Mendez told him that all Argentine actions would stop if Great Britain agreed to negotiate the dispute in its entirety . The Ambassador then requested an urgent meeting with President Galtieri.

All day the Americans gained the impression that the Junta simply did not want to talk to them. It took time to arrange a meeting with Galtieri, possibly because the President was at a meeting of the Junta. The two men eventually met at 16.30 on 1 April (Argentine time).

Schlaudeman gave Galtieri a message from Haig warning that the actions which had apparently been undertaken would jeopardize US–Argentine relations and reported Mrs Thatcher's promise not to escalate the dispute if Argentina would not invade. After a forceful presentation of Argentine views on the history of the negotiations and how it would be difficult to understand if the United States supported colonialism in American waters, Galtieri offered to abstain from the use of force if Britain agreed to negotiations on sovereignty. Not surprisingly the offer was not taken up.

Because of Schlaudeman's difficulties in gaining a meeting with Galtieri, Haig decided to ask Reagan to intervene, as Thatcher had already requested. There were, however, only a few hours before the deadline of 18.00, after which the invasion force could not be halted. Although Schlaudeman may have been told of this deadline, the information had not reached Washington. By the time Reagan, who was delayed by the need for a medical check-up, began to make the call at 18.30 Washington time (19.30 Buenos Aires) it was too late. By the time Galtieri reluctantly agreed to take it at 22.10, it was four hours after the deadline.

During the conversation Reagan urged the need for an alternative to the use of force. Reagan's warnings to Galtieri were clear and explicit. He warned that Britain would not negotiate under threats and would 'respond with force to any military action'.

> Mrs Thatcher, a friend of mine, is a very determined woman and she would have no other alternative but to make a military response. The conflict will be tragic and have grave consequences for the Hemisphere . . .
>
> . . . the relationship between your country and mine will suffer greatly. American and world-wide public opinion will take a negative attitude to an Argentine use of force.

He offered to send Vice-President Bush to Buenos Aires as a mediator. In addition, a formula might be found under the aegis of the United Nations. The American Ambassador to the UN, Jeane Kirkpatrick, was 'ready to assist both parties'.

Galtieri's response to Reagan's points, apart from an assurance that the islanders would be able to 'keep their liberty, their free will and their property', was simply to restate how unreasonable Britain had been and how negotiations had proved fruitless. The only alternative to force now was British recognition – 'explicit and public' – of Argentine sovereignty over the Falkland Islands.[36]

That evening Vice-President Bush was at Henderson's house for the latter's birthday celebrations. He was expecting to go to Buenos Aires to act as a mediator. At 22.00 that evening Haig rang Henderson to report on the outcome of the President's call to Galtieri. Henderson was able to inform Bush that he would not be travelling.

Conclusion

The South Atlantic War of 1982 took place because the Argentine Junta had been planning a military action. If the plans had not been well advanced in March 1982 the intervention could not have taken place. If the Junta had not been so intent on preserving this option then it would not have been so anxious that Britain was removing it by reinforcing its meagre capabilities in the South Atlantic.

This is not to say that if it had not been for the South Georgia incident the intervention would still have taken place. The developing British response to the unilateral communiqué of 1 March, especially if it failed to move beyond talking for the sake of talking, would probably have been insufficient to persuade the military leadership that diplomacy was going to yield results and the military planning would have been developed further. The likely withdrawal of *Endurance* and the steady improvement in Argentina's military capabilities would have made the military option much more attractive and also more liable to succeed.

The start of April 1982 was about the last moment that Argentina could have chosen to allow Britain to mount a counter-response. Within weeks the dispersal of the fleet and the onset of the South Atlantic winter would have made such a response almost impossible. As time passed the loss of naval capabilities would have reduced the ability to put together a task force of the quality of the one that eventually set sail.

If Argentina had not decided to invade the Islands then, the South Georgia incident might well have persuaded the British Government to keep *Endurance* going for some time longer, although this is by no means certain given the unwillingness of the Ministry of Defence to reverse its original decision. The incident alerted the Government, and most importantly the Prime Minister, to the character of the conflict and helped set in motion contingency planning.

It is a truism that military confrontations such as this result from a series of misunderstandings by each side as to the intentions of the other. Most critically, Britain underestimated the military intentions of Argentina while Argentina overestimated those of Britain. While these misunderstandings were fed by the imperfection of the intelligence being received they were essentially the result of the frames of reference with which the two sides viewed each other's strategies.

The planning criterion used by the Ministry of Defence in London to judge the adequacy of British forces in the South Atlantic inevitably produced a gloomy picture because it was assumed that the critical test would be a determined Argentine assault. However, in practice Argentine plans were vulnerable to even a modest British response because they required that the military occupation of the Islands be effectively unopposed. They did not want to fight because they felt that the international community would distinguish between a peaceful and a violent occupation; the former would improve the prospects for negotiation while the latter would create all sorts of problems. As things turned out the distinction proved difficult to sustain.

Part Three

CONFRONTATION

Chapter Eight

OPERATION ROSARIO

The Argentine Plan

It is standard practice for the Argentine military to prepare contingency plans in case any of the territorial disputes with the country's neighbours becomes critical. These plans are known as 'conflict' or 'war hypotheses' and they serve as the basis for military policy for periods ranging from eighteen months to three years. As the political circumstances change these plans are updated or cancelled accordingly. This also tends to happen when commanders-in-chief or governments change.

By and large these plans are developed within individual services. Argentina has not had a strong centralized Ministry of Defence or Joint Staff structure. Each of the chiefs has concentrated on his own service, and so the joint planning process has been minimal. Only at times of crisis do the services work together to any serious extent. This has usually been achieved through *ad hoc* committees rather than through institutionalized procedures. The Falklands War was no exception.

The Navy had always taken prime responsibility for the maritime aspects of all potential conflicts, including the South Atlantic Islands, along with access to Antarctica and the conflict with Chile relating to the Beagle Channel. It had therefore been preparing plans for the Falklands for many years. The first were developed after the breakdown in negotiations in 1968. The major planning exercise prior to

1982 had been at the time of the *Shackleton* incident of 1976.

When Admiral Anaya took command of the Navy in October 1981 he began at once to review its plans. On 18 December 1981, when the new Junta first discussed the Falklands, Anaya listened to Costa Mendez outline the lack of progress in the negotiations with Britain, the pressure to reinstate the *Endurance* and the election of hardliners to the Falkland Islands Council, and he concluded that this could well lead to a conflict with Britain. It was therefore natural to order his own Navy planners to revise the Malvinas plans. At the time there was no need to go much beyond that as the Junta had yet to decide on its approach to the negotiations. According to Anaya: 'I ordered on 22 December 1981 my Chief of Staff, Vice-Admiral Alberto Vigo, to arrange – as a preventive measure – that the recently named head of Naval Operations, Vice-Admiral Juan José Lombardo, should update the plans to occupy the Malvinas.'[1]

The next day Lombardo received a memo ordering him to do this. He ordered his direct commands – the Surface Fleet, the Marine Infantry, the Naval Aviation and his Chief of Staff* – to develop plans for the use of armed force in the event of a continued lack of progress in the negotiations with the United Kingdom. After a week Lombardo arrived at a plan involving helicopters from the naval transports used in the Sub-Antarctic. No warships would be involved: the idea would be to surprise the British garrison and take over the Falklands with the minimum of casualties.[2]

The Junta decided on its approach to the Falklands question when it met on 5 January 1982. A military option was given a higher priority; future planning should be on a joint basis and not just undertaken by an individual service. Such an historic step should not be left to the Navy alone. A planning group was established on 12 January to consider how military force might best be used to support the Junta's determination to regain sovereignty over the Falklands. Lombardo was joined by Army General García and Brigadier Sigfrido Plessl of the Air Force.

---

* Rear Admiral Gualter Allara, Rear Admiral Carlos Büsser, Rear Admiral Carlos García Boll and Rear Admiral Angel M. Rodriguez respectively.

Until 23 March, the real objectives behind all this activity were known only to a handful of high-ranking officers, who were gathering pertinent information and developing a general plan as to how to capture the Islands by force. They met secretly, at different places and kept only hand-written records.

For those involved it seemed a tedious business, in that they had put together plans in the past from which little or nothing had resulted. Capturing the Falklands was a well-known problem, frequently rehearsed at the Naval War School as an exercise in planning techniques, with many studies in the War School's filing cabinets. Few of the officers involved believed that this time the plan would actually be implemented.[3]

The first stage of the planning process was completed by 16 March. This dealt with the political objectives and the problems that would be faced in mounting an invasion of the Islands. There was not yet any campaign plan. The first analyses in January and February suggested plans for an action designed largely to prevent a strengthening of the British position rather than an Argentine seizure of the initiative. However, by March the objective was described as: 'to evict the authorities and the British military forces from the islands so as to restore these territories to the Argentine national sovereignty'.

From early on, the plans had some distinctive features, which were retained: the intervention had to be bloodless with respect to the local population (and if possible with respect to the British troops); it had to be executed by surprise; and it had to be very quick.

The first issue was logical since the population, though they were not sympathizers of Argentina as such, were situated inside Argentine territory and therefore they should be protected as much as possible. The idea of a bloodless operation also meant that no unnecessary destruction should accompany the operation. On the issue of the British troops this meant that the fewer the military casualties for Britain, the less the need for an emotive reaction on the part of the population or of the British Government. There were also notions that, should casualties occur in the population or the defending forces, the Government in London would use the ensuing propaganda against Argentina at a moment when her image had been tarnished because of the issue of human-rights violations in the past.

The second requisite consisted in executing the operation by surprise since this was the only way to achieve a successful bloodless takeover. This demanded that planning and training should be done under the utmost secrecy so as not to alert British intelligence sources.

The third point regarding the rapidity of the operation was also logical since if operations were protracted our objectives would alter and we would not be able to accomplish the mission bloodlessly.[4]

One source describes a plan as developed by 15 February, drawing on Lombardo's first ideas. He wished to use the helicopters from the naval transports to fly in marines, who as two groups would move against the British marine barracks and against the town and radio station. Vice-Commodore Gilobert, the former head of the Falklands air service, would stage just before D-Day an emergency landing at Stanley airport with a group of Air Force staff and check into the Uplands Hotel to ensure the safe landing by troops flying in by Hercules.*

For all plans the preferred date was 9 July (Independence Day); the earliest was 15 May, to allow the transports time to recover after returning to port in April. Two weeks' notice would be needed before the operation could be implemented.[5] When Brigadier General Mario Benjamín Menendez, Chief of Operations in the General Staff, was told on 3 March that he was to be the first Governor of the Islands, Galtieri suggested he would have a force of some 500 men under his command, acting like military police.[6]

---

* On 11 March an Argentine Air Force Hercules did make an emergency landing at Stanley airport. There was speculation that this had been staged as a means of gathering intelligence. In practice it had truly suffered from technical problems. Nevertheless the other services later accused the Air Force of staging this landing and thereby 'warning' Britain.

The Plan Brought Forward

As soon as Lombardo was told on 23 March to bring the plan forward, he ordered Admirals Allara and Büsser to accelerate the operational planning so as to be able to receive the order to sail within forty-eight to seventy-two hours. As a result, and critically for what followed, the rushed plans could only encompass the actual invasion and not a strategy for holding on to the Islands thereafter.

It was clear that the plans could not follow Lombardo's earlier ideas. For one thing, the naval transports were fully preoccupied with the business at South Georgia. Men and material would have to be moved quickly and the only way to do this would be to use units of the surface fleet, while hoping that the British would be convinced that they were still engaged in annual manoeuvres with Uruguay. The major time-constraint was that imposed by the need to prepare the ships.

The basic concept was that the Governor and the garrison should be persuaded as quickly as possible that there was little point in resisting. The detachment of Royal Marines should be prevented from either entering Stanley or retreating into the interior of the Islands. The marines therefore had to be captured in their barracks or intercepted before they reached the town. Routes to the interior had to be blocked. To encourage early surrender the defenders should suddenly face a force that would be impossible to counter. The impression of irresistible force would be heightened by approaching the town from all directions.

This should encourage the population to recognize that they were under total control, that they could not contribute to the defence of the town, and that they should therefore stay in their houses. For this, it would be necessary to gain control of the alarm systems and normal communications within the Islands as soon as possible. Another important objective was to gain control of the airport and put it into immediate operation.

All of this would place great demands on the command and control arrangements. The Argentine troops would need to behave in an exemplary manner. This would be achieved through very close command structures and active participation of the officers in charge of the units. The command structures would also need to be flexible. It was decided that for each objective there had to be at least two alternative operational plans with enough force for each one to be effective in isolation from the other. In effect, this doubled the operational requirements.[7]

General García was designated the Commander for the Malvinas Theatre of Operations. He was responsible for the amphibious task force, the Army units that would remain in the Islands after the occupation, and the Air Force personnel who would come over to supervise the airport operations. Under Admiral Allara, an amphibious task force would be made up of the transport task force, the cover force and the landing force, charged with the capture of the military garrison and the civilian authorities and Stanley itself.

Secrecy too now became more problematic. So far very few officers had been consulted. Among those responsible for the landing forces there had never been more than six aware of what was going on and these had only been able to devote a limited amount of time to the planning because they still had their normal peace-time responsibilities. Now many more officers had to be told and work had to begin at the naval dockyards, even though this might jeopardize the secrecy of the operation. The Army now began to intensify the training of its conscripts, again while maintaining all possible secrecy.

According to Admiral Büsser, the Commander of the Marine Corps and designated commander of landing operations:

The feeling in the Chief of Staff headquarters was one of maddening activity and a general surprise at the level of preparations because there was no time for those who were only then informed of the objectives to get familiarized with the idea of what was going on. The war cabinet looked like a foggy night because of the cigarette smoke. A strange feeling permeated this scene as one entered the room and saw all the charts of the Falkland Islands on the walls and a huge map scale 1/500 of the city of Stanley. It was also curious to see higher officers making coffee, coming and going with trays of sandwiches and sweeping the floors. This was so because at this period only 14 Marine Corps officers were aware of the mission and no other elements were allowed near the war room.

In the units, there was a deluge of orders to be accomplished in a very short period of time, yet the actual purpose of all this frantic activity was not known. Rumours and speculation were rife, centred on the incident in South Georgia rather than the Falklands.

On 26 March Admiral Lombardo was informed by the Junta that a decision had been reached to dispatch the task force to the south, depending only on the diplomatic evolution of the South Georgia incident. He ordered the fleet to prepare to sail on 28 March. As the invasion force began to be assembled at Puerto Belgrano, its final destination was still kept secret from the majority of the officers.

When the fleet sailed on 28 March its course was directly south towards the intermediate area between the Falklands and the Patagonian province of Santa Cruz. To head for the Falklands it was therefore necessary to change route towards the east at a given point. While the intervention task force sailed south the rest of the fleet, with the carrier *25 de Mayo*, remained at a distance to protect the expedition. The Navy's air branch provided reconnaissance and surveillance. Aerial reconnaissance was completed on Tuesday the 30th with photographs taken by a helicopter from the *Santisma Trinidad.*

It was only on Monday 29 March that the nature of the operation was fully explained to the senior officers who were now to be responsible for its implementation. On the next day company commanders were also informed of the objectives. Although it was still possible that the operation might be cancelled at the last minute, it was no longer possible to keep its purpose secret. However, it was not until the evening of 1 April that all personnel in the task force were officially informed of their objective.

Almost as soon as the fleet set sail the weather deteriorated, the going became rough and progress became slow. Although by 31 March planning had been completed and the units sent their instructions, it became necessary to delay the landing by one day, to 2 April.[8] At 12.57 hours on 31 March, the task force changed course and headed directly for the Falklands. At the last moment the code-name was changed – from Operation Azul to Operation Rosario.

The Defenders Prepare

The *John Biscoe* had disembarked Major Mike Norman and forty-two Royal Marines as the new Falklands garrison on 30 March. Normally the outgoing garrison would have departed immediately but because of the situation Governor Hunt had asked that they be retained for the duration of the crisis. Although nine of the previous garrison had been taken to South Georgia, that still left in all seventy-six Royal Marines, plus nine sailors from *Endurance* who had been left at Stanley to make room for the South Georgia party. There were also 100 notional members of the Falkland Islands Defence Force. When it was clear that an invasion was imminent twenty-three of these turned out to join the defence of Stanley but unsurprisingly were reluctant to fight.

On 31 March Norman received a signal to the effect that an Argentine submarine (the *Santa Fé*) was in the vicinity, apparently looking for a likely landing beach.

> we put out observation posts to watch for the submarine but nobody took it as a serious threat and certainly not as a prelude to invasion! It was put into the category of 'yet another incident' which the Argentinians were going to use to raise the temperature. The orders from the Governor, Rex Hunt, were that if the Argentinians landed we were to arrest them – not to shoot them, but arrest them.[9]

It was on this day that the British Government concluded that an invasion of the Islands was likely. However, it took some twenty-four hours before this assessment was passed on to Governor Hunt. At 15.30 hours on 1 April, Hunt received a telex from the Foreign and Commonwealth Office: 'We have apparently reliable information that an Argentine task force could be assembling off Cape Pembroke by dawn tomorrow. You will wish to make your dispositions accordingly.'[10] Hunt observed: 'It looks as if the silly buggers mean it.'

Up to this point Hunt had assumed that the most likely military action by Argentina would be directed towards South Georgia. Even now he could not be sure how serious an operation was being planned; it might still be a modest demonstration to make a political point rather than to seize the islands. The Royal Marines were as unprepared as the Governor. Major Norman had been told little before this tour about Argentine capabilities, let alone the likely conduct of an Argentine invasion.

The garrison's formal task was to defend the 'seat of government' and if possible to hold up the invasion long enough to force the Argentine Commander to negotiate. All they could really hope to do was delay the occupation of the Islands and cause casualties. Norman identified the likely beach on the assumption that the invading force would come ashore in the manner of the Royal Marines – that is on landing craft in deep water. On this assumption he chose between the two possible beaches near Stanley. Needless to say, the Argentine forces chose the other shallower beach because they were using Amtraks (amphibious track vehicles) and conducting their landing in the manner of the American marines who had trained them.[11]

Norman thought that the enemy would land at Cape Pembroke, take control of the airfield and then move up to the peninsula towards Stanley. His strategy was therefore to deploy a series of sections waiting on the route from the airport to Stanley, each firing on the enemy before withdrawing to take up position behind the next section. The suspected landing beach was covered by two men and a machine-gun to give the impression that any landing was being opposed.

Another section was deployed with an 84mm anti-tank gun to fire at any ship that ventured into Stanley Harbour. The support troops, mechanics, drivers and so on were given Government House to defend. Initially it had been assumed that if the invasion could be delayed the Governor could be taken into the country, so denying the Argentine forces access to the legitimate political authority. However, the Governor wished to stay. By switching off the light in the light-house it was hoped that bad weather would make it impossible for the Argentine forces to close in – as it happened the night was clear and moonlit.

Operation Rosario

The delay to the invasion fleet resulting from bad weather meant that the element of surprise had been lost. On the morning of Thursday 1 April intelligence was received by the Argentine command from the Islands to the effect that the British were aware that a landing was imminent and were organizing a defence. The area around the airport was being reinforced and the Falkland Islands Defence Force had been forewarned. It was also known that the Royal Marine detachment which had been due to return to Britain had been retained. That night Governor Hunt's message on Stanley radio, warning the population to expect an invasion, was intercepted. It was decided to concentrate on the main landing and abandon subsidiary raids.

Without surprise the plans for the landing had to be changed. By late on 1 April they took the following form:

At 00.30 on 2 April two groups made up of amphibious commando units and special forces were to land in rubber dinghies and head for their respective objectives (Moody Brook Royal Marine headquarters and Government House respectively). If the Royal Marines were not at Moody Brook then contact would have to be established at the town. Three hours later special forces would land and mark the landing beach at Yorke Point for the main force. This represented a change from the earlier plan, which had been to land to the east of this point, and was the result of the aerial reconnaissance of two days earlier.

At H hour, 06.30, the first amphibious vehicles would land and proceed to the airport. Here this group would split in two, the first taking control of the airport while the second moved on beyond Stanley. Here they would join up with the commandos sent to find the Royal Marines, who should at this point be either at Moody Brook barracks or en route to the town. Once the headquarters of the marines had been captured, the units would continue northwards from the bay until they reached the eastern point of the coast, where they could secure the entrance of the ships.

A second amphibious-vehicle force would land almost immediately after the first, which it would follow until it arrived at the easternmost point of the town, which it would then encircle. Once this had been done, the Governor would be asked to surrender. It was hoped to have artillery batteries installed close to the airport as soon as possible. Other units, including those concerned with civilian affairs, would follow either on the landing beach or by helicopter.

The guidelines remained that the operation had to be as bloodless as possible and should not excessively impinge upon the life of the population.[12]

At midnight on 1 April, the submarine *Santa Fé* observed the Pembroke lighthouse being put out. This intelligence suggested a final change in the landing point to a more distant beach (Mengeary Point).

In the early hours of 2 April the operation proceeded according to plan. The first indication that the invasion was under way came from the vicinity of Moody Brook barracks. The group that had been ordered to take the barracks did not expect to find the marines sleeping there, given that surprise had now been lost. Rather the intention was to deny the defenders whatever stores the barracks contained and their general logistic support, as well as to immobilize any marines still there and persuade the others to return if they had moved away. According to Admiral Büsser:

> I told Captain Sanchez Sabarots that if he captured the headquarters and no one was there, he should mark his presence by making a big noise. A good explosion at the time would alert and attract the enemy troops and tell them that we had arrived in force. General García, smiling, said that he thought the idea was good but that we should be careful not to break the place up unduly since he would have to use it afterwards to house his soldiers. So, as it was, Sanchez Sabarots was given the directive to cause the least possible destruction while at the same time making the greatest noise. In reality, I think that when they executed this mission they took a greater margin and did not care much about destroying some of the headquarters so as not to have any casualties. They managed to comply with the order to produce a great noise with the utmost efficiency.[13]

Even if the attack took this form only because of the absence of the Royal Marines, its enthusiastic nature, involving phosphorous grenades and sub-machine-gun fire, did not help the later effort to demonstrate that the operation had been designed to be as bloodless as possible.[14]

The first indication to the defenders that the invasion was under way came at 02.30 hours when the Falkland Islands Company coaster, *The Forrest*, which had been keeping a radar watch from Port William, picked up a contact with two unidentified ships steaming round to the south. When the noise came from Moody Brook, Norman realized that 'We'd been completely wrong-footed: all our defences were facing the wrong way, all committed to a beach assault and they'd come in behind us.'[15] He ordered his sections to get back to Government House as soon as possible. He returned just before the Argentine attack.

Meanwhile, Argentine forces were landing as planned. At 05.40 hours, the troops embarked on the amphibious vehicles on board the landing ship, and at 06.15 the order was given to launch the vehicles. Once this was done radio silence was broken to ensure that the defenders knew that Argentine forces were arriving *en masse*. When the first vehicles landed fifteen minutes later, the vanguard force was surprised not to be facing the expected resistance. This was both a relief, for this was the point of greatest vulnerability to Argentine forces, and a concern. As news had just been transmitted back from Moody Brook barracks that the marines were not there, this meant that the main defending force still had to be located. The special forces landed by the submarine *Santa Fé* were also soon able to report that they had landed close to the airport without resistance. The airport was soon taken and was being checked to ensure that the Air Force troop carriers could land safely.

The Royal Marines who had been on the airfield and the isthmus by Hookers Point had been pulled back towards Stanley after hearing the attack on Moody Brook. Only one unit was able to get back. Another had a brief encounter with advancing marine infantry. Most were restricted by the steadily overwhelming Argentine strength on the ground.

The Argentine command were unaware of the location of the main body of Royal Marines. If they were outside the town, and could be kept isolated from it, then it all might be over more quickly than hoped. However, if they were in the town, it had to be recognized that the operation might not be so bloodless. All that could be hoped in this case was that knowledge of the loss of Moody Brook and the airport, and the arrival of an Argentine unit close to Government House would make the defenders aware of the weakness of their position.

The advance commando unit had reached Government House and encircled it by 06.00 hours. Initially there were some eighty Argentine troops outside with some thirty defenders inside – mainly administrators and sailors. A snatch squad of six from the Argentine special forces sought to take the Governor, in an attack using stun grenades and calls for Hunt to give himself up. The defenders saw the squad and opened fire. Three fell, including the war's first fatality, Captain Giachino. The other three were later captured by the British.

Although the fate of these men was at first not appreciated, because their radio had fallen with them, the firing taking place around Government House indicated to Admiral Büsser that some British troops were in the town and were prepared to fight: a bloodless operation appeared less likely than ever. In order to compel surrender, the full weight of the invading force would be required and in particular the artillery pieces which were ordered to be brought ashore as soon as possible. These pieces could be used to demonstrate the Argentines' vastly superior firepower.

Sniping then continued for some time. Gradually news came back to Norman from the observers still in place of the size and progress of the Argentine landing. As the overwhelming strength of their forces became apparent, Norman acknowledged that resistance would now be unsuccessful. Breaking out into the country in broad daylight would be possible but would involve casualties. The third option was to ask for a truce. Because the defenders were not actually losing at the time they hoped that it would be possible to negotiate without surrendering. Hunt could not communicate with London and so was unable to consult with the Foreign Office or even inform it as to what was going on.

Using Vice-Commodore Hector Gilobert (the Argentine State Airlines representative) as intermediary, Governor Hunt contacted Admiral Büsser. Eventually a meeting was agreed by Büsser and he met Gilobert at the Catholic church. The two men then walked to

Government House to meet Hunt. According to Büsser, although unarmed he was immediately accosted by a marine. Büsser shook his hand and congratulated him on the quality of the defensive action. The Governor said to Büsser: 'This is British property. You are not invited. We don't want you here. I want you to leave and to take all your men with you.'[16] Büsser had 800 men ashore with another 2,000 about to land – a 'crushing superiority'. He told Hunt:

> he had his job to do and I had mine. His job was to prevent my men killing all his men, and my job was to prevent British soldiers killing some of mine. I invited him to carry out his duty. I insisted that they had no chance and told him we had the airport and were receiving reinforcements, that we had captured Moody Brook and the town, and that Government House was all that was left. The Governor asked the two Royal Marine officers what they thought; I think they answered more with their eyes than anything else. I wanted to get it over with, to tend to my men I knew were wounded.[17]

If necessary they would fight until the defenders had been defeated. Eventually Hunt agreed that he had no option and ordered his troops to lay down their arms. The terms were agreed by 09.25 hours.

Admiral Allara and General García arrived by helicopter at 10.30 hours. Soon afterwards, Governor Hunt met General García, for the moment his Argentine replacement. Again he suggested that it was the Argentines rather than he who should be surrendering. This now struck his captors as 'verging on the ridiculous'.[18] General García told him that he had to leave by that afternoon. At 12.15 hours the Argentine flag was raised in the garden of Government House.

In Buenos Aires General Galtieri, together with the Chairman of the Joint Chiefs of Staff (Vice-Admiral Suarez del Cerro) and Generals Vaquero and Menendez, met at 06.30 hours of 2 April to follow the military operation. As soon as it was confirmed that it had been successfully completed, at 11.20 hours, the Junta considered the next step. Following the original plan, it was agreed that the intervention force should abandon the Islands as soon as possible. This was accomplished but, because Büsser believed that a British submarine could be arriving at any time, the troops were taken back by air rather than sea.

South Georgia[19]

Given the role of South Georgia in the decision to invade the Falkland Islands it seemed natural to the Junta that it should be taken as well, although this was not part of the original plan. The full control of the Falklands, South Georgia and the South Sandwich Islands was deemed indispensable to a strong Argentine hand in the round of negotiations expected to follow the military intervention. This was decided on 26 March, when it was also agreed that this operation should be co-ordinated with the action against the Falklands and placed under the same command. The local Commander would be Captain Trombetta. The Junta issued instructions for the takeover of Grytviken at 07.15 hours on 2 April but the operation was not completed until the next day.

Because *Endurance* was known to be taking twenty-two Royal Marines to the Island the ten Argentine marines under Lieutenant Astiz would not be sufficient. It was therefore decided to send the frigate ARA *Guerrico* with forty additional marines by way of reinforcements. This ship and its men, the *Bahia Paraiso* and the Astiz group, were designated task force 60.1. The *Bahia Paraiso* had two helicopters on board – a naval Alouette and an army Puma.

At the time of the order to sail, the *Guerrico* was undergoing repairs at a dry dock. In less than forty-eight hours it had to be ready to sail, on 29 March, even though its conscript crew had not yet completed its training. As the ship sailed the weather conditions made it impossible to pick up time or to allow the marines to train for the operation. By the time it arrived off Cumberland Bay at 17.00 on 2 April the occupation of the Falkland Islands had already been achieved.

Captain Trombetta's tactics were shaped by the knowledge that *Endurance* had left South Georgia for the Falklands on 1 April but had probably disembarked its marines and, further, that the action on the Falklands meant that all possibility of surprise was lost. By the time his task force was in place on 2 April the hour was late and the conditions poor. Trombetta decided to wait until the next morning. Meanwhile, he contacted the British detachment by radio and informed it that first thing in the morning he would issue an important statement.

By this time the twenty-two marines at Grytviken were completing the preparation of defences. After they had disembarked, on 31 March, *Endurance* had been ordered back towards the Falklands. Their task was to assert British sovereignty and provide protection to the BAS personnel. As to how this was to be achieved there was a remarkable lack of guidance from their superiors. Never before had the BAS had military personnel based on South Georgia and there was concern that its civilian status was being compromised. It was decided that BAS personnel would conduct themselves as non-combatants and that Steve Martin, the Base Commander and Magistrate, would remain in charge until such time as hostilities began. After that, Lieutenant Keith Mills of the Marines would assume responsibility.

Mills had come to South Georgia reasonably well supplied. His firepower included twenty 66mm rockets and a Carl Gustav launcher with twelve rounds plus substantial ammunition for his small arms. On 2 April Mills received his first orders from London. He was told not to co-operate with the Argentines. When he asked for clarification he was told not to surrender. Later *Endurance* passed on a second order: 'The Officer Commanding Royal Marines is not repeat not to take any action which may endanger life.' He was unsure how this tallied with the first order and essentially decided to use his initiative.

Although no warnings came from London the garrison was aware of what was happening on the Falklands. When it had become clear that the Falklands were being occupied and that South Georgia was probably the next target the civilians were evacuated to the old whaler's hut while the marines prepared defensive positions, including mining a possible landing area. The plan was to resist any initial landing and then withdraw into the Island and conduct a guerrilla campaign.

At 10.00 Trombetta established radio contact with Grytviken:

'Following our successful operation in the Malvinas Islands the ex-Governor has surrendered the islands and dependencies to Argentina. We suggest you adopt a similar course of action to prevent further loss of life. A cease-fire is now in force.'

Martin briefly acknowledged the message and asked for five minutes to consider his response. The suggestion that Governor Hunt had surrendered the dependencies he and his companions knew to be untrue.[20] They could not be sure whether a cease-fire had been agreed, as they were aware from the BBC World Service that considerable diplomatic activity was now under way. Mills was concerned that the British Government might have agreed to a formal cease-fire without being able to let him know: one was in operation on the Islands. Martin and Mills hoped to play for time by warning that any attempt at a landing would be opposed. Having failed to get back to Stanley to help resist the invading forces, *Endurance* was now on its way back towards South Georgia.[21] Martin therefore warned Trombetta that the Island would be defended. If a landing was attempted he would hand over authority to the marines' commander. He refused Trombetta's demand that the defending forces should go down to the beach and surrender.

Trombetta was now under severe time pressure because the Argentine intervention was about to be discussed at the UN Security Council and he had been ordered to accomplish his objective before that meeting took place. He therefore did not press the question of peaceful surrender any further. Instead, at 11.00 hours, he ordered the Alouette helicopter to reconnoitre the area (it appears, however, not to have picked out the marines' position), and then the Puma to take a contingent of marines to Grytviken. They landed without mishaps near Grytviken, 218 yards away from the old factory. However, when, soon afterwards, the Puma tried to land a second group of men, it received heavy fire from the British marines who had taken positions in high ground near by. The Puma had to make a forced landing. It suffered severe damage; four Argentine marines were dead and another two wounded.

The Alouette went to its aid, removing the wounded men for attention on board the *Bahia Paraiso*. The rest of the Argentine marines walked to the factory. Meanwhile the first group of marines had come under heavy fire from the British forces. Further reinforcements were brought in on a shuttle by the Alouette.

The Argentine position had now become tricky. To relieve the pressure on the marines, the *Guerrico* decided to get closer to Grytviken by sailing through the dangerous strait leading to the harbour, in order to open distracting fire. This in turn exposed the *Guerrico* to the defenders' fire, especially as it had little room to manoeuvre. The defenders achieved a number of hits which produced considerable damage and five casualties and limited the frigate's ability to use its own guns. It was obliged to withdraw out of British range, staying close enough to fire back even with faulty guns.

By this time the British force had suffered only one casualty but it was clear that its position was not going to improve, especially as the *Guerrico*'s guns steadily became more accurate. Although they could fight on and inflict more losses on the enemy their own losses might also be severe. Mills decided to surrender in return for good treatment for his men. This he did at 13.22 local time. Soon afterwards the Astiz group landed from the *Bahia Paraiso* to take charge of the prisoners and deactivate the land mines with the help of the British marines. *Endurance*, frustrated again at being unable to contribute to the British defence, made north to rendezvous with *Fort Austin* bringing it fresh supplies.

Chapter Nine

THE RESPONSE

Britain Mobilizes

News of the Argentine invasion came through to London haphazardly on 2 April, to the extent that Sir Humphrey Atkins, Carrington's Deputy in the Foreign Office, was still suggesting to the House of Commons that it was only under way when in fact it had already succeeded. A political storm blew up in London, with the Labour Opposition taking the opportunity to embarrass the Government on what was normally its strongest area – defence and security.

Even during the South Georgia crisis, Government critics had seized on the fact that one of the more prominent casualties of the 1981 Defence Review – *Endurance* – was now at the centre of the drama that was currently unfolding in the South Atlantic. The point was made in a debate on 30 March on the Government's decision to opt for the highly capable D–5 version of the Trident missile which Britain was to purchase from the United States to replace its Polaris force. The Opposition argued that it was Trident which had made the 1981 review necessary in the first place.[1]

On news of the Argentine invasion, the Government was criticized not for its lack of concessions to Argentina in previous negotiations but for failing to defend British people from foreign domination. The mood was captured in a speech by Labour Party leader Michael Foot when he spoke to an extraordinary Saturday meeting of the House of Commons on 3 April:

There is no question in the Falkland Islands of any colonial depen-
dence or anything of the sort. It is a question of people who wish to
be associated with this country and who have built their whole lives
on the basis of association with this country. We have a moral duty, a
political duty and every other kind of duty to ensure that this is
sustained.[2]

While the strength of the Opposition's attack may have discomfited the
Government it also endowed any actions they might take to recover the
Islands with a degree of popular support that might otherwise have
been unobtainable. In the same debate the Prime Minister made it
clear that the Government were not going to accept the new situation
created by the Argentine action. There was no suggestion of negotiations with Argentina: 'I must tell the House that the Falkland Islands
and their dependencies remain British territory. No aggression and no
invasion can alter that simple fact. It is the Government's objective to
see that the Islands are freed from occupation and returned to British
administration at the earliest possible moment.' It was clear that
military force was not ruled out as one means of achieving this objective: 'The Government have now decided that a large task force will
sail as soon as all preparations are complete. HMS "Invincible" will be
in the lead and will leave port on Monday.'[3]

This had been decided the day before, after initial hesitation. As the
crisis reached boiling point during the last days of March the Government had decided against sending a task force made up of surface
ships. It would take over three weeks to muster, could not leave
without attracting attention and then would not be able to arrive in the
South Atlantic for another two to three weeks. So warned, Argentina
might be provoked into just the response that Britain was now so
desperate to avoid. The Ministry of Defence was concerned that a
major response would need a carrier to provide air cover. If ships were
taken away from their assigned tasks, problems would be created with
NATO and the exercise could get very expensive, especially in fuel
costs.

When, late in the afternoon of Wednesday 31 March, the intelligence
became compelling, Secretary of Defence John Nott asked to see the

Prime Minister. They met, with Foreign Office and Defence officials, at her rooms in the House of Commons. A critical member of the group was Admiral Sir Henry Leach, First Sea Lord, who had gone to the Commons in search of Nott.[4]

Leach wanted to talk to the Secretary of Defence as he had become convinced that the view in the Ministry of Defence, including that of his own Naval Staff, was too complacent about the implications of the new information coming from the South Atlantic. When he arrived in the Prime Minister's room discussion was under way on how to respond to the latest, disturbing intelligence. The advice being proffered to Mrs Thatcher tended to follow that developed in the Ministry of Defence a few days before: a task force would take a long time to assemble and travel to the South Atlantic and could then fail in its task. According to Leach:

> I think the Prime Minister was very worried, because I think her gut feeling was that we were going to *have* to do something. I think that I sensed, when I went in, that the sort of advice she had been getting prior to that had tended to deflect her from doing anything beyond negotiating, and putting the screws on with words again. She had been receiving advice, I think, that under *no* circumstances should she do anything about it, because it was too far away, and much too difficult.

Leach argued that something could be done, but whatever it was must not be half-hearted, for that was likely to result in a shambles.[5] A full task force with logistic support would be required, not just a small squadron. It could be put together by the weekend. By three weeks it could get to the Falkland Islands, look after itself if subjected to air and sea attack by Argentine forces and so put pressure on Buenos Aires.

Leach was told to begin to prepare the force, although no commitment was made as to whether or not it should sail.[6] During the next day there was considerable activity in Whitehall as the task force started to be put together. The issue at this point was still essentially naval, so, whatever the reservations in the Army and Air Force, they were not pushed to the fore. The Chief of Defence Staff, Admiral Sir

Terence Lewin, was in New Zealand, and attempting to return home as quickly as possible. The Chief of the General Staff, General Sir Edwin Bramall, travelled from Northern Ireland. Admiral Sir John Fieldhouse, Commander-in-Chief, Fleet, who was to command the eventual operation, came back from Gibraltar, where he had been watching the Spring Train exercises and had had a preliminary discussion with Admiral Woodward about the implications of sending a task force to the South Atlantic.

At a meeting of the Cabinet's Defence Committee on the morning of 1 April the preference was still for a diplomatic solution if one could only be found. Moreover, Britain had told the United States that there would be no escalation of the situation while it was attempting to mediate. There seemed little point in the circumstances in ordering troops to the South Atlantic.

By the evening the view had changed. The information coming in suggested little hope of stopping the Argentine landing. The Prime Minister, Carrington (back from Israel) and Nott, now convinced that a task force could be sent, met and decided that troops should be put on immediate notice for deployment to the South Atlantic. Already the ships that had been exercising off Gibraltar were moving south in order to meet up with a force assembling in British ports. From the Defence Committee's meeting Leach went back to the Ministry of Defence and issued a directive: 'The task force is to be made ready and sailed.'

It was only late in the evening of 2 April, with Argentine forces now on the Falklands, that the full Cabinet met and agreed that the task force should sail. Each member was asked by name whether he supported this decision, thus binding in the Government as a whole.[7] Only John Biffen, then Trade Secretary, is said to have dissented. The others felt that there was no other option. In the absence of a serious response to the seizure of British territory the Government could have been forced to resign.[8] Most hoped that the basic purpose of the task force was to strengthen the Government's diplomatic hand; they did not expect that it would need to fight.

By the Monday morning the first units of the task force were preparing to leave port. Admiral Lewin, as he returned from New

Zealand, went straight to the Ministry of Defence to check on the current situation. There he had typed out a draft of the objective for the British military effort. Taking as his guidance Resolution 502, which had just been passed in the United Nations, he described the objective as 'To cause the withdrawal of the Argentinian forces, and to restore the British administration'. From there he went to the first meeting of what became known as the 'War Cabinet', where his wording was agreed.[9] This became the objective for Operation Corporate.

The Structure of Command

The Government machine reorganized itself for the conflict. The first major political casualty was the Foreign Secretary, Lord Carrington. He resigned, as did his number two in the Foreign Office, Sir Humphrey Atkins, and Richard Luce, who had been the junior Minister responsible for the Falklands. Carrington later explained his decision less in terms of a sense of culpability than a recognition that in the face of what he described as a 'national humiliation' someone had to take the blame. Without this it would be difficult for the Government to shake off the post-mortems and consider the major issue now confronting it. His membership of the House of Lords rather than the Commons was a political disadvantage. Exposure to the strength of feeling among Conservative backbenchers at a meeting he attended with John Nott did not dispose him to carry on.[10] His immediate colleagues, however, tried to persuade him to stay for they recognized that the loss of Carrington removed a figure of experience and authority from the Government.

His replacement, Francis Pym, moved from being Leader of the House of Commons. He was given the job because of his strong position in the Conservative Party (had Mrs Thatcher fallen he could well have succeeded her) and because his promotion would not cause major disruption elsewhere. The only other senior Minister who could have taken on the job, and whose relationship with Thatcher was much better, was Deputy Prime Minister and Home Secretary William

Whitelaw, but he did not press for the job. Thatcher's biographer has described Pym as 'the man she least respected and least liked'.[11] Pym soon found himself in the middle of a major international crisis, the details of which were entirely unfamiliar to him.

John Nott had also offered to resign when the crisis broke and had performed poorly in the dramatic parliamentary debate of Saturday 3 April. The conflict was a repudiation of the thrust of the strategic policy he had outlined the previous year, in that it involved a major military effort well away from the NATO area and required capabilities which he had been prepared to scrap. He had an anxious temperament that was not naturally suited to crisis decision-making. Yet if he had resigned as well as Carrington there would have been intolerable disruption at the top in areas where continuity and experience were now vital.

In addition to the Prime Minister, Pym and Nott, the War Cabinet contained William Whitelaw, who added weight as an influential member of the Government and Party, and the Paymaster-General and Chairman of the Conservative Party, Cecil Parkinson. Whitelaw had won the Military Cross during the Second World War and knew something of the unpredictability of war and could warn of the likelihood of serious casualties. Officially Parkinson was responsible for the public relations side of the venture. He was included at the suggestion of John Nott, who had worked with Parkinson before and felt that he would be an ally against the natural alliance of Whitelaw and Pym. In practice the War Cabinet rarely divided on that basis.[12]

The full Cabinet did occasionally discuss policy in the Falklands, especially when it came to major steps such as approving the amphibious landing. But, in general, it was considered too large and potentially leaky and was therefore informed rather than consulted on the progress of the conflict. The Cabinet Office itself played only a minor role, although the Secretary to the Cabinet, Sir Robert Armstrong, chaired a daily meeting of the 'mandarins' – Sir Antony Acland, the new head of the Foreign Office, his immediate predecessor, Sir Michael Palliser, who had been handing over to Acland as the crisis broke, Sir Frank Cooper of the Ministry of Defence and Admiral Lewin, Chief of Defence Staff. This Committee met after the morning meetings of the War Cabinet both to follow through any decisions and to consider the next day's agenda.

The military advice to the War Cabinet was channelled through the Chief of Defence Staff, with other chiefs of staff in attendance when necessary. Reporting directly to Lewin was Admiral Sir John Fieldhouse, Commander-in-Chief of the task force and based at Northwood in north-west London. Under him were the operational commanders.

The choice of Admiral John 'Sandy' Woodward to take command of the First Flotilla was not automatic. To some a more natural choice would have been Admiral Derek Reffell, of the Third Flotilla, with experience of, and current responsibility for, surface and amphibious operations. But Woodward was bringing the ships from Gibraltar and, like Fieldhouse, he was a submariner. As a close relationship between senior commanders is critical no one objected to the choice. Actual submarine operations, however, would not be Woodward's responsibility. They would be tasked from Northwood by Admiral Peter Herbert. General Jeremy Moore as Fieldhouse's Land Deputy was more straightforward. Moore and his staff had a close working relationship with Northwood. Moore's man with the task force was Brigadier Julian Thompson, commanding 3 Commando Brigade. With Commodore Michael Clapp, in charge of amphibious warfare, he would be responsible for any eventual landing. Air Marshall Sir John Curtiss came to Northwood as Air Deputy.

Operation Corporate[13]

If a task force had to be dispatched, the first days of April 1982 were as good a time as any. The fleet was not widely dispersed, nor were critical units undergoing long refits. Unusually the two carriers, *Hermes* and *Invincible*, and the two assault ships, *Fearless* and *Intrepid*, were all at Portsmouth. *Intrepid* was in the process of being taken into reserve. The others had just completed major exercises. *Hermes* was in the early stages of maintenance.

For Task Force 317, frigates and destroyers, including those which had been exercising off Gibraltar, were gathered together. On 3 April the Navy Department gained permission to take ships up from trade (STUFT). Among the first to be taken was the P&O flagship, *Canberra*. Ferries and tankers were also taken up. In an unprecedented operation, stores of fuel, food, ammunition, spare parts and equipment were packed on board.

The political requirement to get the ships loaded and away as soon as possible meant that there was insufficient time to ensure that everything was put on board in the most convenient order so that it could be off-loaded again in the necessary sequence at the other end. The speedy confirmation that the anchorage and airfield at Ascension Island, midway between Britain and the Falklands, would be available eased the concerns here, for the stores could be sorted out and reinforced there. Although Britain owned the Island the airstrip, which was soon to become one of the busiest in the world, was operated by the United States. The local American Commander expressed misgivings that he was being asked to exceed his responsibilities but after a few telephone calls he was overruled.

Initially assigned to be taken to the South Atlantic was 3 Commando Brigade of the Royal Marines, along with the 3rd Battalion of the Parachute Regiment and a 'T' Battery, Air Defence Regiment, with a dozen Rapier air-defence missiles. It was soon apparent that these 3,000 men would not be enough. Crammed on to the two carriers were twenty Sea Harrier aircraft. Again it was hard to believe that these would be sufficient if serious fighting began. It was also clear that throughout the operation every available helicopter would be needed.

Yet the effort to convey even modest land and air power to the South Atlantic required a large fleet, and stretched resources and capacity to the limit. On 5 April the first ships pulled out of ports around Britain and from Gibraltar, with the glare of publicity focused on the two carriers as they left Portsmouth. The cheering crowds indicated a strength of patriotic emotion that was now building up in Britain, following that already expressed in Argentina. The task force represented a popular, national cause.

By 7 April the first wave of the task force was en route. In addition to the two carriers, three submarines and eleven destroyers and frigates there were tankers, landing ships and stores ships. Among the last to leave were *Fearless*, backed up by the Royal Fleet Auxiliary (RFA) *Stromness* with Royal Marines plus their equipment and provisions.

Two days later the *Canberra* left, packed with marines and para-troopers. Another P&O Liner, *Uganda*, was taken up and declared to the Red Cross as a hospital ship, and three small survey ships were fitted out as ambulance ships. Soon other frigates and support ships were also moving south.

The first ships to arrive at Ascension were those that had come from Gibraltar. The destroyer *Antrim*, the frigate *Plymouth* and the tanker RFA *Tidespring* had already been assigned to recapture South Georgia and so they moved with dispatch, arriving at Ascension on 10 April, where they picked up commandos and special force units who had been flown out from England to meet them. This group was later joined by *Endurance*, which after its frustrating adventures of the previous weeks had come north for replenishment before returning.

On 11 April the next group arrived – three destroyers, *Glasgow*, *Sheffield* and *Coventry*, and two frigates, *Arrow* and *Brilliant*. It left three days later, tasked with providing cover for the *Antrim* group and a distant screen for the carrier group that would soon be joining it.

On 16 April *Hermes* and *Invincible* anchored at Ascension. The next day the Amphibious Force, composed of *Fearless*, *Stromness* and five Landing Ships, Logistics (LSLs), began to arrive. On 18 April *Hermes* and *Invincible* left with the destroyer *Glamorgan*, the frigates *Broadsword*, *Yarmouth* and *Alacrity*, and the RFAs, *Olmeda* and *Resource*.

The amphibious group took time to assemble. The final four ships that made it up – the landing ship *Intrepid*, the container vessel *Atlantic Conveyor*, now converted into an aircraft transport, and the ferries *Norland* and *Europic Ferry* – did not leave Britain until 25 April. The two ferries were bringing the 2nd Battalion, the Parachute Regiment, and its equipment, which had been dispatched once it had been recognized that 3 Commando Brigade was not large enough as origin-ally constituted. They were also joined by a new commando company formed from those marines who had been repatriated after resisting the Argentine occupation. The *Atlantic Conveyor* would not only take stores and Wessex and Chinook helicopters, but would also carry a further twenty Harriers, twelve of which were the RAF's. After the necessary modifications they flew to Ascension, using in-flight refuelling, to catch the *Atlantic Conveyor*. Even before these ships had left Britain, the five slow LSLs, escorted by the frigate *Antelope*, had left Ascension. The main body of the amphibious force did not leave Ascension until 7 May, as the *Norland* arrived.

It was reported after the conflict that the task force had carried nuclear weapons into the South Atlantic, not with the intention of using them but because they were part of the ships' normal complement and had not been removed.[14] Some dummy nuclear weapons, which are used for training purposes, may have been seen and mistaken for the real thing.[15] Normally British carriers (in this case HMS *Invincible* and HMS *Hermes*) and some frigates carry nuclear depth charges for anti-submarine warfare purposes. There seems to be little doubt that some ships, especially those that came straight from exercising off Gibraltar, were indeed carrying nuclear weapons. It has been reported that three-quarters of the total naval stockpile set off towards the South Atlantic – but also that ministers were horrified when this was discovered and ordered a Royal Fleet Auxiliary to collect them at Ascension Island.[16]

British Intelligence

The task force left with only the flimsiest idea of the adversary at the other end of their journey. The intelligence sources most frequently mentioned are Portsmouth and Plymouth public libraries, with a considerable amount being gleaned from standard works such as the *Military Balance of the IISS* and *Jane's Fighting Ships*, *All the World's Aircraft* and *Weapons Systems*. These were also in great demand in the Ministry of Defence.[17]

The traumas facing the intelligence staffs were illustrated by the Army's Intelligence Corps, which,

> already fully committed in North West Europe and Northern Ireland, was required to create, at extremely short notice, a complete

intelligence organization to support the Joint Force, operating independently, in a virtually unknown area, against a hitherto friendly country, and 8,000 miles from its sources of supply.

It had to provide resources for supplying combat intelligence both to troops on the ground and to command staffs, which included additional intelligence staffs, linguists, tactical questioners, imagery interpreters, analysts, and electronic warfare operators. For a small corps, which has no central pool or reserve for meeting such emergencies, this was a formidable task.[18]

The immediate intelligence position deteriorated rather than improved. This was the result of a rather classic own goal. Ted Rowlands, a former Labour Minister of State at the Foreign Office who had grappled with these issues during the 1970s, observed in Parliament that 'as well as trying to read the mind of the enemy, we have been reading its telegrams for many years.' The Prime Minister later declared this to be 'totally and utterly devastating in the amount which it gave away' and Rowlands later acknowledged that representations were made to him afterwards by the Foreign Office.[19]

The natural and immediate result was that Argentina changed its codes.* This was at worst a temporary handicap, although with an enemy with more sophisticated means of encryption it could have been much more severe. It is clear that the new codes were broken (possibly with American help) within weeks if not days. According to *The Economist*:

Britain benefited from SIGINT given to GCHQ from NSA listening stations around the South Atlantic. The Americans are believed to have broken the Argentine military codes, thus adding to the British intelligence gathered by HMS Endurance. The Americans claim 98% of British intelligence of Argentine movements came from them.[20]

---

* As irritating to GCHQ was the number of other countries who had been using a similar system to Argentina and who took the hint.

What is not clear is whether this assistance was provided before the American 'tilt' in favour of the UK at the end of April.[21] Certainly Argentine codes were being broken by this time.[22]

By no means all Argentine signals were intercepted and deciphered. According to Lord Lewin, then Chief of Defence Staff, 'interception and deciphering of signals was a lengthy as well as an uncertain business.'[23] Much of the deciphering could be virtually automatic, as material was picked up by the listening posts, passed by communications satellite to GCHQ in Cheltenham where it would then be – if possible – deciphered by computer. The problem would come with deciding which of the many signals intercepted were to be translated. From interception to delivery to the customers could have been 'a matter of hours'[24] but in some cases it appears to have taken longer. Hundreds of 'raw' intercepts were collected and interpretation was demanding.

A major gap in capabilities was lack of decent aerial or satellite reconnaissance. Although some pictures of South Georgia were received in April, it was only in the late stages of the campaign that Britain eventually persuaded the United States to shift the orbit of a military satellite to cover the Falklands area,[25] though little of value appeared. The only satellite pictures which were readily accessible were those commercially available from the LANDSAT satellite. These were also available to Argentina,[26] and were of minimal value.

If it came to fighting the major threat to the task force was clearly going to come from the air, and this was particularly difficult to assess. British figures on the Argentine Air Force were based on reported deliveries. In the case of the Dagger, an Israeli-built version of the Mirage, more had been delivered than announced. More often the relevant equipment had been bought some time before, perhaps as much as a decade, and individual items had since been lost in accidents or mothballed. British intelligence feared that 247 fighter or attack aircraft would be available. The actual number was less than half.[27] This overestimation of numbers was matched by an underestimation of the quality and training of the Argentine Air Force pilots.

One area of uncertainty was the extent of the Argentine ability to marry Exocet missiles to Super-Etendard aircraft. The French informed the British that five Super-Etendards had been delivered. A team from the manufacturers, Dassault, due to go to Argentina to bring the two systems together, had been held back by President Mitterrand. Nevertheless the Exocets were fitted. Argentine sources indicate that they accomplished this alone.[28]

There was enough to know that the mission would be hazardous. According to Woodward:

> The Argentine Navy is a fairly aged force, equipped with plenty of modern weapons. Apart from their carrier, they outnumbered me with surface ship Exocet, they had two modern quiet diesel submarines, and their logistic base was at hand. Their air forces posed a formidable threat, particularly numerically and with the ability to launch Exocet from the Super-Etendard. If the whole could be brought together, I knew I had a problem.[29]

Chapter Ten

RESOLUTION 502

Britain's initial military moves were backed up by an equally crash programme of diplomatic action. The natural forum was the UN Security Council.

Argentina, not Britain, had been the first to consider a move to the Security Council. On 31 March, when the British Government had yet to realize that an invasion was imminent, the Junta was becoming more convinced than ever that British reinforcements were steaming towards the Falklands. It decided to denounce Britain at the United Nations for using a military build-up to avoid serious discussions of sovereignty, as required by past UN resolutions. Any Argentine actions would therefore be justified as an effort to thwart this plan. Also with the UN in mind it was decided to make preliminary contact with Moscow and Beijing. However, as with all Argentine diplomacy over this period it was inhibited by the need for secrecy with regard to Operation Rosario. A faint possibility that American mediation might produce a last-minute concession from Britain also argued against lobbying too hard at the UN.

On 31 March Eduardo Roca, the new Argentine Ambassador to the UN, met the American Ambassador, Jeane Kirkpatrick, who was on her last day as President of the Security Council. He raised the South Georgia issue, which Kirkpatrick still found difficult to take seriously. She argued for low-key diplomacy and suggested that the ambassadors of the two countries meet with her without recourse to the full Council.

At this point the Americans wished the dispute to be handled as a quarrel among friends rather than as a matter for the international community. Kirkpatrick told Roca that Britain did not like to put this sort of issue before the United Nations because the Organization was so unpredictable and anything which hinted of colonialism tended to work against the Western powers. It was true, so far as South Georgia was concerned, that Britain had not considered the Security Council an appropriate forum. It would not be the case with the Argentine occupation, although Roca presumed that it would be from Kirkpatrick's advice. As a result he was even less well prepared when the issue broke.

On 1 April Roca did go so far as to circulate a note to members of the Security Council, which referred to the South Georgia incident, the press reports of a British task force travelling to the South Atlantic and *Endurance*'s order to evict the Argentine workers, suggesting that this constituted the 'beginning of an aggression'.

By this time press reports were also coming through that an Argentine invasion force was sailing towards the Falkland Islands. Before he left for a tour of Europe, the Secretary-General summoned both ambassadors and expressed concern at the rising tension. He made a public appeal for restraint. Around lunchtime, Britain's Ambassador, Sir Anthony Parsons, was told officially by London that an invasion was imminent and he was instructed to call for a meeting of the Security Council. He immediately telephoned Ambassador Kamanda of Zaire, who had just taken over from Kirkpatrick as President of the Council for April. Kirkpatrick warned Parsons that she would 'block' a call for an emergency session of the Security Council. If she attempted to do so, Parsons responded, 'I would demand a vote, procedural vote, on whether we actually discussed the problem. She would have to oppose me on the vote, in public, underneath the television cameras and the rest of it.'[1] The objection was dropped.

Parsons's explanation of the situation to members of the Council when they met that afternoon was received with varying degrees of astonishment and disbelief, as well as considerable ignorance of the nature of the dispute. There was the inevitable inquiry whether this was an elaborate April Fool's Day hoax. Afterwards the President made a statement calling on both governments to 'exercise the utmost restraint at this time and in particular to refrain from the use of force or threat of force in the region'. Parsons promised restraint from Britain and challenged his Argentine counterpart to do likewise: Roca failed to respond.

That evening the British delegation met to prepare further action for the following day when the anticipated news of the invasion would come through. Parsons described two key considerations: 'First we must concentrate on the illegitimate use of force to settle a long-standing political problem. Secondly, we must act quickly and avoid becoming mired in the long negotiations which normally precede the adoption of a resolution by the council.'[2]

The first consideration recognized that on the sovereignty dispute itself Argentina could cite a string of past UN resolutions favouring its position; it was most vulnerable to the charge of attempting to settle this dispute by force. Speed was vital in that early support was likely to be for Britain while delays would allow the eventual vote to be influenced by factors separate from the main issue as horse-trading began. Argentina might well be able to gather votes by making promises on other issues.

By the morning of 2 April Britain had a draft text to present to the Security Council when it reconvened at 11.45. Parsons avoided the series of drafting stages through which Security Council resolutions are normally expected to pass and insisted that no amendments would be accepted. He originally wanted a vote within a day but he agreed to wait until Costa Mendez arrived to present the Argentine case.

Lobbying

There are fifteen members of the Security Council. Five are permanent and ten are drawn from the rest of the membership for two-year periods. To win a Security Council vote it is necessary to have the support of at least nine members. Even then a vote against by one of the permanent members means that the resolution is lost. For Britain to obtain a positive vote in the present case would require an intensive lobbying effort.

Circumstances at the beginning of April found Britain in a better position to argue its case than Argentina. Eduardo Roca, the Ambassador to the UN, had only just arrived in New York and had yet to familiarize himself with its procedures, personalities and political undercurrents. Britain, on the other hand, was a permanent member of the Security Council. Parsons, who was on the point of retirement, was an extremely experienced and popular operator at the UN. Given the speed with which the issue broke, the state of ignorance of many delegates and the lack of well-established positions, this would be one of the few occasions when the quality of the presentations in the debate would actually make a difference.

The draft resolution avoided an extreme statement so that wavering delegations would be more likely to support it. In particular it did not denounce Argentina as an aggressor.[3] The only eventual change was to include the bracketed words '(Islas Malvinas)' after every mention of the Falkland Islands as per normal UN practice.[4]

The British calculation was that at most the draft resolution could get ten votes. The Soviet Union, China and Poland could be discounted as they would not vote on principle for a British resolution. Panama had already identified itself as Argentina's leading supporter on the Security Council while Spain was influenced by considerations of Latin solidarity. On the other hand it was presumed that Britain could count on the United States, France, Ireland and Japan.

The key group therefore comprised the five non-aligned countries: Uganda, Togo and Zaire from Africa, Jordan from the Middle East and Guyana from South America. It was possible to imagine alternatives from each region who would have been much more hostile to Britain. Of these Guyana would support Britain because it perceived a dangerous precedent if Argentina were allowed to settle this dispute by force, given the claim on its own territory from neighbouring Venezuela. Zaire also would give support. The call made by its Ambassador as President of the Council for both sides to show restraint had been disregarded by Argentina. France worked on the Togo delegation on Britain's behalf. This left Uganda, whose eventual intentions remained uncertain, and Jordan. The Jordanian Ambassador, who had originally supported Britain, was told by Amman to abstain. He warned Parsons of this. The Prime Minister was contacted and she immediately tele-phoned King Hussein.[5] As a result Jordan came back into line, pos-sibly influenced by British support for its position on the Middle East.

The Argentine strategy was based on past support for its stand on the sovereignty dispute. On this basis it presumed correctly that it could count on Latin American countries, although only Panama could vote. During the debate many South American countries asked for the right to express their views. Peru, Bolivia, Paraguay and Brazil all stated that they recognized only Argentine sovereignty over the Islands. Yet even these countries reaffirmed their preference for the peaceful solution of international disputes.

Argentine hopes for support from other Third World countries were based on anti-colonialism. These were not its natural allies. It had not given much support to the anti-colonial campaigns of others nor shown much sympathy for those issues which mattered most to this group. It supported Israel, with whom it maintained close links (and which maintained its arms transfers during the conflict), and had just been denounced by Nicaragua for its role in Central America.

As soon as Costa Mendez arrived in New York he went to a meeting of the non-aligned caucus to state his case. It was not his most successful performance. He relied too much on anti-colonial senti-ments and did not argue the merits of the use of force in this instance. Later Roca observed: 'the meeting was bad. Costa Mendez found at the end of his speech that the only head that nodded was that of the Panamanian delegate.'[6]

It was a problem for Argentina that around the world there were many long-standing disputes that one party might decide to resolve by the use of force on exactly the same basis. A number of those voting could imagine themselves becoming the victim of similar arguments. Few were persuaded when, during the Security Council debate, Costa Mendez suggested that the UN Charter's reference to the peaceful resolution of disputes was only relevant to those which began after 1945. This novel principle was being mentally applied to a whole range of other disputes.

It is of course true that in the United Nations anti-colonialism often overrides misgivings about the use of force. It is therefore also likely that non-aligned countries were simply not convinced that this was a true anti-colonial issue, especially given the views of the islanders themselves. It was one thing to lean towards the Argentine view in General Assembly resolutions and urge Britain to negotiate seriously; it was quite another to accept that the position was so intolerable that it could only be resolved by violent means.[7]

Even if Britain could obtain a sufficient majority the resolution could still be lost by a Soviet or Chinese veto. The Argentine ambassadors in both countries had been instructed to explore the possibilities of support but had made little progress. It was never likely that China would use its veto on an issue such as this. A direct appeal was made to the Soviet Ambassador to the Security Council during the debate by Costa Mendez, who asked if instructions had been received from Moscow. He was told: 'the wheels of time do not favour us, sir. You will understand that a veto in the United Nations is a matter of extreme importance; I do not decide it, nor even an assistant secretary in Moscow, and now it is 2 o'clock in the morning over there.'[8]

In fact the Soviet delegation was in constant communication with Moscow. Its eventual decision to abstain was probably based on a reluctance to use its veto on any issue other than one of central importance to the Soviet Union and an awareness that the non-aligned vote, with which it does not like to be out of step, was moving towards Britain. Two days later, on 5 April, when the vote was safely over, word came from Moscow that Argentina could rely on a veto in any subsequent vote. This was never put to the test.

The Vote

At 11.00 hours on 3 April in New York the Security Council met to discuss the resolution presented by the United Kingdom. In his speech Costa Mendez stressed the history of the dispute and argued that Argentina was simply taking back land that had been seized illegally in 1833. He insisted that the military preparations made by Britain in the region explained and justified the actions that 'the Argentine Government has been forced to take in the defence of its rights'. While still expressing a desire for a negotiated settlement he also suggested that now the Islands were being administered by Argentina the issue of sovereignty was non-negotiable.

Panama proposed a procedural amendment to enable the Security Council to adjourn to consider a draft resolution that it had tabled which insisted on sole Argentine sovereignty over the Islands and demanded that Britain withdraw entirely from the region on the grounds of decolonization. Parsons opposed the procedural amendment, which received only seven votes and not the nine needed.

Later Panama argued that Britain could not vote, that as a party to the dispute it should abstain. However, the resolution had been drafted with reference not to the clause of the Charter dealing with dispute settlement but to that dealing with breaches of the peace. Parsons objected to the Panamanian move on this basis and was supported by the Spanish representative, an acknowledged expert on procedure. Panama also suggested that the resolution be amended to require 'mutual [rather than solely Argentine] withdrawal of forces from the region', as it had been reported that a British task force was now being sent. This also failed to gain support.

When the British resolution was subjected to a vote it was approved as Resolution 502/1982 with ten countries voting in favour (US, France, Guyana, Ireland, Japan, Jordan, United Kingdom, Togo, Uganda and Zaire), one against (Panama) and four abstaining (China, USSR, Poland and Spain).

The Resolution stated that:

The Security Council, *recalling* the statement made by the President of the Security Council at the 2345th meeting of the Security Council on 1 April 1982 calling on the Governments of Argentina and the United Kingdom of Great Britain and Northern Ireland to refrain from the use or threat of force in the region of the Falkland Islands (Islas Malvinas).

Deeply disturbed at reports of an invasion on 2 April 1982 by armed forces of Argentina,

Determining that there exists a breach of the peace in the region of the Falkland Islands (Islas Malvinas),

1. *Demands* an immediate cessation of hostilities;
2. *Demands* an immediate withdrawal of all Argentine forces from the Falkland Islands (Islas Malvinas);
3. *Calls* on the Governments of Argentina and the United Kingdom to seek a diplomatic solution to their differences and to respect fully the purposes and principles of the Charter of the United Nations.

To Britain the vote came as a relief. Resolution 502 was taken as a clear statement of opposition to the Argentine action. It linked Argentine action to a breach of the peace. Only Argentina was asked to withdraw its forces. If it failed to do so Britain could claim that it was justified in resorting to force as self-defence, permitted by the Charter. In the event British rationales for the use of force on this basis were generally accepted.

The resolution was a blow for Argentina. It did not ask for mutual – but only Argentine – withdrawal. This meant that if implemented there would be nothing to stop Britain retaking the Islands as soon as its task force reached the South Atlantic. It could then refuse to negotiate seriously in the future.

Nevertheless Argentine diplomats concluded that it could have been worse. The country had not actually been labelled as an aggressor. As it had not been condemned out of hand there was still a possibility that the international community would support eventual negotiation. The resolution did not actually state that the United Kingdom could use force in retaliation nor did it ask for a return of the status quo ante as of 2 April. On this basis Argentina began to say that the problem was not the resolution but the British interpretation of it. In practice, however, it had lost the diplomatic initiative.

Chapter Eleven

OCCUPATION

Argentina Thinks Again

The original objective of Operation Azul/Rosario had been to land on the Falkland Islands and establish an Argentine administration. After this a notional garrison of some 500 troops was to be left to maintain order while the main intervention forces were withdrawn. Although Argentine planners had been thinking for years about how to seize the Islands they had never developed plans for defending them once seized. The presumption in Buenos Aires was that this was not a problem. There was no expectation of such a massive British response. The matter would be settled through negotiation.

The Junta had expected Britain to denounce it in the UN and elsewhere. However, by making the intervention as bloodless as possible it hoped to reduce the force of any condemnation. A more critical hope was that the British reaction would be confined to protests and would not include a strong military response. If these hopes were fulfilled then the next step would be to agree with Britain a cease-fire and the negotiation of the sovereignty question coupled with the withdrawal of Argentine forces as a gesture of goodwill.

Argentina soon discovered that things were not going to be so simple. On 3 April news came in of that day's parliamentary debate. It contained evidence of an awareness of the need for a diplomatic as well as a military response to the crisis. But there was no doubt about the Prime Minister's statement that a task force was being dispatched to the South Atlantic with the objective of reimposing a British administration. The size of the task force was not mentioned but there was no need: it was enough to know that it included the carrier *Invincible*.

UN Resolution 502 agreed later that day did nothing to stop this task force. While it might have been possible to agree to the withdrawal of Argentine forces if British forces were to be kept from the region, now such a withdrawal would appear as weakness in the face of the threat of a British military response.

The possibility of such a reaction had been recognized in the planning process. It represented the most threatening scenario, but also among the least likely, and so no suitable plans had been developed to deal with it. The rushed planning process had barely covered the initial landing let alone a subsequent defence. Now the Junta hurriedly decided on measures to cope with the emerging military challenge.

The previous day's order for an early military withdrawal was reversed. General García asked for immediate reinforcements to be sent to the Islands to complicate Britain's assessment of its military requirements. If possible the reinforcements should comprise the elite forces that had undertaken the intervention in the first place. This led to urgent messages seeking to cancel the original order to fly this force back to the mainland. However, the new order arrived too late. Admiral Büsser had carried out his instruction to the letter and had immediately begun to send back his troops to the mainland. By the evening of 3 April only half the original intervention force was still on the Islands. It was not until 4 April that the decision to demobilize was reversed. The Islands were to be reinforced instead. On 6 April movement by air began of the 8th Regiment to the Falklands, to be deployed at Fox Bay settlement on West Falkland. Two days later the 5th Marine Infantry Battalion with its accompanying artillery units were moved to the Stanley area.

The magnitude of the British military response required that the future defensive efforts concentrate on the Falkland Islands, the central political objective. Once the operation to take South Georgia had been completed an order was sent out to withdraw the naval units involved. A small number of troops could be garrisoned on the Island, but with minimum support and material because little could be done to defend it should Britain decide to attack. This was even more true of the South

Sandwich Islands, where, it was decided, the small presence should be left as it was.

The next day, 4 April, the Junta learned that the US Government had authorized the British use of Ascension Island. News also came of the composition of the British task force. Following the assessments of the previous week, it was expected that nuclear submarines would be arriving imminently as the vanguard. This was thought to be confirmed by the detection on 3 April of a British oil transport, *Apple Leaf*, in the area of the South Atlantic.

The situation seemed even worse than anticipated. The Junta concluded that Britain was attempting a rapid recovery of the territories before pressure mounted for serious negotiations. Whether or not there was an eventual confrontation it was vital to build up military strength on the Falklands to make any attempt by Britain to recover the Islands as difficult as possible and so gain time for the diplomatic offensive. Demonstrating this to Britain would add to the political pressure for a negotiated settlement.

Organization

Argentina reorganized itself for the new situation. Throughout the conflict, the Junta invariably had the last word. It sought to operate on the basis of consensus. There were, however, two other important committees. The Military Committee was composed of all the commanders from the theatre of operations and the chiefs of staff of the services (some ten people including the Junta). This created a Political Committee, known as the Malvinas Working Group, which included Costa Mendez as well as representatives of the services, and which prepared for the negotiations.

At this level there was also an attempt to smooth over differences: further down the command system communications were less than satisfactory. The services tended to operate independently of each other and there were innumerable arguments about the division of roles and responsibilities.

There were continual problems with the military command

structure. Operation Rosario had been the responsibility of the Malvinas Operational Theatre under General Osvaldo García. This was disbanded after the operation and was replaced by the South Atlantic Operational Theatre, which was set up on 7 April under Admiral Lombardo. His Chief of Staff was Rear Admiral Alberto Padilla. General Julio Ruiz was put in charge of Land Forces, Brigadier A. C. Weber of Air Forces and Admiral G. Allara of Naval Forces. The exact role of the Governor, General Menendez, was not made clear in this structure.

Eventually on 26 April Menendez put himself in charge of the Malvinas Joint Command, and gave roles to the three commanders of the brigades which had been sent to him: General Américo Daher (9th Infantry Brigade), his Chief of Staff; General Oscar Jofre (10th Infantry Brigade), Commander of the Puerto Argentino Group of Forces; and General Omar Parada (3rd Infantry Brigade), Commander of the Malvinas Group of Forces. These tasks were themselves disputed. When Jofre first arrived the Army transferred him to Daher's job because of his seniority, before Menendez reinstated Daher.

Parada's position was even more extraordinary and was the result of a visit to the Falklands by Galtieri on 22 April. By the time he arrived it had already been confirmed that British ships were sailing south from Ascension Island. The previous day, a reconnaissance flight by a Boeing counted two aircraft-carriers and eight destroyers or frigates already one-third of the distance from Ascension to the Falklands.[1] Galtieri met with Menendez and Jofre to discuss the situation. They agreed that any British landing would probably be near Stanley. According to Jofre:

Galtieri said we did not have enough reserves, and we agreed; we only had two infantry companies in reserve, with a few helicopters and the twelve armoured cars. Galtieri suggested sending a further regiment of infantry. Menendez and I agreed, providing he could solve the logistics problems we had with our existing forces, plus that of the new regiment.[2]

However, Galtieri had become so concerned that when he returned to Buenos Aires he decided that, instead of sending an extra regiment, an extra brigade should be sent. In addition to the problems of defending Stanley, he was concerned that there were insufficient troops to occupy the whole area and that this could weaken his bargaining position should there be a fight. Another brigade could fill up the spaces. Without consultation with other members of the Junta or with the Military Committee, Galtieri decided to send the 3rd Infantry Brigade. It moved to the Falklands from 24 to 29 April.

The 3rd Infantry Brigade was normally based in Corrientes. It was not at all prepared for this task, and had no plans for such a move. It was in fact in the process of redeploying to the south-west to strengthen defences against any attempt by Chile to take advantage of the conflict with Britain. Conditions in the Falklands were quite different from those in Corrientes, and were beyond the experience and training of the troops. They lacked the appropriate equipment and little regard was paid to the problem of logistic support. Yet the role assigned to the Brigade meant that it had to deploy in some of the more distant and desolate parts of the Island (the 12th Infantry Regiment at Darwin; the 5th in Howard).*

General Parada was unable to establish a brigade headquarters at Darwin. He was required by Menendez to stay at Stanley to organize the unexpected influx of troops caused by his Brigade's move. As some of his men were deployed more than 62 miles away and visits were extremely difficult, because of the complete lack of roads and the scarcity of available aircraft, he could only keep in touch by radio.[3]

The arrival of 3 Brigade added to the strain on the already stretched logistic resources and meant less rations all round. The *Formosa* had just arrived bringing desperately needed food reserves, extending them to fifteen days. The arrival of 3 Brigade now cut this in half. When Britain announced the Maritime Exclusion Zone on 12 April four ships loaded with rations and equipment were still at home port waiting to sail to the Islands. They were held back by the Junta because

---

* The infantry units of the Argentine Army are known as 'regiments' and are the equivalent, although slightly smaller, of British battalions, normally around 600 men.

Alexander Haig was just about to start his mediation effort and it was decided not to take any step which might provoke early military action. Only belatedly was it realized that Britain would probably not attack solitary merchant ships. The ships eventually arrived but two were then trapped in the Islands and were unable to return to the mainland, while a third, the *Ciudad de Cordoba*, hit a rock en route and had to return home, without being able to deliver 3 Brigade's equipment. The air bridge was able to deliver some 5,500 tons of cargo by 29 April, but shortages of food and equipment remained thereafter.[4]

In general each service retained responsbility for its own logistics. This worked to the disadvantage of the Army as it was dependent upon air and sea transport. On the Island the Air Force transports shared their space with the Army.

During April ships were allocated to the Army to take over supplies but after May, when the ships could no longer get through, the naval air transports seem to have confined themselves to looking after naval units.

Strategy

Menendez himself was not the best person to prepare a stout defence. He later commented: 'we had no definite idea that the English would indeed attack.' When news came that a task force was to be sent it was seen as a 'form of military pressure to aid the diplomacy to get the best advantage for the negotiated settlement that would ensue'.[5] On 4 April, as Menendez was about to leave to take over as Governor, he was told by Lombardo that he did not want to get involved in the defence of the Islands. Lombardo said: 'I will give you freedom of action because you will be isolated. Tell me what you need.' Menendez answered that he had only been prepared to be Governor.[6]

He had not been chosen for his qualities as a fighter but, rather, for a conciliatory temperament that would help him govern the Islands. It was expected that he would return to the mainland by December 1982, by which time a proper diplomatic settlement would have been reached. Throughout he remained stubbornly convinced that military action must remain subordinate to diplomacy, and this may well explain his later behaviour when he found himself serving as a military commander rather than a political governor.

Given the new circumstances, the possibility was considered of replacing Menendez with someone more suited to armed conflict. Galtieri decided against. He felt that it would cause undue anxiety among both the armed forces and the Argentine people generally if there were 'chops and changes' at the top. In the event, and as he might have predicted, Menendez proved to be a less able military commander than political governor.[7]

Neither Lombardo's command in Puerto Belgrano nor Menendez in Stanley acted as if they expected anything other than a diplomatic resolution of the conflict. Little military planning was done. On 9 April Lombardo visited the Islands with his senior staff. On 14 April he sent a directive – MTQ 68 – to Menendez suggesting how the Islands might be defended in an emergency, but the Governor found these too vague. He does not seem to have produced an alternative, but only to have discussed Lombardo's ideas with him over the telephone.[8]

The main effort was put into reinforcing personnel on the Islands in order to buy time for the negotiations. It was assumed simply that British military calculations would become more difficult the larger the number of Argentine troops they had to face.

It was difficult for the Argentine leaders to free themselves from the idea that the critical battle was to be fought at the diplomatic front, and that therefore military operations must be subordinate to political requirements.

Occupation or Negotiation

The Military Committee had begun the crisis with the assumption that every military action must be geared to the negotiating process and it continued in this vein. At its meeting on 6 April it resolved that no new military actions should be initiated by Argentina in case they created an unfavourable climate for negotiations. Three days later it ordered restrictions on the use of weapons. No Argentine troops or units could initiate hostile activities under any circumstances.

Yet the very act of sending Menendez, especially as this was done with great ostentation, reduced Argentina's flexibility. When he arrived at Stanley (now Puerto Argentino) on 7 April he was with representatives of all the political parties, heightening the symbolism of the occasion. Immediately it meant that his return would become an issue in any future negotiations. If an Argentine governor was later replaced by a non-Argentine authority this would entail a loss of domestic and international prestige.

Costa Menendez had been anxious as soon as he heard of the plan to take the politicians to Stanley because it suggested a permanence inconsistent with the image of flexibility that he was seeking to create. On 6 April, just before Menendez arrived to become Governor, Costa Mendez urged that he should not 'take up this post until the situation was clear'. However, the popular enthusiasm for the occupation had its diplomatic consequences. Up to this point the Junta had not intended to insist on a prior recognition of Argentine sovereignty as a precondition for the negotiations. It was only at this time that the transfer of sovereignty by a fixed date (the end of the year) became part of the Argentine position. As Costa Mendez noted: 'The reaction of the Argentine people was extraordinary and much greater than expected. Many believed we could keep the Islands forever, without concessions. This reaction limited the Government's negotiating stance.'9

Chapter Twelve

ALLIES, FRIENDS AND MEDIATORS

Regional Support (i) Latin America

In seeking diplomatic support it was natural for Argentina to turn to its Latin American neighbours. However, relations there were not warm. The recent tendency in Argentina had been to isolate itself from its regional context, looking instead to Europe. The isolation was further exacerbated by the Military Government. During 1980 a number of countries had become democratic, notably Peru and Bolivia, and in late 1981 the democratic countries of South America had launched a political offensive through the Quito Declaration against the authoritarian governments of the south – Argentina, Chile, Paraguay, Uruguay and Brazil. Of these Chile was the most logical ally of Argentina, except that relations had been undermined by the Beagle Channel dispute.

Further north, in Central America, Argentina had alienated most potential sympathizers when, in 1981, it had pledged military support for the United States in its policies towards El Salvador and Nicaragua. In addition, the more left-wing countries in Latin America regarded Argentina with enmity because of the severity of the repression of the insurgency it had faced during the 'dirty war'. Finally, Mexico – along with Spain, Italy, Canada and France – had attacked the Argentine Government for its human-rights abuses and provided a political haven for many of the persecuted Argentines fleeing from the Junta.

Obviously Argentina had to work quickly to improve its position in the region. Costa Mendez found this task easier than some of the other diplomatic challenges he faced. He stayed on in the United States to address a meeting of the Organization of American States in Washington DC on 5 April. There he stated pointedly that Argentina would comply fully with the resolutions of the General Assembly of the United Nations – that is, those resolutions which favoured the Argentine position on sovereignty – and that it would protect the interests of the islanders. Costa Mendez did not doubt that the principle of Argentine sovereignty would be endorsed. His task was to gauge the level of support for its current stance should Argentina decide to raise the issue under the Rio Treaty.

Costa Mendez had received instructions from the Junta to inform the regional community that while Argentina would not initiate hostilities it would respond if the country were attacked. Should the British fleet come as near as 200 miles from its coast, now including the Falklands, Argentina would maintain freedom of action to defend its national interests.

Over the next few weeks Latin American declaratory support for Argentina grew, perhaps less because of Argentine diplomacy than because of the opportunities the conflict provided for Peru, Venezuela and Brazil to make their mark in regional politics and extend their influence with Washington.

By the time Costa Mendez returned to Buenos Aires on 7 April his staff at the Ministry of Foreign Affairs had concluded that it might be possible to live with Resolution 502, and even use it to the Argentine advantage. This view depended on an ingenious interpretation which noted that the resolution did not accuse Argentina of actual aggression; that the first demand, for a cessation of hostilities, had been met and that any renewal of hostilities would be Britain's responsibility; that the second demand, for the withdrawal of Argentine forces, did not mention the date of execution (although, rather awkwardly for this interpretation, it did say 'immediate'); and that the third clause calling on both parties to negotiate precisely reflected Argentine objectives. Thus, they argued, if this resolution were to form the basis of future negotiations it must be taken as a whole and not clause by clause.

Return of the British task force to home base was required for the cessation of hostilities (clause one) which would then be coupled with Argentine troop withdrawal (clause two) and the beginning of negotiations (clause three).

Whether or not this could be sold to the international community was another matter. On 8 April Costa Mendez reported to the full Cabinet on his trip to Washington, aware now of the problems he faced. The major powers, he noted, wished to preserve the international status quo and were unhappy with the precedent created by Argentina in the South Atlantic. Meanwhile the very small countries identified themselves as probable victims of similar interventions in the future.

Regional Support (ii) Europe

While Argentina looked naturally to Latin America for support, Britain looked to Europe. It was able to achieve a quick condemnation of the Argentine action, on the day of the occupation. Practical support was also requested. A number of countries – France, Italy, Germany – had sold arms to Argentina and Britain was anxious for an embargo. This was effectively achieved within a week. It also wanted economic sanctions, for which it asked the EEC formally on 6 April.

The Presidency of the Council of Ministers at that time was held by Belgium, whose Prime Minister, Leo Tindemans, was an enthusiast for political co-operation among Community members. Support for Britain was based on the argument that the Argentine action contravened international law (this had been reflected in Resolution 502) and that the territory itself was associated with a member state. Other member states could conceive of similar instances where small groups might find themselves under threat – from West Berlin to French colonies.[1]

The main problem was less in agreeing in principle to economic sanctions than deciding on how it was to be achieved. Britain's initial preference, because it would have quickly taken effect, was that action should be taken under Article 242 of the Treaty of Rome, which requires member states to implement common action through national legislation. However, this could have led to variations in implementation which other states, notably Germany, were anxious to avoid. Article 113 could mean that sanctions would arise as trade policy, and so more a Community rather than national responsibility. This, however, was awkward for the Danes, who could not move until their Parliament had been consulted. So although the principle was soon agreed, the proposed text could not be endorsed until 14 April. Regulation 877/82, imposing an embargo on Argentine goods, came into force on 16 April for one month.

On the question of the arms embargo the attitude of France was critical. It was in the process of delivering Super-Etendard aircraft to the Argentine Navy with Exocet anti-ship missiles. Another deal was for armoured vehicles. France also provided engines for Pucara aircraft.

Although a socialist government might not have seemed a natural supporter of conservative Mrs Thatcher, in practice members of the French Government were more anglophile than the Gaullists. President Mitterrand, Foreign Minister Claude Cheysson and Defence Minister Charles Hernu had all spent the Second World War in Britain. Mitterrand rang Thatcher personally on the morning of 3 April to pledge his support to Britain.

Hernu had a routine meeting with John Nott on 1 April. He learned of the situation in the South Atlantic, although the matter was not raised formally. The next day Hernu was not in Paris when the news of the Argentine occupation came through. However, after a quick consultation among members of his *cabinet*, the department responsible for arms sales was contacted and told to halt immediately all deliveries to Argentina. On the following Wednesday, 6 April, this *de facto* embargo was formalized by the full Cabinet, without opposition.

A greater difficulty for France came later in April when Peru suddenly decided to press for early delivery of air-launched Exocets, which had been ordered to be carried on (British-made) Sea Kings. Peru even offered to divert a warship to a French port to pick them up. This created a quandary because France had no quarrel with Peru and had no wish for a diplomatic row, especially as Peru was within its contractual rights. On the other hand the likely destination of the Exocets was clear. French officials dreamed up a series of excuses (including the risk of British sabotage) to delay delivery.

Another element in the embargo was the removal of French technical assistance from Argentina. Initially little attention was paid to this question, although with modern weapons the accompanying software is often as important as the hardware. Eventually it was realized that there were still industrial support teams in Argentina and withdrawal was ordered, though this was not accomplished until the middle of April.

On 4 April Hernu was contacted directly from London and asked for technical assistance, especially with regard to the French aircraft sold to Argentina. This was agreed at once. Mirage crews were told to fly to Britain: they left so quickly that their arrival caught the host base by surprise. The aircraft exercised with British Harriers, playing both attacker and defender to enable the British pilots to get the measure of their likely opponents. Throughout the conflict, France provided a stream of technical information to help Britain counter the French-made systems its forces were facing.

The final key element in France's assistance was to encourage its former colony Senegal to allow British aircraft to use the airport at Dakaar on their journey to Ascension. It also helped persuade Togo to support UN Resolution 502.

The Formulation of US Policy

The efforts by both Argentina and Britain to gain support from their regional partners were secondary to their courting of the United States, a friend of both governments and so in a central position.

In the United States, as in the United Nations, it took some time before the conflict could be taken seriously. There were frequent references to comic operas and disbelief that in the modern age countries could believe that what Reagan later referred to as 'that little ice-cold bunch of land down there' was worth fighting for. Gradually the seriousness of the situation became apparent and, in particular, its perilous implications for American foreign policy.

There were three possible criteria against which US policy might be judged: the underlying dispute over sovereignty; the balance of US interests with regard to the two belligerents; and the broader principles raised by the nature of the dispute.

On the first of these issues the United States had sustained a studious neutrality and this hardly seemed the moment to depart from that policy. As to where the balance of US interests lay the Administration soon divided into the 'Europeanists' and the 'Latinos'. The President played little part in guiding this debate. His Adviser for National Security Affairs, William Clark, had recently moved into the office and, although he had had a brief spell as Haig's Deputy, knew little of foreign policy. He was an old friend of Reagan and his main interest appeared to be to protect the President's high personal popularity.

The leading 'Latinos' were Thomas Enders and Jeane Kirkpatrick. Kirkpatrick was the best-informed person on Latin American issues in the Administration; even Enders had spent most of his career working on European affairs. They argued for neutrality: Argentina had shifted towards the United States and was now a valuable supporter in critical areas, most notably in the attempt to undermine Marxist strength in Central America. This was a central policy objective of the Reagan Administration and could now be threatened should the United States back Britain. Moreover, such support would confirm the often expressed South American view that the United States cared far more for Europe than it did for the rest of the Americas. There was no obligation to back Britain at all times; this was certainly not Britain's approach with regard to American actions.

The Europeanists, such as the Under Secretary for European Affairs, Lawrence Eagleburger, stressed the implications of failing to support a NATO ally which had been the victim of aggression. Eagleburger later explained:

I was driven essentially by one very simple argument – an ally is an ally. I believed ... that one of our most serious general foreign policy problems is a growing perception – correct perception – that we are no longer as reliable partners and allies as we were, [and] under those circumstances, in a case that was so important to Mrs Thatcher . . . we had no choice.[2]

Although the North Atlantic Treaty itself did not oblige the US to come to British aid the circumstances of the Argentine occupation and the fact that Britain was the ally in question made support even more vital. The special relationship was even closer than usual with Margaret Thatcher as Prime Minister. She had provided President Reagan with invaluable political and ideological support on a number of issues. The US position in Europe was at that time bound up with a fierce debate over the introduction of cruise and Pershing missiles into Europe. Mrs Thatcher was one of the most stalwart supporters of missile deployment.

Her political fate was now tied to the resolution of the conflict. There was also awareness that ever since the Suez débâcle of 1956, when the United States forced Britain to terminate its military action in Egypt, there had been suspicion in London that when it came to the crunch the United States could not be relied upon.

Haig was not convinced that the matter could best be understood as Latin America versus Europe. On the one hand he was aware that hemispheric solidarity with Argentina was by no means total: neighbours of Argentina were wary that success this time might encourage other uses of force to solve disputes. Support in Latin America seemed to grow with distance from Argentine territory.[3] On the other hand he knew Britain could not be sure that the broad support it enjoyed from its allies would endure, especially if it engaged in military action. Some countries, such as Italy, had their own close relations with Argentina.

Haig was naturally a strong Europeanist. He was aware of the widespread sympathy in America, soon expressed by politicians and the media, for Britain's predicament. It could draw on years of close political alliance and cultural bonds. Argentina, by comparison, was best known as an abuser of human rights and a military dictatorship. The sort of geopolitical arguments favoured by the 'Latinos' were based on hard but controversial strategic calculations. They were not calculated to go down well with US public opinion, for which a readiness to support clandestinely controversial policies in Central America would not earn high commendations. Galtieri's brusque behaviour towards Reagan when he called on the night of 1 April did not count in Argentina's favour.

A clinching argument in Britain's favour was that the Argentine action seemed such a clear violation of the principles of the rule of law. Mrs Kirkpatrick, the most influential of the Latinos, suggested that as the US was neutral on the dispute over sovereignty it could also be neutral as to whether Argentina had been wrong to use force. She noted later: 'if the Argentines own the islands then moving troops into them is not armed aggression.'[4] None the less, this was still an attempt to resolve a dispute under negotiation by force.

This meant that in practice the options for the United States were to support Britain or to maintain a neutral stance. Support for Argentina was not an option. Yet, despite his instincts, Haig inclined towards initial neutrality. He felt that this natural sympathy must be qualified. As with many other international issues at that time, he was strongly influenced by calculations of potential Soviet advantage. At the time of the US grain embargo, Argentina had supplied the Soviet Union. The risk of the Junta turning to the Soviet Union for direct aid, a risk which was greatly over-estimated, was the Latino argument that most impressed him: 'If the US aligned itself, from the outset, with Great Britain, either because of our traditional relationship with Britain . . . or on the broader grounds of being an advocate for "rule of law", it offered great opportunities for Soviet mischief-making, either directly, or through their Cuban proxies, in Argentina.'[5]

On the most pressing question facing the State Department – how to vote on Resolution 502 – the Europeanists argued successfully that this must be supported. Ambassador Kirkpatrick proposed that the United States should try to get the vote postponed but it was known that the British would not agree to this. She distanced herself from the decision by not going to New York for the vote. Her place was taken by Charles Lichenstein, the second in command at the UN delegation.

How much further the US should go was a much more difficult matter. On 3 April the UK Ambassador, Sir Nicholas Henderson, pressed for straightforward support from America with a strong statement condemning Argentine action and with the withdrawal of the US Ambassador to Argentina. In addition, he suggested that the United States embargo arms shipments to Argentina. The last request was the easiest to deal with: the sale of arms was already forbidden by Congress under a policy linking such sales to progress on human-rights violations. British forces would be facing more British than American modern weapons.

It was agreed that any appeal to the Organization of American States would be the height of folly.[6] Argentina would win votes simply through inter-American solidarity. Indeed reports that Argentina might call a meeting of the Rio Pact (Inter-American Treaty of Reciprocal Assistance – IATRA) were disconcerting precisely because that would exert pressure on the United States from this other direction.

The decisive factor was whether or not the United States would act as a mediator. If it were to do so it would need to adopt, at least in the first instance, a relatively neutral stance. Haig decided in favour of mediation. He was influenced by the damaging implications for American policy towards Latin America if Britain were given unequivocal support from the start. He also felt that Britain, having clearly equivocated on the Falklands in the past, was under some obligation to seek a negotiated settlement.

The United States was well placed to act in this quest. It had good relations with both countries. In the lead-up to the crisis Britain had turned naturally to the United States to help resolve the situation. Since the crisis had broken there had been a number of indications from Argentine diplomats that they would be very happy for the US to play this role.

Nor were there any other obvious alternatives. Britain could not expect to gain satisfaction from the Organization of American States. There were indications that it was not confident that it would do much better with a UN mediation, which had a reputation for cumbersome processes and being over-influenced by extraneous Third World pressures. The new Secretary-General, Perez de Cuellar, was untried in this sort of crisis and his impartiality might be questioned as he came from Peru, a country which supported Argentina. Notably and unusually for Security Council resolutions, Resolution 502 had failed to ask the Secretary-General to do anything such as arrange consultations or prepare a report. At any rate Perez de Cuellar was now in Europe, away from his office.

The risk of mediation was quite simply that it would fail. Haig suggests that it was recognized from the start that there was only an 'outside chance of success'.[7] The hope was that neither side wanted war and therefore both would be prepared to make compromises. Accordingly it was decided that the best option was to offer American services as an 'honest broker'.

This approach at least had the apparent advantage of enabling the United States to avoid offending one of its friends, although the consequences certainly failed to impress Britain. Haig explained to Henderson:

> While my sympathy was with the British, I believed that the most practical expression of that sympathy would be impartial United States mediation in the disrepute. The honest broker must, above all, be neutral. We chose to preserve our neutrality by avoiding extremes of language [and] declined to withdraw our Ambassador on grounds that such an action would eliminate our ability to communicate with Argentina as a friend of both belligerents.[8]

The next question was to identify the mediator. Vice-President Bush chaired the Working Group for Special Situations and this was one of the possible roles envisaged for him when he was given that responsibility. But Reagan had already offered Bush as a mediator to Galtieri on the evening of the invasion and this had been rejected. He could not be offered again.

In the same conversation the services of Mrs Kirkpatrick had also been mentioned. She was now unacceptable to Britain. She was known to have a close interest in Latin America and to have argued strongly in favour of a neutral stance to avoid undermining American interests.[9] Her major crime, in British eyes, was to have attended a dinner in her honour on the day of the invasion given by the Argentine Ambassador to the US, Esteban Takacs. At the dinner there were nine senior US officials, including Walter Stoessel, Haig's deputy, and Thomas Enders. Later she explained that the White House had been asked whether it was proper that they should attend and the answer had come back that to cancel would be seen as a snub to Argentina that could damage later efforts at mediation.[10] Henderson observed publicly that it would be as if he had dined with the Iranians on the night that the US hostages were seized.

Haig was soon identified as the obvious candidate. He was at a sufficiently high level to have authority. The London Embassy had warned that the British Government was unlikely to take much notice of anyone at a lower level. As a former Supreme Allied Commander, Europe, he was well known and respected in London; as a former military man the leaders of Argentina might find him easy to talk to. Naturally many assumed personal motives: a desire to emulate his early sponsor, Dr Henry Kissinger, who had achieved notable successes with his Middle East shuttles in the mid-1970s, and who had gained a Nobel Prize for bringing the Vietnam War to a close. Haig's position in the Administration had been under fire for some time from both the White House and the Pentagon.* A major diplomatic triumph would enhance his standing. This was recognized in the White House where, according to one of Haig's aides, 'people seemed equally worried Haig would fail or succeed: the former might hurt the President in obvious ways unless it could be pinned on Haig; the latter might make it impossible to get rid of Haig, something quite a few people sought.'[11]

In fact Argentina assumed that Bush would be the mediator. They did not believe that Galtieri had specifically rejected Bush in his conversation with Reagan; his negativism was directed more against the broader American call for restraint. The choice of Haig therefore came as a surprise to them and there was considerable suspicion of his motives. One supposition was that if Bush was the man for a crisis, and

---

* The tensions came out later as Haig left for London. He refused to fly in the KC–135, allocated to him by the White House, because it had poor communications and was uncomfortable for long journeys. He wanted a VC–137, which he eventually got after much negotiation and some delay in his departure to London. The story, suggesting that Haig's vanity was at issue, was soon leaked to the *New York Times* (15 April 1982).

he was not coming, then the United States did not consider this to be a real crisis.

Costa Mendez reported, much later, a conversation with Kissinger, who told him:

Haig, before taking on the job, consulted me. I told him not to take it, that it would not be convenient for him, that it was difficult and that in any case no one in Latin America would believe that he would be impartial. I told him that should he take it, he should go first to Buenos Aires and then to London.[12]

The President agreed on the evening of 5 April that Haig should attempt to mediate. The next morning a National Security Council planning group met to ratify this. According to one participant:

The NSC meeting was rather chaotic and unstructured in the sense that most of the senior members of the president's party were just about out the door on the way to their aircraft to go down to the Caribbean . . . to visit Claudette Colbert [an actress and friend of the President]. The State Department, led by Al Haig, always well prepared, came in with the idea that what we ought to do is try a mediatory role here and get these guys to see sense. He said, 'Look, we'll go down and talk some sense to those generals. I'll take [special envoy] Dick Walters with me. Dick can anecdote them in Spanish, you know, and bend their ears back.'[13]

Secretary of Defence Caspar Weinberger uncharacteristically gave wholehearted support to Haig. His support for Britain was in part based on his personal ties with the country. However, although there were military officers and Pentagon officials with close links to Latin America and preoccupied with Central America, especially in the Office of International Security Affairs, there were many more officers and officials with close links with Britain. Moreover, even those less sympathetic to Britain were not as convinced as the other Latinos that this readily translated into policy.

Kirkpatrick argued strongly in favour of a more sympathetic stance with Argentina. Deputy CIA Director Robert Inman strenuously disagreed: 'I couldn't disagree more with Jeane's statement, it's the most wrongheaded thing I've ever heard.' He listed the various arguments · for tilting in Britain's favour, adding one of his own: 'I want you to remember the problems we have with Argentina on the non-proliferation front; if we let the Argentines get away with aggression now using conventional stuff, who is to say that ten or fifteen years down the road they won't be tempted to try it again with nuclear?'[14]

The meeting concluded with it being decided officially that Haig would mediate and that, contrary to Kissinger's advice, he would go first to London to learn 'what was possible'. The President told him to do his best and left to visit Miss Colbert.

Part Four

COMPROMISES

Chapter Thirteen

HAIG'S SHUTTLE: ROUND ONE

It is difficult to reconstruct a process of negotiation. Not all is captured in a formal record. Critical meetings are often in the corridors, over lunch or conducted in the utmost secrecy in a private room. Official minutes are often brief, noting only the headlines rather than the cut and thrust of debate. Even when they are fuller they fail to convey atmosphere, the tone of voice, the nodding heads, the meanings attributed to words and statements as they are delivered.

In reading the following account it must be remembered that the task of a mediator is to gain the confidence of both sides and identify future areas of compromise while the protagonists remain fixed in their original positions. In this effort, confidentiality is critical; one of the few weapons available to the mediator is that only he has the full picture of the state of the negotiations and he can be selective in his disclosure. This is a record, therefore, that was never meant to be seen as a whole; it is not surprising to find Haig saying different things to each side and not simply acting, as he at times claimed to be, as a mere transmitter of ideas. It is also important to remember that many of the principals were suffering from fatigue during this process. The negotiations were arduous and difficult in themselves. It did not help that they were often conducted after hours in flight with little sleep and a confusion of time-zones.

Because he was not acting as a simple channel of communication but was seeking to introduce his own ideas for the resolution of the conflict, Haig created the risk of confusing his interlocutors at times as to whether he was speaking for the United States or the other side. This problem was aggravated by his lack of familiarity with the issues prior to embarking on his shuttle diplomacy. Nor could the United States act as a truly impartial mediator. It preserved as neutral a posture as possible so long as the mediation was under way but the pull towards full support of the United Kingdom was very strong throughout, reinforced by a number of factors: Haig's own view of the balance of American interests and the inadmissibility of the Argentine action of 2 April, close intelligence and military ties that could not be broken to preserve the neutral posture, and the steady pressure of American public opinion.

One of those involved with Haig described the objectives of the effort:

> US aims throughout the crisis were clear and simple: to avoid a conflict – but not at any cost. For the United States the worst outcome would have been for Argentina to be successful in resolving the Falklands dispute through force either because the British failed to act or because they acted and failed. The United States wanted a solution which did not depart so significantly from the *status quo ante bellum* that it could be widely read as any kind of significant reward for the use of force. This was really the most delicate aspect in trying to construct an outcome that not only was acceptable to both sides, but was also acceptable to the United States.[1]

The other important consideration was that the most desirable outcome was negotiations which decided the disposition of the Islands once and for all so that there would be no repeat performance.[2] American interests were thus bound up wth the conflict from the start and this inevitably influenced Haig's efforts. Apart from the desire to avoid bloodshed Haig was acutely aware that if his diplomatic effort failed and the US was obliged to come down on Britain's side then this would damage America's standing in South America. One of his objectives throughout April was to limit this sort of damage for as long as possible. This added extra urgency to his efforts and can be seen in his continual requests to Argentina not to convene the Rio

Treaty, at which the United States would find itself in an uncomfortable minority position. Meanwhile he had to persuade Britain that the United States had abandoned neither its ally nor its respect for the rule of law in order to preserve its South American interests.

The Problem Identified

The first tentative proposals developed in the State Department suggested a solution based on the diversion of the British fleet and the withdrawal of Argentine forces from the Islands and interposing a peacekeeping force made up of personnel from Canada and the United States and two Latin American countries.[3] This would be followed by negotiations.[4]

When Haig tried this out on Henderson on 6 April, before he left for London, the response was less than enthusiastic. There would be no negotiations on the future of the Islands until Argentine forces had withdrawn and British administration was reinstated. Haig explained that Galtieri could not survive if Argentine troops were withdrawn without something in return, to which Henderson replied that it was not Britain's purpose to help Galtieri survive. He then emphasized the strength of feeling in Britain. At issue was whether differences were going to be settled by force or by the principle of self-determination.

All this Haig accepted but he noted that it still did not get Argentina out of the Islands. Perhaps it might be possible to appoint a commission comprising 'a distinguished but impartial American figure, a Canadian, some Latin Americans and one or two others, who might act as intermediaries and serve as some kind of interim administration'. Henderson expressed little interest in these ideas and saw no point in a return to the United Nations. Haig's assertion that the US had to maintain credibility with Argentina in order to exert influence brought the rejoinder that Buenos Aires was more likely to be influenced by economic pressure from the United States. In reporting all this back to London, Henderson absolved Haig from putting forward a 'clearcut plan of action. He was simply testing reactions.'[5] But the conversation did little to stay developing British suspicions over the American position.*

Haig's meeting with Costa Mendez in Washington on the same day was easier and Costa Mendez left it feeling very satisfied. The Argentines were generally pleased with the idea of American mediation: securing it had been one of the original objectives behind the occupation of the Islands. Costa Mendez had drawn the same conclusion from the 'Kirkpatrick dinner' on the evening of the occupation as had Henderson, and he had also noted the UN Ambassador's absence from New York when the vote on Resolution 502 had been taken. On the evening of 4 April he had dined himself with Mrs Kirkpatrick and had been taken with her conviction that a peaceful solution to the dispute must be found. Now as he met with Haig he felt even more encouraged that the Argentine strategy might be working:

> He does not say a single word of condemnation of the Argentine attitude or position. He does not ask for the unilateral withdrawal of our troops from the Island. Instead he talks of the intervention of third countries, of joint administrations and of the need to save Mrs Thatcher's face as well as the need to transfer sovereignty.[6]

In stressing the problems faced by the other side, such as helping save face, Haig was following a similar line to that adopted with Henderson. Costa Mendez said that he was happy to provide reassurances that the rights of the islanders would be guaranteed and that if it would help Britain he would happily agree to such things as the joint exploitation of resources around the Islands. What could not be discussed was sovereignty except in terms of its formal recognition as belonging to Argentina.

---

* Matters were not helped by Reagan's comments to journalists on 5 April in which he placed Britain and Argentina on an equal footing:
  It's a very difficult situation for the United States because we're friends with both of the countries engaged in this dispute and we stand ready to do anything we can to help them, and what we hope for and would like to help in doing is have a peaceful resolution of this with no forceful action or bloodshed.

The most that could be offered was a joint Argentine–British administration in the Islands during the interim period while arrangements were made for the formal transfer. At this point Argentine troops would withdraw and British administrators could come back, although this would only be for some four months or so, and some face and honour would thereby be saved. He did not see any value in getting third parties involved, except possibly the United States. With two small islands and 1,800 inhabitants, administration ought not to be that difficult.

On the basis of this conversation, including Haig's apparent interest in the idea of a joint administration, the Argentine Government were pleased to accept US mediation and Costa Mendez was encouraged to persuade Haig to take the Argentine offer to London and convince the British Government of the need not to send its task force further south.

Thus from the start Haig was faced with a dilemma. Britain was prepared to talk but only without preconditions and only when Argentine forces had left the Islands; Argentina would withdraw its forces only if it was guaranteed that any subsequent negotiations would confirm its sovereignty. Neither had any reason to trust the other.

Visit to London

It was this particular problem that greeted Haig when he visited London to begin his diplomatic effort. Britain was growing restless with the American approach. The first casual responses to Carrington's requests for intervention at the end of March were now being followed by a stress on even-handedness. Worries were expressed to the effect that the United States was again going to fail to provide Britain support when it was needed. Haig was aware of this. Henderson observed how:

Haig went out of his way the following weeks to promise me that there would be no repeat of Suez. Given the possible parallels, I do not think his assurances were otiose. The Falklands crisis touched on certain American nerves that had proved sensitive at Suez: a recessive feeling about colonalism; concern that the Americans were eventually to pick up the cheque; worry about the Russians; and the fear that what Britain was doing would rally other countries in the area against western interests.[7]

Haig was met in London on 8 April by Edward Streator, the Chargé d'Affaires at the US Embassy, who informed him that the British position was one of 'unconditional withdrawal' and that the country was in a 'bellicose mood, more highly strung and unpredictable than we had ever known it'.[8] The point was underlined by that day's announcement of the Maritime Exclusion Zone, to take effect from 12 April, which was understood by the American team as a signal intended for its benefit but was simply a reflection of the fact that *Spartan* was about to arrive in the area. The signals were somewhat clearer when later that day Thatcher drew on her surroundings in No. 10 Downing Street to emphasize the dangers of appeasement (pointing to the table where Neville Chamberlain sat at the time of the Munich agreement with Hitler) and British readiness to use force as necessary (singling out pictures of Wellington and Nelson). Haig was left in no doubt that the Prime Minister was not searching for an easy way out of the crisis. As he reported to Reagan she had the 'bit in her teeth'.[9]

The British were anxious to discover just how 'neutral' Haig was inclined to be in practice. They intended to stress the broad principles, supported by the British action, and their unwillingness to contemplate any other outcome than the withdrawal of Argentine forces and the return of a British administration. No proposals for a settlement, other than the implementation of Resolution 502, were prepared. The Prime Minister, in particular, considered the issue to be one of dealing with aggression rather than settling a dispute. The main value of Haig's mediation would be in convincing Buenos Aires of London's resolve.

The two teams met – Thatcher with Pym and Admiral Lewin, and Haig with General Vernon Walters and Enders. Thatcher opened by stressing that her concern was to ensure that Washington understood that certain principles could not be compromised: 'Do not urge Britain to reward aggression, to give Argentina something taken by force that it could not attain by peaceful means and that would send a signal round the world with devastating consequences.'

Haig noted with admiration the Prime Minister's resolve, but he was not convinced that she enjoyed the unreserved support of her colleagues. Her Cabinet still contained many senior Conservatives who were unhappy with both her leadership and her policies. Elsewhere in government there was a greater emphasis on a negotiated solution. Before arriving at Downing Street Haig had gone first to the Foreign Office, where the new Foreign Secretary, Francis Pym, and his team were keen to discover the character of his proposals. At a later discussion about the capabilities of the British task force, Pym observed, 'Maybe we should ask the Falklanders how they feel about a war.' The response from the Prime Minister was sharp: 'Aggressors classically try to intimidate those against whom they address, saying that things far worse than the aggression itself could happen.'[10] Haig concluded that it was only really Lewin, the Chief of the Defence Staff, who supported the Prime Minister, and that the position in Cabinet 'was a microcosm of a potentially less than united British opinion'.[11]

None the less Thatcher was in charge and Haig did not wish her to gain the impression that he was requesting compromise of her principles. However, he did want to find a way of solving the dispute without more violence. He therefore opened his discussions with the promise that there would be no repetition of Suez: 'I am in London to help the British. We are fully sensitive to the depth of British feeling on the Falklands issue. But we must, if possible, avoid armed conflict.'

He warned of the strength of feeling in Argentina, the dangers that would accompany any use of force and the possible opportunities for a growth of Soviet influence in South America (a possibility that the British found difficult to take seriously). To gain an Argentine withdrawal Galtieri would have to be offered something to prevent a loss of face. Haig's ideas for achieving this required that Britain should avoid an uncompromising assertion of its sovereignty while some international umbrella was put over the Islands to indicate a change in status that might be more apparent than real. He spoke of an international force to be interposed on the Islands, an interim administration and negotiations on the status of the Islands on the basis of self-determination.

All this Thatcher said was too 'woolly'. There had to be a return to British administration. Some vague international presence would be no substitute. 'I am pledged before the House of Commons, the Defence Minister is pledged, the Foreign Secretary is pledged to restore British administration. I did not dispatch a fleet to install some nebulous arrangement which would have no authority whatsoever. Interim authority! – to do what?'[12]

Attempting to resolve the dispute through self-determination would produce a reaffirmation of British sovereignty, which was already the position. She could not see Argentina agreeing to that, while, on Britain's part, it would be insulting to negotiate on these matters under duress. Admiral Lewin, who had known Haig when they had both been NATO commanders, pointed out the problems Britain would face in sustaining its military option if the task force were asked to hold back some distance from the Islands for any length of time. In making a practical military point, Lewin also underlined the degree of determination to use the military instrument if necessary.

From all this Haig concluded that the Prime Minister was indeed ready to go to war if Argentine forces did not leave the Islands peacefully. If there was a hint of a compromise it was that negotiations on the future of the Islands might be possible so long as the islanders had the final say. This, of course, had been the British position for many years and was the reason why previous negotiations had reached an impasse. Haig was aware that there was little here likely to gain Argentine acceptance and if war was to be avoided Galtieri had to be offered something substantial. Somehow Mrs Thatcher would have to be persuaded to alter the administrative structure of the Islands to give Argentina a degree of presence that it would not otherwise have had.

The American team recognized that Argentina would have to move the furthest. It would have to be persuaded that the British task force would not turn round until Argentina withdrew its troops, that otherwise Britain was prepared to use force, and that if it came to a confrontation Britain would win. The balance of power should be reflected in the balance of compromise. However, this military assessment was by no means universal. There were many in Washington who had grave doubts that Britain could succeed in a military confrontation. Certainly Buenos Aires would not share Haig's prognosis.

To Argentina

Aware that the British had been stressing to Haig the degree of popular support for a tough stance, the Argentine Government had determined that Haig should be left in no doubt as to the feeling of the Argentine people. As he arrived late in the evening of 9 April after a sixteen-hour journey he was met by Costa Mendez and evidence of great patriotic fervour in the streets. The following morning much of the city's population had gathered in the Plaza de Mayo, having been urged by the media 'to show Haig the spirit of Argentina'. If anything the American team found this less impressive than the 'rage' of the professional diplomats over Britain's attitude and behaviour – 'if anything more intense, though of course less frenzied, than the rage in the streets'.[13]

At 10.30 hours the next morning the two delegations met. The American side was again led by Haig, Enders and Walters, who interpreted. Argentina was represented by President Galtieri, Costa Mendez, Under Secretaries Ros and Pena from the Ministry of Foreign Affairs and the three members of the Malvinas Working Group.* Haig noted that the other members of the Junta were not present.

The Argentine strategy for the talks required not only that the United States should know the strength of popular feeling, but that it

---

* This was a group that had been established on the previous Thursday by the Military Committee to support the Ministry of Foreign Affairs during the negotiations and to keep the Junta informed of their evolution. It consisted of General Iglesias (Secretary-General of the Presidency), Rear Admiral Moya (Head of the Military Household) and Brigadier Miret (Head of the Planning Commission) as well as Dr Costa Mendez. The position set out to Haig on that first morning was based on the first report of the Malvinas Working Group, entitled 'Basis for the Negotiation to be Presented to Mr Haig'.

should also be keenly aware of how its own interests were at stake in the dispute. The US would lose credibility in its hemispheric policies if it supported a colonial power and failed to find a solution to the dispute. Should this happen its adversaries would benefit in the region. If war came it might soon spread through South America. It would also require the purchase of new weapons which could not depend on Western countries. Commerce in the southern cone would be disturbed.

The US decision to make Ascension Island available to Britain already meant that an extra-regional power would be able to blockade an American country in American waters and this undermined the Rio Treaty. The Argentine interpretation of the Treaty's provisions suggested that if British forces moved far beyond Ascension Island they would enter the security zone as defined by the Treaty, and this could be the trigger for Argentina to call a meeting of the Organ of Consultation of the Pact. This prospect, the Argentines knew, alarmed Haig. It could be used to encourage him to put pressure on Britain to hold the task force back and also discourage him from succumbing to British pressure for more assistance.

The Junta's principles for the negotiations were that sovereignty was not negotiable; the rights and interests of the islanders would be guaranteed; once the task force stopped and withdrew Argentina would withdraw militarily from the Islands; in subsequent negotiations Argentina would be prepared to discuss everything *except* the sovereignty issue, including government, armed forces, nationality of the population, economy, strategic presence and Antarctic projection.

The specialists in the Malvinas Group had concluded that concessions would have to be granted to the United Kingdom. However, these were not in any of the areas where the British – and the Americans – were looking for them. Rather they addressed what were judged to be the interests of the islanders and Britain in the region. Thus possible concessions included British participation in the exploitation of natural resources; replacing the Argentine military presence in the Islands by a third party (UN or another country); allowing British citizens to hold the highest administrative posts in the Islands; and allowing Britain freedom of navigation in the South Atlantic and Sub-Antarctic areas.

Galtieri conveyed the flavour, if not the details, of this approach when he addressed Haig's delegation on the Saturday morning. There is no evidence that Haig was aware that Argentina had offered anything that might be considered a concession.

Haig's strategy for dealing with Galtieri was the same as that employed with Thatcher. He had stressed to Thatcher his desire to help Britain and his agreement on fundamental principles; now he complimented Galtieri's regime and spoke of the value of relations between their two countries. He understood – contrasting this with the views of the Carter Administration – the Argentine fight against subversion and described the counter-insurgency campaign as 'successful' despite the 'irrational and illogical' international criticism. He expressed concern over the US position in the Americas at this time, which was 'fragile' because of the problems in Mexico, Nicaragua and El Salvador. Argentine help on these matters was appreciated.* He did not want good Argentine–US relations and the overall situation on the continent undermined because of '1,000 Scottish shepherds'.

In the same way as he had sought to persuade Thatcher to make concessions by explaining how Galtieri needed something to save face, so he told Galtieri how Thatcher (a 'vigorous leader' and supporter of the United States) was in a corner. At that moment she had no other position than an ultimatum: Argentine withdrawal from the Islands before there could be any negotiation. He indicated that he had told the Prime Minister that this position could not be sustained.

He warned of the dangers of war. If the British task force continued south, emotions would be exacerbated and the conflict would escape from all control. According to Haig he expressed his view that Britain was the superior force and would win if it came to hostilities: 'I must be frank. In the United States, the support for Britain is widespread. In the liberal world the sentiment is overwhelmingly in favour of Great Britain and would remain so if it comes to a confrontation.'

As his discussions progressed, Haig became concerned that this message was not getting through. Later he sent Walters to see Galtieri alone and to explain to him in Spanish that without a negotiated

---

* Galtieri interjected to report that the former Cuban Ambassador to Argentina had made a surprise visit and was now waiting to see him. This was, he noted, an indication of just how complicated the situation was becoming.

settlement the British would fight and win, and that the United States would back Britain. Walters recalls:

> I said, to Galtieri, 'General, they *will* fight, and they will win. They have technical means that you simply do not have. They have an experienced career army in which everybody has been shot at, and everything else. You've got seventeen-year-old conscripts, some of whom come from tropical areas to this very cold, very unpleasant, very windy climate.' But he was absolutely, viscerally, convinced that the British would not fight. At one time he said to me, 'That woman wouldn't dare.' I said, 'Mr President, "that woman" has let a number of hunger strikers of her own basic ethnic origin starve themselves to death, without flickering an eyelash. I would not count on that if I were you.'[14]

Haig believed it was necessary to be blunt to ensure that the Argentines understood the true position; the continual disbelief that Britain would fight reaffirmed his conviction that Galtieri and his colleagues did not understand the true parlousness of their position. To the Argentine delegation the continued assertion of these points began to raise doubts whether Haig really was neutral, while they encouraged the military to insist that they could take on the British.

Still Haig believed that he had the basis for the solution of the dispute. This could not be founded on Argentine sovereignty as this would be rejected by London. In fact the sovereignty issue should not be mentioned at all. His proposal began with the simultaneous withdrawal of forces, followed by the creation of a zone from which British forces would be excluded. He then focused on the area where his team had decided there would be the greatest scope for compromise: a possible interim administration for the Islands. If this were international in character, at least Argentina would be denying Britain direct control even though it would not have gained control for itself.

All this, however, was completely removed from Argentine interests and expectations. Haig was excluding Argentine participation in the government of the Islands, reference to the underlying dispute over sovereignty and Argentine rights in the region. He wanted recognition of an autonomous, local administration run by the islanders. Galtieri presented a stark alternative: Argentina taking charge of the government, with some islander involvement and guarantees from the US, OAS or UN. This government would administer the Islands so long as the negotiations on sovereignty lasted.

The meeting broke for lunch and in the afternoon the two delegations were set to work to see if there was any basis for a compromise. The discussions were difficult and it was not until 21.00 hours, much later than expected, that they met again with the President in his official residence, the Casa Rosada.

The Americans had seen little point in drawing upon any of the Argentine proposals, for none provided the basis for an agreement with Britain. Instead they sought to refine their ideas on the administration of the Islands. The key element was a consortium of states – the United States, Canada and two Latin American countries – who would monitor demilitarization. Communications and movement of people between the Islands and the mainland would be maintained and the two sides would undertake to negotiate a final settlement to the dispute by the end of 1982, taking into account the rights and interests of the islanders. The final paragraph read: 'The traditional local administration shall continue, including the executive and legislative councils. Argentina shall name a senior official as its coordinator on the islands to act as liaison with the consortium and to assist it in its tasks.'[15]

With Galtieri and Costa Mendez now involved the discussions moved slowly. The Argentine side seemed happier with a smaller consortium involving only Britain, Argentina and the United States. It also pressed for representation on the islanders' committees. The Americans pointed out that there would not necessarily be a governor above the councils.

Haig thought that General Menendez, now acting as the Governor, might remain – but he could not have ultimate authority. He returned here to Mrs Thatcher's problems. She would 'fall' if such a loss of authority had to be accepted. 'Let's tread softly around this lady who outfaces statues.' She had to be able to assure Parliament that British administration had been re-established. But then it might be phased out gradually. Haig suggested a secret protocol signed by the Prime Minister and guaranteed by President Reagan to the effect that this would happen. Galtieri was unimpressed: 'They took away our flag for 150 years. Now that we've reinstalled it we can't ask the Argentine people to accept our taking it away again.' This, Haig pointed out, would be 'political suicide' for Thatcher. To achieve a solution it appeared that one leader would have to commit political suicide.[16]

During this discussion a critical issue was raised which was to dog the negotiations thereafter; since 1971 the United Kingdom had refused Argentine citizens entry into and property on the Islands. Argentina now demanded for its citizens the right to live and work in the Islands if they so desired.

Galtieri reported back to a meeting of the Military Committee just before midnight. His two colleagues in the Junta exerted conflicting pressures: Anaya argued that the basic purpose of the negotiations was to consolidate the gains of the occupation, while Lami Dozo expressed the need for flexibility. All in all, however, the response was not enthusiastic. The Junta decided not to adopt the new American ideas but to restate the original Argentine requirements: the immediate implementation of Resolution 502 in all three clauses simultaneously and acceptance of an Argentine administration. Participation of islander committees in this administration might be acceptable, as might the presence of an international body to oversee and guarantee the new procedures. These should be written up in a form that Haig could present to Britain. This work was set in motion.

Haig had already indicated that the negotiations would break down completely if there was no movement in the Argentine stance. He was therefore asked if he would meet privately with Galtieri, accompanied only by Costa Mendez and Rear Admiral Moya. They sought to impress on him that, while they too were prepared to negotiate, they could not give in to threats. They cited the mass demonstrations witnessed by Haig as evidence of popular backing. They expressed concern that Britain only seemed interested in returning to the position prior to 2 April and was using the threat of military force – and from that day economic sanctions[17] – to achieve that end. Argentina wanted to negotiate but, if this were impossible, it would defend the Islands. Successful negotiations had to be based on a viable alternative and this had not yet been offered.

At this point there was one of those misunderstandings to which such negotiations are prone. Haig gained the impression that he was being offered a concession. As the meeting ended at 01.15 he indicated to his hosts that the impasse had been broken and that he would cable London to say that he would return there immediately. Even so, as the Argentine press officer told waiting reporters, 'There was no agreement.'

What was the basis for his new optimism? According to Haig, Galtieri:

> took me aside and, all bravado abandoned, said that only soldiers could understand how critically important it was to avoid conflict. Then, with moving candor, he told me that he could not withdraw both his military and his administrative presence from the Malvinas and last a week. If the British attacked, he would have to accept help from whomever it might be obtained.

It is by no means clear from this account why Haig should have thought Galtieri was showing flexibility. Even so, he seems to have concluded that the real problem, under the current scheme, was that once the Argentine military had withdrawn there would be no Argentine presence at all. Perhaps if sufficient Argentine flags could be seen on the Islands then honour would be satisfied.

In agreeing that there might be an interim administration the Argentines had accepted that formal transfer of sovereignty had yet to take place. But there was no wavering in their view that the formal transfer must eventually occur. This was not reflected in the American proposals. They could not accept only a minimum Argentine presence prior to the transfer, nor that a more substantial presence could be an alternative to a transfer.

Yet Haig regarded the development of the administrative presence as the key to Argentine military withdrawal.

Now that we knew Galtieri's requirements, the work went quickly. In less than an hour, we produced a new draft that was essentially the same as the one I had brought from London, except for two important modifications. Argentinean troops would leave the islands and the British administration would be restored. But economic and financial measures against Argentina would be terminated within two weeks, the flags of the six nations would be flown at the headquarters of the consortium, and, finally, national flags could be displayed at the residences and on the official automobiles of all countries represented on the islands.[18]

It may well be that 'we' in this quotation refers to the US team.[19] Haig does not say that Galtieri and his aides either appreciated the construction that was put on the President's remarks or endorsed the new proposals. There is some evidence that Haig's team had already begun work on a new draft to kill time as they waited for him to come out of his private meeting with Galtieri in the early hours of the morning.* None of the Argentines involved in the discussions knew of its existence or its contents. However, now that he felt that he understood how to deal with Argentine concerns, Haig became more confident for his return trip to London.

His confidence did not last long. Before he left Buenos Aires to return to London at 09.30 hours on 11 April, he had a brief meeting with Costa Mendez, who later remarked on his good humour. He noted that the British and Argentine governments could fall as a result

---

* This draft proposed that (1) all forces would be withdrawn from the area within two weeks; (2) the Islands would be demilitarized as of that date; (3) there would be observers from Argentina, the United Kingdom and the United States of America; (4) all sanctions and restrictions imposed until then would be removed; (5) the local administration would continue in the Islands as per legislative and executive committees. The decisions, laws and regulations would be ratified by a higher body involving the US and the UK (who would act as Governor) and with one Argentine representative; (6) communications and transport between the Islands and the mainland would be improved; (7) the transition period would end on 31 December 1982. Both parties would negotiate until that date. On that date the local police would be allowed back on the Islands, and one Argentine representative would be allowed to report to the administering group consisting of the UK and US. There would be no Argentine representatives in the local committees.

of the present situation; if anything, the British Government was less stable. He made no complaints about the way that Argentina was handling the issue, and again stressed his concern lest Argentina call a meeting of the Rio Treaty.

Costa Mendez handed him a paper. Haig did not look at it until his plane was in the air. Haig recalls Costa Mendez saying that it contained some 'personal thoughts' of his own. In fact it contained the official Argentine proposals to transmit to Britain. When he read it he saw it as 'a retreat from everything we had accomplished at the Casa Rosada the night before'. His sense of betrayal was not calmed when the next day in London he found that the same thoughts had been leaked to the *New York Times*.[20]

The paper did not reflect Costa Mendez's own views but, rather, those of the Military Committee as of its meeting prior to Galtieri's final discussion with Haig. The main feature of this paper was to offer Britain a choice between two options. Either the Governor of the Islands would be designated by Argentina, and the Argentine flag flown (without sovereignty necessarily having been transferred) or else the Argentine Government must be given a guarantee that any negotiations would conclude with sovereignty reverting to Argentina by 31 December 1982. Meanwhile Argentine citizens must have the same rights as British citizens to enter the Islands and demilitarization must be implemented along the lines of Resolution 502.

While Haig exaggerated the extent to which the Argentines were reneging on a concession, he had some grounds for complaint in that the Argentine proposal had not been discussed during his visit to Buenos Aires and reflected none of the ideas brought to the negotiations by his team.

Back in London

All of this made Haig very gloomy. In conversation with Reagan he received the unhelpful suggestion that if only Britain could sink an Argentine ship perhaps honour would be satisfied. William Clark, the President's Adviser on National Security affairs, who had never been convinced of the value of Haig's mission, wondered whether it all ought to be called off. Enders and Walters were anxious Haig persevere. Haig decided to persist.

That day's meeting in London with the British did not raise his spirits. All day long he, Enders and Walters sat round a table with the War Cabinet and its advisers hammering out a position. The conversations continued over lunch. Unlike in Buenos Aires, where he was never quite sure who he was dealing with, there was no doubt who was in charge. The British team did not need to retire to reconsider its position. When the Prime Minister decided that a concession was in order she made it known immediately. If she did not, that was equally clear.

Haig decided to carry on working with the American draft proposals, influenced by his most optimistic interpretation of the Argentine room for manoeuvre. As the British team examined these ideas there was little evidence of flexibility. Haig hoped to convince Thatcher that 'while her strategy of pressure and threat was having the right effect in rattling the Argentine leaders, it could not produce an Argentinean withdrawal from the islands. Only diplomacy could do that, short of military action.'[21]

Britain's position remained unchanged: before anything else could be done Argentine forces would have to withdraw from the Islands as required by Resolution 502. As with Haig's previous visit, Britain offered no other ideas on a negotiated settlement. Enders later characterized the British stance as a 'willingness to listen, be drawn along in a process, but not as an active . . . search for a solution'.[22]

Prior to Haig's arrival the War Cabinet had met and considered the advance telegrams from the American team. They agreed that they could not move from the basic principles that had been established.

Under pressure from Haig they agreed that there could be some minor Argentine role in the administration so long as in major respects it was 'recognizably British'. The Argentine representative might fly the Argentine flag, but they were not going to have this flag flying all over the place. They refused to agree to British forces being moved back to operational bases, which for Britain would be 8,000 miles from the Falklands. They were not happy with the idea of both sides going back 400 miles (the distance from the Argentine bases). For Britain, this would have meant sticking men on ships that would, as Lewin put it 'wallow about in the South Atlantic'. In the end they agreed to leave this vague: if there had been an agreement on this basis, British forces would probably have been based in South Georgia (after its recovery), 900 miles away.

According to Hastings and Jenkins: 'The best Pym could offer was that the "trauma of invasion" might have induced the islanders to soften their previous intransigence. Mrs Thatcher unhelpfully added that they would hardly be softening in a pro-Argentine direction.'[23]

Mrs Thatcher described the day's talks to Parliament as follows:

Mr Haig put forward certain ideas as a basis for discussion – ideas concerning the withdrawal of troops and its supervision, and an interim period during which negotiations on the future of the islands would be conducted. Our talks were long and detailed, as the House would expect. Some things we could not consider because they flouted our basic principles. Others we had to examine carefully and suggest alternatives. The talks were constructive and some progress was made.

By the end of the morning news of the leak of the hardline Argentine position in the *New York Times* confirmed that it represented more than the personal thoughts of Costa Mendez. At 14.30 (London) Haig contacted the Argentine Foreign Minister to seek clarification.

He told Costa Mendez that little progress could be made in London on the basis of the paper handed to him on his departure and that therefore he was continuing to work along the lines he and his team had been developing while in Buenos Aires. Costa Mendez stated that the paper contained the true Argentine position; any other draft had no official status in the negotiations. They agreed to talk again later in the day.

The conversation left Costa Mendez and his team concerned that Haig was keeping them in the dark. Haig had refused to give them details of the British position or its negotiating ideas during his stay in Buenos Aires, and now he was refusing to transmit their own ideas to the British. The view began to form that Haig was not a very capable

All

negotiator, together with concern that Britain was interested only in a return to the status quo ante bellum. The Haig mediation started to appear haphazard and of doubtful value. Further conversations with the Americans during the day led Costa Mendez to suspect that Haig was simply trying to apply pressure by threatening to abandon the talks immediately and back Britain.

For his part Haig now felt it necessary to warn Costa Mendez, through a message carried by the US Ambassador, that the negotiation was reaching a crisis point. Little progress was being made even on the basis of his draft: there would be no hope with the Argentine draft. The British task force would continue until an agreement was reached. Costa Mendez could only repeat that the official Argentine posture was that presented to Haig on his departure.

At 20.20 Argentine time (00.20 on 13 April in London), Haig phoned Costa Mendez again,[24] to stress the need to work with the American draft rather than the airport document which he described as little more than an ultimatum. He had been irritated by the hardline position suddenly emerging:

> I am only trying to help, that is all I am trying to do. I will be happy to see you again on the terms of last Friday. We were thinking of flying tonight to Buenos Aires but now I must think it over because the circumstances have changed. I also do not consider myself as a negotiator, merely a transmitter of ideas between both parties that have profound differences. I think that both are going to end up in a war that will have very damaging consequences for all.

With little success Costa Mendez attempted to argue that Argentine flexibility could be found in its proposals to secure the rights and interests of the islanders and allow Britain a role in the South Atlantic, while stressing the importance of the Argentine Governor and the Argentine flag.

Haig threatened to pull out of the negotiations. Costa Mendez complained that he had not even had a formal response to the Argentine position. He thought that it was too soon to interrupt the negotiations but if that was what Britain wanted then Argentina was ready.

Haig said that the impulse to end the effort was his and not Britain's and that it was the shift in the Argentine position that was to blame. His 'orders' (from the White House) were 'to place everything in suspense unless I have the security that the talks are a help and not a hindrance or a commitment to the U.S.'.

Costa Mendez offered to send one of his aides to London if that would help or to go himself to Washington. Haig accepted neither suggestion. When Costa Mendez hinted vaguely at flexibility the response was more positive. The problem, Costa Mendez suggested, was only one of finding a suitable formula that might make the Argentine alternatives more acceptable to the United Kingdom. Haig had been given a 'clear and precise' official proposal, but, Costa Mendez noted, 'words and clauses are what make international agreements. We must look for a language, that is all . . . let us see if we can translate those principles and concepts into a language that will be acceptable to both peoples. But let us not abandon now the negotiations.' Haig did not wish to continue the conversation – 'it is very late here and we have worked all day. I am very tired. I cannot coordinate ideas' – but said he would ring back the next day. According to Haig's account of the conversation he concluded: 'Talk to your President. Tell him we are close to a workable solution if we are not faced with these kinds of alternatives. I'll call you in the morning.'[25]

The next morning's conversation helped keep the negotiations going. On the Argentine side there is no record of a concession being either discussed or offered. None the less Haig clearly felt that he had been offered one, and it was one that did appear in the Argentine document drawn up prior to Haig's arrival on the next round of the shuttle. As Haig put it, Argentina:

> would not insist on an Argentine governor if the agreement contained a British acknowledgement that it intended to 'decolonize' the Falklands in compliance with the 1964 United Nations Declaration on Decolonization. However, Costa Mendez was not prepared to submit this proposal formally without some advance indication of flexibility from London. Argentina also required a guarantee that the British fleet would limit its movements and, from the United States, a firm statement that the US was not assisting Britain militarily in any way.[26]

It is possible that Costa Mendez was trying to suggest a potential area of flexibility in order to keep the negotiations alive, even though he could not make this firm until he had indications of a comparable response from London. All he told the Military Committee was that Haig had been more positive and thought that it was still worth pursuing the negotiations.

In the previous night's conversation Costa Mendez had referred to the 1964 Declaration on Decolonization largely to make the point that Britain had indicated then that the Falklands might be decolonized and that this had spurred the Argentine Foreign Ministry at the time to explore the possibility of a negotiation on sovereignty. He was simply contrasting Britain's earlier willingness to discuss sovereignty with its present intransigence.

There was, however, a difference between decolonization and the transfer of sovereignty. The Falkland Islands were categorized as a non-autonomous territory. Britain had indeed indicated some time before that it might be prepared to end this status. But that, of course, did not in itself mean that the alternative status of joining Argentina was inevitable in principle, whatever might be thought likely in practice. It could be independent (which for the bulk of the territories in this category was the preferred and likely outcome) or even develop a much closer association with Britain.

Possibly clutching at straws, Haig decided to ask Pym whether, on this basis, it was worth carrying on. Neither was familiar with the Declaration. British officials were aware of it and its role in the formulation of General Assembly Resolution 2065, which linked the broad principle of decolonization with the particular case of the Falklands. If there was a hint of a compromise then this could be because the 1964 UN Declaration contained language on self-determination. This might be worth pursuing. In practice it had been no part of Costa Mendez's objective to signal such a concession. Far from stressing self-determination, he clung to Resolution 2065, which contained the proposition that only the islanders' *interests*, rather than their *wishes*, should be considered.

Yet Haig was prepared to hope that Costa Mendez had been giving a nod in the direction of self-determination. As this was a critical principle for Britain any flexibility on this score was naturally encouraging. The Prime Minister agreed that there might be something worth exploring here, although by now her own scepticism and that of her colleagues was growing. Everything they had heard about the Haig team's experiences in Buenos Aires convinced them that mutually acceptable terms could not be found.

At 14.00 (London) Haig rang Costa Mendez back and told him that he had 'spoken to the highest figures in the British government', and saw 'grounds for a breakthrough'. They agreed that he would return to Buenos Aires after first visiting Washington. For the moment at least the mediation could continue.

Later that day (Tuesday 13 April) as Haig arrived back in Washington he told the press: 'the parties have received some new ideas today which they are considering, and this will give me an opportunity to discuss the situation directly with President Reagan ... before proceeding on to Buenos Aires and the continuation of our efforts.' After Haig described the difficulties he was facing to the National Security Council, the President observed: 'Imagine when – if – you do settle this, Al. We'll be the envy of the world.'[27]

While Washington was discussing the issue on 14 April the Prime Minister reported to Parliament on the state of the negotiations. After stressing her commitment to a 'peaceful solution by diplomatic effort' she set down her terms: 'We made clear to Mr. Haig that withdrawal of the invaders' troops must come first; that the sovereignty of the islands is not affected by the act of invasion; and that when it comes to future negotiations what matters most is what the Falkland Islanders themselves wish.' After describing Monday's discussions she explained how the proposals received by Haig from Costa Mendez 'we could not possibly have accepted'. The position now appeared to have eased, further ideas were being considered and Secretary Haig would soon return to Buenos Aires. 'That meeting, in our view, will be crucial.'

If the negotiations failed she refused to rule out the use of force:

In any negotiations over the coming days we shall be guided by the following principles. We shall continue to insist on Argentine withdrawal from the Falkland Islands and dependencies. We shall

187

remain ready to exercise our right to force in self-defence under Article 51 of the United Nations charter until the occupying forces leave the islands. Our naval task force sails on towards its destination. We remain fully confident of its ability to take whatever measures may be necessary. Meanwhile its very existence and its progress towards the Falkland Islands reinforce the efforts we are making for a diplomatic solution.[28]

Chapter Fourteen

HAIG'S SHUTTLE: ROUND TWO

American Military Assistance

The initial contest in Washington between the Latinos and the Europeanists, over the basic American orientation to the conflict, was
settled as a draw. In another arena it was settled decisively in Britain's
favour. Immediately the dispatch of Britain's task force was
announced, Caspar Weinberger, the US Secretary of Defence,
decided that maximum practical support should be provided.

Weinberger, a passionate anglophile, admired the decisiveness of
the British response to what he felt was blatant aggression. He was,
however, also concerned that most of the military advice he was
receiving suggested that Britain could easily fail. It would have to fight
a staggering distance from home and without the sort of air superiority
that American forces would have deemed vital. A British defeat would
be a disaster for American policy – not just in terms of the humiliation
of an ally but also as a demonstration that aggression might prosper.
Accordingly a British defeat must be prevented and that required
American assistance.

One of the major areas was intelligence support, especially signals
intelligence (SIGINT) from US listening posts that was passed on to
Britain's GCHQ. To some extent the traffic was automatic, but a more
concentrated effort was made as the conflict developed and there was a
drive, albeit limited in results, to provide satellite photography. As the
Americans exercised with Argentine forces (especially with the Navy in

189

the UNITAS exercise) assessments of their operational effectiveness were requested, and received.

The first major policy issue to arise was triggered by the British request for the use of Wideawake air base on Ascension Island. A decision was made relatively easy because Britain actually owned the Island and, under the leasing agreement, had reserved the right to use it in an emergency. The US had little choice but to permit use of the airfield. Denial would have caused a major crisis, as the British military position would then have been hopeless, while US officials were conscious of the many US facilities on other British territories where the US enjoyed a virtually free hand. After the Base Commander's reservations had been overcome through some transatlantic telephone calls, the US began to provide aviation fuel, critical stores and spare parts, as well as weapons systems, including a variety of missiles – additional and more modern air-to-air Sidewinders, anti-aircraft Stingers, radar-seeking Shrikes. By the end of the war the aid bill, excluding the Sidewinders and the fuel, was $60 million.[1]

The decision to support Britain was largely taken by Weinberger himself. Implementing it was straightforward. The intimacy of Anglo-American defence relationships meant that there was a network of agreements and understandings readily available to provide the bureaucratic and financial guidelines. The President was informed, although whether the full implications for the policy being pursued by Haig were explained to him is less clear. The assistance was not discussed at the National Security Council and it appears that Haig, specifically, was not told.[2] Walters has claimed that he did know, although he suggests that it was less than Argentina suspected. John Lehman, then US Secretary of the Navy, claims that no attempt was made to hide the extent of the support, but nor was any effort made 'to educate people on what was really going on'. He explains the ignorance by the ease with which support could flow through established channels – 'it was really just turning up the volume.'[3]

Eventually, as happens in Washington, the scale of the American support effort to Britain leaked. ABC News reported on 13 April the provision of satellite communication links, weather forecasts, intelligence and jet fuel. The next day the *Washington Post* provided more detail. This article was written by Carl Bernstein, whose Watergate fame added credibility to the revelations. They were immediately brought to the notice of the Argentine Junta. It seemed that, despite everything they had been promised on the issue of neutrality, the US Government had already decided to side with the United Kingdom.

The Pentagon initially denied the story but then, three hours later, refused to comment on it. Haig was furious, but he appears to have been satisfied that the story was inaccurate:

> My day in Washington, which I had hoped to devote to a fresh examination of the Falklands crisis and other acute problems, was spent instead in trying to convince an outraged and deeply nervous Argentina that the U.S. government was telling the truth and that my return to Buenos Aires should not be cancelled as the result of a mischievous press report based on a mendacious leak. Finally, I succeeded, but it was an arduous process. In addition to being the enemy of results, leaking is the thief of time.[4]

At 11.00 hours (Argentine time), Walters contacted Galtieri to inform him that the story was incorrect and that Haig knew nothing of any military support. An emergency meeting had been called in Washington, he said, in an attempt to discover the sources of the information and Haig would soon be in touch with Costa Mendez to comment. This Haig did at 13.00 hours. He promised a public denial,* and reiterated his previous statement that Washington was not granting London

---

* The statement read as follows:

> From the outset of this crisis, the United States has viewed its role as that of assisting the two sides in finding a peaceful solution. Our ability to do this is based on our longstanding relations with both the United Kingdom and Argentina. We have been careful to maintain these relationships in order to preserve our influence with both governments. Failure to live up to existing agreements – or going beyond them – would obviously jeopardize our ability to perform the role both countries wish to perform.
>
> Since the onset of the crisis, the United States has, therefore, not acceded to requests that would go beyond the customary patterns of cooperation based on existing bilateral agreements. That will continue to be our stand while our efforts are underway.

Press Release 131 of 14 April 1982.

requests which went beyond the 'customary patterns of cooperation'.

Up to this point the main problem for Haig on the matter of American support for Britain revolved around the use of Ascension Island. This, though, could be justified on the basis that it was British to begin with. Beyond that, 'customary patterns of cooperation' between Britain and the United States could include a considerable amount of activity.* Whatever Haig believed to be covered by this phrase the level of assistance to Britain exceeded that described to the Junta. Even if, for the moment, the Junta was prepared to believe him, the episode fed their anxieties about America's role thus far.

Argentine Anxieties

The Junta also felt uneasy about the actual state of the negotiations; it believed it was being kept in the dark. On 14 April the Military Committee studied a copy of Mrs Thatcher's speech to Parliament, rushed from London.

It did not sound very conciliatory: the fleet was continuing to move south: economic sanctions were in force; the Security Council and the European Community gave Britain strong support (while Latin American support to Argentina was minimal); the rights of the islanders would be protected and force would be used if Argentine forces did not withdraw. The Junta did not feel inclined to be conciliatory either.

The Committee had resolved the previous afternoon that, as soon as Haig arrived from Washington, he must provide a full account of the British position and demands. No new Argentine proposals were to be offered until this was done. This was the stance Costa Mendez was instructed to adopt when he next spoke to Haig – although that discussion turned out to be dominated by the level of American military assistance to Britain.

Costa Mendez also sought assurances that the task force would not sail south of Ascension Island. If it did, he warned, Argentina would

---

* There was even a precedent for the current support: at a time of formal American neutrality in 1940 Roosevelt had agreed lend-lease, by which Britain received 100 warships.

call the Rio Treaty, order the blockade to be broken and allow its forces freedom to fire on those of Britain. Haig's anxiety to calm Argentine passions provided Costa Mendez with an encouraging signal. Haig's information was that the fleet was not advancing and had no intention of doing so. When asked to explain Thatcher's parliamentary remarks – which Haig had not seen and the tenor of which Costa Mendez exaggerated – the Secretary of State replied that he had asked Thatcher 'very firmly to avoid doing precisely that; I am very angry because of this and will contact her immediately'.

Costa Mendez's search for information on whether or not Britain had 'new ideas' was less productive. If there were any, Haig was not telling. Haig was equally unsuccessful in his effort to find out whether Argentina had anything new on offer. He said there had been analysis of the 'decolonization' concept but as yet he had no firm proposals from Britain. 'I left them some ideas and asked them to analyze them and to answer them as soon as they could.' Costa Mendez expressed his reluctance to pass on his 'memorandum ... on the problems of the islanders' if there was nothing from Britain. Haig agreed that he should insist that Britain 'should present something so that we can reach some sort of accord'.

Later he told Costa Mendez that he would be arriving in Buenos Aires from Washington late the next day. There were new British ideas. These concerned the flag, the islander committees and the date when negotiations would finish. Costa Mendez then offered to send the new Argentine ideas. In one key area Haig qualified his previous remarks:

COSTA MENDEZ: Let me tell you two things: we have a strong pressure from our public opinion and people within the Government to call the Rio Treaty in our assistance if the British fleet is mobilized south of Ascension.

I understand, from our previous conversations, that while you come here and for the next forty-eight hours, the fleet will not advance towards the south. Am I right?

HAIG: No, no, it is not correct.

I cannot make the United Kingdom change the fleet movement until we have reached an agreement. Nevertheless there is some reference to this in the proposals I am carrying with me.

As a further reflection of the nervousness felt by the Junta as to the direction of American policy it was decided that President Galtieri should contact President Reagan. On the morning of 15 April the two men spoke. Galtieri explained his anxiety at the consequences of the steady advance of the British fleet to the South Atlantic. He sought to win over Reagan by playing on his fears of Soviet exploitation of the conflict and the anti-colonial history of their two nations. Reagan expressed his confidence in Haig, reassured Galtieri that the US had done nothing 'at variance with the role we have assumed as neutral and objective intermediaries' and asserted the need for 'a flexible attitude and moderation' in the effort to find a 'peaceful working solution to this grave situation'.[5]

The Argentines prepared to receive Haig with growing misgivings. There was now suspicion about the true state of American neutrality, based as much on Haig's past performance as on the press leak. His pressure seemed to be directed solely in the direction of Buenos Aires: to obtain information on Argentine proposals and ask for unilateral modifications without providing sufficient information, just to help the American team formulate its ideas and without making any equivalent demands on London.

The memorandum prepared for the next Haig visit was therefore drawn up partly with a breakdown of relations in mind. The objective now was as much to be seen to be reasonable if negotiations failed as actually to encourage a breakthrough. The Junta decided to make its proposals public should there be no progress.

The Argentine draft envisaged that the withdrawal process would take two weeks. After the first week half the Argentine forces would have returned to the mainland while the task force would be back at Ascension Island. By the end of the period all forces would have left the area. The logic of this was that Britain would lose its military options far more quickly than Argentina and would be put in a position where the option could never be recreated. The Islands and the surrounding zone would remain demilitarized until 31 December

1982, the date for the completion of negotiations.

During the transition period the Argentine Government would appoint a governor. The Executive and Legislative Councils would be retained but the islanders would be joined by equal numbers of Argentine representatives, if possible selected from those Argentines already allowed to reside in the Islands. The Governor would appoint the police force, including local members in service prior to the occupation (of which there were two). Argentines from the continent and the inhabitants of the Islands would enjoy equal rights and obligations and the Argentine flag would fly. Transport and communications between the Islands and the mainland would be improved.

Where the Junta believed itself more conciliatory was that in adding to its promise to respect the rights and way of life of the inhabitants it would also 'be disposed to pay a just price for the properties of persons or companies not wishing to continue their activities in the [Islands], thus giving compensation to those wishing to emigrate'.[6] In negotiations the 'interests' of the islanders would be taken into account, as would those of the United Kingdom in considering exploitation of the region's resources. A group consisting of an equal number of representatives of Argentina, the United States and the United Kingdom would verify the implementation of the agreement.

Haig Returns

At 09.45 hours on 16 April, Haig met with Galtieri in the Casa Rosada while simultaneously both country's delegations met to start negotiations in the Ministry of Foreign Affairs. Haig informed Galtieri that he had prepared seven points as a basis for negotiation. These in part reflected concessions that he had extracted from Britain late on 14 April. He felt that he had enough from the British to allow him to make progress: an agreement that there could be an Argentine administrative presence prior to the completion of negotiations, as well as a date for the completion. The seven points were:

1 stop the British fleet
2 keep the Argentine flag flying in the Islands
3 expand the Argentine role in the Islands little by little during the period of interim administration
4 guarantee that the negotiations would finish by the end of the year
5 guide the process according to the principles of decolonization
6 normalize communications between the continent and the Islands
7 lift sanctions and guarantee US assistance in the Islands during this process.

The main response received to this was a complaint from Galtieri with regard to the 'unfriendly spirit' demonstrated by the American Embassy in Buenos Aires, which had asked for visas so that all the diplomatic personnel of that mission could be transferred to Uruguay.* Haig also had to reassure Galtieri that a declaration of support for Britain from Caspar Weinberger carried no authority. However, he added that in the event of war public opinion in the US would push the Administration to side with London.

Galtieri informed Haig that the Argentine proposals guaranteed the rights and way of life of the islanders, the economic interests of those who would wish to remain in the Islands, as well as the present and future strategic needs of the United Kingdom in the South Atlantic. Galtieri promised to be available if needed while Haig promised that nobody in Washington 'had the impression that people were intransigent here in Buenos Aires'. Haig stressed again that he was convinced that the attitude of the United Kingdom Government had nothing to do with economic interests in the area so that compensation or the promise of joint exploration would not sway British opinion.

I want to be sure, Mr. President, that we all understand the British attitude. I know you are involved in other things, but I am now

---

* The flight of US staff made Argentina look like Iran. Although the parallel upset Galtieri it was precisely the one that Haig had in mind. The demonstration of the previous Saturday, and its potential to turn nasty if the United States were blamed for the onset of war, reminded Haig of Tehran and the taking of the diplomatic hostages whose fate had dominated the last year of the Carter Administration.

convinced that the attitude of Great Britain has nothing to do with economic interests. After years of occupation it is difficult for them to see only economic interests there.[7]

The meeting finished at 10.40 hours. Haig and Costa Mendez went to the Ministry of Foreign Affairs to continue negotiations. Two hours later a stalemate had been reached. The two sides' formulas were not compatible; they were addressing the problem from completely different angles. It was only in the few areas of overlap (such as demilitarization) that there was any progress. At lunchtime Haig returned to the American Embassy with his aides while the Argentine delegation met with Costa Mendez.

Looking at the American proposals, the Argentine delegation had few problems with the provisions relating to the cessation of hostilities or the removal of economic sanctions. There were some difficulties with the provision for withdrawal of forces because it was unclear whether these included all types of British forces (such as submarines). Demilitarizing a zone that extended up to 400 miles from the Islands would include Argentine troops on the mainland.

Once again the definition of the interim administration raised major difficulties. The Americans proposed retaining a British government through the Islands Councils and the police; an Argentine representative would be included in the committees only if he were a long-term resident in the Islands.* A special interim authority would ratify future laws but all the previous laws and mechanisms were to remain in place; the authority would be formed by the US, the United Kingdom and Argentina. Given the inclinations of the United States, Argentina could anticipate being in a semi-permanent minority in any votes.

The Argentines were also concerned that there appeared to be no way of modifying the monopolistic position of the Falkland Islands Company. The discussion of rights and guarantees was phrased in such general terms that it included not only the islanders but also the

---

* They must have stayed for an equivalent time as that required for foreigners in the United Kingdom to be considered resident.

Company. Another clause referred to the property rights of those with investments in the Islands.

With regard to sovereignty the Argentine delegation still did not feel that the position was sufficiently clear. By 31 December 1982, at the end of the interim period, negotiations would be concluded. In UN language, the Islands would no longer be non-autonomous territories. However, while they would no longer have their old status, the new status might take several forms: an independent territory, some sort of association with Great Britain or a transfer of sovereignty to Argentina. Among others, the favourable UN resolutions – 1514(XV) and 2065(XX) – would be taken into consideration but they would not necessarily be decisive.

Taken together the American proposals began to look like a trap. By demilitarizing the Islands the Argentine military option would be completely foreclosed and Britain would not even have to bear the burden of maintaining military forces in the region. Yet the British administration would be perpetuated, with only a minimal Argentine representation lacking any real influence. The control of the Islands and the progress of the negotiations on their future status would be the responsibility of a group in which Argentina could be consistently outvoted by Britain and the United States. This would be even less acceptable than hitherto because now the United Nations would not even be involved.

Part of the trap was that if the negotiations broke down Argentina was going to be blamed. So the Argentine delegation sought ways to modify its position to meet some of the American points.* When the two delegations met again at 16.30 hours Argentina proposed modifications to the American proposal. They accepted the clause on sovereignty: this would not now be recognized prior to the negotiations nor was it to be confirmed as the final objective of the negotiations. The stress was on the interim administration and the negotiating process.

* One idea considered was to include as representatives on the Executive and Legislative Councils members of the Anglo-Argentine community that held dual nationality instead of Argentine residents, so that all members of the Councils would be British citizens.

At 19.00 hours Costa Mendez went to the Casa Rosada to explain these latest developments. Galtieri decided to call an immediate meeting of the Military Committee by 20.15. The Minister of Foreign Affairs explained the position so far. He outlined the American ideas, the objections of his delegation and the amendments it had proposed to demonstrate the maximum flexibility. The Americans had no commitment to the transfer of sovereignty in the long term. He warned that the American position could harden further; already it kept on using the threat of imminent war. As far as he could see the United States was attempting to isolate Argentina within both the OAS and the UN.

The Military Committee agreed to concentrate in counter-proposals on the interim administration, which had to be subject to much greater UN and Argentine influence. It formulated a complex scheme. In overall terms any agreement could be backed by a US guarantee. However, the administration and the negotiation would be overseen by the UN in the form of either the Secretary-General or the Committee on Decolonization. Beneath them would be a UN Commissioner who could be American. Next in the hierarchy would be a British and an Argentine administrator (neither would have a governor), with the system completed by the Executive and Legislative Councils, composed in equal measure of British and Argentine representatives, with the latter having dual nationality.* Decolonization would be completed by 2 April 1983.

The Junta'a new draft also required that Argentine citizens would

---

* The relevant clause was drafted:

> Pending a definite agreement, all the decisions, laws and regulations that will be implemented in the islands will be subject to rapid ratification by the special interim authority, except in those cases in which the interim authorities consider that these decisions, laws and regulations are not in accordance with this agreement or its implementation. The traditional local administration shall continue through the executive and legislative councils, that will be broadened to include equal numbers of representatives named by the Argentine government from its local residents. The local police will be subject to the general supervision of the special interim authorities. The flags of the three countries members of the special interim authority shall be raised in their respective residences.

have the same rights as the present islanders.* On the crunch clause relating to sovereignty the Junta suggested the following:

> On December 31, 1982, the interim period will conclude at which the signatories will conclude the negotiations that relate to the removal of the islands from the lists of territories without autonomous government as per Chapter XI of the Charter of the United Nations. The negotiations will also confirm the definite situation of the islands on the basis of the implementation of the principle of Argentine territorial integrity taking into total consideration the interests of the inhabitants of the islands in accordance with the purposes and principles in the Charter of the United Nations and of the Resolutions 1514(XV), 2065(XX) and other pertinent resolutions of the General Assembly of the United Nations.

This used the standard language to deny the paramountcy of the wishes of the islanders and came as close to saying that sovereignty would be the outcome of the negotiations without actually using those words.

The meeting lasted over two hours. When it concluded – at 22.45 hours on 16 April – Costa Mendez took the draft clauses to Haig. Haig reacted by saying, 'I am sure that the British will shoot.' Costa Mendez urged him not to do anything hasty until he had met the Junta and added, 'I am truly surprised that the British will go to war for such a small problem as these few rocky islands.' Haig called Reagan, who agreed that he should return to Washington the next day unless progress was made.[8] Before that he was to have one last try. Haig requested a meeting with the three members of the Junta together.

Costa Mendez scuttled back to the Junta within half an hour to

---

*Thus Clause 8 on transport and communications read:

> Total freedom to travel, transport, individual movements, residence, property dispositions, communications and commerce between the continent and the islands will be recognized for the inhabitants of the islands and for Argentine citizens that come from the continent under equal conditions. The interim authorities will arrange for specific regulations in this sense so as to implement this freedom including arrangements to compensate those islanders that wish to leave the islands.

report Haig's negative reaction. His request for an audience was agreed for the next morning. The Junta also began to make its plans for the breakdown of the negotiations. Haig's hard line was reinforced by confirmation that the British task force had sailed from Ascension Island and was moving south. Once he had left Buenos Aires the political leaders of Argentina would have to be brought together to have the situation explained, the Argentine proposal would be published, the Rio Treaty would be called at once and Argentine–American defence co-operation would be re-examined.

Haig Meets the Junta

At 10.00 on 17 April Haig met with the full Junta for the first time. Inevitably the meeting was tense, most particularly between Anaya and Haig. One account has Anaya, on the basis of his own Washington contacts, telling Haig that he was lying when he said that the United States would tilt towards Britain if negotiations broke down; another has Anaya telling Haig that the Argentine media were telling the truth when it accused him of being pro-British.[9] Haig's own description of this meeting is notable for his report of an exchange with Anaya, who expressed his pride that his son, an Army helicopter pilot, was serving in the Islands and was prepared to die for the Malvinas – 'it is my family's point of view that we would be proud to know his blood had mingled with this sacred soil.' 'Let me assure you, Admiral,' Haig replied, 'that you don't know the meaning of war until you see the corpses of young men being put into body bags.'

Haig also reports that it was a remark of the moderate Lami Dozo that gave him his opening. The Air Force chief said that both sides should withdraw – 'but the situation had to be resolved by 31 December 1982'. Haig explained that there need be nothing in any final agreement that 'precludes Argentina from saying that it has received satisfaction'.[10] In his book, Haig does not elaborate further. However, central to the discussion was his attempt to persuade the Junta that it would get what it wanted in the end if it would only accept a degree of fudging in the actual agreement.

In support of his case he described the consequences of a break-down in the negotiations. He expressed his concern that the dispute was being internationalized (code for Soviet involvement) and that the United States faced a rupture in its relations with Latin American countries, as public opinion would drive his Government to back Britain. He urged the Junta to accept a restructuring of the local government of the Islands, overseen by the United States, as its gain from the dispute. They had to accept the return of British influence. Certainly a better Argentine proposal was needed than the one he had received the previous night.

He needed to persuade the Junta of two things. First, that it should trust the United States. This was, for example, relevant to the interim administration. He had insisted with Britain that the decision-making structure for the Islands should be based not on unanimity in the Special Interim Authority (which would have given Britain veto-power over any changes it disliked), but instead on a majority. Argentina could well be the beneficiary of the American 'swing' vote in future decisions.

Second, he had to persuade Argentina that Britain cared far more about the administration of the Islands than about eventual sovereignty. Argentina should therefore demonstrate maximum flexibility on the question of the interim administration, especially as its own priority was sovereignty.

Britain did not want another recurrence of this sort of problem. It had already proved economically and politically costly and it would never be able to mount a military operation of this sort again. So long as it was not seen to be giving in to force it would be happy to have the problem off its plate in the future. As the Islands were only 400 miles away from Argentina, once they were removed from the list of non-autonomus territories by London, they could be nothing else but Argentine. He indicated, on the basis of his conversations with Mrs Thatcher, that Britain had little interest in long-term sovereignty over the Islands.

I can't speak for Mrs Thatcher, at times I don't speak very well to her, but I know they don't care about the sovereignty of the islands.

They are prepared to renegotiate but we must permit her to do it gracefully and on honourable terms. But I can assure you we will drive it to a solution. Secondly, I personally am convinced that Britain wants this problem off the plate. They will never be able to face another crisis of this kind. They could not politically, and they could not by their own assessment of the cost.[11]

What Haig therefore wanted was an ambiguous and grey framework that would suggest rather than define the final solution to the dispute. This would allow Britain the appearance of an actual negotiation yet it would be clear both in Argentina and internationally that the eventual solution could only be Argentine sovereignty. If Thatcher were forced to decide now on the future status of the Islands she would choose to fight, if only to survive politically. As justification she would use the principles of international law.

Haig's basic argument was that any permanent political solution would almost inevitably involve restoration of the Islands to Argentina. All that he asked was that this should not be expressed too explicitly in the text.

After hearing Haig's exposition, the Junta still required that, at the very least by the conclusion of the negotiations on 31 December, it should be clear that the Islands would become part of Argentine territory. There were warnings of other forms of external interference,* complaints over US tolerance of the British use of Ascension Island and demands that the British fleet be stopped while negotiations continued. Haig should understand the depth of feeling and frustration on this issue in Argentina.

None the less the Junta agreed to explore the possibility of introducing greater flexibility into the Argentine text so as to accommodate the points raised by the Secretary of State. Haig was pleased with the outcome of the meeting and agreed to continue mediating.

The Junta ordered the Malvinas Working Group to rewrite the Argentine proposal. The group decided to follow Haig's suggestion to

---

* Throughout the negotiations the Junta was concerned that a Soviet submarine was in the area and that it was going to sink a British ship so as to cast blame on Argentina.

withdraw opposition to the clause on government and administration, apparently of the utmost importance to London, while placing greater emphasis on sovereignty. This seemed to offer a possible compromise. At 11.30 the two delegations met to see if the compromise could be negotiated.

Sovereignty and Administration

Haig opened by identifying three requirements for the clause on sovereignty. It had to avoid attracting opposition through the stress on a deadline (31 December); it had to avoid an undesirable solution (such as independence or government from London); and it had to be phrased in a way acceptable to both sides. He therefore objected to:

1 prefacing 'territorial integrity' with 'Argentine';
2 the use of the term 'interests' as in 'the interests of the inhabitants of the islands'; and
3 mention of precise UN resolutions. Words of less political impact for Britain should be used in the text. Though a number of UN resolutions supported Argentina, others were more favourable to the British position.

Haig suggested eliminating from the Argentine proposals the phrase 'on the basis of the implementation of the principle of Argentine territorial integrity and taking into total consideration the interests of the inhabitants of the islands' and, instead, inserting phrases such as 'according to Chapter X of the United Nations Charter' and 'in mutually accorded conditions'. Admittedly this formula did not rule out an outcome unacceptable to Argentina at the end of the year. Argentina had to rely instead on the logic of the situation. Additional support derived from America's role in the negotiating process. After all it was in the US interest to ensure a rapid and peaceful settlement.

The Argentine delegation were not convinced by Haig's arguments. They did not share his confidence that Britain would not respond to a new crisis in December by sending a task force once again. It might even be more – and not less – capable than the one currently moving towards the South Atlantic. Nor were they convinced, on the basis of seventeen years' experience, that the British were interested not in the Islands as strategic or economic assets but only in due consideration being given to the islanders. Argentina needed much more than wishful thinking about what Britain might or might not do. By all means have a clause that would be inoffensive to London but it must offer something much more concrete to Argentina. By 31 December 1982 the position could not be one of continuing negotiations with some distant hope of a solution; this was what the General Assembly was told every year. 'We need something more concrete, positive and objective.' How could Argentina be sure that London would not simply revert to her old procrastinating stance once the Argentine military occupation had been dismantled?

Haig appreciated the problem but insisted that international law did not permit Argentina to resort to force to solve the dispute. Costa Mendez answered:

I agree with you but I think no one can challenge Great Britain on her title of world champion on the use of force in the conquest of her territories. On the contrary, Argentina always criticized the use of force for the purpose of conquest and there is no square metre of her territory that has been obtained through conquest. We lost much territory, instead, for not wanting to use force to avoid the loss. As Admiral Anaya has said, we have occupied our own territory without causing British deaths though some of our men were lost in the process and this was done with the only purpose of trying to get Great Britain to agree to negotiate with us on the issue of a definite solution to this problem. India occupied Goa, there were criticisms but, at the end of the day, it was accepted.

Haig again expressed his sympathy: 'I have studied all the debates and documents on this issue and, to me, it is clear that you are right and that if one could obtain an impartial body to adjudicate the islands, I have no doubt that this body would support the Argentine thesis.'

However, the issue now was not who was right or wrong but one of finding a formula to avoid war. There followed some discussion of referral to the international courts (which Britain would probably have had to accept) but this soon foundered on uncertainty over the British position and Argentine frustration, expressed by Costa Mendez:

> I do not know the position of the United Kingdom; you are talking to us and you know what we feel and want but it is very difficult for me to analyse options when I do not know what London wants.
>
> I think we should start from the analysis of the British position. You have been in London and you know their position. Please let us know what it is, otherwise this is a very difficult negotiation that has no possibilities of working out.

Haig reaffirmed his own approach. He was aware that if Costa Mendez were given an accurate account of Britain's views the negotiations would end forthwith. All he could do was indicate that the proposals under discussion did not originate in London but were those he considered the most likely to bear fruit. Discussion returned to the substance, especially the proposition that the Falklands would cease to be a colony but its final status would remain uncertain, with which the Argentine delegation was generally satisfied.

After a short break the American delegation produced a new idea. The best way to replace the wording referring to 'Argentine territorial integrity' (which was unacceptable to Britain) was to quote certain phrases in the decolonization Resolution 114 of the United Nations. These read: 'taking totally into account the will and the wishes clearly expressed of the interested population and the principle of avoiding the partial or total rupture of national unity and territorial integrity'. This wording should be tolerable to Buenos Aires. After all London could still quote other phrases of the same resolution against Argentina, including references to 'independence' (Chapter 5 of UN decolonization Resolution 114).

Unfortunately the word 'wishes' appeared and this was over-burdened with meaning in the history of the dispute. To Argentina the inclusion of this element would simply encourage self-determination for the inhabitants of the Falklands, while the principle of territorial integrity would be devalued. The Argentine delegation decided to meet alone. When they returned Costa Mendez went through the history of the negotiations to demonstrate why Britain could not be trusted and how the injunctions of the UN had been disregarded.

Haig grew restive. He said that no one was bound to abide by a decision of the United Nations and that in all its history this Organization had never been able to solve anything. He threatened to abandon the negotiations. Even so Costa Mendez continued to describe the frustrations of the previous seventeen years. Haig insisted that there was no possibility of stopping the British military advance unless the delegations produced a credible alternative. Argentina had violated the principles of the United Nations by refusing to deal with the problem in a peaceful manner. The United States was trying to avoid a tragedy but could not do so without greater Argentine flexibility. Costa Mendez replied:

We have not spent the whole day here to amuse you but to strive to find an acceptable document for both parties . . .

The first country to use force was not Argentina but the United Kingdom. She has continued with this use of force continuously and coupled now with perpetual negotiating intransigence. It is only now, because of a personal situation that Mrs Thatcher faces in her own Parliament, that the British Government is actually negotiating with us. Two months ago we proposed to the British a document of negotiations that they have not even answered: this is also the use of force on the part of a country that has a superior position in the United Nations and that aborts our possibilities of talking in that forum so as to avoid negotiations. For our people the Islands are ours and the least thing we can ask is for these to be restored to us. We have never, in any moment in our history, made use of force against the United Kingdom; it was the British who used their power to force a situation on us, and therefore it should be them who are forced to reduce their aspirations.

Haig insisted again that the British would eventually have to concede, whether or not its presence in the South Atlantic was legal or illegal. This led to the following exchange:

COSTA MENDEZ: I believe you are sincere when you say this but this is more in your spirit than in a paper that registers this idea. Nor is there a written guarantee relating to the commitment of the US to the solving of this dispute.

HAIG: I don't know what greater guarantee than the fact that we are participating in these talks.

COSTA MENDEZ: We have offered the islanders a very generous status, they are a very small population of 1,800 people but they should not be used as a political instrument to block future negotiations.

Haig now felt that discussion of the sovereignty clause had been taken about as far as it could go. They should now look at the clause relating to the interim administration, which was the area he had marked as the one in which Britain should be favoured.

The key difference, explained Haig, was that for Argentina the issue was one of principles and rights, but for Britain it was only a transitory problem. Its interest in the Islands was only 'temporary'. Once an agreement had been reached the British Government would honour it but parliamentary interference must also be prevented. He therefore suggested wording to say that 'neither of the two governments will undertake any action that is incompatible with the purpose or dispositions of the present agreement or with its application.'

Costa Mendez raised the question of whether Argentine citizens would be allowed to invest in property on the Islands.* Soon the discussion reverted to the vexed question of the consequences of decolonization. Costa Mendez insisted on 'a more specific reference to territorial integrity'. If he did so, warned Haig, 'I can assure you that there will be no agreement with the British.'

With this deadlock the meeting ended at 22.00 hours. At this point, according to Haig, he played a 'wild card'.

---

* He claimed that there was a particular problem because of the legal requirement that the British company Coalite, which controlled the Falkland Islands Company, could not sell shares without Parliament's permission.

Although the British in fact told us nothing of their military plans, the Argentinians plainly believed that we knew everything they did. Possibly this misconception could be useful. I called Bill Clark [the President's National Security Adviser] at the White House on an open line, knowing that the Argentinians would monitor the call, and told him in a tone of confidentiality that British military action was imminent. At 2.00 AM on April 18, new proposals were delivered to me with an invitation to resume the negotiations at the Casa Rosada at two o'clock in the afternoon.[12]

There is no Argentine confirmation of this and so whether it could have influenced the Junta is unclear. Argentine records do show Haig making the same threat overtly the next day. At any rate there was good reason to expect initial British attacks by this time. What is certain is that when the Military Committee met with the Malvinas Working Group just after 23.00 on the night of 17 April it was agreed that they should demonstrate maximum flexibility. With this in mind and in order to sustain the negotiations the Argentine delegation worked on a revised text until the early hours of the morning.

The decolonization clause included the most significant amendments: for the first time the word 'rights' appeared, instead of the 'interests' of the islanders. The word 'Argentine' was taken away from 'territorial integrity'. Thus the clause now read:

On December 31 1982 the period of transition will end. During this period of transition the signatories will have concluded negotiations over the mode of cancellation of the islands from the list of non-autonomous territories under Chapter XI of the United Nations Charter and under mutually accorded conditions for its definite status, including due consideration for the rights of the inhabitants as well as for the principle of territorial integrity applicable to this dispute, in accordance with the purposes and principles of the Charter of the United Nations and the resolutions 1514(XV), 2065(XX), and other pertinent resolutions of the General Assembly of the United Nations in the question of the Malvinas Islands. The negotiations that are mentioned here will begin within fifteen days following the signing of the present agreement.

The new clause on the interim administration also revealed some concessions:

(a) During the period of transition, all the decisions, laws and regulations that in future should be adopted by the local administration of the islands, shall be subjected to and rapidly ratified by the special interim authority, except in those cases that the special interim authority should consider that those decisions, laws, and regulations are incompatible with the purposes and provisions of this agreement or its implementation. The local traditional administration shall be maintained through the island executive and legislative committees, that will be widened to include equal number of Argentine representatives from among the local population.

(b) Pending a definitive agreement, none of the governments will undertake actions that are incompatible with the purposes and provisions of this agreement or its implementation.

After the American delegation had had a chance to discuss the new text in the morning the two delegations met in the Government House. Negotiations began at 15.00 on 18 April; they did not end until 01.55 hours on 19 April.

Haig now had renewed heart. He praised the 'very important progress that the Argentine delegation has achieved in the underlying matter of the dispute'. Especially 'miraculous' was what had been achieved with the decolonization paragraph. But more concessions were needed. He still did not think that the package was going to be acceptable to London.

This made the Argentines suspicious, for they still had little idea of where exactly Britain was and was not prepared to be flexible. This was not going to be revealed until Haig had extracted the maximum possible concessions from Argentina.

Haig's line was that the logic of the situation would persuade Britain to transfer sovereignty. The Argentine delegation had taken this to mean that the United States would guarantee this tacitly, though it could not appear explicitly in the agreement. In the course of the discussions it became clear that the United States would not force Britain to recognize this logic. Haig said: 'I do not say that this agreement will represent British acceptance of an eventual transference of sovereignty at the end of the negotiations, but that Great Britain will accept the inevitable end of this long process.' Costa Mendez reacted immediately. If, in the end, sovereignty was not transferred, 'the terms that we have agreed to use here, which are so diffuse and ambiguous so as to be acceptable to the British Government today, will add a very risky threat to our position as of 31 December.'

Nevertheless Haig continued to press for further modifications of the Argentine text, attempting to remove all references to the United Nations resolutions that referred specifically to the Islands and also to the name 'Malvinas'. The wording 'in accordance with' should be changed to 'in the light of' when referring to the United Nations. Finally he wanted to add the word 'fundamental' to the reference to 'rights of the inhabitants'. These modifications would have allowed for self-determination of the islanders, the established British position.

With the decolonization clause Haig sought to substitute 'during this period of transition' when discussing the government of the Islands with 'pending a definitive agreement'. As the Argentine delegation pointed out, this would allow the British administration to continue, should the talks reach a stalemate by December 1982. Haig countered that all this must rest in indeterminate terms. For Thatcher to accept the agreement it must include the concept of self-determination.

At this point the Argentine delegation retired to another room. They felt themselves faced by increasing rigidity in the American stance, based apparently on a complete lack of flexibility in London (for Haig still refused to inform them fully of the British position). What was proposed was the return to the status quo ante bellum and self-determination for the islanders. The disillusion with the Haig mediation was all but complete. It was assumed that he had been in constant communication with Britain and had been gearing his diplomatic endeavours to British military preparations. As Haig would not specify areas of British flexibility the Argentine delegation now presumed that there were none. Britain's strategy had been to wait for Argentine reactions to American ideas without having to reveal its own intransigence. Argentina would be accused of aborting the negotiations even though Britain had not been ready to reach agreement on any terms.

Faced with this the Junta reverted to a tactic which was to be followed at the conclusion of later negotiations. Instead of the next effort opening with past concessions taken as read, the original Argentine stand now had to be reasserted. It was as if each set of negotiations was akin to haggling at a bazaar. With one customer the price for the goods might be reduced in the bargaining. If he still refuses to buy, the price is not kept down. It is raised again for the next customer and the haggling begins anew. Thus the Junta insisted on adding another sentence to the decolonization clause: 'As from December 31, 1982, and until such time as the agreement on the final status comes into force, the leadership of the government and administration will be exercised by an official appointed by the Argentine Government.' Costa Mendez notes that he knew this would be unacceptable. It was added 'so we could later negotiate it. I think we made a mistake.'[13]

The Argentine records suggest that, as expected, Haig rejected the addition. He was now angry. The advance of the British fleet made war imminent. The Argentine Government could fall. From now on he would blame Argentina for scuttling the negotiations.

Haig's view appears to be that the talks had actually run into the ground the previous evening (18 April) on a less crucial matter that had been agreed the day before – the withdrawal of military forces – but that he had, even so, persevered with his draft.

[B]y 2:40 AM on April 19, we had produced a draft, acceptable to the Argentinians, providing for an immediate cessation of hostilities and the withdrawal of forces, an Argentinian presence on the island under a U.S. guarantee, and negotiations leading to a resolution of the question by December 31, 1982. I believed that Mrs Thatcher would have great difficulty in accepting this text.

A further meeting in the morning helped clear up some unresolved points. By 13.00 'there was a modified text that met some of the British objections.' The text was sent off to London for consideration. If it was worth returning to London, Haig would do so. Otherwise he would go back to Washington (which is where he told the press he was going). The White House staff was worried that the effort was going nowhere:

the president had been in office just over a year. Everyone was still acutely conscious of press [accounts] about the gang that couldn't shoot straight, that didn't have a clue about foreign affairs … [about] sheer amateurism … And those in custody of the president's image were very, very concerned about this. And if the mission was gonna fail, they didn't want it to fail because we looked like we were being made fools of. [They were also afraid that some of the US team] might be seriously affected by the fatigue factor. And having invested so much physical and psychic expenditure in this enterprise [they] might not be fully capable of judging when the moment had come to break it off.[14]

Haig had hoped to see Costa Mendez at 14.00 but the Foreign Minister was closeted with Galtieri. Eventually he was informed that they would meet at the airport. Haig told the press: 'In these more than 3 days of very detailed talks, there has been a further refinement of the Argentine position. We have now finished this stage of our work. I am making the results available to the British Government, and I am returning to Washington to report to the President.'[15]

When Costa Mendez arrived Haig was handed a note. Once again this was to be read when airborne; once again it went back on what had been previously agreed: 'It is absolutely essential and *conditio sine qua non* that negotiations will have to conclude with a result on 31 December, 1982. This result must include a recognition of Argentinian sovereignty over the islands.'[16] The copy of the final Argentine proposal attached included an additional sentence on Argentine administration from the beginning of 1983. Argentina would not continue to make concessions if the British remained intransigent.

Whether or not Haig had been alerted to this shift earlier, he was now convinced that the Argentine decision-making process was a shambles. He saw the Argentines continually going back on their word, largely because of the diffuse nature of that process:

> if Galtieri did not hold the power of decision, neither did the Junta. On every decision, the Government apparently had to secure the unanimous consent of every corps commander in the Army and of their equivalents in the Navy and Air Force. Progress was made by syllables and centimetres and then vetoed by men who had never been part of the negotiations.[17]

While he may have been exaggerating the problem, in that the final decision did rest with the Junta, the nature and role of the Military Committee (which included the Chiefs of Staff and senior commanders) was hidden from him. The Malvinas Working Group, with whom he spent most of his time, was subordinate to the Military Committee. Moreover the Junta's members all had to be sensitive to the shifting currents of military opinion, expressed in a number of meetings which took place over the few days that Haig was in Buenos Aires. There was also of course domestic, civilian pressure demanding both details of the negotiations and a promise that the sovereignty of the Islands would not be negotiated away. The impact on Galtieri of the crowds outside the Casa Rosada is remarked upon by many of those who witnessed it. At any rate Haig's experience of decision-making in Buenos Aires gave him little confidence in future negotiations.[18]

The Argentine perception of Haig was scarcely more flattering. His mediation was now seen as little more than a smokescreen while the British fleet closed in on the South Atlantic, discouraging Argentine action while negotiations were under way.

Having promised to pass on new proposals to London Haig felt bound to do so. Clearly the latest Argentine addition would be rejected out of hand, so he simply excluded it. In another message also sent from his aircraft Haig informed Costa Mendez (via the American Embassy in Buenos Aires) of this decision. Haig added that he knew this was not the final Argentine position but that he hoped that Costa Mendez's Government would understand his reasons. Costa Mendez complained immediately to the American Ambassador, but there was little he could do about it.

London Receives the Proposals

When the War Cabinet received the ideas on the Monday evening, it did not find them encouraging. Because of a desire not to be seen to be responsible for the breakdown of the negotiations they were not rejected out of hand. On the other hand a message was sent to Haig which dissuaded him from diverting his plane to London when he stopped at Caracas to see the Venezuelan Foreign Minister.[19] The Prime Minister explained her objections to Parliament the next day:

> I cannot disguise from the House that the Argentine proposals at present before us fall far short in some important aspects of those objectives and of the requirements expressed in this House.
> . . . Among the many problems presented by the Argentine proposals is that they fail to provide that the Falkland islanders should be able to determine their own destiny. The House has always said that the wishes of the islanders are paramount.

However, the negotiation was not yet over: 'We are examining the proposals very closely and will seek to put forward our own proposals to Mr. Haig. With that in mind my Right Hon. Friend the Foreign Secretary plans to visit Washington on Thursday.'

On Tuesday 20 April Haig contacted Costa Mendez again to tell him of the British reaction:

> 1) I have the first British reaction to the paper drafted in Buenos Aires. It is a disappointment. London, of course, concedes that it is worth careful study, but it finds the basis for a mutual withdrawal very inequitable.
> 2) The question of sovereignty is stated too explicitly, and it finds that the wishes of the islanders have not been taken into account sufficiently.

3) London will issue a press release, placing emphasis on the failure to consider the wishes of the islanders as paramount, but it has not closed the door.

4) Tomorrow I shall be in a better position to advise you, but I would urge you to pass on the first reaction to your colleagues in the Government.

5) It is clear to me that a substantial mutual adjustment of position will have to be made if war is to be avoided. When I have seen the British proposal in detail I shall get into contact again concerning future steps.[20]

At least Costa Mendez could not complain that he was not being informed about the British views. However, by this time he assumed (correctly) that Argentina was not seeing the British proposal in detail because Haig did not wish to pass it on rather than because it was not available.

Although the negotiating pressure had been on Buenos Aires it was now recognized in London that matters were coming to a head. Haig's strategy of seeking the reaction of each side to the most realistic draft available at a given time put both sides at risk of rejecting not just the adversary, which was comparatively easy, but also the United States, which neither wished to do. Although a short and sharp response had been sent to Haig on receipt of the latest draft there was concern in the Foreign Office that a display of intransigence by Britain could postpone the overt American assistance that was deemed both necessary and long overdue.

While Pym was searching for some sort of compromise Thatcher was becoming increasingly irritated by the whole exercise. She was not herself over-impressed by Haig, and had never understood why the United States had not simply supported Britain in the first place. Officials sought to explain his problems, the competing pressures on the US Administration, and the need to give him something to work on. With great reluctance the Prime Minister allowed herself to be convinced. Some concessions might be taken to Washington by Pym:

The only concessions Pym was able to take with him were an offer that other flags might fly beside the British during the interim period and an acceptance that sovereignty would be open for discussion after an Argentine withdrawal. This could not be to any fixed deadline and there would be no 'creeping transfer of sovereignty'. There also had to be recognition of local Falkland opinion in any deal.[21]

Before he left for Washington Pym told the Commons on 21 April that 'there is undoubtedly life in the negotiations', but he gave no evidence for this. His speech was most notable for a false impression he gave, which he had to return to Parliament to correct. He would not, he said, exclude the resort to military force. However: 'I will exclude it so long as negotiations are in play.' He explained later that what he really meant was that 'however hard I was trying to achieve a peaceful settlement, the use of force could not at any stage be ruled out.'[22]

Chapter Fifteen

HAIG'S SHUTTLE CONCLUDES

Operation Paraquat

On 25 April Britain did use force. The decision to retake South Georgia had been one of the first made by the War Cabinet. Politically, it had the advantage of demonstrating resolve, reinforcing domestic morale and strengthening Britain's diplomatic position. South Georgia was not a negligible asset in itself: in terms of the exploration of Antarctica it was even more important than the Falklands.

The attack was made on military advice. The senior commanders were concerned about morale, and an early victory could provide a psychological benefit. They also saw advantages in gaining access to a deep-water harbour, and in denying this to the enemy, who might eventually use it to mount operations against British forces from the rear.

The advice given to the Government was that the recapture of South Georgia should be comparatively easy: the Argentine garrison was small and lacked air support. Sufficient forces could be dispatched to the Island to overwhelm any likely defences. Within the Ministry of Defence there was a contrary view that it would make far more sense to press on to the Falklands without diversion of effort and unnecessary expenditure of scarce resources. There were 800 miles between South Georgia and the Falklands – plenty of sea in which a small detachment might find itself vulnerable to submarine attacks. The terrain itself was forbidding. There is no such thing as a risk-free military operation: a disaster could have the opposite political effect to that intended. Even after the political decision had been taken and central planning completed, there was still pressure from some senior officers within the task force to abort the operation.

Just as one of the first military operations approved by the British War Cabinet had been the recapture of South Georgia, one of the first decisions taken by the Junta had been to make no serious effort to defend it. As we noted earlier, concern as to the magnitude of the British military response required that future defensive efforts concentrate on the Falkland Islands.

On completion of the Argentine occupation of South Georgia naval units involved had been ordered to withdraw. Only a small number of troops were to be garrisoned on the Island, with minimum support and material. Should Britain decide to attack, little could be done by way of defence. It was too far from the Argentine mainland to provide air cover. This was even more emphatically so for the South Sandwich Islands.*

From 19 April on, after Haig's warnings, the Junta had been expecting some sort of military action. Although Haig had said that an attack could take place as early as 20 April, on that day the Junta's military staff advised that 25 April was more likely. An attempt was made to discover the whereabouts of the British fleet using aerial reconnaissance.

The Argentine Air Force had been obliged to improve its aerial reconnaissance using Boeing 707 320–Cs. It was not easy. When a Boeing first encountered the task force south of Ascension on 21 April it was intercepted by a Sea Harrier and the mission had to be abandoned. None the less it had seen enough to know that the task force was entering American waters, as defined by the Rio Treaty, and had begun to divide. Argentine planners concluded immediately that the British were planning to retake South Georgia. On 24 April it was reported that two destroyers and a tanker were near the Island. The Joint Chiefs of Staff assessed that an attack was imminent.

* Interestingly no consideration appears to have been given at any time to the removal of the very small Argentine garrison on South Thule, which would have been a comparatively easy exercise, if necessary just using *Endurance.*

On 7 April Captain Brian Young, the Captain of the destroyer HMS *Antrim*, had been put in charge of a 'forward combined force' to re-establish a presence on South Georgia. Named Operation Paraquat, the relevant orders were signed by Admiral Fieldhouse on 12 April. There was a need to issue them quickly. They were too long and too sensitive to send by radio and if they were to be dropped to the relevant elements in the task force in time it was necessary to take account of the maximum operational range of a Nimrod aircraft.

In London the Army was concerned that the Navy had taken only one company of the Royal Marines, which might not provide sufficient strength to overwhelm properly organized defences. It was, insisted the Navy, too late to add further support. However, the concern was eased when it was discovered that D Squadron SAS, on its own initiative so as to be involved in any action, had embarked on the *Antrim* group at Ascension Island. This meant that there were some 200 troops available for the operation.

The order was to reoccupy South Georgia with the minimum loss of life and with minimum damage to property. The first requirement ruled out a frontal assault; the latter, reflecting the need to preserve accommodation for a future garrison, meant that it would not be possible to use naval gunfire. This increased the importance of secrecy, which in turn meant that it would be impossible to demand surrender before the attack. The initial landing target date was 21 April. It was subsequently put back to 23 April.

The restrictions on the character of the attack meant that it was essential to have good intelligence as to the situation of the defenders. In this one, exceptional case it appears that Britain did have satellite pictures from the United States, taken on a satellite's final orbit. This made it possible to identify the location, as well as note the weakness, of Argentine defences.

Special services were to be put ashore to survey the Argentine positions. In the discussions of where to land the marines and the British Antarctic Survey felt that the SAS were underestimating the problems of terrain, and advised against their choice of Fortuna Glacier.

On 19 April the submarine HMS *Conqueror* conducted surveillance in the waters surrounding South Georgia and concluded that there were no Argentine ships in the area. This was confirmed the next day from the air. An aerial-reconnaissance Victor flew from Ascension on 20 April, but was forced to turn back because of operating problems. Another Victor took its place, conducting a radar search which discovered no Argentine warships of any size in a 200-mile zone around the South Georgia coastline.[1]

The Fortuna Glacier did turn out to be unsuitable: the landings were almost a complete disaster. The SAS units were inserted on 21 April but they soon found the weather conditions intolerable. Unable to make progress they asked to be removed. Two of the three helicopters sent to extract them crashed and it was remarkable that the third managed to get everybody off without serious casualty during a break in the bad weather. Late on 22 April another attempt was made using Gemini inflatables from *Antrim*, which manoeuvred uncomfortably close for its own safety into Stromness Bay. The Geminis were hit by a failure of outboard motors and a sudden gale. Three boats landed without detection; two others were swept out to sea and had to be rescued. The SAS men who did land were able to establish the limited capabilities of the small Argentine garrison at Leith. Meanwhile it was decided to insert three SBS teams on 22 April on the beach at Hound Bay, on the north coast of the Barff Peninsula. One unit was delivered by a Wasp helicopter and discovered what the BAS civilians who had stayed on after the Argentine occupation already knew: that there were no Argentine forces in this area. An attempt to deliver the other two units by helicopter was defeated by bad weather; they reached the shore in Geminis.

On the morning of 23 April an Argentine Hercules made contact with *Antrim*; it moved quickly away before it could be attacked (although the British rules of engagement still did not allow an attack). It then came across the *Brambleleaf*, *Tidespring* and *Plymouth*. At 14.56 hours electronic-warfare operators on board *Endurance* detected an Argentine submarine. This was later confirmed by signals intelligence, which suggested that this was the *Santa Fé*.[2]

Young was now becoming concerned. He had received little useful information from the surveillance teams; he had been detected by aircraft and a submarine was now in the area. There were queries from London as to why there had not been more progress. A request to change the rules of engagement to allow attacks on aircraft was only being considered. They were later changed to allow attack, but only if the aircraft posed a direct threat. This did not include surveillance aircraft. Young's inclination was to move his more vulnerable ships to a safer distance while mounting an attack at Leith which he knew to be a reasonably straightforward operation. However, another Hercules flight made him nervous that his position had now been pinpointed and that the *Santa Fé* would find *Antrim* in Stromness Bay, where it would be vulnerable to attack.

Increasingly attention focused on the *Santa Fé*. Its mere presence was complicating all British plans. During 24 April intelligence suggested that the submarine intended to reinforce the Argentine garrison and withdraw. Thereafter she would be a threat to the British ships. Analysts at the task force HQ at Northwood had calculated that she was likely to arrive in Cumberland Bay for Grytviken, rather than Stromness Bay for Leith. This was confirmed by the interception of a call on an open line between the submarine and Grytviken.

The decision to send the *Santa Fé* had been taken by Vice-Admiral Lombardo after a request by Captain Trombetta for reinforcements, although this went against the Junta's original order not to reinforce South Georgia. Admiral Anaya only discovered that this had been ignored late in the day, but he decided to back the responsible commanders.* The submarine was virtually obsolete. It had left Mar del Plata on 9 April and arrived in Grytviken after a long journey, much of

---

* Admiral Anaya told the Rattenbach Commission:

Unfortunately, nowadays we live in particular circumstances that make the Commander-in-Chief of the Navy of today very different to the Commander-in-Chief in other days. Today we cannot do what we would like to do but we must look into very many issues that are not specific to the Navy. That is why I permitted my admirals to take these decisions. When one has commanders like them (the two best admirals that the Navy had in the professional field) and they tell me that they are doing this action, I support their decision.

Testimony of Admiral Anaya, *Gente*, 8 December 1983, p. 89.

it on the surface for its batteries were almost spent with age. Its weaponry was limited and it could not expect to achieve the surprise necessary to launch its torpedoes. During the journey it had been damaged by strong wind and waves. None the less, it managed to avoid detection and reached Cumberland Bay by the morning of 25 April, when it landed some forty men and material to reinforce the defenders. It hoped to withdraw from the Island before sunrise.

However, British helicopters were now actively searching for the *Sante Fé*. A Wessex from *Antrim* picked up a slight radar echo which it correctly interpreted to have come from the submarine; it then attacked it with a depth charge. This was followed by attacks by a Lynx from *Brilliant*, which was only just reaching Young's group, and a Wasp from *Endurance*. The submarine suffered one casualty, but it had been crippled by the attack. It limped with great difficulty into Grytviken, under continual fire from the helicopters, and the crew abandoned it.

Despite the lack of reconnaissance the local British commanders decided to exploit the evident confusion in the Argentine garrison and mount an improvised attack. It was not possible to use marines on board the tanker *Tidespring* because this was now too far away. A small scratch force was put together of the various units on board *Antrim*. This produced seventy-five men, who were divided into three groups. The guns of *Antrim* and *Plymouth* were used to unnerve the enemy further while the troops were landed by helicopter. They moved cautiously, suspecting opposition. When the first group got close to King Edward Point they saw a white flag flying, raised soon after the start of the intense naval bombardment. Captain Bicain from the *Santa Fé*, now the senior officer, announced on radio his wish to surrender. This was formally agreed at 17.05 hours on 25 April. At Leith Lieutenant Astiz was reluctant to surrender but soon he changed his mind.

Before the surrender the Argentine Air Force had sought to mount an attack. A Canberra squadron (three bombers, a Boeing 707 support plane and a KC–130 exploration plane) was detailed to the Rio Grande airstrip for this purpose. The Boeing 707 had discovered part of the British flotilla in the morning – the *Endurance*, *Plymouth* and *Tidespring* – but not the *Brilliant* and the *Antrim*. Soon after noon on 25

April the Canberras took off with orders to attack British ships so long as they were isolated and away from Cumberland Bay. It was judged that the aircraft would have little chance of survival within the Bay if they were fired on, nor would they have sufficient space to descend to release their bombs. Just before they were due to arrive the KC–130 informed them that the meteorological conditions around the islands were poor and that the British fleet was already inside the Bay. The aircraft returned without being able to provide support to the defending forces. The surrender later that day halted any further Air Force plans for sorties to South Georgia.

The British assault had succeeded without any serious resistance. In London the news of the success was greeted with relief, especially after the anxious moments on the glaciers. On the afternoon of Saturday 23 April Nott and Lewin had gone to 10 Downing Street to report the disturbing news that both helicopters and men might be lost. The news was greeted with silence. Lewin moved quickly to reassure the shaken Prime Minister that this was not a disaster and that, with the weather so awful, these sort of set-backs were inevitable. Soon he was able to report back that there were no casualties. When the operation eventually succeeded, so great was the relief that she went with Nott into Downing Street to inform the press and tell them to 'rejoice'. The military had given the politicians the early victory they had wanted and thereafter found it much easier to get the politicians to trust their judgement.

The Rio Treaty

From the debate on Resolution 502 onwards Argentina had found the Organization of American States a congenial forum. It could count on the support of most Latin American states for its stance on the sovereignty issue. Although initially there was disapproval of its use of force to achieve its ends, over time this became muted as considerations of American solidarity came to the fore. Attempts by some of the Commonwealth countries in the Caribbean to get Argentina denounced in the OAS were easily defeated. On the other hand, at its meeting on 12 April the Caribbean countries were able to prevent anything other than an innocuous resolution being passed, which expressed concern over the crisis and offered to co-operate in the search for a peaceful solution.

Argentine diplomats remained confident that they could obtain the necessary votes to call the Rio Treaty, a forum in which the Caribbean countries counted for much less.[3]

The Rio Treaty or the Inter-American Treaty of Reciprocal Aid (IATRA) had been established during a Conference of American Foreign Ministers in Rio de Janeiro in 1947. Article Three of the Treaty states that:

an armed attack by any State against a State Party shall be considered an attack against all the State Parties and, consequently,
each of them undertakes to assist in meeting any such attack in the
exercise of the inherent right of individual or collective self-defence
recognized by Article 51 of the Charter of the United Nations.

It describes a security zone which includes the Falkland Islands and the dependencies. There are twenty-one contracting parties.* Not all members of the Organization of American States are members of IATRA – significantly those who are not include a number of the smaller Commonwealth states.† This lack would make it easier for Argentina to obtain the two-thirds majority required for the imple-mentation of collective measures.

On 14 April the Junta had discussed the circumstances in which the Rio Treaty would be called: should Chile become an effective ally of Britain in the conflict or if the task force sailed south from Ascension Island. Five days later it appeared that both sets of circumstances obtained. Intelligence sources suggested a degree of Anglo-Chilean

---

* The contracting parties are Argentina, Bolivia, Brazil, Chile, Colombia, Costa Rica, Dominican Republic, Ecuador, El Salvador, Guatemala, Haiti, Honduras, Mexico, Nicaragua, Panama, Paraguay, Peru, Trinidad–Tobago, United States, Uruguay and Venezuela.

† Members of the OAS who have not joined IATRA: Antigua and Barbuda, Barbados, Grenada, Jamaica, Bahamas, Santa Lucia and Surinam.

collusion as the task force moved away from Ascension Island.

On 19 April, therefore, the Junta decided to call the Rio Treaty if the current round of the Haig mediation failed to produce a result. Haig himself had been anxious about this possibility from the start. In almost every communication with the Argentine Foreign Ministry he urged that there should be no recourse to the Treaty. So long as the negotiations were under way he saw it as a distraction that would encourage public posturing when private diplomacy was vital. He was also well aware that the United States would be in a minority position and at the receiving end of inflamed rhetoric. Haig argued that the Treaty would not be appropriate because the reciprocal obligation of the signatory states was to lend assistance in the case of attack upon one member by an extra-continental state (the US obviously had the Soviet Union in mind). One could not cite extra-continental aggression in the present case, given that Argentina had initiated the use of force.*

The procedure of the Rio Treaty required that Argentina first call a consultation of member countries within the framework of the OAS. The Junta decided on this course for several reasons: pressure from within Argentina, Britain's example in gathering supporting statements from her neighbours in the European Community and NATO, as well as the expectation (encouraged by Haig) that British military action would take place in the late hours of 20 April.

The consultation took place that day. Against American opposition Argentina asked formally for a meeting of the Rio Treaty countries. The resolution indicating that there was a threat to the area and that the Treaty should meet in formal session was supported by eighteen countries, with no votes against and three abstentions: Colombia, USA and Trinidad and Tobago. Only sixteen votes were necessary for the meeting to be agreed. This was the first time since the creation of the Rio Treaty that it had been invoked without the participation of the United States of America. The meeting of the Rio Treaty, with all the

* IATRA defines aggression as 'the use of armed force by a State against the sovereignty, territorial integrity or political independence of another State, or in any other manner inconsistent with the Charter of the UN, the Charter of the OAS or this Treaty' (Article 9, Clause 1).

Foreign Ministers of the member countries, was arranged for Monday 26 April.

The Military Committee discussed with Costa Mendez an appropriate strategy for the meeting two days before it took place. Costa Mendez asserted that the objective was to obtain for Argentina the maximum number of positive votes and that the text of the resolution must therefore be weaker than a straightforward exposition of the Argentine position. The resolution should exhort the parties to the dispute to negotiate, taking into account Argentine sovereign rights over the territory. Great Britain should abstain from the use of force in the area defined in Article 4 of the Rio Treaty. Member countries of the Treaty should be urged not to undertake individual actions that could affect the conflict. Finally, it should allow for IATRA to be kept open for further consultation. The Military Committee also added that it should be made clear that the final objective was to settle the underlying dispute once and for all. Argentina would continue to work with every possible organization or third party to obtain this.

Before the meeting took place Britain recaptured South Georgia. This represented a rebuff to one of the consistent demands made by Argentina during the negotiations – that the British task force should not move south from Ascension. Haig had not tried seriously to persuade Britain to do this and he would have failed had he tried. Haig had in fact consistently stressed the likelihood of a British attack – in an effort to induce Argentina to be more conciliatory. He contacted Costa Mendez twice before the Rio Treaty was convened in an effort to arrange a meeting and both times warned that in twenty-four or forty-eight hours there would be a violent British attack in the South Atlantic.

At the meeting Costa Mendez fared somewhat better than he had done at the UN. In his speech he condemned the British attack on South Georgia, blamed the crisis on Britain, offered his interpretation of Resolution 502, and denounced British colonialism and the measures of political and economic coercion imposed on Argentina. He concluded:

Mr. President: the use of force against an American state by an extra-continental power is happening before our eyes. Peace in

America is seriously endangered and with it the territorial integrity of Argentina ... This situation cannot be prolonged ... we must demand that the British forces withdraw immediately from the area of security defined by Article 4 of the Rio Treaty and that they should return to their natural bases in the United Kingdom. This is the first and the most important step ... The British fleet has its place in another part of the world and colonialism has no more place in the world ...

At the end of the presentation, Costa Mendez was applauded for twenty minutes in a standing ovation by all present with the single exception of Alexander Haig, who remained seated and unsmiling.[4] In his presentation Haig insisted that the United States had to follow the dictates of international law and could not allow disputes to be resolved through the use of force. He reminded members of the OAS that many of them were involved in territorial disputes with neighbours, warned that unless a settlement were achieved within the 'next few days' more intensive fighting could break out and suggested that the passage of the resolution would hinder rather than help his mediation effort.

At 04.00 hours of 28 April the OAS resolved in favour of Argentina by seventeen votes for, none against and four abstentions. The resolution:

- urged Great Britain 'to cease the hostilities it is carrying on' within the security region defined by the Rio Treaty and (along with Argentina) 'to refrain from any act that may affect inter-American peace and security',
- urged 'those governments immediately to call a truce that will make it possible to resume and proceed normally with the negotiation aimed at a peaceful settlement of the conflict, taking into account the rights of sovereignty of the Republic of Argentina over the Malvinas (Falkland) Islands and the interests of the islanders',
- offered OAS assistance in the search for a peaceful solution,
- noted and supported the Haig mediation,
- deplored sanctions 'of coercive measures of an economic and

political nature' imposed on Argentina by the EEC and other states and exhorted them to be lifted as incompatible with Resolution 502, the Charter of the UN, the Charter of the OAS and GATT.

In Buenos Aires the resolution was seen as a triumph for Argentine diplomacy in the same way that Resolution 502 had been seen as a triumph for British diplomacy. It had gathered a substantial number of votes to support its stand. However, as with Resolution 502, the OAS resolution could be interpreted as being only a half-measure. The Treaty, for example, allows in Article 8 for a variety of collective measures – from recall of chief of missions to the use of armed force.[5] Argentina did not press this issue, knowing that if it had done so regional support would have evaporated. (For similar reasons British diplomats had been careful not to label Argentina as an aggressor in the UN.) This made possible a British interpretation of the IATRA resolution similar to the Argentine interpretation of Resolution 502. It could be noted that British withdrawal was not actually demanded and that the UN resolution was supported.

The Mediation Concludes

As Argentina moved towards calling the Rio Treaty, Haig struggled to salvage something from his mediation. In Argentina the two were seen as linked: calling the meeting had put pressure on Haig. In practice Britain had seemed slightly more conciliatory than he had anticipated – in particular it had not rejected outright, 'contrary to newspaper reports from London', the paper sent from Buenos Aires – and so he felt that Argentina might still be persuaded that further concessions were not only necessary but could be worthwhile. Haig wrote to Costa Mendez that he had urged Pym to reduce his amendments to an 'absolute minimum'. Pym was coming to Washington on 22 April; Costa Mendez would be arriving on 25 April for the Rio Treaty meeting.[6]

Haig was now moving towards the last act of the negotiation. He had decided that an American proposal should be presented to the two sides. Central to this idea was the notion of self-determination, which Haig regarded as crucial to the British position and far more important than sovereignty itself. The proposal therefore allowed for the transfer of sovereignty but 'preserved the basic British position by providing for free choice by the islanders as to whether they would be associated with one or the other parties, opt for independence, or even accept compensation for leaving the Falklands'.[7]

He had hoped to present the 'draft to Pym, negotiate down to the bottom line, and then pass the proposal on to the Argentineans'. However, by the time the two men met, Pym had already been told the details at a breakfast meeting with William Clark. As a result Thatcher had been contacted and a response elicited which was, unsurprisingly, negative. She could not accept it and even if she did she could not sell it to her parliamentary supporters. Nevertheless, she had agreed that it could go forward to Argentina. This did not imply acceptance of its provisions, but it showed that Britain would negotiate a settlement 'as long as the islanders were given the opportunity of deciding their own future'.[8]

After concluding his discussions with Pym, Haig wrote to Costa Mendez:

> We have just ended our second day of tiring discussions with Francis Pym and his colleagues. As we had anticipated, the text that I brought with me from Buenos Aires is unacceptable to the British. We found strong resistance in those areas that I told you about.
>
> Nevertheless, we have made a serious effort and are trying to achieve some progress. Now I hope to have a new text soon that you and I can review when we meet on Sunday.

Early in the morning of 25 April Costa Mendez and the Malvinas Working Group arrived in Washington DC. They already knew of the attack on South Georgia, though not its outcome. They were informed on arrival that Haig wished to see Costa Mendez immediately in order to hand him a simultaneous proposal that the US was making to both Argentina and the United Kingdom.

The Argentine party decided not to visit Haig. They were now extremely wary of the Secretary of State's methods and intentions. They suspected that the proposal was not simultaneous but that in all probability it had been handed first to the British on 22 April or had been concocted when Pym met Haig on that day. More importantly, such a meeting was now out of the question because the British had initiated military action before the conclusion of the Haig negotiations. In these circumstances to continue as if nothing had happened would give quite the wrong impression – especially in South America, which was increasingly the focus of Argentina's diplomatic effort. Costa Mendez spoke over the phone to Galtieri:

> personally, I am not inclined to go, while the present circumstances are unclear. I would prefer to search for some alternative way for him to give us the proposal; handing it over to Takacs [the Argentine Ambassador in the US] for example. We will, nevertheless, strive in all ways possible not to break up the negotiations today but with what is happening we cannot exhibit publicly any conduct that is not firm and dignified.

They decided that a proposal could be received from Haig, but only simultaneously with Britain and after the Rio Treaty meeting.

Having received the rebuff from Costa Mendez, Haig telephoned him at 18.45. He expressed concern over the South Georgia action and his desire to continue with the negotiating effort. He would even return to Argentina if necessary.[9] President Reagan himself was now getting involved: he was issuing a proposal to both parties so as to avoid a tragedy for the West. Haig regretted the trend of events but he had warned of this possibility.

Costa Mendez explained that he could not meet Haig in these circumstances: it would be unfavourably interpreted by Argentine public opinion if he appeared to be seeking aid or acknowledging a military problem. Haig said that there was no reason why it should be seen in that way because the visit had been arranged before the attack. Nevertheless he understood and asked only that the meeting be post-poned and not cancelled. Costa Mendez reassured him that his President wished to continue with the negotiations despite the attack. More important from Costa Mendez's point of view was the impact that a meeting with Haig would have had on other Latin American countries just before the IATRA meeting.*

Meanwhile in London, Pym met with the rest of the War Cabinet on Saturday morning on his return from Washington. He knew the outlines of Haig's 'new text' and recommended that it should be accepted as the best negotiated solution available, in that it would have the twin advantages of avoiding war and preserving Britain's position in Latin America. The Prime Minister was unconvinced and anxious lest Pym had given Haig the same positive impression (he had not) and that this might have been passed on to Argentina.[10] By this time, relations between the two were becoming increasingly strained, as Pym sought desperately to avoid a war which Thatcher was coming to accept as almost inevitable.[11]

At this time the operation in South Georgia was at an uncertain stage; if it had ended in a shambles then the position might have changed. The delicacy of the South Georgia operation also distracted the attention of the Prime Minister and her colleagues. They were much more interested in the drama of Operation Paraquat than the intricacies of Haig's proposed settlement.

The anxiety in London that it might be put under pressure is evident in Pym's call to Haig on 26 April that he had 'new ideas', which basically involved a return of the task force if Argentina withdrew, some participation of Argentine residents on the Islands in the local administration, renewed negotiations and other provisions, including a US guarantee. These would have been viewed by Argentina as 'surrender terms'.[12] This communication was less than helpful in that Haig got the idea – which irritated him – that Britain had been working this out behind his back with the Mexicans, who had thrown in the idea of an international conference. There had been discussions with Mexico, largely because London was being polite to any Latin

---

* At a press conference later he explained that he had not met with Haig because of the attack on South Georgia, but he did make an effort to sound conciliatory: 'Argentina appreciates the efforts that the Secretary of State is undertaking with Buenos Aires. I am very surprised that this attack happened the morning before the meeting of the Organization of the American States and before negotiations have ended.'

American country who offered to help, but this was in no way a separate negotiating track. None the less Haig's conviction that it had been led him to assume that the British Government was more anxious for a compromise settlement than it had let on to him.

The American Proposal

On 27 April the two sides were sent the American proposal. Britain – which knew in broad terms what to expect – replied extremely quickly: it would not react in detail until it had the Junta's reaction. Later in the House of Commons Mrs Thatcher explained her position:

> Mr. Haig has put formal American proposals to the Argentine Government and requested an early response. I stress the status of those proposals. They are official American proposals. Mr. Haig judged it right to ask Argentina to give its decision first, as the country to which Security Council Resolution 502 is principally addressed . . . Mr. Haig has also communicated to us the text of his proposals . . .
>
> The proposals are complex and difficult and inevitably bear all the hallmarks of compromise in both their substance and language. But they must be measured against the principles and objectives expressed so strongly in the debates in the House.

In the same debate, Pym outlined the central principles by which the American proposal might be judged and which might lead him to argue for acceptance: 'Our basic position is that Britain is ready to co-operate in any solution which the people of the Falkland Islands could accept and any framework of negotiation which does not pre-determine and does not prejudice the eventual outcome.'[13] Britain was spared the problem of decision by an Argentine rejection.

In the early morning of 27 April the American proposal was received in Buenos Aires. In the covering letter, Haig indicated that he was giving Argentina up to midnight of that day to reply. At 09.30 the Military Committee began its analysis; at 13.00 a working group started its scrutiny at the Ministry of Foreign Affairs. At the same time it was being considered by the Malvinas Working Group and the Minister in Washington. Both groups had reached very similar conclusions by the end of the day.

It was noted that the American proposal was divided into three parts: a memorandum of understanding, a protocol and the letter of acceptance. It lacked a time-limit for the negotiations and Argentine participation in the Legislative and Executive Committees in the Islands. It included a new phrase referring to the 'will and wishes of the islanders'. It lacked reference to the 'territorial integrity' issue and the treatment of the Islands as a whole. The British Government would be in possession of the Islands for an unlimited period. The essence of the proposal was to favour self-determination for the islanders. There would be no possibility of any Argentine military action or diplomatic pressure in the future.

The Military Committee met at 20.30 in Buenos Aires and agreed on its guidelines and recommendations for Costa Mendez should he meet with Haig. The proposal as it stood could not be accepted; acceptance would only be possible with modifications that brought it back into line with the text drafted by Argentina on 19 April.

1) the proposal of the US Government raises complex issues that require a detailed analysis. The Argentine Government is studying this proposal carefully.

2) the Argentine Government wishes to highlight that *prima facie* the proposal contains elements that help towards the progress of the negotiations, though there are other elements that are not adequately treated and that we believe are essential for the satisfactory solution of the issue, in particular we refer to the clauses on the administration of the islands after the lapse of the negotiations proper; the terms and minimum references for these negotiations and the consequences of an eventual prolongation without results further than the date assigned for the end of the negotiations. These present elements are not balanced and prejudge in favour of one of the parties of the dispute.

3) the Argentine Government considers it indispensable to have

more time for the analysis of the proposal so as to be in a position to detail its own points of view and allow for the continuation of the present talks on a basis that allows for a minimum success.

4) the Argentine Government reiterates its readiness to exploit all the available options so as to reach a peaceful solution to the present crisis, so long as the other party to the dispute does not demand preconditions that signify the irreversible rejection of the basic principles that Argentina has sustained for 150 years.

5) the Argentine Government values the efforts of the American Government especially when faced by the growing threat of an aggression by the United Kingdom that today indicates an imminent attack on the Malvinas islands.

Haig had wanted a response by midnight on 27 April. His failure to get one on the grounds that the Junta was still considering it had added to his frustration. He was aware of the likelihood of imminent action by Britain and this could be stopped only by a favourable Argentine response. There was little time left. Although the official response did not come until the next day, a meeting with Costa Mendez on the Wednesday made it clear that the mediation was over.

The Secretary of State warned that Argentina would not obtain a solution through the United Nations; all it would obtain were 'bad alliances' (i.e. Soviet support). It must recognize that it faced war; the British fleet could not now return and an attack should be expected on 30 April. The United States wished Buenos Aires to accept self-determination for the islanders – afterwards it would press the British Government to consider future negotiations. Costa Mendez reported that he would send an answer to the proposal shortly. At this point Haig announced that if Argentina opted for war 'we, Great Britain and the NATO countries will create such pressure that the Argentine Government will fall.'

To this Costa Mendez replied that the Malvinas was a national cause and not one of the military regime; that they had already received the solidarity of the inter-American community, which recognized only Argentine sovereignty over the Islands and that Argentina could not understand why efforts to obtain peace could not continue.

235

He indicated that there were two alternatives open: efforts through the good offices of the US Government or the mediation of the United Nations.

Then he asked whether the United Kingdom had rejected the American proposal. He was told that the British did not like the document and that Thatcher would certainly express her disagreement with it as she believed that the crisis was entirely of Argentina's making. The document offered a fundamental change in the status quo of the Islands but the implications could not be made more explicit by being couched in any other language; it could not prejudge the outcome of the negotiations. If a war broke out, he continued, then the US would have to back Britain.

Costa Mendez informed Haig of those aspects of his proposals which raised the greatest problems for Buenos Aires: the lack of effective guidance as to what would happen if the negotiations should stall by 31 December 1982, and the reference to the 'wishes' of the islanders and the proposed referendum. This was all contrary to Argentina's long-standing position as well to the United Nations resolutions. Argentina did not wish to reject the document but wanted to discuss these two points further.

Haig then said that the document was very good as it was; if Argentina accepted it, he would force Great Britain into doing likewise. Costa Mendez returned to the problem of the dichotomy between the wishes and interests of the islanders. Argentina was not overly worried about the actual wording of the text but more so as regards the final result of the proceedings.

Haig told Costa Mendez that everything could be reduced to a question of trust and that the United Kingdom would not be able to confront another crisis of this sort. Costa Mendez reacted by indicating that the United States was the Western world's superpower and that he could understand the emotional bonds between the US and the United Kingdom. However, Washington should not forget that its interests in Latin America were at least as important as those that tied it to Britain.

Finally, after a long silence, Haig said that if war came the United States would have to apportion blame. He also insisted that, even if

Argentina answered the proposal positively, it should not expect President Reagan to force the outcome of the negotiations because the President would not survive politically if he did so. Costa Mendez left after promising to send the official Argentine reply the next day.

The official response followed the lines agreed by the Junta and outlined by Costa Mendez to Haig: Argentina asked for more time and for changes in some of the clauses. At 13.45 hours Enders brought the reply from Haig: the changes proposed by Argentina were unacceptable. This would be made public the next day, when he would inform the press that the American efforts had failed and that Argentina was responsible for this. He also indicated that the text would state that the British Government had been ready to accept the proposal. He would conclude by asking the US Government for military and economic sanctions against Argentina. In the same letter to Costa Mendez, Haig mentioned the possibility of even greater sanctions against Argentina and added that he would advise all American citizens to leave the country.

The US Tilt

Throughout this period support for Britain had been building up in the United States. The British Embassy in Washington mounted a major public relations campaign to persuade American opinion to support Britain, which could be presented as not only the aggrieved party but also democratic and a close and long-standing friend and ally. Ambassador Henderson made regular appearances on television and radio.[14]

Within Congress pressure grew for a more pro-British stance. Contact with British officials (including Pym when in Washington on 22 April) and the influence of anglophile members of the Administration (such as Weinberger) and of key Senators led to the drafting of a resolution supportive of Britain. On the evening of 28 April, the day before Senators Joseph Biden and Daniel Moynihan were to put the resolution before the Senate, Haig briefed Senators on the fate of his mediation, blaming Argentina for intransigence. The resolution was passed,* 79–1, with only the right-wing Jesse Helms voting against.[15]

Not long afterwards, at 21.00 Washington time, Haig contacted Ambassador Takacs to warn him that the United States would tilt in favour of Britain the next day. His statement on 30 April, along lines agreed at a short National Security Council meeting, described the reasons for his attempt at mediation and the final proposal. As Britain had not exactly accepted his compromise he chose his words carefully: 'We had reason to hope that the United Kingdom would consider a settlement along the lines of our proposal, but Argentina informed us yesterday that it could not accept it.'

Given Argentina's refusal to accept this compromise he reported on the 'concrete steps' now to be taken to demonstrate that the US 'cannot and will not condone the use of unlawful force to resolve disputes'. The steps took the form of limited economic sanctions and a presidential directive 'to respond positively to requests for matériel support for British forces'. He did however conclude with a warning for London: 'A strictly military outcome cannot endure over time. In the end, there will have to be a negotiated outcome acceptable to the interested parties. Otherwise, we will all face unending hostility and insecurity in the South Atlantic.'

Conclusion

Was the Haig mediation doomed from the start? There can be little doubt that the Secretary of State brought to the effort considerable personal energy and commitment. A number of personal motives have been attributed to him, from trumping the achievements of his former boss, Henry Kissinger, in his successful shuttle around the Middle

---

* Senate Resolution 382, 29 April 1982:

Resolved: that the United States cannot stand neutral with regard to implementation of Security Council Resolution 502 and recognizes the right of the United Kingdom and all other nations to the right of self-determination under the United Nations Charter, should therefore prepare, through consultations with Congress, to further all efforts pursuant to Security Council Resolution 502, to achieve full withdrawal of Argentine forces from the Falkland Islands.

East in the aftermath of the 1973 Yom Kippur War, to obtaining a Nobel Peace Prize.

The United States also had national interest involved. There was every incentive to end the conflict as soon as possible before serious fighting began and the United States was obliged to choose sides. Both Argentina and Britain had good reason to expect American support and if either were let down there would be a price to pay in the respective region.

Haig's image as a mediator in this case is tarnished by the fact that he failed. To some extent this reflected personal limitations; tact, patience and calm temper were not his strengths. He was also, but by no means unusually, unfamiliar with the details of the Falklands dispute. It was difficult to prepare properly for the mediation, and this meant that he did not always appreciate the nuances of the dispute and the symbolic baggage carried by words such as 'interests' and 'wishes' when considering the views of the islanders.

Haig was not helped by the character of the decision-making in the two sides. In Britain some problems were caused by the fact that Francis Pym had come suddenly to his position and did not enjoy the full confidence of the Prime Minister. However, at least Haig was able to deal directly with Mrs Thatcher and he was in no doubt as to who was in charge. In Argentina he became increasingly exasperated with a lack of a clear line of authority and consequently a series of confused and at times contradictory messages. In practice the problem was less that of every senior officer having his say – the soundings being taken among the military were not much different in kind from those being undertaken among backbench MPs in Britain. It was more the lack of co-ordination between the Argentine negotiating team, President Galtieri and the rest of the Junta. This meant that apparent concessions did not always survive the scrutiny of the Military Committee. At least twice this put Costa Mendez in the position of delivering last-minute messages to Haig as he left Buenos Aires which substantially qualified the most recent understanding and helped to weaken the credibility of Costa Mendez as an interlocutor.

The very simplicity of the issue created its own difficulties, for it was not possible to draw on a range of interlocking issues to produce a series of complex trade-offs. Basic principles of sovereignty and self-determination were at stake and these do not leave a lot of room for compromise, especially with the addition of prestige. Because it was easy to measure the degree of compromise being offered at any time, both sides had to be careful as to how far they could be seen to be moving along that path lest they offend their domestic constituencies.

During and after the war both sides accused the other of intransigence. In practice both did make concessions that were significant in a domestic context, and this was even more markedly so in the later UN mediation. However, although the concessions were not trivial they steered clear of the central question. Argentina considered that it was offering a great deal in respecting the way of life of the islanders and allowing Britain a continuing role in the South Atlantic, but it had to be confident that it had broken through on the sovereignty issue.

Thatcher agreed changes to the character of the administration of the Falklands which would have been unthinkable a month earlier and were direct gains to Argentina from the occupation. An interesting comparison is the controversy surrounding the Anglo-Irish agreement of 1984, which was severely criticized for allowing a foreign government special privileges in the governance of British territory. Thatcher also agreed to change the status of the Islands, and if the Haig plan had been accepted then it might have been hard to avoid some change to the ownership of the Islands. What she could not do was to reward Argentine aggression by handing over the Islands.

Haig's difficulty was compounded by the fact that it was by no means clear to what extent either side *needed* to compromise because battle had yet to be joined. Here a comparison with Kissinger's shuttle diplomacy after the October 1973 Arab–Israeli war is instructive. Then the participants had just been through a war and nobody wanted another round. The power balance had been shaken but Israel did have the upper hand militarily. On the other hand, its need for resupply meant that it could not disregard American pressure to compromise.

In April 1982 the United States lacked that sort of leverage over either side, although Argentina believed that Britain was as dependent on the United States as Israel had been in October 1973. It was uncertain whether either Government would go through with a military confrontation and, if both did, what the likely result would be. Haig believed that if Britain went to war it would win, but this was by no means a unanimous view even within the American Government. Many on the British side were also nervous. Yet they had sufficient grounds for optimism to create few grounds for compromise. The true strength of the parties was only going to become apparent in the fighting. In these circumstances every concession could appear to weaken a future negotiating position and could be criticized as negotiating under duress. So long as Argentina was unconvinced that Britain would actually fight or that, if it did, it would succeed there was no need to renounce its fundamental objective.

A final problem was that the United States was not disinterested. It could not but lose out if the two parties came to blows, hence its interests would be best served by a peaceful settlement. But it also could not be seen to be pressing Britain, of all countries, to reward a breach of international law, nor could it allow Britain to be defeated. Haig was not simply making himself available as a channel of communication to two parties who refused to speak directly. He was continually developing and refining an American position.

Thus even-handedness characterized the diplomatic formalities necessary to maintain the channels of communication with the two parties. However, it never described the American attitude to the issues at hand. From the first official reaction on 2 April to the speech at the Rio Treaty meeting on 27 April the US had consistently and publicly condemned the Argentine use of force to settle the dispute. Haig made it clear to the Junta that if war came the United States would have to back Britain. It therefore never occurred to him that he should ask for equal concessions from the two sides. As this dawned on the Argentine negotiators they became annoyed at what they perceived as unfairness and felt frustrated because they believed that the true nature of the British position was being concealed from them.

The essence of the shuttle was to extract sufficient concessions from Britain to allow Argentina to get itself off the hook. This strategy involved two major gambles. First, that in the end concessions could be extracted from Thatcher on the basis of American proposals that went beyond those agreed in prior discussions. Britain did not endorse Haig's final proposal and had clear reservations. Even if Argentina had accepted it Britain was not obliged to do so. Haig sought to convince Argentina that he could persuade Thatcher to agree. He would have had some support within the Cabinet and Thatcher would have been hard put to ignore him. But it could well have led to a crisis in Anglo-American relations.

A more serious gamble lay in seeking to persuade Argentina that as a result of these concessions there was a good possibility that the occupation had changed everything and that the process being set in motion would most probably result in a transfer of sovereignty even if that could not be stated explicitly. In part this would result from the administrative structure and negotiating process that Haig hoped to create. It also reflected the view that few in Britain believed that the Falklands were a great strategic asset that must be clung to at all costs. Britain would be happy to hand the land over to Argentina. But this had been the case for years; the problem was that it could not be seen to be handing the people over against their will.

In this context the principle of self-determination was inconsistent with a transfer of sovereignty and it is hard to see how, in the aftermath of the conflict, with promises having being made to Parliament that nothing of importance had been compromised, the principle of self-determination could have been jettisoned. The Argentine use of force had itself changed the issue and would make it doubly difficult to be seen to compromise.

The British approach to the negotiations, including the retaking of South Georgia as key decisions were about to be made, confirmed Argentine doubts that Haig would be able to deliver British concessions in the sovereignty negotiations – or even try to do so – unless there were firm guarantees. Operation Paraquat rebuffed a consistent Argentine demand during the negotiations – that the British task force should not move south from Ascension.

Argentina had argued for a cease-fire so long as the negotiations had any chance of success. Of course, by the British calculation the negotiations had no chance of success unless the task force kept moving. It was not something that could easily be withheld. It was a perishable asset, with the problems of supply, the condition of the service personnel and the onset of winter prime considerations. The British Government would consider holding the task force back only if Argentina withdrew from the Islands; instead Argentina had been reinforcing its position.

Haig had not been disposed to argue the point with London. He himself felt that only the prospect of a confrontation with Britain induced any sort of flexibility in the Argentine posture.

As a result, by the time the Haig mediation came to an end and the tilt to Britain was announced, the task force was in position to begin the operations leading to the reoccupation of the Falkland Islands. In this way Haig's diplomacy benefited Britain. It gave the subsequent use of force an international and domestic legitimacy that it would have lacked without this sort of backing, especially as Haig clearly blamed Argentina for the failure of his mission.

Part Five

COLLISION

Chapter Sixteen

THE SINKING OF THE *BELGRANO*

Rules of Engagement

There was no formal state of war between Britain and Argentina. Such a state would have carried with it many awkward implications for Britain, Argentina and other important nations, such as the United States. The lack of a declaration of war meant that Britain was obliged to justify Operation Corporate in terms of the 'inherent right of self-defence under Article 51 of the UN Charter', which it reinforced by reference to Resolution 502.*

There is always a question of whether acting in self-defence imposes any limitations on the sort of military action permitted. At what point might it exceed the requirements of self-defence? Exercising this 'inherent right' *after* the seizure of territory by another country is likely to require the use of sufficient force to eject the enemy from that territory. If one is forced to stay on the tactical defensive, in respect of some concept of proportionality, then all the advantages flow to the aggressor, whose offensive action has been completed.

There is therefore no reason in principle why self-defence cannot involve going on to the offensive. The commander of the task force was charged with bringing about the withdrawal of the Argentine

---

* Article 51 states: 'Nothing in the present Charter shall impair the inherent right of individual or collective self-defence if an armed attack occurs against a member of the United Nations, until the Security Council has taken the measures necessary to maintain international peace and security.'

forces from the Falkland Islands and re-establishing British administration. Once military operations have begun in earnest the question of what constitutes minimum force becomes moot and the casualties likely to result from any given exercise almost impossible to calculate.

None the less, in order to maintain some political control over military operations, the forces were required to follow rules of engagement. These varied in scope from strategic to detailed tactical instructions. They defined the freedom of action of the commander on the spot rather than controlled matters directly through precise instructions. The military interest is normally to encourage the enemy to assume that the commander's freedom is greater than it actually is. So, in addition to the rules sent to the task force command, the British Government issued a series of public statements which defined the terms under which it would take action against Argentine forces. In general the rules under which British forces were actually operating were more restrictive than those communicated to the outside world.

As British forces drew closer to the South Atlantic the potential scope and intensity of hostilities grew. In the weeks before the bulk of the task force arrived all the British could do was inhibit Argentine reinforcements. This was the purpose of the Maritime Exclusion Zone (MEZ) announced on 7 April to take effect from 12 April. The military would have been content to call it a blockade, but this created problems under international law, and so the more neutral terminology was adopted.

The MEZ took the form of a circle of 200 nautical miles from latitude 51° 41' south and longitude 59° 39' west, approximately the centre of the Islands.

> From the time indicated, any Argentine warships and Argentine naval auxiliaries found within this Zone will be treated as hostile and are liable to be attacked by British forces. This measure is without prejudice to the right of the United Kingdom to take whatever additional measures may be needed in exercise of its right of self-defence, under Article 51 of the United Nations Charter.

The zone was not a territorial zone, which would have been an awkward shape and would have led to ambiguities in interpretation. A circle was more precise although this did mean that some parts of the Islands were only 100 miles from the edge of the Zone. Despite the fact that 200 miles was similar to the distance used in economic zones, it was actually chosen to provide, according to Lewin,

> enough room between the edge of the zone and the safe haven of a port in the Falklands to be able to signal to a merchant ship, invite it to stop, chase it if it did not stop, fire a shot across it bows, continue to signal to it . . . Our experience in fishery wars has shown us that this takes quite a lot of distance.[1]

However, when the MEZ was declared, merchant ships could not be covered by its provisions. This was because the only means of enforcing the MEZ was by the use of nuclear submarines – the first of which arrived in the Zone on 12 April – and which are unsuitable for mounting challenges to merchant ships. The advantages of nuclear submarines are lost if they are obliged to surface in order to issue warnings and invite a reversal of course (which would be required if challenging a merchant ship).

On Wednesday 28 April the British Government announced the establishment of a Total Exclusion Zone (TEZ) around the Falkland Islands to take effect from 11.00 GMT on 30 April.* This made it clear that the British would attempt to seal off the Argentine garrison from all further reinforcement. The announcement stated that:

> Any ship and any aircraft whether military or civil which is found within this Zone without due authority from the Ministry of Defence in London will be regarded as operating in support of the illegal occupation and will therefore be regarded as hostile and will be liable to be attacked by British forces.
>
> Also from the time indicated, Port Stanley airport will be closed; and any aircraft on the ground in the Falkland Islands will be

---

* Argentina met both the 7 and 28 April declarations with declarations of its own. The United Nations was informed of both sets of declarations in the form of Circular Notes to the Security Council.

regarded as present in support of the illegal occupation and accordingly is liable to attack.

As with the previous warning there was the same rider to the effect that the measures were 'without prejudice' to what else might be done in exercise of the UK's right of self-defence under Article 51 of the UN Charter. This proviso was later stressed by Britain in explaining why there was no reason for Argentine forces to believe that the TEZ was a combat exclusion zone.

This latter point had already been emphasized on 23 April in amplification of the statement establishing the MEZ. The 23 April statement explained the reference to 'additional measures' as follows:

In this connection, HMG now wishes to make clear that any approach on the part of Argentine warships, including submarines, naval auxiliaries, or military aircraft, which could amount to a threat to interfere with the mission of the British Forces in the South Atlantic will encounter the appropriate response.

All Argentine aircraft including civil aircraft engaging in surveillance of these British Forces will be regarded as hostile and are liable to be dealt with accordingly.

According to Lewin this statement was made necessary because of the various threats faced by the task force from Argentine submarines, carrier-based aircraft and surface ships as it approached the Falklands and the lack of sufficient surveillance capability to provide early warning. 'We could not wait for them to fire first, because if we did our ships would be hit, such is the accuracy of modern missiles.' Ministers were initially reluctant to change the rules of engagement to allow for attacks against warships which were deemed a threat simply because they were approaching the task force, but eventually they were persuaded.[2]

Submarines had received rules of engagement earlier than the surface ships, permitting them to attack Argentine warships in the MEZ. There was no need for them at this time to be allowed to attack warships outside the MEZ: submarines ought not to be at risk from surface warships as they can prevent themselves from being detected and usually take effective evasive action if they are. Right from the start they had been allowed to attack any submarine that they came across. It had been learned from the United States that, in exercises, the Argentine Navy's diesel 209 submarines were quieter than nuclear-powered submarines and might catch them unawares. The order was to shoot another submarine on detection. Special measures were taken, including informal contacts with the Brazilian Navy, to ensure that if another submarine were detected it could only be Argentine.

The reference to the civilian aircraft in the warning was prompted by the earlier reconnaissance by an Argentine Boeing 707 transport. There was concern that this might result in the position, course and speed of elements in the task force being passed on to a submarine.

The passage concerning a 'threat to interfere with the mission of the British forces' could be invoked to describe almost any Argentine military activity. The statement was released just before the attack on the Argentine submarine *Santa Fé* and the retaking of South Georgia on 25 April, operations undertaken well outside the MEZ and for reasons other than the direct defence of the task force. This passage was understood by Argentine commanders, although they thought it might be preparing the ground for an attack on the mainland air bases.

In a speech to the Commons on 29 April the Prime Minister referred to the retaking of South Georgia as an exercise in self-defence and made it clear that the Government was willing to take further military steps, given that the UN was unable to enforce compliance with UN Resolution 502.

In reinforcing this stance, Pym implied that further exercise of the right of self-defence was bound up with the enforcement of the TEZ. However, the possibility of action outside the TEZ should negotiations fail was not ruled out; nor was it suggested (for example in connection with the retaking of South Georgia) that the obligation to inform the Security Council of all actions undertaken under Article 51 had to be respected prior to the measures actually being implemented.

After our re-taking of South Georgia by the carefully limited use of force – the minimum use of force is the present instruction and rules of engagement – Argentina surely abandoned any lingering doubts that Britain would exercise her right of self-defence. We shall certainly do so again if Argentina was so reckless as to violate the total exclusion zone. We are ready to do so, if unhappily, Argentina cannot be brought to accept a negotiated settlement . . .[3]

In the afternoon of 30 April, with the task force now virtually in position, the Haig negotiating effort having failed and American support for Britain announced, the War Cabinet decided on the next military steps to be taken. The key actions proposed were that a Vulcan bomber would leave Ascension Island that evening in order to mount an attack on the runway at Stanley airfield and that this would be followed with Harrier attacks on the airport, backed up by naval bombardment.

The main area of controversy surrounded the desire of the task force commander to attack the aircraft carrier *25 de Mayo*, wherever it could be found. Up to 23 April the nuclear submarine *Splendid* had kept a watch on *25 de Mayo* as it exercised close to the Argentine coast. Requests from the task force to torpedo the carrier were refused, because it was considered too high-profile and therefore politically sensitive a target. Now as matters were shifting into a higher military gear and *25 de Mayo* had moved out of territorial waters, permission was granted 'to attack the *25 de Mayo* on the high seas, that is both within and outside the Total Exclusion Zone, in circumstances in which it posed a military threat to the task force'.[4]

It is clear from this that ministers wished to ensure that any attack should be mounted only if there were evidence of a direct threat to the task force, and they had restricted this permission to the single most threatening unit of the enemy fleet. *Splendid*, which had by now lost contact, was not ordered to hunt and kill the *25 de Mayo* but to move to a patrol area where any contact would in itself be incontrovertible evidence that the carrier was constituting a threat to the 'mission' of the task force.[5] This, therefore, was why the War Cabinet accepted that the carrier might be sunk, rather than as a means of turning the military balance in Britain's favour. Even then the military advisers found it difficult to persuade their political masters that the carrier, given the range of its aircraft, should be viewed as a warship with guns of 250-mile range that became a threat almost as soon as it left port. Here they found an ally in the Attorney General, Sir Michael Havers, who had served in the Fleet Air Arm during the war.

However, with the Foreign Secretary, Sir Michael was not without misgivings. It was decided that the 23 April statement would suffice as warning to the Argentine forces. But Pym queried this before leaving for Washington on 1 May. Having consulted with Havers, he wrote to Thatcher with regard to:

> the way in which our action would have to be publicly justified and its legality defended. I believe our position would be immeasurably strengthened if we had given a warning to the Argentine government, requiring the aircraft carrier to stay within the narrow zone we discussed yesterday, or within territorial waters south of about 41 degrees South.

He attached:

> a draft of a possible warning message which we could ask the Swiss to convey urgently to the Argentine government. This is no way alters the substance of the decision we took yesterday. But I believe it would greatly strengthen our hand in dealing with criticism at home and abroad once an attack on the carrier had been carried out.

Pym's draft specifically mentioned the *25 de Mayo* and warned that it would be at risk if it ventured beyond territorial waters. It went on to say that 'if any attack anywhere in the South Atlantic is made upon British naval or air forces by an Argentine unit, all other Argentine naval units operating on the high seas, including the carrier "THE 25TH OF MAY", would be considered hostile and are liable to be dealt with accordingly.'[6]

If such a message had been sent then it would not have eased Britain's political position in the aftermath of the sinking of the *Belgrano* because it mentioned only the carrier. It was unlikely that the military would have accepted it because of the requirement that

Argentine forces must fire first. This was considered too much of a risk, in that the first shots can be decisive in any engagement. At any rate no such warning was sent. By the time the War Cabinet next met the military situation had changed dramatically.

When Pym arrived in Washington he did not appear to expect further military action to follow from the previously agreed change in the rules. In a press conference he explained that the day's action had been intended to 'concentrate Argentine minds'. 'No further military action is envisaged for the moment other than making the Total Exclusion Zone secure.' Even this statement was not without ambiguity. What were the requirements for making the TEZ secure? The natural presumption was no more than preventing Argentine aircraft or ships entering the zone.

Although this statement reinforced perceptions that further military action was unlikely on 2 May, Pym was in no position to offer reassurance. He was not up to date on the military developments that had taken place on the day of his journey and which were not to be confined to the first of the month.

British Military Operations on 1 May

It had been hoped initially that the first actions to enforce the Total Exclusion Zone would take place on the day that it came into effect, 30 April. Bad weather on 27 April had hindered the progress of the task force by a day, although at one point it was feared that it might be two.[7] The directive to Woodward was to enforce the TEZ. He chose to do this with an eye to the future requirements of a landing.

> My initial plan was to lay on a major demonstration of force well inside the Exclusion Zone to make the Argentines believe that landings were about to take place and thus provoke a reaction that would allow me to conduct a major attrition exercise before the amphibious force actually arrived to complicate my problem. And at the very least, I might discover whether they had a coherent defensive plan.[8]

Woodward's objective therefore was to tempt Argentine forces into engagements. The other requirement was reliable intelligence on the disposition and strength of the Argentine units on the Falklands. In the absence of decent satellite or aerial photography it was necessary to insert Special Air Service and Special Boat Service patrols on the Islands to obtain the necessary information. All this was set in motion on 1 May.

The attack was in three stages. First, in the early-morning darkness the airport at Stanley was attacked by a single Vulcan bomber, which had been operating from Ascension, and managed the trip using seven in-flight refuellings. A bomb was put in the middle of the runway. Through radio communications with an Islander, Woodward asked General Menendez to surrender.

Second, at dawn, after the British had learned of the success of the Vulcan raid, Sea Harriers launched low-level attacks on the airfields at Stanley and Goose Green. After these attacks they returned to the task force to operate in an air-defence role to meet the expected Argentine response. Third, in the late afternoon a small contingent of warships moved close to the Falklands, bombarded the Stanley airfield and generally gave the impression of preparing for seaborne landings. In addition, throughout the day two frigates and several Sea King helicopters maintained a constant anti-submarine patrol.[9] Intelligence information had come in two days earlier that a submarine had been ordered into the area. A number of inaccurate contacts were made and depth-charges released, but to no effect. Before the bombardment by the warships had ceased just before midnight, the first special services' patrols had been inserted on the Islands.[10]

The Vulcan attack on the airfield was a considerable technical achievement. As far as was known on 1 May it had damaged the runway but problems of post-attack reconnaissance made it unclear exactly what had been achieved. In practice it was all that might have been expected but less than hoped.[11]

The Argentine Air Force had been tempted out and there had been major engagements. It lost two Mirages, one Dagger and a Canberra to Sea Harriers. In addition an Islander and a Pucara had been hit at Stanley and Goose Green airfields respectively. There was reason to be well satisfied with the performance of the Sea Harriers in aerial combat with the Mirages. Only one Sea Harrier was damaged but not so that it could not land and be repaired.

On the other hand, the actual attrition achieved had been limited. The Argentine Air Force was not severely depleted and thereafter conserved its resources until the main landings actually did take place. Although no Argentine aircraft had successfully penetrated the screen protecting the carrier group, those attacking the detachment bombarding Stanley had been more successful. *Glamorgan* and *Arrow* received slight damage. The commanders were all too aware of how the damage to *Glamorgan* in particular could have been much worse.

Meanwhile, despite intensive anti-submarine activity the Argentine submarine believed to be operating was not found. It was hoped that it had been given an unpleasant time. More seriously, the Argentine Navy was believed to be at sea but it had yet to be engaged by the Royal Navy. In particular, *Splendid* had not come across the *25 de Mayo*, although it has been reported that it made long-range towed-array sonar contact with the carrier's escorting destroyers.[12]

At the end of the day Admiral Woodward felt that 'The reactions we got indicate that the plan succeeded, at least initially. There was considerable Argentine air activity on 1 May. We made some limited attrition and we learned quite a bit.'[13]

Argentine Operations

Argentine sources describe the same pattern of activity. There are, however, two significant differences which are extremely important in relation to the following day's events. The first concerned the damage to Stanley airfield, which was immediately assessed to have been of only limited effectiveness. More important it was firmly believed that air defences had successfully shot down two Sea Harriers during their early-morning raids. The implications for the British task force, if this were so, were grave for this would represent 10 per cent of its total capability. Moreover, reports suggested that serious damage had been inflicted on the British warships that had been conducting the naval bombardment.[14]

The Argentine explanation for the withdrawal of the task force was therefore quite different. The Argentine commanders had been readily convinced that the British had been attempting a landing, probably, it was thought, to gain a foothold on the Islands to strengthen their negotiating position. Instead of coming to recognize it as a feint, they assumed that the British activity represented a not very efficient version of the real thing. This had been abandoned because of the performance of the Argentine resistance, in particular by the air defences around Stanley and those aircraft which had inflicted severe damage on the bombarding warships.

There had been disappointments – the apparent failure of the submarine's torpedoes[15] and, rather significant in terms of later events, the failure to mount an attack with two Exocet-armed Super-Etendards as a result of problems with the initial refuelling.[16] Nevertheless, the overall feeling was positive. Taking on the British task force did not seem such a hopeless task.

The Argentine Chiefs of Staff assessment on the morning of 2 May was that the withdrawal of the British fleet beyond the radius of Argentine air operations implied a wish to avoid further losses and for an opportunity to consider its capacity to continue military activities.[17]

On 27 April the Argentine Navy had been deployed to counter an anticipated landing by British forces.[18] On 29 April the fleet split into two groups, moving into position to cover the Falklands. The larger group comprised the *25 de Mayo* with two guided-missile destroyers, plus four smaller destroyers and frigates. This later split into two (Task Groups 79.1 and 79.4) and took positions just outside the MEZ and to the north-west of the Islands (TG 79.1 was 270 nautical miles east of the Gulf of San Jorge in Patagonia, and TG 79.4 north-east of the same position). The smaller group, including the cruiser *The General Belgrano*, plus two destroyers (Task Group 79.3), moved into position, 260 miles to the south of the Islands. Their orders were to 'find and destroy the British fleet if the Islands or the mainland were attacked'.[19] The Navy had been ordered to respect the British-imposed 200-mile zone and also not to initiate attacks.

At 15.13 on 1 May Admiral Allara commanding GT.1 (Task Group 1) on *25 de Mayo* had received aerial reconnaissance to the effect that seven British warships were some 120 miles away, north of Stanley. Lombardo later recalled:

> Our people in Falklands, in Malvinas, they began to say there was a disembarkation ... A landing by helicopters and by craft, by boats, both things in several points, near Puerto Argentino, near Port Stanley ... So I must accept that this was the day of the landing.
>
> We thought that the British were going to concentrate near Port Stanley and we tried to attack isolated ships or small groups of ships out of that region. The Air Force were going to attack the ships near Port Stanley.[20]

At around the same time information came from Rear Admiral Otero of the South Atlantic Command that there was a 'landing underway north of the Islands'. Ships were reported to be distributed between 010 degrees and 145 degrees off Stanley, at intervals of 90, 40 and 10 nautical miles, with Sea Harriers providing cover.[21]

At 15.55, on receipt of Admiral Allara's information, Lombardo gave him 'freedom of action to attack'. This was interpreted by Allara as a revision of the Argentine rules of engagement. He could now take action against the British fleet and he ordered the groups under his command to do so. This change was agreed without reference to higher authorities. There is no reason to believe that if it had been there would have been second thoughts. Admiral Anaya, the Commander-in-Chief of the Navy, was anxious that the Navy was not responding quickly enough and that all the battle honours were going to the Air Force. He sent orders to Lombardo to get the Navy involved and then relented, feeling that this was unfair. Lombardo was 'nearer the action' and so must do what he judged 'necessary and adequate'. In fact Lombardo had already ordered the attack.[22]

On being given freedom of action, Allara started to move towards the task force. At 20.07, with more evidence coming in of British bombardments and possible landings, Allara gave a general order to initiate offensive operations.[23] As late as 20.39 General Menendez in Stanley was convinced that a landing was taking place. At 20.55 there was intense naval fire over the airstrip and helicopters came near the coast. However, just before midnight the ships stopped firing and withdrew.[24] There had been no Sea Harrier attacks since 19.00.[25] At around this time, the first SAS units were being landed on East Falkland. If, as has been suggested, Argentine shore radars detected the Sea King helicopters delivering the SAS men, then that might have reinforced the impression of an attempted landing.[26]

At midday a Tracker aircraft, engaged on a reconnaissance mission, discovered six of the British ships. On board the *25 de Mayo* Allara was informed. He hoped to be able to fly off six Skyhawks with a 240-mile combat radius and each armed with six 250kg bombs. He needed 40 knots of wind to be able to achieve this. At 22.00 the wind started to drop. He now calculated that it would take until 06.00 before he could be in a position to mount the attack. Two hours later at midnight the wind had dropped further. To get the planes off the carrier they would need to carry less fuel and weapons. Their radius of action was reduced to 140 miles and the load to two bombs. It was now estimated that an attack would not be possible until 11.00 on 2 May. None the less Allara decided to continue to move towards the task force.

At 00.30 on 2 May an echo was detected at some 110 miles distance coming towards GT.1. This was soon identified as a Sea Harrier. The aircraft circled some 60–70 miles away from GT.1, which it had apparently spotted. At 01.19 Lombardo sent Allara the following signal: 'Your 012007: There have been no further air attacks on the Malvinas after 011900. I do not know the position of the enemy aircraft carriers. The free-ranging enemy still constitutes a strong threat to task force 79.'[27]

If the enemy were not now attacking Stanley then they could be anywhere within a wide radius. So not only was there now not an immediate *need* to attack the Royal Navy, for there was no landing taking place, but there was now a threat to the Argentine fleet. This was not an order to withdraw but the implication was clear. Allara was well aware of the risks, having just been spotted by an enemy Sea Harrier. At 01.45 he reported back to Lombardo that there was little point in continuing because the wind conditions rendered an attack impossible, and the forecast for the next day suggested that there would be no improvement. He therefore ordered the task groups to go 'back to their former positions ... That is to say, the two groups in the north to their continent and the group in south to their Staten Island.'[28] He wanted to return to shallower waters to reduce the risk of falling victim to submarine attack. When Admiral Anaya arrived at Operations Headquarters at 02.30 he confirmed the messages by Allara and Lombardo and annulled the orders to take offensive action.

Meanwhile, the *Belgrano* and its two accompanying destroyers were patrolling between the Isla de los Estados and Burdwood Bank to the south-west of the Falklands, with the twin objective of preventing any British warships joining the task force from the Pacific and providing warning of any movement towards the mainland.[29] It was also acting as a counter to any Chilean intervention. On the afternoon of 1 May it received orders not to approach the Exclusion Zone or engage the enemy without further authorization, but to pose a lateral threat so as to force the enemy to divide. It shared orders with the rest of the fleet to intercept enemy units that were damaged, isolated or had strayed from the main body of the British task force if the opportunity arose. It was not engaged in a frontal attack.[30]

At 02.50 the Commander of the *Belgrano* received Allara's order of 01.45. It was not until 05.11 that he actually began to turn. This manoeuvre was completed at 06.00, by which time the cruiser was pointing in the direction of Staten Island. Some ten hours later it was hit by two torpedoes on the port side. It immediately lost power and began to list. Half an hour later evacuation was ordered and then at 17.02 the *Belgrano* sank. An accompanying destroyer, *Hipolito Bouchard*, believed it had been hit by a third torpedo which had failed to explode. With the other destroyer, *Piedra Buena*, it engaged in anti-submarine measures and moved away.

Lombardo later explained why the destroyers had not helped to pick up survivors by reference to 'the first spectacular submarine action' in the Great War in the Channel. A German submarine torpedoed one British ship, which began to sink, and then picked off the two accompanying ships in turn as each stopped to pick up survivors. 'Ships aren't at sea to pick up survivors,' he added, 'but to fight and not to be sunk.'[31] In the most costly single engagement of the war, 321 of the *Belgrano*'s crew lost their lives.

Woodward's Request

Coming so many hours after the fighting on 1 May this British attack appeared unrelated to the earlier combat. However, this was not the case. It followed closely the previous day's action. To explain this it is necessary to return to the British understanding of the military situation.

On 30 April *Conqueror* had been sent into the area of Tierra del Fuego and told to look for the *Belgrano*. The information that the cruiser was in the area may have come from sources in Chile: according to one account a message was sent from the Chilean Naval Command in Punta Arenas to the British Military Attaché in Santiago in late April, through an intermediary.[32] Late that afternoon *Conqueror* picked up the first noises on towed-array sonar. In fact this was an oil tanker accompanying *Belgrano*.

Conqueror's orders, received at 21.00 local time on 30 April, were to intercept the *Belgrano* and attack it when it penetrated, as was expected, the Total Exclusion Zone. The next morning it sighted *Belgrano* and the two accompanying destroyers being refuelled by the tanker. At 11.00 the three ships began to sail off south-east at 8 knots. The *Conqueror* began to trail and signalled to Fleet Headquarters at Northwood on the outskirts of London that it had made contact and gave its current position and course.[33] The signal also reached Admiral Woodward on board *Hermes*. At 01.00 on 2 May *Conqueror* reported that it was still on the trail of the *Belgrano*.

Admiral Woodward wanted the *Conqueror* to attack the *Belgrano*. He issued a direct order to *Conqueror* to attack at 04.10 (08.10 BST) on the morning of 2 May.[34] This had to go through Northwood, where Admiral Herbert, commanding the submarines, countermanded it because he recognized that it would require political approval. Woodward had authority to attack threatening Argentine ships with his own surface ships or aircraft, and could have done so in this case, though not so easily. What he now requested required a change in the rules of engagement, a move that Northwood was already considering. A signal was sent from Northwood to a probably surprised Captain Wreford Brown on *Conqueror* at 06.15 ordering him not to mount an attack until the rules were changed.[35]

Although Britain now appeared locked into a possibly unlimited naval engagement with Argentina, the task force was limited in the use it could make of its most lethal weapons – the nuclear submarines – by the established rules of engagement. At Northwood there was irritation with Woodward. It has been suggested that Admiral Fieldhouse signalled his displeasure.[36] None the less, Woodward's request threw into relief an issue that was already being addressed. Fieldhouse endorsed Woodward's view that the rules should be changed to allow for the attack.

At Northwood it was calculated that there was time to obtain a change in the rules of engagement before the *Belgrano* could reach the task force. Not long after Woodward's signal had been received, at 09.15 BST on the morning of 2 May, Admiral Lewin reached Northwood and considered the position with other senior officers before going on to Chequers for a meeting of the War Cabinet. It was agreed that Lewin would press the War Cabinet for a change in the rules of engagement.

Admiral Woodward has explained his concern as follows:

> Early on the morning of 2 May, all the indications were that *25 de Mayo*, the Argentinian carrier, and a group of escorts had slipped past my forward SSN* barrier to the north, while the cruiser *General Belgrano* and her escorts were attempting to complete the pincer movement from the south, still outside the Total Exclusion Zone. But *Belgrano* still had *Conqueror* on the trail. My fear was that *Belgrano* would lose the SSN as she ran over the shallow water of the Burdwood Bank, and that my forward SSN barrier would be evaded there too. I therefore sought, for the first and only time throughout the campaign, a major change to the Rules of Engagement (ROE) to enable *Conqueror* to attack *Belgrano* outside the Exclusion Zone.[37]

Woodward's concern therefore was with the immediate tactical situation in which he found himself. His own past experience in Royal

* SSN – nuclear powered submarine.

Navy exercises with the United States Navy made him aware that carrier groups were not invulnerable to surface action groups. He sent his request to *Conqueror* not long after having received intelligence that the more substantial Argentine group was moving towards him, and the two pieces of information together raised the possibility of a 'pincer movement'. The destroyers accompanying *Belgrano* were known to carry Exocets, and it was possible that the cruiser itself carried this missile.* At any rate its 6in guns outranged the 4.5in British guns. All he had available with which to attack the cruiser were Harriers and the SSN. The Harriers were needed for their air-defence task – especially while there was still a risk of Skyhawks being launched from the *25 de Mayo*. This left *Conqueror*. Here the concern was that should the *Belgrano* move across the submerged ridge known as the Burdwood Bank, *Conqueror* would be hard-pressed to stay in contact, particularly so if it wanted to remain undetected.[38]

On the basis of available intelligence, the assessment at Northwood was also that the Argentine Navy was attempting a pincer movement. What was known at this time about Argentine movements? According to a number of accounts Admiral Allara's signal of 15.55 (19.55 BST) ordering the groups under his command to take the offensive against the British fleet had been intercepted, and it was this that affected the *Belgrano* and her escorts.[39] Lewin has also indicated that the assessment was based on an awareness of a substantial amount of radio traffic between the different units of the Argentine Navy and an 'assessment of what you would have done if you were Argentina'.[40]

The reference to radio traffic reflects an analysis of the position and progress of the Argentine carrier group made by Woodward's staff on the basis of interpretation of 'wireless traffic patterns and observation of the direction of approach of shadowing aircraft from the *25 de*

* Lord Lewin (*Foreign Affairs Committee Report*, p.88) noted:

Every surface ship, according to Jane's Fighting Ships, in the Argentine Navy, with the exception of *Belgrano*, was fitted with Exocet. We knew the Argentinians had spare Exocet launchers and they had plenty of surface-to-surface Exocet missiles. We bolt on our Exocet missiles in two to three weeks outside a dockyard refit. We therefore had to assume that *Belgrano* was equipped with Exocet. We would have been extremely imprudent to assume otherwise. We now know that she was not.

Mayo'. After a radar contact with one of the Tracker search aircraft from the *25 de Mayo*, Sea Harriers flew off to see if they could find the carrier. It was one of these which detected four or five ships not long after midnight local time. The pilot immediately realized as well that he was being illuminated by a Type 909 Sea Dart tracking radar. With this alarming confirmation that he had come across enemy ships he hastened back to *Hermes*.[41] As we now know, this contact itself was a critical factor in the Argentine decision to withdraw and this was being implemented as the officers at Northwood considered how to cope with a threat which they still assumed to be developing.

It has been suggested that Lombardo's signal of 01.19 (05.19 BST) had also been intercepted by GCHQ but had not been decoded.[42] This signal was more of a warning than an order to withdraw (which came later from Allara), though the implication was there. Other signals may have been intercepted that might have given a clearer picture had they been decoded, but even if this had been achieved the actual deciphering would have taken a number of hours. According to the House of Commons Foreign Affairs Committee, who were shown the available intelligence material: 'the classified evidence we have seen and other evidence authoritatively and conclusively shows that no intercepted orders for a withdrawal of Argentine forces reached the British Government before the sinking of the *Belgrano*.'[43] The most recent direct evidence would have confirmed the impression that the Argentine fleet was still pressing forward. *Conqueror* had signalled at 05.00 London time that it was still trailing *Belgrano*, which was clearly skirting the Exclusion Zone but moving towards the task force at 13 knots.[44]

So the tactical picture was in some ways disconcerting. The Argentine fleet, and in particular the aircraft-carrier, had been drawn out as planned, but the plan had gone awry in that *Splendid* had been unable to make contact with the *25 de Mayo*, which was now leading an Argentine offensive. The only part of this offensive with which there was any contact was the *Belgrano* and the two destroyers accompanying it. It probably did not carry Exocet anti-ship missiles but it might, and the escorting destroyers were so armed. Equally, while the current speed was slow, it could still reach the task force. This was calculated on the basis of the 'Furthest On-Circle' – one whose centre is the last reported position of the enemy and whose radius is the enemy's known maximum speed multiplied by the time that has elapsed since last seen. This circle expands with time. The last reported speed of the *Belgrano* of 13 knots was under half its maximum speed of 30 knots, but a prudent commander getting nervous about the vulnerability of the ships under his command would have felt obliged to assume the worst.[45]

Another tactical risk was that the *Belgrano* could have been part of an effort to retake South Georgia, which was not properly defended at the time. Meanwhile, the need to keep a look-out for it would be an added burden on the hard-pressed helicopter and Harrier resources of the task force.

Yet another factor weighing on the minds of the commanders was the risk of delay in getting special forces ashore to reconnoitre the Islands. According to Lewin:

> So having arrived within range of the Falklands he [Woodward] had to insert special forces covertly, to obtain intelligence of the Argentine dispositions. To do that, he had to approach the Falkland quite closely every night, either to put in or to re-supply the special forces which were involved. He could not do either of those jobs if the Argentinian fleet were at sea. He did not know where they were, and the appreciation was that their intention was to attack him. He could only preserve his safety by going off to the eastward and keeping out of range of the Argentinians. If he did that he could not do his mission.[46]

In addition to concern that the *Belgrano* might have been part of an imminent offensive, there were other reasons why the task force commanders strongly supported an attack. First, one of the original objectives of the previous day's operations had been to create opportunities for attrition against the Argentine Navy and Air Force. The full impact of the loss of the *Belgrano* may not have been anticipated but the opportunity was still one that the commanders were reluctant to miss. To quote Lewin again: 'In war opportunities must be taken while they exist; there may not be a second time.'[47]

There was a further point. These arguments were in themselves symptomatic of the fact that the restrictions on the submarines appeared anomalous. All the information coming in from the South Atlantic on the previous day's activity indicated that the fight had been well and truly joined. The close shave with *Glamorgan* and the evidence that at least one Argentine submarine had been hunting for prey made this clear. That morning's reports from Buenos Aires reinforced the impression. The Argentine claims of their successes of the previous day, though obviously exaggerated, were none the less taken to be a reliable indicator of their intentions – and in themselves helped create the climate for the later decision of the War Cabinet. Whatever the particular reasons provided by the *Belgrano*, Lewin would have been pressing the War Cabinet for a change in the rules of engagement. If the particular tactical situation on 1–2 May had not forced the issue the matter would have been raised the next day when the War Cabinet met. The change would put all Argentine warships at risk from British submarines – and not just the *Belgrano*.

Lewin took Admiral Fieldhouse with him to Chequers to emphasize the military case. When he arrived he immediately told the Prime Minister of the situation and requested the change in the rules.[48] The War Cabinet itself did not discuss the matter. The Chiefs of Staff other than Lewin were not brought in, although they all concurred with Lewin's recommendation. Because the matter was urgent, Thatcher brought together those ministers and officials who had been invited for lunch before the formal body met in the afternoon. There was therefore no minuted record. There was little time to consider the implications of the step beforehand. The discussion itself took fifteen to twenty minutes. One account suggests a rather comprehensive discussion,[49] but in practice it appears to have been more perfunctory, with a general unwillingness to challenge the military judgement. Whitelaw later recalled it as 'one of the simplest decisions that I personally found myself involved in' once he understood the risk of losing contact with the *Belgrano* if the *Conqueror* were not allowed to attack.[50]

The absence of the Foreign Secretary perhaps meant that

diplomatic questions were not as fully discussed as they might have been. The Head of the Diplomatic Service, Sir Antony Acland, might have been present but his immediate predecessor, Sir Michael Palliser, now serving as an adviser to the War Cabinet, had not yet arrived. Sir Michael Havers was concerned about the possible impact on international public opinion, but there was no consideration of the effect on peace negotiations as none were believed to be taking place at the time.

The change agreed was 'to permit attacks on all Argentine naval vessels on the high seas, as had previously been agreed for the *25 de Mayo* alone'.[51] Again no need was seen for this change to be communicated immediately to Argentina. Once it had been decided to send the signal Lewin warned that by the time the *Conqueror* received it it might well have lost the *Belgrano*. At the time he thought that there was a 75 per cent chance of the *Conqueror* being successful.[52]

At 13.00 BST Lewin contacted Northwood from Chequers and thirty minutes later Northwood conveyed this change to the task force. The communications involved slots on a US communications satellite which were only available every few hours and allowed for only short, sharp messages. Moreover, if the SSN was not expecting a message, and if it was also taking steps to avoid detection by the enemy, then it might not receive the message.

This is apparently what happened at 13.30 on 2 May when Northwood signalled the change in the rules of engagement. The Captain of *Conqueror* is reported to have recorded the signal 'garbled'. He had been experiencing communications problems the previous day as a result of damage to his masts from heavy seas. In addition, he was probably anxious to ensure that the position was fully understood before taking such a momentous step.[53] Using its next available slot at 15.00 BST (11.00 in South Atlantic) *Conqueror* reported that its quarry had reversed course at 09.00 that morning. The course was now 270 degrees and the speed 14 knots.

The order from Northwood could not be repeated until 17.00 and this time, at 17.30, *Conqueror* acknowledged receipt and appraised Northwood of its intention to attack. The information that the *Belgrano* had changed course reached Northwood at 15.40, but reportedly did not go higher than Admiral Herbert, Flag Officer Submarines. This does not appear to have been assessed as significant at the time: the cruiser might have changed course again as it had done in the past, or moved against South Georgia.[54]

On board *Conqueror*, Wreford Brown had decided to attack with the older, closer-range Mark 8 torpedo because of its larger warhead, which gave it a better chance of penetrating the warship's armour plating and anti-torpedo bulges. He was also at close range.[55]

I spent more than two hours working my way into an attack position on the port beam of the cruiser. It was still daylight. The visibility was variable; it came down to 2,000 yards at one time. I kept coming up for a look – but when at periscope depth we were losing ground on them – and then going deep and catching up. I did this five or six times. They were not using sonar – just gently zigzagging at about 13 knots. Twice I was in reasonable firing positions but found they had moved off a few degrees.

At 20.00 *Conqueror* was in a position to launch three torpedoes at the *Belgrano*. At 20.30 BST (16.30 local time) it reported back to Northwood that *Belgrano* had been successfully hit. *Conqueror* itself had to escape quickly for it soon faced an intensive anti-submarine attack from the cruiser's escorts.

It was not until 3 May that the news broke in Britain of the sinking of the *Belgrano*, and the extent of the loss of life only gradually emerged.[56] The initial presumption was that, because the cruiser had not sunk immediately, most of the 1,000 on board would have been saved. As it became clear that many had lost their lives, there was concern over the effect on Britain's overall international position. The suggestion that the casualties had been the direct result of the two escorting Argentine warships failing to stay around to pick up survivors provided only small comfort. Nor were the reasons for the action clear. Secretary of State for Defence John Nott explained to Parliament on 4 May:

The next day, 2 May, at 8 p.m. London time, one of our submarines detected the Argentine cruiser, 'General Belgrano', escorted by two destroyers. This heavily armed surface attack group was close to the total exclusion zone and was closing on elements of our task force, which was only hours away. We knew that the cruiser itself has substantial fire power, provided by 15 6in guns, with a range of 13 miles, and Seacat anti-aircraft missiles. Together with its escorting destroyers, which we believe were equipped with Exocet anti-ship missiles with a range of more than 20 miles, the threat to the task force was such that the task force commander could ignore it only at his peril.[57]

Aware of the international concern that the *Belgrano* had been attacked outside the Exclusion Zone, the War Cabinet agreed to its formal extension to up to 12 miles from the Argentine coast. The Chiefs of Staff were also thinking ahead to any eventual landing when the task force would be at its most vulnerable. On 7 May this was announced to take effect from 9 May.

From then on no major Argentine warships ventured beyond 12 miles of the Argentine coast. The sinking contributed to the Argentine decision to keep the Navy at port, although it was not the only factor. As relevant was the attack the next day on the *Alferez Sobral.*

This attack, on 3 May, was a continuation of the previous day's activities. Late on the evening of 2 May, radar contacts, which turned out to be misleading, were made with what appeared to be a group of Argentine ships approaching the task force. Early in the morning of 3 May, a Sea King helicopter sent out to investigate followed up a radar contact and came across a darkened ship which fired at it. The hostility was reported back and Lynx helicopters armed with Sea Skua missiles were sent to join the Sea King. As one of the Lynx flights approached it was fired upon again by a gun, and sent Sea Skuas back by way of response. The British view was that the ship sank, although it has since proved impossible to identify the ship in question and Argentine sources deny that any ship was lost. The other Lynx flight came upon an Argentine patrol vessel, *Alferez Sobral*, which was part of the rescue effort for the *Belgrano* and the same pattern followed: it was fired upon and responded with Sea Skuas which hit their target; the target, although damaged, in this case survived.[58]

This, along with the loss of the *Belgrano*, convinced Admiral Anaya that the British were benefiting from American satellite intelligence.[59] Following the attack, and without consulting the Military Committee, he sent round an internal naval communication warning of this and confirming the decision of his commanders to withdraw to coastal waters. Thereafter he challenged his officers to come up with ideas for employing the surface fleet given its presumed vulnerability to American surveillance. The fleet sailed between Comodoro Rivadavia and Rio Grande waiting for an opportunity to return to the attack. None came. Instead it was given a more defensive role, to protect the mainland and the air bases at Rio Gallegos and Rio Grande from sea attack. The aircraft of the *25 de Mayo* were disembarked and put to use in operations against the British task force from land bases.[60]

On 9 May a trawler, *Narwal*, which had been spying on the movements of the task force, was strafed by Harriers. The crew abandoned ship; they and the trawler were taken prisoner. On 10 May HMS *Alacrity* was making a run down Falkland Sound to see if it was mined (this was relevant to the plans for the landing) and to counter any Argentine resupply efforts. It came across the *Isla de los Estados* taking aviation fuel round to the garrisons at Fox Bay and Darwin. *Alacrity*'s gunfire ignited the aviation fuel and the transport went up in a ball of flame.[61]

Not long after this the *Alacrity* met up with HMS *Arrow* to return to the battle group. They were spotted by the Argentine submarine *San Luis*. The submarine had problems with its fire-control system. An attempt to launch one torpedo manually failed; a second was fired but its guidance system malfunctioned and it appears to have hit *Arrow*'s towed torpedo decoy. The submarine was unable to launch another attack.[62] It faced some twenty-five hours of depth-charge attacks but escaped unscathed. On 11 May the *San Luis* returned to base after a thirty-six day patrol. It was not ready again for operations until the war was over. The other submarine, *Salta*, had noise problems and did not get out on a patrol. It is worth noting that although the Argentine submarine threat was limited it caused enormous bother to the task force, as the area around the Falklands was judged to be ideal for conventional submarine operations. This led to continual activity by both surface ships and helicopters – 'really one enormous ASW operation from beginning to end'.[63]

The only other maritime targets which presented themselves to the British were ships caught by the blockade in the Falklands – the freighter *Rio Caracara* and the naval auxiliary *Bahia Buen Suceso* – which were attacked effectively on 16 May.

Chapter Seventeen

THE PERUVIAN INITIATIVE

Just before the fighting began in earnest Francis Pym, who was still anxious to continue to explore diplomatic options, gained agreement from his colleagues to meet with UN Secretary-General Perez de Cuellar. But this was not the only reason why he left for the United States on 1 May. He was to discuss with the US Administration how best to implement its latest declaration of support for Britain. On his arrival in Washington he underscored the changed circumstances by observing that whereas the previous week he had come to visit a negotiator, now he came to visit an ally. According to Sir Nicholas Henderson (then British Ambassador in Washington) this remark 'made some members of the Administration wince'. The effect was not wholly unintentional.[1]

Pym's first meeting was with Secretary of Defence Weinberger to discuss US military assistance. A meeting with Secretary of State Haig was arranged for the next morning and dinner with the UN Secretary-General in New York for the evening of 2 May. On the British side there was therefore no expectation of an imminent new peace initiative and so there had been no prior discussion of how best to handle such an initiative.

Since much of the Argentine diplomatic strategy had been, throughout, to persuade the United States to put pressure on Britain to reach a settlement, the end of the American initiative had reduced their options. It has been suggested that as a result of the military action on 1 May the Argentine Junta was anxious for a settlement.[2] However, as was noted above, the Argentine view of the day's events had been much more positive. The assessment of the Chiefs of Staff was that a British attempt to land forces on the Falklands had failed – partly through their own incompetence and partly through the resistance shown by Argentine forces. The losses suffered by the task force were significant, especially in terms of its limited air power, and would render it difficult to mount further attacks. An analysis of the British media revealed a concern with casualties, which explained the apparent unwillingness of the British Government to acknowledge those that had been suffered.'[3] With this assessment there was no reason for a more conciliatory attitude and every reason to expect one from Britain.

The Origins of the Initiative

From 30 April, after the announcement of the US 'tilt', there appears to have been some contact between Peruvian and American diplomats. They had alerted the State Department team working on the Falklands to a possible Peruvian initiative. However, when the British Ambassador to Lima, Charles Wallace, met the Peruvian Foreign Minister on the morning of 1 May, he was not given any indication of an imminent effort at mediation.

Wallace had asked for a meeting with the Deputy Minister to explain current British policy. He was then invited to see the Foreign Minister, who asked if there were ways 'in which the Peruvians could help break the diplomatic deadlock'. Although he lacked instructions from London, Wallace took the opportunity to reiterate the importance of Resolution 502, stress the difficulties faced by Haig as a result of 'the different lines taken by some of his interlocutors in Argentina' and to suggest that 'it was clear that Argentina attached great importance to the attitudes and opinions in Peru ... Peru could usefully exert its influence ... in convincing Argentina to implement Resolution 502 without any preconditions as soon as possible.' In the ensuing conversation reference was made to Pym's forthcoming visit to Washington.[4]

President Fernando Belaunde Terry, apparently alarmed by the surge of fighting on that day, decided to set in motion his own initiative. During the morning his officials worked on some ideas of their own, possibly in contact with Argentine officials. After the President and his advisers had met to analyse the situation,[5] he decided to ring President Reagan, who was out of town at the time. Half an hour later Haig rang back. According to Belaunde:

> He told me: 'President Reagan's not in Washington right now. He's in Knoxville, opening an exhibition. But I know that you are very concerned, and so are we. What can we do? How can you help us?' I told him plainly that I was on very good terms with Argentina and that I understood his negotiations with her had not succeeded. 'That's right,' Haig agreed, 'there was intransigence on both sides.' I said then that some acceptable formula had to be found. We talked by phone for three-quarters of an hour, and I finally asked him please to dictate to me the essential points from Britain's viewpoint. Haig read them over to me, and I for my part told him what word was unsatisfactory and what condition unacceptable for Argentina. We finally agreed on a plan which covered seven points, and I left it that I should call President Galtieri at once to put that formula to him.[6]

The resulting plan was clearly derived from the Haig plan and was so judged by everyone who considered it. Enders has claimed that he drafted it with Haig that afternoon in Washington.[7]

Haig had seen the Belaunde interest as a way of keeping the negotiating process going. His belief that the British had toyed with a Mexican initiative convinced him that there was still an appetite in London for a settlement, although here, as with the subsequent Peruvian initiative, the only real motive was to show willing to Latin American governments and not reject their ideas out of hand. US officials had sustained contact with the Foreign Office.[8]

There were, however, differences from the original plan. One was a matter of presentation: it was much shorter than the final Haig plan. According to Haig, Belaunde said: 'Simplify and we can still do it.'[9] When Belaunde later described it to President Galtieri he suggested that the 'shortened version' of the Haig proposals might be more 'viable'.[10]

This simplicity may explain why the initial British reaction was that the proposals were 'vague and indeterminate'.[11] This problem may not have been fully appreciated by the Peruvians at first because Haig apparently supported the drive for simplicity. This in turn indicates the basic problem with the initiative in its early stages in that there was no direct negotiation with London – only a set of American comments on what might and might not be acceptable to the British.

The second, self-evident but important feature of the initiative is that it involved Peru. What was clearly of most interest to Haig was that Peru could put pressure on Argentina in a way that was now impossible for the United States. Haig noted that a proposal from 'the head of state of a neighbouring country that clearly was very close to Buenos Aires ... could not be taken trivially'. It was understood in Argentina that it would be difficult to rebuff Peru. None the less, Peru could only deliver Argentina on the assumption that Haig could deliver the British. As we shall see, the impression of progress that was achieved on 2 May was based on the erroneous assumption that Haig was in a position to speak for the British.

Whether or not the initiative would work depended on whether the two belligerents would accept it as an alternative to mediation by the United Nations. For their own reasons both Haig, who saw it as the last chance for his effort, and Belaunde, who would receive a great boost to his international reputation, keenly wished it to succeed. When the first high-level contacts were made between Peru and Argentina on the evening of 1 May the first issue was the acceptability of Peruvian mediation. Costa Mendez appears to have suspected that in the long term the UN was the most promising, but there was nothing else under way at the time and so Peruvian mediation appeared as a viable alternative.[12]

Peru–Argentina

The Peruvian Prime Minister, Manuel Ulloa, contacted Costa Mendez around midnight on 1 May and told him that Peru was about to offer mediation, which would start with Argentina. Costa Mendez suggested that Belaunde call Galtieri immediately, and then rang Galtieri's office to warn him of what to expect. At 01.30 Belaunde spoke to Galtieri, who expressed interest in the proposals and suggested that they would be considered in detail the next morning. After speaking with Belaunde he told Costa Mendez at 02.00 that he had accepted the mediation. They agreed to meet in Galtieri's office at 08.00 to consider their response to Belaunde's plan.[13]

The transcript of the conversation between Belaunde and Galtieri provides not only the detail of the offer but also the nature of the appeal being made to Galtieri:

So what I'd like to insist, Mr President, is that you think deeply about these conditions [of the proposal] and if possible have ready by 10 a.m. tomorrow* – that's the time when the Secretary of State is meeting Pym – some agreement on these points of view because if you could that would support the hope that we could achieve a solution.

Not surprisingly this is followed by a clarification of the problems posed by the time differences. Galtieri indicated that it might be difficult to meet this deadline but Belaunde urged him to try. The Peruvian's objective was to get agreement on the Sunday and then send delegates to Washington to begin work on Monday in the Contact Group that would be established as part of his proposals.[14] There was a degree of urgency in the plea, but, as Galtieri recognized, it was unreal. Belaunde's hope was to get quick agreement on a simplified formula in the belief that this would be more 'viable' than an elaborate proposal – 'naturally they're not exhaustive, they're necessarily short and in some cases vague, but that's what makes them viable, isn't it?'[15]

* This was actually 10.00 the same day.

It was not possible for agreement to be reached in time for the Pym–Haig meeting. By the time it started Costa Mendez was still engaged in an extensive series of conversations with Peru. There was no reason to suppose that Argentina would accept the plan. Peru could not tell Haig what would be acceptable to Costa Mendez prior to his meeting. All they could do was urge military restraint. There is some evidence that in Peruvian contacts prior to his meetings with Pym, Haig was asked to encourage the British to sustain what was erroneously believed to be a tacit cease-fire.

It can be seen how in Argentina the possibility of a tacit cease-fire could have appeared quite realistic. As we have seen, the Argentine assessment of the previous day's events was that the British had tried and failed to land forces on the Islands, and that they had suffered serious losses in the process. British claims to the contrary were seen as an attempt to manipulate public opinion. It was assumed that support for the task force would erode in the event of British casualties and that the British Government was therefore attempting to hide the truth.[16]

Consider the following discussion between Costa Mendez and Belaunde during the morning of 2 May. Belaunde asks if there have been any military attacks that morning; Costa Mendez replies that there have not and, more positively, that 'the British ships have withdrawn. I think they have suffered considerable damage . . .' Belaunde then reports what he has been told by Haig about the previous day's events, especially with regard to Argentine claims about British casualties. He reports Haig saying: 'According to our sources, we know that the four Harriers have not been lost. We do know that there has been minor damage to one airplane that has returned to base and minor damage to a surface vessel.' Belaunde reports Haig adding that from Britain's point of view the previous day's operations had been 'successful, and he anticipated worse actions in the future.'

Belaunde was hoping that the lack of activity thus far was an 'excellent symptom'. After some effort Costa Mendez interjects with a rebuttal of the State Department's assessment: 'tell them that in the Islands there are four completely destroyed Harrier airplanes as well as a helicopter and that it seems to me that the satellite information that gets to the State Department is not too correct.'

Whatever the reasons for their emergence, the new proposals were extremely interesting to Argentina. The Peruvian plan as originally submitted to Galtieri involved:

1 Immediate cease-fire.
2 Simultaneous and mutual withdrawal of forces.
3 Third parties would govern the Islands, temporarily.
4 The two governments would recognize the existence of conflicting viewpoints about the Islands.
5 The two governments would recognize the need to take the viewpoints and interests of the islanders into account in the final solution.
6 The contact group which would start negotiating at once to implement this agreement would be Brazil, Peru, West Germany and the US.
7 A final solution must be found by 30 April 1983 under the contact group's guarantee.[17]

When Costa Mendez reviewed with Galtieri the latter's conversation with Belaunde their reaction was positive. Although the new plan clearly reflected American thinking it was seen as an improvement in two ways. First, there would be no direct British role in the new administration. In the Haig plan Britain, Argentina and the United States would have jointly administered the Islands pending an eventual settlement. Argentina had objected to this on the grounds that the Argentine role was too limited and could lead to 'a predominantly British administration with no fixed expiry date'.

Second, 'viewpoints and interests' was more admissible than the previous 'wishes', which had carried a more decisive connotation. During the conversations Belaunde reported a suggestion to reintroduce 'wishes' (which the plural 'they' implied came from both the United States and Britain). Costa Mendez refused and suggested a weaker version of the original – 'points of view *concerning* the interests' (*puntos de vista sobre los intereses*). Later, in consultation with Belaunde, Costa Mendez suggested 'aspirations' as a synonym which was not as loaded as 'wishes'.[18] This appears to have been incorporated into the plan,[19] although Belaunde was still referring to 'viewpoints concerning interests' when speaking to Galtieri in the late afternoon.

It is worth noting that in the previous Haig plan an objectionable point to Costa Mendez had been a provision to take a 'sounding of the opinion of the inhabitants, with respect to such issues relating to the negotiations, conducted in such manner as the Authority may determine' (Paragraph 8.1), which he described as a 'virtual referendum'. The vague nature of the new plan implied something less but it still left open the critical question of how these wishes were to be taken into account.[20]

The second important issue was the composition of the contact group. In the first discussion, Galtieri objected to the United States because of its recent 'public attitude'. Belaunde said that Canada had been mentioned as an alternative, but it had been suggested that it was even less acceptable, and that anyway the United States was balanced by Peru ('a country that's frankly on Argentina's side'). In a curious observation Belaunde worries whether Britain would find Germany acceptable as they once fought a naval battle around the Falklands.[21]

In the morning negotiations Costa Mendez said that the 'elimination of the US' from the contact group was 'fundamental'. Costa Mendez was quite happy with Canada (indicating the depth of feeling against the United States rather than concern over being pro-British). Belaunde was apparently worried about this but, according to one account, the matter was solved when Haig reported that the British would object to Peru. Belaunde said, 'Magnificent, we're on equal footing. We can both withdraw and look for two other countries.'[22] Costa Mendez's main priority was to ensure that there was no return in any way to a British administration.

Britain–United States

Francis Pym had no authority to accept either a cease-fire or a new peace proposal without agreement in London. Furthermore when Haig met Pym on the morning of 2 May the Peruvian plan lacked later

Argentine refinements or any clear endorsement from Argentina. Not surprisingly in these circumstances the British response was sceptical. Sir Nicholas Henderson describes the meeting as follows:

[Haig] relayed President Reagan's conviction that British forces were 'doing the work of the free world', but then balanced this with an ardent plea that we could and should avoid a large-scale battle because it would be unnecessary and risky. He briefly outlined certain ideas which had originated in a Peruvian initiative and which had not been formulated in any definitive way. These were very similar to those which he himself had advanced earlier and he thought they would be more acceptable in Buenos Aires if they were put forward by a South American government. They could not possibly be described as 'proposals'.

Pym replied to the effect that he wondered whether Argentina would be more likely to respond positively to these views than to Haig's earlier proposals, to which they bore a strong resemblance. Pym also emphasized that he would need to discuss any new ideas with his colleagues on his return. 'Haig fully agreed that more time and more detailed work were needed.'[23]

None of the other accounts contradict this version. Pym has recalled that it was 'perfectly clear that the Peruvians were in touch with the Argentines ... and ... naturally the Peruvians were hopeful that the plans ... had a reasonable chance of success'. He remembers discussion at 'considerable length' of matters that were no more than 'outlines' that were 'undeveloped'. 'We discussed ideas and headings which, of course, bore a relation to the attempt that Al Haig had been making himself to get an agreement ... but there was no actual piece of paper with a text being altered.' This does not contradict Haig's assertion that 'We were down to words, single words,' for the words in question were those that composed the 'headings' which Pym mentions. Pym agrees that he was 'positive': 'I said, "yes, work on them, work on them, tell me more. Let's see what they look like."'[24]

Presumably after this meeting finished at 12.00 (Washington time) Haig was back in touch with the Peruvians. Belaunde may have begun to report back also on his conversations with Costa Mendez as well as Haig on Pym. However, the conversation had to be cut short because Haig was going off to have lunch with Pym at the British Embassy at 13.00.[25]

The lunch lasted about an hour. According to Pym 'we further reviewed the whole scene as it was and how we were going to continue in the future.'[26] There does not appear to have been any discussion of the Peruvian proposal. While Haig and Pym lunched Belaunde spoke again to Galtieri, drawing on his understanding of his own and his ministers' conversations with Costa Mendez earlier in the morning and his own conversation with Haig.

A reading of the transcript indicates the concerns that Haig had put to Belaunde, and those of Belaunde himself. Belaunde first sought to ensure that the position adopted by Costa Mendez had adequately reflected Galtieri's own. His main concern was to communicate a sense of urgency. Haig had indicated to him that there could well be more 'violence'. Belaunde had asked Haig to urge the British to be restrained and he asked this also of Argentina. He appears to have believed that after the previous day's activity there was a 'tacit cease-fire' which he hoped would continue. Galtieri confirmed that there had been no further military action that day, suggesting that the British 'have taken a holiday'.

In order to maintain the negotiating momentum he needed to obtain the Junta's authorization. Galtieri replied that he was predisposed to say 'yes'. When asked if the 'document can prosper' he replied: 'With a few changes, it definitely can ... we are willing to sign a cease-fire ... but if the British violence continues we will answer back in the same form and with even more violence.' Galtieri did not rule out further changes in the text, although Belaunde discouraged this.

Galtieri stressed that he could not make the decision by himself but would need to consult the other members of the Junta, who would be meeting that evening at 19.00. Belaunde again argued the urgency of the situation and said that once agreement had been reached he was prepared to have a signing ceremony of the two Ambassadors to Lima in order to ensure that there could be an immediate halt to hostilities. On hearing that the Junta would meet at 19.00 Belaunde offered to ring back at 20.00 to get a reply. It is significant that his press conference announcing progress was scheduled for this time. However, Galtieri was more cautious: 'Don't be such an optimist.' He promised to contact Belaunde at 22.00.

Belaunde gave the impression of American support, and that pressure was being put on Britain, and that somehow Britain was a participant in an active negotiation. Earlier he had told Costa Mendez, 'they say England might have other objections,' from which the Foreign Minister naturally assumed a close British involvement. Now he told Galtieri that 'negotiations with Pym will not be interrupted,' and later that 'the Americans support it and this is vital because their influence over the British is definitive. Haig has told me that he will patronize the proposal.'

When Belaunde later gave his news conference he stressed the American role. After explaining that Peru had been talking directly to Argentina, he added: 'In the course of the morning evidently work was done on this document, and although the Secretary of State didn't say it to me, he did make two or three interjections which did perhaps come from his talks with the British minister.'[27]

Unfortunately when this conversion took place there was no longer the potential for a serious negotiation with Pym.[28] By the time Belaunde could talk again with Haig and report that Galtieri had at last promised his 'best predispositions' towards the proposal Haig was back from lunch with Pym with no more meetings scheduled. All Haig could do was try to catch Pym at the airport before he left for New York and the UN Secretary-General. Pym describes the fate of the call:

Haig had rung to say that he wanted to impress upon me – and this is having left after lunch – the importance he attached to the Peruvian proposals and I, because I didn't want to miss the plane and had my date in New York, authorized Sir Nicholas Henderson to ring back and tell Al Haig to be in no doubt whatsoever that I regarded that, and I would regard any other, proposal as extremely important and no stone would be left unturned, as far as I was concerned, in the search for an agreement.

Henderson's account suggests a less effusive message: 'what had been put forward so far seemed only vague and indeterminate and provided no basis on which to do business.'[29] He repeated that Pym could take no decisions by himself and would need to consult London.

It would not be surprising if the Peruvian initiative was more acceptable to Argentina, because Argentina had been directly involved in its formation. What made it appear significant in Lima and Buenos Aires is that they believed that it had been endorsed by Britain, or at least that endorsement would soon be forthcoming as a result of American pressure. There was absolutely no reason for that view, but it was clearly derived from the impression that Belaunde had received from Haig. The South Americans in their memoirs of this event all stress their belief that Pym was actively contributing to the negotiations, that London was being kept fully informed, and that Haig was in any case a virtual spokesman for Britain (a view reinforced by his conduct the previous month). Thus Dr Arias Stella, Peruvian Foreign Minister: 'We understood that Pym and Haig's contact was so close that whatever Haig accepted was all right with Pym – that is, Pym passed it on at once to London, Pym spoke with London's voice.'[30]

But while Pym knew of the Peruvian initiative there was little in it to impress him and no reason to contact London urgently. By the time that Belaunde could extract a tentative endorsement from Galtieri, Haig was no longer in direct contact with Pym. Haig, for his part, seems to have assumed that Britain's Ambassador to Peru was in constant touch and was the means by which London was in touch. But Ambassador Wallace was only provided with the detail of the Peruvian proposals after Belaunde's press conference at 18.30 Lima time, by which time the Junta in Argentina had heard the news of *Belgrano*.

Wallace has described Stella explaining to him that the plan was the result of a series of conversations with Haig, that Costa Mendez and Galtieri were 'well disposed', but that they had to convince the Junta. Peru was anxious not to lose any momentum and, if the formula was acceptable, hoped to sign soon an interim document in Lima. Wallace records his view that 'the Peruvian assessment was rather optimistic and if they hoped that the signature of a document was to take place imminently it was going to be jolly difficult to do it that evening because . . . it was already tomorrow morning in London.'

Wallace sent a telegram back reporting the contents of his meeting with Dr Arias Stella at 20.03 Peruvian time, which was 02.03 3 May BST. His staff reported Belaunde's press conference at 20.44 local time. Before these telegrams were sent two had arrived from Ambassador Henderson in Washington. At 17.15 Washington time Henderson reported the outline of the Peruvian proposals as they had been identified by Haig in his morning meetings with Pym. At 17.30 Henderson added a report of his own telephone conversation with Haig.[31] All these messages were received well after the fateful decisions had been taken to change the rules of engagement and indeed after the *Belgrano* had been sunk.

The Impact of the *Belgrano*

Although it has been alleged since the war that the sinking of the *Belgrano* was ordered so as to sink the Peruvian initiative,[32] this was not the case. One decision was quite separate from the other. The British Government could not have foreseen that the action would have these political consequences, and it is now clear that the attack did not have any political motive. If the effect on the negotiating process had been a primary consideration it might have argued for such a blow in order to keep the pressure on Buenos Aires.

The sinking affected the course of the initiative taken by President Belaunde but it is quite wrong to suggest that it was responsible for its loss. On 2 May it was not in a form that the British Government could or would have agreed. The impression that this might have been so resulted from an optimistic assessment of the military situation following the action on 1 May, as well as the belief developed by Belaunde and communicated to Buenos Aires that Haig was virtually speaking for Britain. Haig had of course given Argentina the impression during his shuttle that he could deliver British concessions and he may have communicated the same confidence to Peru. If he based this confidence on anything that Pym might have said to him then he should by now have understood the limited freedom of manoeuvre allowed the Foreign Secretary by the Prime Minister.

Nor was there any specific reason why the sinking need have led to the rejection of the initiative. Galtieri and Costa Mendez had been enthusiastic. According to Costa Mendez their position was that they 'both knew that the proposal was not perfect and that it would carry many inconveniences but we also knew that it was much better than the situation previous to 1 April. We also knew that if we rejected it we would lose a friend in Peru and many Latin American countries' support.'[33]

It was by no means certain that these arguments would have carried the day with the Military Committee. Galtieri's warning to Belaunde not to expect too much too soon indicated that a lengthy discussion was expected. In the event the discussion did not materialize. The meeting began at 19.00 but at 19.30 Admiral Anaya reported the news of the loss of the *Belgrano*. The mood was not conducive to a discussion of a diplomatic settlement. The Peruvian initiative was not rejected outright but the Junta did decide to suspend consideration.[34]

That the news of the sinking arrived coincidentally with the start of the meeting to discuss the proposal did not help rational decision-making. As the Rattenbach Commission is reported to have observed, the Junta missed an opportunity: 'the most rational and productive course would have been to accept the proposal in spite of the sinking of the *General Belgrano*.'[35] Coupled with the international reaction to the sinking this would have put Britain under considerable pressure.

For the Junta this was the first major tragedy of the war and those at the meeting were keenly affected by the news. As Haig was seen to be behind the Peruvian plan, all the suspicions of the Secretary of State that had developed during his shuttle resurfaced. Once again collusion with Britain was assumed. He had led them on without any evidence of British flexibility. If he had been in communication with London then the British Government must have escalated its military action in the full knowledge of the new proposals and indeed used him – and the Peruvians – to gain time for the attack. The result was a new element of duress. If Argentina accepted the proposals now it would appear to have been weakened by the disaster.

After the Military Committee broke up, the three members of the

Junta continued their discussions. As they did so, news came in of the UN Secretary-General's offer of mediation, which had been set in motion by Perez de Cuellar without any knowledge of the Peruvian initiative. This provided the Junta with an honourable way out of its predicament. A UN mediation would be less vulnerable to British – and American – manipulation. By midnight the UN proposal had been accepted in principle, although it took two days' of discussion before the official acceptance was delivered on 5 May. The Junta also decided to send two members of the Malvinas Group, Moya and Iglesias, to explain to Peru why its initiative was being rejected.*

The Mediation Continues

Just after this meeting at 00.30 Galtieri spoke to Belaunde and expressed his feelings: 'the Argentine government will not, in the face of this military pressure, accept any negotiations relating to peace in the South Atlantic in these circumstances. We would rather die on our feet than live on our knees.'[36]

Belaunde commented during the conversation on the role of Haig. He described how prior to the news of the British bombardment of the Islands on 1 May Haig had been 'euphoric' and ready to impose terms on Britain. Then he became frustrated. Now he was 'speaking of Mr Pym as a man who simply has no interest in peace and only wants to obtain facilities to continue the war'. The next morning Peruvian Prime Minister Ulloa informed Costa Mendez that Belaunde had told Haig 'how disappointed he was in a very emphatic way' and that the United States must now take action to 'repair the almost irreparable damage that the US had caused'. Ulloa, with some prescience, noted: 'My personal opinion now is that Haig has his days numbered. We told him this . . .'

---

* In general Junta decisions were unanimous during the war. However, after the war, Lami Dozo of the Air Force indicated that the Air Force had voted to accept the Peruvian initiative. The proof of this dissent was said to be the lack of an Air Force man in the group going to Lima. However, there is no other record of this, and all three men appear to have agreed on the UN mediation.

There was great disappointment in Washington. Enders confesses to having had two hours of optimism that the initiative might turn into something, only to go to Haig's house and find that Belaunde had just called to tell him 'It's all off.'[37] Haig, having been on the receiving end of Belaunde's anger, proceeded to pass some of it on to the British Ambassador, whom he met the next day. The United States was now starting to suffer in South America for the support shown to Britain, especially as it was now being put about that the *Belgrano* could not have been sunk were it not for American help with satellite information. Costa Mendez had told Ulloa, 'we have the conviction that the information that allowed the attack came from US satellites.'

Haig warned of opinion in the West becoming less favourable to the United Kingdom. 'People might say that Britain was over-reacting.' When Henderson retorted that the Argentines had not been behaving peacefully, Haig queried whether 'hitting the Argentines was the only thing that brought them to negotiate or whether it made them more inflexible'. Henderson responded that they had shown no great flexibility during the weeks that they had not been hit. At this point Haig asked directly for a cease-fire on receipt of an Argentine agreement to withdraw. Henderson repeated the Government's previous position that they would not let up on military pressure without categorical assurances that 'the Argentines were going to stop military action and withdraw'.

When the two met again later that day Haig had again spoken to Belaunde, who was demanding that Britain agree to a cease-fire. According to Henderson: 'Haig insisted that military action must be stopped. He did not think that the Argentines could do anything to prevent the British sinking the whole of their fleet. This would bring about the collapse of any authority in Buenos Aires; the whole of Latin America would be alienated.'

Henderson demurred and observed that London would not agree to an armistice just because Argentina was now doing badly. Haig repeated his worry about the consequences of Britain appearing to 'drive things too far'. He later maintained pressure by sending a document containing the Peruvian plan with a suggested cease-fire statement for the British Government. The statement began:

'Whatever happens militarily there must be a negotiated solution to the Falklands crisis if we are to avoid open-ended hostility and instability.'[38]

A further source of pressure on Britain resulted from Belaunde's press conference. Francis Pym's Private Secretary contacted Ambassador Wallace in Lima in the 'middle of the night' to instruct him to acknowledge the Peruvian proposals and to say that time was required to consider them.[39] When Arias Stella spoke to Costa Mendez the next morning (3 May) Stella informed him that Wallace had been in contact and that he had said 'the door is not totally closed within the framework of what has been proposed.'[40]

The Impact of the *Sheffield*

The last source of pressure was the successful Argentine strike against the Type 42 destroyer, *Sheffield*, by an Exocet missile fired from a Super-Etendard late on 4 May.

On that day the British military objective was once again to deplete Argentina's air capability. As on 1 May it began with another raid against Stanley airport, but this time the Vulcan missed the runway. Again the carrier group moved close to Stanley during the night so that when day broke they were 100 miles from the capital, with the three Type 42 destroyers serving as a picket line to provide protection. Again Sea Harriers flew missions from early morning. But this time the Argentine Air Force was not to be drawn.[41]

One of the main differences from the previous Saturday was that this time two Super-Etendards got away from their Rio Grande base and refuelled successfully as they moved towards their targets – three Type 42 frigates. The Super-Etendard squadron had been practising against the two Argentine Type 42s, also armed with Sea Dart missiles, to assess how best to avoid radar detection. Although there had been some discussion of a joint operation with Air Force Daggers during April, the Navy had decided to go it alone, stressing surprise as the basis of their approach. This could not have been achieved with a Dagger accompaniment.[42]

The British Type 42s were detected by a Neptune aircraft on a reconnaissance sortie at 9.15. Thirty minutes later the aircraft took off, with the Neptune keeping them informed of their targets' position. Flying low through bad weather, and refraining from use of their radars to avoid detection, they moved closer. As they approached *Sheffield*, they were detected by *Glasgow* to their east. A Harrier patrol was alerted and the radars of the Sea Dart air-defence missiles were switched on to acquire the incoming aircraft. *Sheffield* made radar contact, but too late. In the minutes leading up to the attack the destroyer had been transmitting on its satellite communications terminal, which had a frequency similar to that of the Etendard and Exocet radars and so had 'inadvertently deafened itself'.[43]

The Super-Etendards closed in to 12 miles, fired a missile each at 12.04 and then made their escape. The Exocets took a minute to reach the *Sheffield*. One flew past, the other hit the destroyer amidships. The warhead did not explode but its fuel ignited on impact causing blast damage and fires that led to twenty deaths and twenty-four injuries. Frigates in the area came to the stricken ship's aid, but it was soon without power or communications. The order came to abandon ship.[44]

Later that day three Harriers took off from *Hermes* to mount an attack against the airfield at Goose Green. The Argentine radar at Stanley picked up the flight and warned the anti-aircraft batteries at Goose Green of the incoming attack. As the Harriers approached, the batteries opened fire, downing one of them.

The day's experiences were sobering for the British command. The reality of the Exocet threat was now clear, and the risks associated with Harrier attacks against land targets, when the stock of Harriers was so limited, now had to be weighed carefully. For Britain's political leaders the day's events also came as a shock. The news of the sinking was broadcast abruptly on the evening news, before the full extent of the casualties were known. Now Britain was having to face the human cost of war.

Whereas at the start of that day the problem had appeared to be of appearing too much like bullies – to the extent that Pym had told Parliament that no military humiliation of Argentina was sought – now the risks to the task force had been brought home. On 3 May the War

Cabinet had authorized Henderson to explore further the Peruvian initiative. On 5 May the full Cabinet met. According to one account:

> Pym's arguments, which before had been tedious obstacles on the path to glory, now seemed to many a ray of hope. All talk was now of Peru. Was a third-party interim administration acceptable? Could the Commons swallow only a vague reference to self-determination in the longer term? Was a balanced withdrawal quite what they had envisaged at the start?[45]

Another source quotes a minister suggesting that it was necessary to make a generous offer so that, if it was rejected, it would make 'the British understand why they had to go to war'.[46]

Later that day Henderson met again with Haig and offered a series of British amendments to the Peruvian plan. Haig told him that these would be rejected out of hand by Argentina and presented a different set of proposals which he asked Henderson to transmit to London. These proposals 'presented considerable difficulties' as now there would be no British administration but were none the less accepted.[47]

The British position was set out by Pym in a statement to the Commons on 7 May in which he stressed the need to link a cease-fire to the unambiguous commencement of a supervised Argentine withdrawal. Without mentioning any names he accepted that a 'small group of countries acceptable to both sides' could have a role supervising withdrawal, undertaking an interim administration 'in consultation with the islanders' elected representatives, and perhaps . . . in negotiations for a definitive agreement on the status of the islands, without prejudice to our principles or the wishes of the islanders'.[48]

Late at night on 5 May Belaunde once again spoke to Galtieri. He reported that he had received through the United States the British reaction to the document containing his proposals:

> In general, they accept it; they make it a bit more concise, because they reduce it from seven points to six, but they make some changes in editing. They leave the first part, for example – immediate cessation of hostilities. They talk of a mutual withdrawal, but also of

a ... non-redeployment or non-reintroduction ... of all forces, that is to say a non-return of the forces during this period. They then go on at once to insist that the Contact Group be those countries originally mentioned – despite the fact that I had been very clear that this was not acceptable to you, above all in one case – and that its mission should be, first, to verify the withdrawal of forces, second to administer the government of the islands during the provisional period in consultation with the elected representatives of the islands' population – you see here they want to give prominence to the existing organizations, and make it certain that no action is taken on the islands that contravenes this interim accord – and, third, to ensure that all the other terms of the agreement are respected.

He then asserted that the Americans would 'make them accept these accords in a discussion' but noted that the British were insisting on a very tight schedule for the discussion – twenty-four hours for giving orders and instructions for the cease-fire, forty-eight hours for the work, but only twelve hours, once the cease-fire had started, to reject or approve a previously presented but not necessarily approved document.

This last condition reflected the British concern that the Argentines would begin to stall once a cease-fire had been agreed, which would then make it very difficult to retain any sort of military initiative. Otherwise, in Belaunde's presentation, the return of the US into the contact group went against an original Argentine position. Absent from Belaunde's account to Galtieri but present in Pym's statement to Parliament was the 'wishes' of the islanders – a word that had been deemed unacceptable on 2 May. The tight schedule and the reinsertion of the US were enough for Galtieri to reject the proposals.[49]

However, even if they had been more palatable, Galtieri would probably not have accepted. The diplomatic forum had now switched. At lunchtime on 5 May, Argentina had formally accepted UN mediation. Galtieri informed Belaunde of this that evening, even before the latter had begun to outline the British response to the Peruvian proposals. 'Argentina has lost faith in the United States,' noted Galtieri.

Chapter Eighteen

UN MEDIATION

Although Resolution 502 had not required anything of the Secretary-General, Perez de Cuellar made an effort from the start to keep in touch with the development of the dispute. As early as 8 April he had established a working group headed by Under Secretary-General Rafee Ahmed of Pakistan to develop some plans in case Haig's mediation should fail.* This group assembled its own data on the crisis. Although it had voluminous files, going back to 1964, covering the decolonization aspects of the dispute it lacked such simple things as detailed maps covering islands like South Georgia. Possibilities for UN operational involvement – perhaps in the form of a peace-keeping force – were also examined.[1]

On 19 April, without any invitation to do so, the Secretary-General gave the two sides, as well as the United States, an account of the ways in which the UN might be able to help with a negotiated settlement. This floated such possibilities as a small UN civilian presence, together with military observers, which might help supervise a military withdrawal and interim agreement. Options ranged from a UN umbrella for whatever arrangements were agreed to a temporary UN administration.[2] Haig never showed much interest in a UN role in a

---

* He could not ask either of the two Under Secretaries-General for Special Political Affairs to take on this task – although in other circumstances they would have been natural candidates – because one, Mr Brian Urquhart, was British and the other, Mr Diego Cordovez, was Ecuadoran. There was no West European or Latin American on the working group.

settlement and tended to be dismissive when it was discussed.

Although the Secretary-General was not kept well informed at an official level of the development of the Haig mediation he appears to have been kept in touch informally. On the other hand the Peruvian initiative came to him as a complete surprise, despite the fact that he himself was Peruvian. This may be explained by his own background, which contained a degree of rivalry with President Belaunde. The only time he was contacted by the Peruvian Foreign Minister was because the latter was curious to know whether he was doing anything.[3] None the less, as a result of the preparations, almost as soon as the Haig mediation came to an end, Perez de Cuellar was ready to initiate his own. To some extent it was vital for his own position that he should scotch the view that the Secretary-General's role was becoming increasingly passive.

On 2 May, coincident with the sinking of the *Belgrano*, he presented a 'set of ideas' on one sheet of paper which suggested that the two sides take a series of simultaneous steps as provisional measures.[4] These were described as 'not prejudicing the rights, demands or positions of the parties', and covered such familiar areas as mutual withdrawal, removal of sanctions and exclusion zones, interim administration and long-term negotiations to end the dispute. They were not dissimilar to the proposals made at the concluding stage of the Peruvian Plan.[5]

At the same time Ireland, uneasy at the raising of the military temperature, was pressing for a round of more public diplomacy in the Security Council in order to urge the two parties to 'exercise restraint'. This was precisely the sort of move Britain feared most. Having obtained the backing it sought with Resolution 502 it did not want any amendment, especially a notionally even-handed call for a cease-fire, that would leave it in an impossible position militarily. Britain therefore objected that the exercise of restraint was meaningless so long as Argentine forces continued to occupy the Islands. It would only support a UN effort if it were unofficial and confidential.

The Secretary-General agreed that a public debate was not going to help and that private diplomacy should continue a little longer. With both sides accepting the mediation offer – Argentina on 5 May and Britain on 6 May – Ireland was persuaded to suspend its request.

There remained some pressure on Britain within the Security Council not to take any military action so long as the negotiations were under way, but no assurances were given.

Nor were any given during the subsequent negotiations. As they began Britain announced the new 12-mile Exclusion Zone. This was seen in Buenos Aires as further intimidation. The Secretary-General might have preferred Britain to hold back on such moves but he did not make it a precondition for his continuing efforts. Britain felt unable to contain its military activities, because it only had a short period in which to mount a landing before the task force would be obliged to turn back. This served as a deadline in British minds, although others could only guess at the relationship between British diplomacy and its military preparations.

Initially, Argentina assumed that Britain was anxious to block referral to the Security Council because it was concerned that its support was declining in the aftermath of the sinking of the *Belgrano*. Equally there was some confidence that not only was the Argentine position holding up in Latin America but that support for Britain in the United States and Europe had eroded. The UN framework provided the opportunity to give the lie to the idea that Argentina was uninterested in negotiations, while the UN, given the history of favourable General Assembly resolutions, was considered a congenial forum.

Round One

Unlike Haig, Perez de Cuellar did not have to spend hours in an aircraft travelling from one party to the other. He could hold a number of conversations with each on the same day. Also unlike Haig, he was a more natural neutral. Not only was he not pursuing his own foreign policy agenda, but it was vital to the integrity of his office that he was seen to be impartial. This was reflected in a critical feature of his approach that was also quite different from Haig's: he was careful to ensure that he said exactly the same things to each side. While this might have reduced the potential for creative ambiguity, it also meant that he was less vulnerable to the suspicions that had eventually clouded Haig's role as a mediator.

For almost two weeks he met regularly with the British Ambassador, Sir Anthony Parsons, and Enrique Ros, who had been brought in to strengthen the Argentine delegation, but who also appears to have irritated de Cuellar by his preoccupation with details and his reluctance to stray far from his brief without clear instructions. Ros, of course, had had his fingers burned during the February negotiations and was anxious this time not to alienate the Junta. Each man met with the Secretary-General once or twice a day – some thirty times during the course of his effort. This was a much more professional negotiation than Haig's or Belaunde's. The direct contact created far less scope for misunderstandings.

At the start of the process Britain passed on for consideration a ten-point proposal to Perez de Cuellar, largely based on the position adopted at the end of the Peruvian negotiation. Parsons promised that all these points were negotiable, but only so long as Argentina accepted that the final outcome of any discussion of the status of the Islands could not be prejudged. The Secretary-General asked Argentina to provide its own ideas so that he could compare and contrast the points before he made his own proposal. At this early stage he was interested in general ideas rather than detailed documents.

Just as Haig had done, Perez de Cuellar seized upon the question of the Island's administration as the key to the success of his exercise. This was central to both the conduct of the demilitarization of the Islands and the withdrawal of forces, as well as the prospects for future negotiations. Because of the size of the population the administration itself need not be large; its composition, however, would be critical.

On the morning of 8 May he moved from generalities to specifics. He had heard enough the previous day to convince him of some possibility for agreement. One theme that he had promoted with his original set of ideas was simultaneity in the cease-fire, the withdrawal of forces, the lifting of sanctions and exclusion zones, and the start of negotiations. Britain had little problem with the first two elements in the list, but was cautious with regard to the others lest it weaken its bargaining position. Even so, the Secretary-General persuaded Britain to accept these five elements as a coherent package rather than pick and choose among them.

Neither side was very clear on the schedule for a military withdrawal. Perez de Cuellar had two quite different dates for the conclusion of the negotiations – Britain wanted a year from the date of an agreement, whereas Argentina insisted on 31 December 1982. He considered suggesting an intermediate date somewhere between the two.

The question of the administration dominated the next few days. The Secretary-General explored a variety of possibilities, including combining UN supervision with the continuation of the Island Councils, which might be made more acceptable to Argentina by the removal of all British members, leaving only those from the Islands.

Both sides accepted that during the interim period the administration would be uniquely neither British nor Argentine. Argentina had indicated that it preferred to see the UN in the administrative role with negotiations located in New York. It wanted to see the UN prominent in all aspects: in the administration, the supervision of the negotiations on the underlying dispute and, by means of the past resolutions, in setting the terms for these negotiations.

Britain remained attached to the idea of a contact group of nations, as Haig had proposed. Without actually precluding it, Britain appeared to see little role for the United Nations even in observing the military withdrawal. At most it would play a back-up to a four-nation contact group.

Yet there were indications that Britain was prepared to contemplate some UN participation in the transitional administration. In response to a question by the Shadow Foreign Secretary, Denis Healey, during a parliamentary debate on 7 May, the Foreign Secretary said that the extent of UN involvement 'remains to be seen'. He would not 'rule out . . . the possibility of trusteeship'. In the same debate, he also stressed his readiness to talk about sovereignty:

Our position is that this is British sovereign territory. We are totally clear about that. We acknowledge, however, that the Argentines feel that they have a claim to it. We believe that this claim is invalid but acknowledge that they have a claim. Let that be negotiated about in a peaceful way. That is perhaps the crunch point.[6]

With pressure growing for a shift in the British position, Parsons asked on Saturday 8 May for a short delay while he consulted with London. This was assumed in Buenos Aires to reflect a British desire to play for time or else to consider abandoning the mediation, given that during the Haig mediation the British had refused to contemplate a change in the traditional administration. Plans were made to ensure that, if the negotiations did end in this way, Argentina would not be held responsible, as it had been after the Haig shuttle had ground to a halt.

However, by Sunday evening the response came from London that while it was willing to move in its attitude to the role of the UN it still wished to maintain the local Councils in the Islands. Coupled with this were ideas on future negotiations. These stressed the need for a framework designed to resolve the full range of bilateral problems rather than the particular issue of sovereignty. Another shift, to which Argentina soon objected, was to exclude South Georgia and the South Sandwich Islands from any negotiation. In the past Britain had always accepted that these should be considered as a single administrative entity with the Falklands. The most important British point was that there was little point in continuing if the final outcome of the negotiations was to be prejudged.

After the British concession on administration came an Argentine concession on sovereignty. The Argentine delegation, apparently on its own initiative, offered to omit the word 'sovereignty' from its proposals. This was to be done on the understanding that the relevant UN resolutions – which gave implicit support to the Argentine position – would be specifically mentioned in the formal text. This, however, the British were reluctant to do. None the less, the concession on sovereignty had been noted by Parsons, who now sought to follow it up by asking the Secretary-General to gain Argentine confirmation that the parties would conduct the eventual negotiations 'without prejudging the outcome'. On the same day Costa Mendez told a group of American reporters that Argentine sovereignty was now to be the 'objective' of the negotiations; it was no longer a 'prior condition'.[7]

On 10 May Perez de Cuellar asked the Argentine delegation to agree to the following paragraph:

> The parties commit themselves to undergo negotiations in good faith, under the auspices of the Secretary-General of the UN, to achieve the peaceful solution of their differences and to try to complete these negotiations urgently before 31 December 1982. These negotiations will be conducted without damaging the rights and the claims or the positions of both parties and without prejudging their outcome.

He argued that this clause was vital if the stalemate were to be broken. In return Argentina would get not only its preferred date for the conclusion of the negotiations (the end of the year) but also UN administration of the Islands. Ros and his delegation asked the Junta to agree to this formula. In Buenos Aires Costa Mendez argued that it should be accepted on the grounds that opinion in the United Nations, and possibly even in the United States, was moving towards Argentina. Meanwhile there were other provisions which, taken as a whole, would ensure a reasonably favourable final document.

The Junta agreed to the concession to the extent that sovereignty would not be mentioned specifically, but would do so only if this were part of a broader package of measures. The Argentine position now stated that:

1 the accord will be signed in the framework of the Charter of the United Nations; and would take into consideration Resolution 502 of the Security Council as well as the pertinent resolutions of the General Assembly of the United Nations on the specific case of the Islands;

2 the accord will not damage the respective rights, claims and positions of either party;

3 the geographical setting will include the three groups of islands in dispute;

4 the government and the administration will be the exclusive

responsibility of the United Nations. Observers of both parties to the dispute will be able to raise their respective flags in the Islands;

5 there will be freedom of transit and residence for the citizens of both parties, with the power to buy property in the islands;

6 withdrawal of forces will be carried out under the supervision of the UN;

7 the parties will commit themselves to start negotiations in good faith under the auspices of the Secretary-General for the peaceful solution of their differences and with a sense of urgency. They will commit themselves to finishing these negotiations by 31 December 1982.

The next day the Argentine delegation discussed these ideas with the Secretary-General, who then took them to the British delegation. In these first meetings little progress was made. The British insisted on the inclusion of the phrase 'without prejudging the outcome of the negotiations'. The Argentine delegation pressed Buenos Aires for further movement. After intensive consultations between the delegation and the capital, and equally intensive meetings with the capital, the concession was agreed. By the evening the delegation could tell Perez de Cuellar that this critical phrase was now part of the Argentine position.

Argentina still stressed the need to cite the appropriate UN resolutions in the text, and would tolerate only a minimal advisory role for the Island Councils. The administrative structure would be in UN hands. The need to assure access for Argentines to settle on the Islands and to buy property remained central.

Perez de Cuellar was very pleased to receive this news from Ros. At last it seemed that a negotiated settlement was possible. Parsons too was hopeful:

I began with little optimism but I was inclined to revise this when, on 11 May, the Argentine delegation agreed to a formulation under which the outcome of the diplomatic negotiations would not be prejudged at the outset, i.e. establishing that the outcome need not be the transfer of the Falklands to Argentine sovereignty. This was a major concession, or so it seemed.[8]

Perez de Cuellar now decided that it was time to firm up a settlement as soon as possible. He asked the two parties to submit their formal proposals not later than 13 May so that he could bring them together in a document which he would then pass back for consideration. The Argentine draft, which went as far as the country ever went during the course of the conflict, was submitted on 12 May. The preamble concluded: 'These negotiations will begin without prejudice to the rights, claims and/or positions of the parties and without prejudging its outcome.'

Later that day the British proposals were passed on to the UN Secretary-General. The two sides were still far apart on the questions of administration, communications, troop withdrawal and geographical framework. Perez de Cuellar sought further clarification, asking for it by Saturday 15 May so that he could make a formal proposal of his own. Within forty-eight hours of receiving it the parties would be required to answer whether they were in agreement or not. If not, he would withdraw his good offices.

On 14 May he discussed informally with the Security Council the progress of his mediation. He would not go into details because the discussions were confidential but he did warn that a quick result would be very difficult to achieve. 'Time does not favour peace.' After his presentation Parsons informed the Council that he had to travel that same day to London and expected to return on 17 May.

Panama, which had taken a pro-Argentine line from the start, responded to Parsons's announcement by asking Perez de Cuellar if this meant that the negotiations were over. He received the reply that they continued in good faith. At this point the Spanish Ambassador, who had taken a more moderately pro-Argentinean line (and had been keeping the Argentine delegation informed of the climate of opinion within the Security Council) urged the benefits of a cease-fire on the negotiations and asked Parsons to take to his government the message of the Council on the need to maintain a truce while negotiations lasted. The USSR, Poland, Panama, Togo, France, Japan and Ireland concurred.

Final Positions: (i) Britain

It had been Parsons's idea that he should return to London.[9] Matters were clearly coming to a head and he did not want the Government to get itself committed to a position that would cause problems later on when the full implications were appreciated. Both diplomatic negotiations and military preparations were under way without those involved in each activity being fully aware of the others' plans and assessments. This could no longer be achieved through transatlantic communications. Henderson was also asked to return to London from the Washington Embassy for the critical meeting with senior ministers and officials.

There was at this point a range of pressures working on Britain. The task force was not yet ready to mount a landing but it would be so in about a week. That was really all the time available; if the military option was not exercised at that point it feasibility would steadily decline. Parsons could report on the growing sentiment in favour of a cease-fire, while Henderson described the anxiety in the Reagan Administration over the damage to its relations with Latin America. If it were going to sustain its position in the UN, in Europe and with the United States it had to be seen to be negotiating seriously. Such an impression would be undermined by undertaking an amphibious landing while the negotiations were under way. But the landing could not be delayed. The negotiations, therefore, could not be allowed to drag on much longer.

The Secretary-General's intention to come up with his own formula after considering the drafts of the two sides seemed to fit the British timetable. It did, however, contain an obvious danger. Britain had found itself in an awkward position at the end of the Haig mediation when the Secretary of State had submitted his own proposal. It had been let off the hook by an Argentine rejection, but, without this, it would have faced intense pressure to agree to a formula which would have offered major concessions to Argentina and thus rewarded aggression. While the Secretary-General had impressed everyone with the conduct of his mediation it was clear that he was much more genuinely neutral than Haig and was more likely to try to find an intermediate point between the two sides. There remained the possibility of an Argentine rejection, but this could not be assumed. Britain might therefore find itself facing even greater pressure to agree to a formula which breached those principles that had, from the start, been presented to Parliament as inviolable.

The debates in the Commons that week had provided a foretaste of the arguments that might then ensue. The opposition parties had been giving a lot of support to the Secretary-General's efforts. Some Conservative MPs had also shown sympathy, perhaps most notably the former Prime Minister Edward Heath. In terms which had done little to ease the ill will between himself and the Prime Minister, Heath had praised Pym extravagantly in the debate on 13 May and dwelt on the virtues of conciliation. However, Pym had been subjected to the full blast of Conservative feeling when, after the same debate, he addressed the backbench 1922 Committee and had been warned of the vices of conciliation.

To pre-empt a divisive internal debate and external pressure it was necessary to make a final peace offer which went as far as the Government could go without violating its principles. But this could not be subject to further discussion. Negotiations had to conclude one way or the other two days after the submission of this offer.

During the previous week the groundwork for the main compromises that had been agreed during the UN mediation had been laid in the Commons. Up to this point Britain's position had been based on an assertion of sovereignty, which in turn involved a British interim administration. Now the principle of sovereignty had become less important;* now the key principle was self-determination and the continued expression of islander views through the established Councils even if under a UN administration. On 11 May the Prime Minister had stressed the importance of a cease-fire being linked to a speedy military withdrawal on a specific time-table and of not prejudging the outcome of the negotiations. She did not, however, reply directly to

---

* Indeed at one point Pym got into trouble by stating, 'We must have an undertaking from them that sovereignty is not committed, but is negotiable.' He later made it clear that it was the Argentine position that had to be rendered negotiable – and not the British. House of Commons, *The Falklands Campaign*, p. 235.

Enoch Powell when he asked whether there would be a return to sole British administration: 'Sovereignty cannot be changed by invasion. I am very much aware that the rights of the Falkland Islanders were to be governed through the means of an executive and legislative council, and that is what democracy is all about.'[10]

Pym outlined the new position on 13 May:

It may or may not be the case that the United Nations will have a role to play. But we could not, of course, agree to a structure, however temporary, which ignored the past and disregarded the administrative experience of the British inhabitants of the islands . . .

There are officials and administrators who know their jobs; there are democratically elected members of the councils who know the feelings of their fellow islanders. They must be fitted into whatever is agreed if the islands are to be run fairly and efficiently during whatever interim period proves necessary . . .

If we get an agreement, long-term negotiations may begin quite soon. I want to make it clear to the House that we have no doubt whatever about the British title to sovereignty. All British governments have taken the same view. However, we did not, before the invasion, rule out discussion of sovereignty in negotiations with Argentina. Again, successive governments of both parties have taken the same position. We still remain willing to discuss it as one of the factors in negotiations about the long-term future . . .

The islanders will wish to consider, after a period of respite and recuperation, how their prosperity and the economic development of the islands can best be furthered, how their security can best be protected and how their links with the outside world can best be organized. These questions at present are some way ahead and the Government retains an open mind . . .[11]

On Sunday 16 May the text of the proposed agreement was hammered out at the Prime Minister's country residence at Chequers. Much of what passed was a dialogue between the principal negotiator, Parsons, and the principal minister, Thatcher. By this time public opinion was clearly behind the task force and the Government.

Thatcher now dominated the War Cabinet and the other ministers present backed her view that, as the aggrieved party, Britain was under no obligation to make any concessions at all. It was left to the professional diplomats present to warn of the adverse consequences of the appearance of intransigence. Henderson in particular stressed the importance of the flow of military support from the United States to Britain and the risk of that flow being stemmed if opinion in Washington turned against Britain. Gradually the diplomats won the Prime Minister over to the need for a document that represented a genuine attempt at compromise, without conceding the fundamental principle of self-determination.

Parsons understood that a softer diplomatic impression might be created if some of the critical passages were left vague. However, he was also concerned that vague clauses could lead to dangerous misunderstandings. He was exercised as much by the political trouble that the Government might find itself in with Conservative backbenchers as by international opinion. Clarity was particularly important with regard to the mechanics of military withdrawal, which could soon be under way, even though this interested ministers less than the more fundamental issues of principle.

One intriguing feature of the British position was the distinction drawn between the Falkland Islands themselves and the dependencies of South Georgia and the South Sandwich Islands. Although the case for British sovereignty was quite separate in the latter territories and, as we saw during the March crisis, the 1971 Communications Agreements did not apply to them, in practice it had always been accepted that they could not be maintained as a separate entity. During the Haig mediation they had been considered with the main Islands.

Having recaptured South Georgia, Britain saw no reason to make them subject to further negotiations, and this was partly the reason for excluding them from the draft interim agreement. This, of course, was what Argentina feared would happen if the Falklands were returned to British administration without any guarantees on the outcome of an eventual negotiation. There was also, however, a more subtle point. The British attitude to the Falkland Islands would, as a result of the agreement, largely depend on the islanders themselves. Their political institutions should be sustained while their wishes were respected during the negotiations on their long-term future. South Georgia and the South Sandwich Islands lacked a settled population. Here the British position on sovereignty had to rely on assertion rather than self-determination.

Britain's draft agreement provided for mutual withdrawal to a distance of 150 nautical miles around the Islands within fourteen days. A UN administrator would take over the government of the Islands.

> He shall discharge his functions in consultation with the representative institutions in the Islands which have been developed in accordance with the terms of Article 73 of the Charter of the United Nations, with the exception that one representative from the Argentine population normally resident on the Islands shall be appointed by the administrator to each of the two institutions. The administrator shall exercise his powers in accordance with the terms of this Agreement and in conformity with the laws and practices traditionally obtaining in the Islands.

The reference to Article 73 which makes the interests of the inhabitants of non-self-governing territories paramount and refers to the need to take account of their political aspirations was considered to be sufficient to safeguard self-determination.* As Thatcher later explained to the House of Commons: 'If the islanders wished to go to Argentina, I believe that this country would uphold the wishes of the islanders. After their experience, I doubt very much whether that would be the wish of the islanders. Indeed, I believe that they would recoil from it.'[12]

Representation of Argentine interests would be permitted by one of its few permitted local residents (of which there were 30 out of 1,800 total population). In addition, Argentina could have three observers on the Islands – as could Britain. Negotiations on the fundamental dispute should be concluded by 31 December.[13] This completion date

---

* The Article covers non-autonomous countries, such as the Falklands. It speaks of 'developing self-government' and the need to take 'into account the political aspirations of the inhabitants'.

was an aspiration and not a requirement. If no definitive settlement was reached then the interim administration would stay in place.

Final Positions: (ii) Argentina

The Argentine stance was also shaped with a sense of the growing pressure on Argentina to take a softer line as well as the imminence of military action. The British Government had reason to be concerned that it was losing ground in Europe: the problems faced in getting sanctions renewed had been noted. On the other hand, although Argentina still had sympathizers at the highest level in the US Administration, there was no evidence of a change in the American posture. A 14 May speech by Reagan reaffirmed the pro-British line. In Latin America, support for Argentina was strengthening. Colombia, which had abstained at the last Rio meeting, now indicated that it would vote in favour of Argentina. There was to be a meeting of Ministers of Foreign Affairs of the Andean Pact in Bogotá and this would issue a favourable declaration.*

As before, Argentine policy-makers attempted to read the British mind. In the War Cabinet and, more generally, in the Conservative Party there was clearly confusion. Some newspapers were reporting the Argentine concession on sovereignty and suggesting that Britain would have to respond in kind. But equally there was still strong pressure to move quickly to military action. Analysis of the parliamentary debates picked up the tougher statements from ministers and took these to reflect a hardening line. But there was little feel for the nuances of the debate. The divergence of view between Thatcher and Pym was noted but the shift away from the focus on sovereignty and on to self-determination was missed. Perhaps this is not surprising, for in Argentine eyes a stress on self-determination was tantamount to a denial of Argentine sovereignty.

Argentina had hoped to use the negotiating process to delay British military action, especially as it remained extremely uncertain of the form this action was likely to take and when it would occur. The return of

---

* The Andean Pact countries are Peru, Bolivia, Ecuador, Colombia and Venezuela.

Parsons to London indicated that matters had now reached crisis point. The possible British motives for this move dominated Argentine discussions. Ros's assessment from New York was pessimistic.[14] The British were attempting to stretch out the negotiations either to increase pressure on Argentina or simply to obscure preparations for further military operations. This latter interpretation was given added credibility by the raid on Argentine aircraft at Pebble Island on 15 May (see below pp. 327–8). Britain had been wrong-footed by Argentine diplomatic flexibility and so deprived of an excuse to abandon the negotiations for military action. In order to pre-empt what was now becoming a serious negotiation it could well be tempted to move rapidly to achieve a military victory.

Although Britain had insisted that the return to London of Parsons and Henderson did not signify any interruption of the diplomatic process, Roca reported back that senior figures in the UN, including the President and Secretary of the Security Council as well as the Spanish Ambassador, with whom he was in regular contact, were concerned that Britain was taking advantage of the weekend period to complete its military preparations. It was possible, he suggested, that Perez de Cuellar would issue a statement accusing Britain of obstructing his efforts at mediation.

The basis of this rumour is not altogether clear. Undoubtedly Perez de Cuellar and his senior aides would have preferred Parsons to stay in New York and for the proposed time-table to be followed exactly. But the Secretary-General was a pragmatist. Up to this point he had not found Britain especially difficult in the negotiations and Parsons had explained fully his reasons for returning to London. Nothing would be gained by making a public fuss. The origins of the rumour appear to be middle-ranking UN officials on the periphery of the mediation effort from the non-aligned bloc, who had little natural sympathy for Britain. They were suspicious of Britain's motives and proposed a public rebuke to London. Perez de Cuellar never had any intention of following such a course of action.*

---

* When no rebuke came it was assumed that Perez de Cuellar had lost his nerve, so diminishing him in Argentine eyes. The inevitable belief that this was the result of American pressure also diminished the likely instrument of that pressure – Ambassador Kirkpatrick.

If Parsons returned on 17 May with either unacceptable conditions or a formal withdrawal from the negotiations the resolution of the crisis would depend on the outcome of the military confrontation. However, in the event of protracted fighting the political climate could begin to favour Argentina, and even lead to a review and amendment of the troublesome Clause Two of Resolution 502 (which required immediate Argentine withdrawal), so removing the basis of American support for Britain. If Britain were obliged to use its veto, this would demonstrate to the international community that it had never seriously considered a negotiated settlement.*

If the British approach was to be fully exposed then it was necessary for Argentina to have its own position ready at the time that Britain's was presented. This appeared to be the painful diplomatic lesson of the last days of the Haig mediation. In terms of the substance it had to be recognized that there was little that could be done with regard to South Georgia and the South Sandwich Islands, where Argentina had few military options. Nor was there now much possibility of ordering the British fleet back to home base; Ascension Island was about as far as they would go.

At its meeting on the morning of 15 May, the Military Committee decided that Argentina had to create the best diplomatic image possible. Its answer should be ready for Perez de Cuellar at the precise moment that the British proposal was delivered. All channels of communication with the United States should be kept open. No bellicose statements should be issued to the press, notwithstanding the military attacks. However, in order to add to the pressure on Washington

---

* Buenos Aires received a report from New York based on a purported conversation between the Spanish Ambassador and the Secretary-General in which the latter was said to have expressed concern that the return of the two British Ambassadors to London reflected a declining interest in negotiations, that the task force might go on to the attack immediately and that it was felt politic to have Parsons spared the necessity of making diplomatic excuses when the attack came. Perez de Cuellar was also said to believe that his own mediation was almost at an end because of the continued military activity. Ros's assessment was that the Security Council was waiting for the conclusion of the Secretary-General's mediation. In any future vote the Council would align itself in the following manner: China, USSR, Panama, Spain and Poland in favour of Argentina; US, France and Guyana voting with the United Kingdom. The other countries involved were fluctuating between one party and the other.

preparations should be made to call for a meeting of American presidents in the OAS so as to propose breaking the organization and creating instead an Organization of Latin American States excluding the US.

The Military Committee met again on 16 May at 18.00. Costa Mendez reported on the UN delegation's expectations. Three possibilities were considered. First, the Secretary-General's plan would be followed and Britain would provide its proposal as requested. Taking this into account, with that of Argentina, Perez de Cuellar would present a written proposal of his own to both parties, who would then respond. This could happen between 19 and 21 May.

Second, this procedure would be followed but in the middle of this process Britain would invade the Islands. Should this happen Argentina would call at once for a meeting of the Security Council.

Third, Britain might simply harden its posture and increase military pressure by escalating the war. In this case the Argentine proposals should be presented to the Secretary-General immediately to show up Britain for its inflexibility. Then there should be a call for a meeting of the Security Council. With both the second and third possibilities it was assumed that the Security Council would back a cease-fire and encourage continuing negotiations.

The recommendation from both Ros and Roca at the UN was that they should be allowed to present the Argentine proposals to Perez de Cuellar without waiting for Britain, so as to demonstrate goodwill. However, Costa Mendez disagreed. He felt that Argentina had been at a disadvantage during the Haig mission because it continued to put forward its ideas without any notion of what Britain was proposing. This information had been used by Britain and the United States to revise their positions. This time Argentine ideas should not be forwarded to the mediator before the British paper was received.

This advice was accepted. The Military Committee decided that Ambassador Listre should take the Argentine document to Ros and Roca at the UN but that they should not present it to the Secretary-General until Britain had first presented its own document. In practice this meant conceding the initiative to Britain, for the possibility that had not been considered was Britain submitting a document that appeared reasonable, but on a take-it-or-leave-it basis.

Argentina's revised position differed in a number of respects from Britain's. It covered the dependencies as well as the main Islands. Forces would withdraw to 'their normal bases and areas of operation', which for Britain would mean a complete withdrawal from the South Atlantic. The interim administration was to be the exclusive responsibility of the United Nations, with no role for the Island Councils. The administration itself would be made up of individuals of nationalities other than of Britain and Argentina, whose interests would be represented only by advisers drawn in equal measure from Argentine nationals and the islanders. There would be no 'discriminatory restrictions of any kind for the parties, including freedom of movement and equality of access with respect to residence, work and property'. This would mean that Argentine settlers could potentially change the demographic character of the Islands, and so the implication of self-determination.

With regard to the question of sovereignty, the new draft still included the earlier concession, but removed the phrase 'without prejudging the outcome' when referring to negotiations between the two parties. It agreed to initiate the talks without 'prejudice to the right and claims or positions of the two parties and in recognition of the fact that they have divergent positions'. The objective of these negotiations was compliance with those UN resolutions judged by Argentina to be favourable to its case. The negotiations had to be completed in the time allowed. As a concession the deadline of 31 December 1982 was not final: there could be an option to extend to 30 June 1983. The whole of the Argentine position was to be declared as negotiable.

The Last Stage

On 17 May Parsons carried the British proposal with him on the early-morning Concorde from London to New York. By noon he was with the Secretary-General going through it. Perez de Cuellar was impressed by its flexibility. His initial reaction was 'optimistic'; he thought that it might be considered favourably by Argentina.[15]

He was concerned about the disruption of the process he had outlined, although he also accepted that the negotiations had to conclude within forty-eight hours: there had been plenty of time for discussions but they could not be allowed to drag on indefinitely. Parsons gave to Perez de Cuellar the same assessment that he had given the Prime Minister: there was a less than 50 per cent chance of it being accepted by Argentina but that it would be well advised to do so.

Later that afternoon the Secretary-General met with the Argentine delegation and described the British proposal. He explained that it was final and could not be amended. It was non-negotiable.

Jeane Kirkpatrick, who was considered by Argentina to be its most senior sympathizer in Washington, saw Ros and Roca that evening to persuade them to accept the British proposal or at least, even though it was described as non-negotiable, suggest modifications rather than reject it outright. She believed that it was the best that Argentina could hope for. Britain was not asking for Argentina to acknowledge British sovereignty over the Islands, nor insisting on the return of a British administration; there were specific dates for negotiations and there was an Argentine presence on the Islands. However, she found the Argentine Vice-Minister unwilling to modify his own negotiating position.[16]

The Malvinas Group and Costa Mendez concluded their analysis of the British proposal on the morning of 18 May. Not surprisingly they found unacceptable the exclusion of the dependencies, the continuation of the Island Councils, the open-ended character of the temporary administration, the use of Article 73 of the UN Charter to indicate that the eventual solution for the Islands would be based on self-determination, and the continued inaccessibility of the Islands and their property to Argentine citizens.

At 11.00 they took this analysis to the Military Committee, which had already been meeting for two hours. A quick response was needed: Ros was anxious to hand over the document that Listre had taken to him, with whatever amendments were now deemed necessary. Costa Mendez suggested a new clause which would allow the issue to be passed to the General Assembly if the negotiations stalled: 'the Secretary-General shall draw up a report addressed to the General

Assembly of the United Nations, in order that the latter may determine, as appropriate and with greater urgency, the lines to which the said final agreement should conform in order to achieve a speedy settlement of the question.' In addition, it was suggested that the Secretary-General should be encouraged to reject the British reference to Article 73 given that Argentina had refrained from mentioning 'sovereignty' and, further, that it was necessary to insist on equal rights for Argentine citizens.

Speaking to Ros in New York, Costa Mendez stressed the importance of continued negotiations. If, however, this was impossible then the responsibility for their collapse must be seen to be Britain's, rather than due to 'Argentine intransigence'. 'Our differences', he noted, 'are not so great so as to justify a total war.'

Ros was less sure. He thought that the differences were 'substantial'. There was a strong possibility of a British rejection. More seriously:

I do believe that we have to present a paper that is as flexible and as rational as possible but we also must understand that this exercise does not have much future, because the British position is hard and does not admit any variations or alterations and in so doing reveals its intention ... We will see the reaction of the Secretary-General now but it is possible that he will decide not to offer an intermediate paper but report directly to the Security Council on the negative result of the mediation.

In a later communication Ros argued that the matter would now be referred to the Security Council. Costa Mendez should come to New York for a likely meeting on Thursday 20 May.

This exercise in negotiations is reaching its end. Even in the most optimistic light, it is ending because both the Secretary-General and the British have talked of deadlines. So it is logical to assume that the Security Council will take over. So, what we have here is the beginning of a new political exercise that will coincide with the imminent British military escalation.

At this point the final Argentine stance was fixed – not to create the image of reasonableness but to restate its basic position – on the assumption that the present attempt at mediation no longer had a future. It was decided not only to include a clause which sought to refer the issue to the General Assembly but also to remove the concession of the previous week with regard to 'not prejudging the outcome'.

This was the opposite of what Britain had feared. Although it had insisted that its proposal was non-negotiable, an Argentine response that was at all close to this proposal but required a few, apparently small, concessions would have led to enormous pressure, not least from the United States, to continue negotiating. British diplomats had persuaded their political masters – with difficulty – that international support required an image of reasonableness. Argentine diplomats were aware of the same need, but they had apparently failed to persuade their leaders.

This is partly explained by the Junta's understanding of the nature of the negotiating exercise. From the start its objective had been a transfer of the Islands' sovereignty. Any negotiation should be about the modalities of the transfer, the guarantees to the islanders and whatever consolation prizes were to be offered to Britain.

The occupation had raised popular expectations, to the point where any deviation from the basic objective was viewed as virtually treason-ous. But with the task force on its way Britain saw no need to allow Argentina to dictate the terms of the negotiations. The role of any mediator in these circumstances was extremely difficult; it was neces-sary to persuade Britain to offer Argentina some gain after an act of blatant illegality while persuading Argentina to accept something manifestly less than sovereignty.

Argentina blamed Haig for the failure of the previous mediation efforts – both his own and the Peruvian, which was an extension of his. In part this was because of his diplomatic technique, but also, more importantly, because it was almost impossible to believe that anything could occur in the region without US knowledge or acquiescence: any Argentine reversal had occurred because Haig had planned it. He had used the mediation to explore the concerns and vulnerabilities of

Argentina and had then used this intelligence to Britain's advantage, above all in providing it with time for the task force to reach its destination. Suspicions of Haig were such that when Belaunde reported that his initiative was backed by the US (which the Peruvian President considered a major selling point) this was actually a cause for concern, seen to be all too justified by the sinking of the *Belgrano*. Hence the relief at the possibility of UN mediation.

But the preoccupation with what was believed to be Haig's deception hid from the Junta the fact that *no* mediator could have given Argentina much more. Britain was widely seen – not just by the US – to be the aggrieved party. Its bargaining position was also getting stronger all the time. Perez de Cuellar was as aware of this as Haig. He was attempting to reconcile the differences; that was not simply a matter of 'splitting the difference' but of attempting to offer each side the maximum that it could realistically expect from the exercise. The two sides could be treated equally but their views could not be given the same status.

If the Junta assumed that the Secretary-General would in following his original procedure come up with an intermediate proposal and that, in this case, by staking out a more extreme position the median spot would be pulled further towards Argentine interests, then disappointment was inevitable.

But the facts were more complex than this interpretation allowed. The Junta could not accept that Britain had made any significant concessions because the end result of any deal that it proposed would be a return to something approximating the status quo ante bellum. It therefore assumed that Britain was not negotiating in good faith but was procrastinating in order to gain time for its military operations. (This is also of course almost exactly what was believed in London about Argentina.) The sudden disruption of what appeared to be an orderly negotiating procedure when Parsons returned to London, coupled with further military actions by Britain, alerted the Junta to the possibility that once again Britain had just been buying time. Comments by representatives of other countries at the UN had reinforced this perception, including those that urged Argentina to make concessions to 'avoid bloodshed'.

The hardening of the Argentine stance was therefore based on the assumption not that Perez de Cuellar would split the difference, but that the mediation was all but over. In these circumstances, and whatever had been said privately to Perez de Cuellar, the final proposals for publication had to restate the basic Argentine position. As at the end of the Haig mediation, previous concessions were withdrawn so as to have a full set ready for the next mediator and to demonstrate to public opinion that the Junta was still firm in its convictions.

The Mediation Concludes

Having received the Argentine proposals late on 18 May, Perez de Cuellar considered them. As the recent amendments had hardened rather than softened the Argentine stance, following on a British position that offered no new concessions and lacked any further flexibility, he realized his mediation effort was coming to an end. Near midnight he asked the Argentine delegation whether he should transmit these proposals to Britain and whether he could describe them as 'Argentine ideas' rather than a final statement. He was told that he could.

Perez de Cuellar then rang Parsons and told him that he had received the Argentine document but that it was in Spanish. Could he wait until a translation was ready in the morning? Parsons said he could not because the loss of another day was unacceptable. So Perez de Cuellar provided Parsons with a rough translation in his office. Parsons's immediate reaction was that the document was rhetorical and failed to address the detailed points in the British position. This seemed to be the end of the negotiations. He praised Perez de Cuellar for his negotiating effort and described the result as a tragedy.[17]

As had been understood from the start, any final bridging of the gap would have to be done by Perez de Cuellar. The British had shown some flexibility but now insisted that there could be no more: Argentina had yielded little, and had gone back on a previous concession, but it indicated that it might show more flexibility. It was hard to be optimistic.

None the less, the Secretary-General persevered with his attempt. He sought an extension of the period allowed him by the Security Council to complete the negotiation. He suggested sending an envoy, Dr Cordoves, to talk directly to the two parties, before he presented his own proposal. He suggested this first to Costa Mendez in a telephone conversation. Costa Mendez asked whether the envoy would go to London and, if so, whether he would be welcome. Perez de Cuellar replied that his aides were exploring the possibility. Costa Mendez offered to arrange talks with Galtieri, and to do whatever was necessary himself, including even meeting the British Foreign Minister. He was ready for all 'negotiations that lead to peace and a peaceful solution as long as there is symmetry and equivalence in the treatment so that there is equity both inside and outside the negotiation procedures. I trust on your decision.'

Perez de Cuellar warned him not to expect too much:

I am trying to see now what the reaction on the other side will be [to the sending of an envoy]. Unfortunately I believe the reaction will be negative. It seems that Mrs. Thatcher is under enormous pressures from Parliament. There is a great urgency that undermines the possibilities for talking. I am trying to obtain another 48 hours but I have the impression that the other party is not willing to give me this breathing space . . .

Perez de Cuellar did speak to President Galtieri. He described the progress that had been made up to 17 May but also the major differences that remained in the areas of interim administration, geographical framework, force withdrawals and outcome of the negotiations. Although Britain had ended the mediation effort he nevertheless still believed he could continue with his good offices and asked for more hours.

Galtieri agreed to an envoy so long as he also went to London. If an envoy were sent only to Argentina it would appear as if it were his country that was being intransigent. He also suggested to Perez de Cuellar that Thatcher should be asked to send Pym to New York to confer face to face with Costa Mendez. Perez de Cuellar said he would suggest this to the Prime Minister.

Perez de Cuellar met informally with the Security Council on the evening of 19 May. He explained that, although the two proposals he had received diverged, he still wished to continue his efforts. He believed that he could benefit from another two days. Parsons explained that there could be no qualifications to the British position – and certainly not until after the House of Commons debate scheduled for the next day. It was agreed that the Secretary-General should be allowed another twenty-four hours (midnight on 20 May) to develop his own proposal and send it to both parties. Late that night, Perez de Cuellar sent his proposal to both parties for analysis and comment.

Exactly what happened then is unclear. According to British sources, when Perez de Cuellar spoke to Thatcher on 19 May he suggested a few small and apparently insignificant changes to the text. He then sent an *aide-mémoire* containing his own formulations. This was brief on most points, but full on the two critical questions of interim administration and the subsequent diplomatic negotiations. It contained, according to Pym, 'no specific proposals on the practical details of mutual force withdrawal.'[18] – the area in which Parsons had convinced the Government that ambiguity could be treacherous. According to Parsons, the Secretary-General's idea 'did not agree with our own proposals (although it was not far removed from them)'. Thatcher told Parliament on 20 May that the Secretary-General's *aide-mémoire*:

> differs in certain important respects from our position as presented to him on 17 May and which we then described as the furthest that we could go. Moreover, it differs fundamentally from the present Argentine position as communicated to us yesterday.
>
> ... Some of his suggestions are the very ones which have already been rejected by the Argentine response to our own proposals. Even if they were acceptable to both parties as a basis for negotiation, that negotiation would take many days, if not weeks, to reach either success or failure.

This was the seventh set of proposals received and, as they were again closer to the British than the Argentine position, the Prime Minister saw no reason to delay military action. Her words to Parliament, however, do not make it clear whether she had actually ruled out further negotiations on the basis of the *aide-mémoire*: 'Even if we were prepared to negotiate on the basis of the aide-mémoire, we should first wish to see substantive Argentine comments on it, going beyond mere acceptance of it as a basis for negotiation. At the same time we are reminding [the Secretary-General] . . . that negotiations do not close any military options.'[19] Pym's speech indicated slightly more interest in the Argentine response, although no more confidence that it would be positive.[20] At the same time Parsons was telling the Secretary-General that Britain would need to see the Argentine response before commenting in detail.[21]

Having concluded that the Argentine document constituted a definite rejection of its proposals, the British Government made public its own version of events as Mrs Thatcher was speaking to Parliament. Argentina later complained that this action directly contravened the procedures agreed with the Secretary-General and at a time when he was still considering his position after receiving the ideas of the two parties. He would now find it even more difficult to construct his own intermediate proposals. One UN official has agreed with this:

> Once the British text was released to the press, the possibility of confidential, quiet, mutually developed formulations disappeared. While there are some very positive points in the British proposal, which the Argentine government may subsequently have considered a pretty good deal, its release to the public greatly inhibited the prospects of the secretary-general's efforts to reach an agreement that would seem to be the result of mutual Argentine–British efforts.[22]

In practice, however, Britain believed that the process of negotiation had come to an end. Argentina seems to have taken a similar view. There was some discussion about making a response by the evening of 20 May. However, Thatcher's comments in Parliament were apparently taken as a rejection by Britain. Then intelligence was received in Buenos Aires of orders to Admiral Woodward to start landings. At just this time the President of Peru introduced yet another proposal. Its main effect was to distract Argentina from responding at all to the Secretary-General's ideas, and Perez de Cuellar now appears to blame this, together with a false expectation that more could be achieved, for the final collapse of his efforts.[23]

Time had now run out. As the mediation closed the landings began.

Part Six

COMBAT

Chapter Nineteen

BUILD-UP TO SAN CARLOS

The British Chiefs of Staff had concluded at an early stage that if diplomacy failed to produce an Argentine withdrawal there would be little choice but to land troops in the Falklands. There was some political support for the idea of a blockade, for example from Defence Minister John Nott. This could put diplomatic pressure on Argentina while reducing the risks of war. Nott recognized too that once Britain had put forces in great numbers on to the Islands it would, thereafter, be difficult to get them off. A permanent Falklands garrison, he believed, was not in Britain's long-term defence interests.[1]

The military would have none of this. Admiral Lewin was insistent that a blockade would be difficult to sustain, because of enemy action and the weather, while excessive delay could render an eventual landing impossible because of the problem of maintaining the task force in increasingly stormy and inclement weather over an extended period. Stuck on board ships the soldiers would lose combat readiness. Options to harass the enemy by small-scale raids or even troop landings on remote parts of the Islands would scarcely inconvenience the enemy and might hazard the islanders. As time went by British commitments to NATO would suffer and international support would diminish. There was little choice but to attempt a landing.

On 16 April Admiral Fieldhouse and General Moore arrived on *Hermes*, anchored off Ascension Island, for a 'council of war' with the brigade staff and Woodward's staff. Fieldhouse told those present that the Government was committed to the repossession of the Falklands by whatever means necessary. He also warned that 'this is the most difficult thing we have attempted since the Second World War.'[2]

However the landing was to be achieved, the planners were concerned to ensure that they had sufficient forces and that they could cope with the enemy threat, especially the air threat.

The Operational Directive set just before this meeting was to 'prepare to land with a view to regaining the possession', which left open the type and extent of fighting which might take place after a landing. It did not involve planning beyond that stage. A week later, as the Haig mission faltered and Lewin became convinced that fighting was virtually inevitable, he changed the mission to the simple 'repossession' of the Islands.

Planning on the basis of the first directive provided for only enough forces to land and then to protect the landing area. That could be done with one brigade; anything more would require two brigades. The paper prepared by 3 Commando Brigade[3] for the meeting warned that it would have insufficient forces to take Stanley:

> The imbalance of forces, lack of initial assault capability and subsequent inability to maintain a rapid rate of advance across country with appropriate fire support for a practical period, precludes an attack against Port Stanley by 3 Commando Brigade (without reinforcement) in any time frame. The landing force as currently constituted cannot retake Port Stanley.[4]

There had already been some preliminary discussions between Moore, in charge of land forces, and the Army about the possibility of sending 5 Infantry Brigade to the South Atlantic as well but there was no formal advice from the Ministry of Defence. It was agreed to reinforce 3 Brigade with 2 PARA, then assigned to 5 Brigade. Thereafter, 5 Brigade began to be prepared for service in the Falklands.

No formal decisions concerning its dispatch to the South Atlantic were taken until late April. After a visit to Northwood, the commander of UK land forces reported to General Edwin Bramall, Chief of the General Staff, his belief that more troops were necessary. This Bramall reported to Lewin, who responded that he had received no such request from Admiral Fieldhouse, commanding the task force from Northwood. When asked by Lewin, Fieldhouse was annoyed that the argument had not been put to him directly. There was some suspicion that the Army's main concern was that the Marines were taking the lead and that the Army were being left out of the action.

However, now that the issue had been raised the question of 5 Brigade's role was addressed. The change in the operational directive to 'repossession' of the Islands argued for extra forces. Reports were now coming through of the arrival of Parada's 3rd Infantry Brigade in the Falklands and this raised the requirements. All this plus the deteriorating prospects for a peaceful settlement persuaded the Government to take the high-profile step of ordering 5 Brigade to mobilize and requisitioning the liner *Queen Elizabeth II* to take it to the South Atlantic, with Moore as divisional commander. The *QE2* left on 12 May.

Argentine Air Power

Another major issue at the Ascension Island council was how to cope with the air threat. Thompson and Commodore Clapp, Commander of the amphibious fleet, had stressed the importance of air superiority at a meeting in Northwood just before the task force sailed and now did so again. They had become concerned that Woodward was failing to appreciate the gravity of the air threat. In part this was a result of Woodward's difficulty at the time in achieving the right balance between prudent recognition of the risks and sustaining morale. (This difficulty was also reflected in press interviews after the retaking of South Georgia which appeared to give contradictory assessments of the dangers facing the task force.) In practice he was just as concerned about the threat, and this was indicated in some of his ideas – in themselves impractical – which would have geared the landing to establishing an airstrip. Although the amphibious force commanders were offered reassurances at Ascension they were not reassured.

Argentine Air Force Daggers and Mirages deployed to airfields in Patagonia and Tierra del Fuego during the second half of April. But the air strength was not as great as the British had feared: the initial estimate suggested that as many as 247 aircraft might be available.[5] In the event the Argentine Air Force deployed seventeen tanker and reconnaissance aircraft, with sixty-five fighters and strike aircraft – eight Mirages, nineteen Daggers (an Israeli version of the Mirage), thirty-one Skyhawks and seven Canberras. In addition the Navy deployed four Super-Etendards and eight Skyhawks to the Air Force base at Rio Grande. Other Air Force squadrons were kept back to their normal bases to deal with either a Chilean or a British challenge to the mainland. In addition a number of light aircraft, of which the most capable were the Pucaras, were employed.

The British task force was also fortunate that Argentina had not worked out how to turn the runway at Stanley into one that could support high-performance jets. During April a Super-Etendard was sent with a dummy missile load to Stanley airport to see if it could be used for operations. It was concluded that the runway was too short and generally too wet for this sort of operation. Some consideration was given to the possibility of lengthening it, but there was insufficient time and the runway was in heavy use by transport aircraft.[6] A scheme to install a metallic (aluminium) runway was postponed because there were other priorities for the scarce sealift capacity during April. Air Force planners were concerned that even if they had managed to establish a base at Stanley it would have been almost impossible to sustain the supply network for armaments, fuel and spare parts.[7]

In the event only light aircraft were based at Stanley. Two other landing strips were also found to be of use for light aircraft. Darwin served as a base for the Air Force's Pucara light aircraft while the Navy took over a landing strip at Pebble Island for four Beech armed trainers and six Pucaras.

In order to reduce further Argentine air capabilities the British task force sought to put Argentine bases out of action on the Islands and draw out those aircraft on the mainland in the hope of shooting down as many as possible prior to any landing.

As we have seen, the first attack on Stanley airfield was made on 1 May by a Vulcan bomber, backed by Sea Harriers. It was initially unclear how effective this had been. An attempt by a Harrier to photograph the damage was thwarted by heavy anti-aircraft fire and bad weather, although a visual observation suggested some damage.[8] Eventually, two days later, a picture was obtained showing a crater in the middle of the runway and three shallow craters going down the runway and slightly across. An unwillingness to risk Sea Harriers, which were in increasingly short supply, meant that it took until 12 May before another photograph was obtained. It appeared as if there were still craters. In fact, by this time the Argentine garrison had partially repaired the damage, but had made two mock craters out of mounds of earth that were removed each night to allow Hercules transports to land.[9]

The British knew that some transports were using the runway and that it would probably be difficult to close it altogether, but they hoped that continued harassment through air and naval gunfire attack could interfere with its effective operation. Despite all this, over thirty Hercules flights reached Stanley from 1 May until the end of the war on 14 June.

More success was achieved in dealing with aircraft on the Falklands. The intelligence staff at Northwood had checked the details of all the many possible landing strips on the Islands with Argentine aircraft specifications and concluded that none was appropriate. Islanders who had returned to Britain after the invasion suggested a few possibilities, including Pebble Island, and this was then checked through reconnaissance.

The SAS had already identified Pebble Island as an Argentine garrison on the basis of radio traffic, and had wanted to mount a raid to demoralize the defenders. Permission for this had been denied. However, Admiral Woodward had taken a renewed interest when he became concerned that Pebble Island might be used as a helicopter base. This variety of interests came together, and the SAS was given permission to mount the raid.

On 15 May, forty-five SAS men were landed by helicopter three miles from the Argentine airstrip on Pebble Island, unsure what they would find but expecting a fight with the defenders. In the event they found few defenders but eleven aircraft, against which they detonated charges. Under cover of naval gunfire, they were taken back to the fleet without serious casualty. All the aircraft were destroyed and the raid appeared as a surgical, bloodless operation, somewhat different from the SAS's original expectation. The runway was disabled and was not used thereafter, although the aircraft losses, especially the Pucaras, were made up by extra deliveries from the mainland.

Given the difficulties of putting even a crude airfield out of action, attacks on the bases on the Argentine mainland would have had only a limited chance of success. The possibility of an attack on a carefully delineated target, for example the base of the Super-Etendards, was not ruled out, but the view in London from early on was that the political costs of this sort of escalation, its doubtful status in international law, combined with the practical problems of making it a success, rendered it unattractive.

From the British perspective, the encounters of early May, when a Mirage and two Canberras were shot down, appeared to have discouraged the Argentine Air Force from further engagements so as to conserve resources for a British landing. On being spotted by Harriers, Argentine aircraft returned home.

Certainly the Argentine Air Force mounted few sorties – only sixteen – from early May to 20 May. But eighty-five were planned and Argentine sources suggest that the main reasons for the lack of air activity were poor weather conditions and the fact that the task force was keeping its distance after being caught on 4 May. Woodward's need to protect his ships from air attack meant that he could not tempt the Argentine pilots as he had done in the first days of May.

The Argentine perception was that British airpower had yet to prove itself. On 1 May the Harriers bombing Stanley airport had not got close enough to mount an effective attack and in the process a number had got shot down. Although this assessment was based on an optimistic reading of the performance of air defences (see Chapter 16) it was none the less firmly believed in Buenos Aires. In early May the Argentine view was that the Harriers had been overrated.

For whatever reason the attrition of Argentine air capabilities was not as great as the British command had hoped. An Aeromacchi and three Skyhawks were lost in accidents (one shot down by Argentine anti-aircraft fire near Goose Green on 15 May) and another three

Skyhawks to Sea Wolf missiles from HMS *Brilliant* on 12 May. Meanwhile the British had lost three helicopters and two Sea Harriers in accidents while another Harrier had been lost to anti-air fire near Goose Green on 4 May.

The bulk of the Argentine Air Force was still intact. Frustrated by his failure to draw it out, Woodward signalled to Northwood his concern just as the amphibious force was leaving Ascension Island. He concluded: 'A ticket on the train about to leave Ascension will be very expensive.' Thompson also expressed his continuing concern, only to be told not to worry, that it was being 'dealt with' – an assurance that left him quite unconvinced and helped create the later tension that developed between the Commander of 3 Brigade and Northwood after the landing. From Northwood's perspective the decision to order an amphibious landing was political and not military. If the risks could not be eliminated then its responsibility was only to ensure that the politicians were aware of them.

Landing Site

Woodward's idea, discussed at the Ascension council, was to land on West Falkland in order to establish an airstrip from which British air superiority could eventually be asserted. Phantoms would be brought over from the UK and Hercules transports could land to bring stores.[10] But Thompson's planners saw glaring faults in this approach: yet another amphibious landing would then be needed to gain access to the main Argentine force on East Falkland, while West Falkland would be much more vulnerable to Argentine land-based aircraft and less easy to protect using carrier-based aircraft.

Nor could any landing be too close to Stanley. A variety of options had been considered at an early stage, including an SAS raid, after a landing at Stanley airport, which would drive into town to seize the Argentine commanders. The paper from 3 Brigade noted: 'given the imbalance of force ratios . . . and our very limited assault capability . . . a frontal assault on Port Stanley would have little chance of success.' The same conclusion was reached quite separately by Moore's staff at

Northwood and in a paper prepared for the War Cabinet.[11]

East Falkland offered many alternative landing sites, most of which would be undefended. Some were discarded because they were within range of the Argentine artillery at Stanley or easy to attack from sea or air or land; others were too obvious or too exposed to the fierce winds of the area; still more offered beaches that were too confined. However, because of the lack of an internal road network and the limited number of heavy-lift helicopters, the site had to be within reach of Stanley. Gradually the options were narrowed down for checking by SBS patrols, who reported back on surf conditions, the beach gradient, the exits from the beach and whether elbow room could be found for 5,000 men, 24 guns, about 36 helicopters initially and 4,500 tons of stores, fuel and ammunition, as well as for its defence.

Finally, three options remained – Cow Bay, Uranie Bay and San Carlos. Since April San Carlos had been favoured by both Clapp and Thompson, and by Northwood.[12] The others were only suitable if the objective had been to take an Argentine surrender, for they had poor anchorages and would be easier to defend. At San Carlos the beaches were good. It was well out of the range of artillery and the layout of the bay made it very difficult to mount air attacks on the landing forces. With the attacking aircraft coming from the west, they would have to pass first a Harrier cordon, then a picket line of ships with a variety of anti-air defences and eventually the anti-aircraft weapons of the ground forces. The disadvantage was that many warships would have to sit for a number of days in highly vulnerable positions. By way of compensation Falkland Sound allowed for reasonable protection against Exocet anti-ship missiles and submarines (because of the narrow entrance at each end).

The principal disadvantage, however, was the distance from Stanley. Moore, along with the Army staff, would have preferred a much shorter distance to allow the land forces to close quickly on the enemy.[13] If there were any sort of serious Argentine resistance the forces might get stuck in the middle of the Islands in deteriorating conditions. However, General Bramall, Chief of the General Staff, overruled his staff once he became convinced, as did Moore, that the alternatives were all much more exposed to attack. At the time of landing, British forces would be at their most vulnerable; thereafter superior British professionalism should assert itself. Moreover, the distance also meant that the Argentine command would probably assume that San Carlos was simply too far away for a landing to be likely; they had certainly made no attempt to guard against it and there was only a small Argentine presence in the area.

By May the Chiefs of Staff had accepted that San Carlos was the optimum site, the concern about the distance from Stanley outweighed by the possibility of a relatively protected anchorage. On 10 May at a conference on *Fearless* there was formal agreement on San Carlos. On 12 May Thompson received confirmation that his preference was shared by Northwood; two days later he sent out his orders, already prepared, for Operation Sutton – 'operations related to the repossession of the Falklands'.

Timing

There was a ten-day period within which to make the landing. After that time the troops would have been embarked for one month and would need to be taken back to Ascension. Then it would be midwinter and the operation could not be repeated.

It was calculated that maximum intensive flying from carriers could probably not continue for more than a month – from 1 May to 1 June. After that there would be weather damage and equipment failures. However, after the landing the equipment being carried on *Atlantic Conveyor* would make it possible to operate and maintain Harriers from a landing strip at San Carlos, though this would take some time. For these reasons Northwood and Admiral Woodward hoped that a landing could be organized for 16 May.

In the event, a delay until at least 19/20 May was unavoidable because of the time taken to get key ships of the task force, such as the ferry *Norland* and the *Atlantic Conveyor*, into position. 2 PARA only arrived at Ascension on *Norland* in early May. They were given some time to catch up with the training that had been under way for the past couple of weeks and then, on 8 May, the War Cabinet ordered the amphibious task force to set sail.

3 Brigade would have preferred more time at Ascension – to train and practise, but also to get everything prepared for the eventual landing. They needed to restow kit so that men and equipment would come out in the sequence in which they were needed rather than that in which they had happened to be packed while loading in Britain. In the event some problems with the Rapier air-defence missiles were only discovered at San Carlos.[14]

Intelligence

The optimum date for the landing allowed only two weeks for special patrols to gather intelligence on possible landing sites and the state of Argentine defences. This led to arguments at the council of war because the admirals were fearful of the consequences of delay, while those responsible for the actual landing saw this as further evidence of the naval officers' insufficient grasp of the imperatives of amphibious landings. In the event the special forces were allowed three weeks, which is what Thompson had asked for in the first place. According to his account this was 'barely enough': 'The gathering of intelligence was a long and painstaking business, a point not readily appreciated by those who forecast that it could be done in two weeks.'[15]

A potential source of delay was mitigated because one officer, Major Southby-Tailyour, a keen yachtsman, had charted the waters surrounding the Falklands in 1978. His copious notes made it possible to identify likely landing sites early on so that the special forces had to look at relatively few beaches. It was thus possible 'to gather in three weeks the sort of detailed information that had taken months to collect before the Normandy landings in 1944'.[16] Although the Hydrographer of the Navy provided considerable detail to Northwood for its planning, for tactical detail Southby-Tailyour was invaluable. Moreover as a landing-craft specialist he looked at the coast-line in terms of how to beach a boat, while the naval officer's natural concern is to avoid that.

In general intelligence was poor. The lack of satellite photography has already been noted. The helicopters and Harriers could provide some tactical reconnaissance, but with their limited capabilities they could not travel far afield and, as scarce resources required for a variety of other tasks, there was a limit on how often they could be used for this purpose. Specialist Canberras or Phantoms would have been ideal for photo-reconnaissance, but they were not available. An Airborne Early Warning and Command System (AWACS) would have been useful for more general surveillance and early warning but the US would not provide one as that would have involved committing US personnel to the conflict.[17] The UK equivalent, based on the Nimrod aircraft, was not yet operational (and indeed never became so).

Some capability was gradually built up based on Ascension Island. Nimrods began arriving on Ascension as early as 5 April but their limited range meant that they could do little more than watch over the task force as it approached the base and then departed for the South Atlantic, as well as watch against any attack on Ascension itself. On 18 April, six Victor tankers arrived, at least one of them fitted with aerial cameras. But not until 11 May was it possible to use the Nimrods over a longer distance, by adding an air-to-air refuelling capability. These appeared to have been used primarily for radar and electronic reconnaissance rather than photographic. Their main task, capturing the world record for long-distance reconnaissance flights in the process (1,300 miles and a 400,000 square mile sweep), was to check that the Argentine Navy was staying in port after its experience with the *Belgrano*.[18] Nobody seems to have thought to take what might have served as a valuable and comparatively invulnerable form of photographic reconnaissance – remotely controlled vehicles (drones) which were in service in Germany and Britain.

Thompson noted:

Not until the very end of the campaign were there any air photographs showing enemy dispositions, defensive positions, strong positions, gun positions and so forth. Even they arrived so late and were so poor that they had no influence on planning. So, for the first time probably since Gallipoli in 1915, an amphibious operation was to be mounted with no air photographs of the enemy. Detailed intelligence would therefore have to be gleaned by the 'mark one eyeball'.[19]

'Mark one eyeball' referred to the SAS and SBS patrols active on the Falklands from the beginning of May. Patrolling of this sort would have been essential with or without other forms of tactical intelligence, but they were given more importance as a result of the limitations elsewhere. The first SAS and SBS men were inserted on East Falkland on the night of 30 April. The four-man patrols were landed at night by Sea King helicopters. With so few helicopters and occasional bad weather it was not always possible to land patrols as planned. They had to be put down up to four nights' march away from their targets and they would move at least one night's march away before pickup.

Some notion of where the patrols should be looking came from reports by those who had been on the Islands after the occupation. The marines repatriated by Argentina from South Georgia and the Falklands, who had the first – if short – combat experience in dealing with the Argentine forces, were debriefed, as were two RAF technicians who had been inspecting the Stanley runway and provided MoD with information on its condition (which it ought already to have had but could not find – the plans were with the Overseas Development Administration).

More useful than the marines, who had not seen Argentine forces beyond Stanley, were the islanders who had left the Falklands after the invasion. Because Argentina was anxious to demonstrate that the islanders were being well treated and were not prisoners, they were specifically told that they could 'come and go' as they pleased. Trips out of the Islands were not stopped until 1 May. The civil population of the Falklands fell by more than 800 to fewer than 1,000 within about three weeks.[20] They had come from various settlements around the Islands and were able to report on where they had seen substantial bodies of troops, as well as the sort of equipment they carried and the uniforms they wore – even on patrolling patterns, though they could not be precise on numbers. This information was used to task the SAS and SBS patrols. The first opportunity to interrogate Argentine PoWs came after the capture of South Georgia on 25 April. Spanish-speakers were attached to the HQs of both 3 Commando Brigade and 5 Infantry Brigade and there were other Spanish-speakers available.

By the time the first orders were prepared for Operation Sutton on

14 May it was assessed that Argentine strength was about twice that of 3 Brigade, and had had time to select the best defensive ground. It enjoyed air mobility (200 troops could be moved at one go) and, most frighteningly, air superiority. On the other hand morale was expected to be low. One senior British commander told his officers: 'They are isolated from mainland Arg and in cold damp conditions if deployed in the field. The ratio of cas [casualties] in previous contacts with the RM may worry them. Some conscripts will be at the end of their year's service.' It was also suspected – possibly on an optimistic assessment of the impact of the attack on Stanley airport – that the Army's rations would soon run out.

Argentine Assessment

When Galtieri met with Menendez and Jofre at Stanley on 22 April they concluded that a British landing would probably take place to the south of Stanley, although they recognized the possibility of a diversionary, or even the main, landing at Uranie Beach on Berkeley Sound, one of those which had been seriously considered by the British planners. San Carlos was noted but was considered too far away.[21]

Menendez's basic strategy was to concentrate defences around Stanley as the key to the conflict. Deployment of the troops had to take account of the need to establish a presence in the most important civil locations. The extensive and complicated coast-line rendered it difficult to maintain forces at every possible point of entry for British forces, which, when and if they arrived, were expected to have superior equipment and mobility to the Argentine forces. The only major garrison other than Stanley was that of the 12th Infantry Regiment under General Arenales based at Darwin. This would be able to defend the airstrip there, as well as keep watch over possible landing sites in the vicinity, with those on West Falkland particularly in mind. Because there were insufficient forces to guard against every possible site, it was decided only to deploy small detachments in secondary sectors, such as San Carlos, and tasked only to provide early warning.

The situation of the troops was less than satisfactory. They had inadequate protection against the wet and cold. Hygiene was poor, communications extremely difficult, and the blockade had prevented the delivery of extra transport. Argentine forces went on the alert as soon as the first elements of the task force arrived in the South Atlantic and they were ready to believe that the British would attempt to land at the first opportunity (see p. 258). The assumption that a British landing had been attempted and then rebuffed on 1 May was not revised during the subsequent days.[22]

Thus the assessment by the Joint Chiefs of Staff in Argentina on 6 May was that the enemy would probably act again soon. Any lull in the combat could be attributed to its need to reinforce its air power (which was still assumed to have been seriously damaged on 1 May). Knowledge that the British task force had been strengthened by the arrival of an auxiliary merchant ship and an assault ship with landing troops encouraged the view that a massive landing attempt was imminent, and might be attempted during the week beginning 8 May.

This suspicion was not modified by the news from London that a further forty-five merchant ships were leaving Britain with reinforcements, as these were assumed to be geared to the replenishment of the fleet rather than preparation for an invasion. Indeed, unless these ships were bringing their own air cover the need to protect them would diminish the air support for a landing by almost a third, thus providing another reason why the British commanders might want to get on with the landing before they were required to cope with this extra responsibility. The 7 May assessment also warned of possible covert landings of small special forces units in the Islands. These, of course, had already begun on 30 April, although not for the purpose assumed by the Argentine military – penetration of the local population – but for reconnaissance. Given the lack of dedicated landing ships in the British force, another possibility reviewed by the Argentines was that of an imminent helicopter landing in some part of the Islands. Thus an attack might be expected from the next day onwards. The previous priority given to an airlift of matériel and logistical support to the Islands was reaffirmed, as was the need for intensified sea surveillance.

When the attack came it was not quite as expected, although within the time-frame. On Sunday, 9 May at 01.40 the British attacked both Stanley and Darwin, as well as an Argentine fishing vessel inside the 12-mile limit imposed by the Exclusion Zone. This altered the Argentine appreciation only in so far as it was now believed that the British would mount small operations while they prepared for a massive landing, which would probably take place on 12 May. It was judged that the enemy would want to conquer an important sector of the Islands as a matter of some urgency so as to negotiate from a position of strength in the United Nations.

An analysis by Costa Mendez of the diplomatic context of British actions in the past reinforced this presumption of an imminent attack. He believed that all previous attacks had been connected with negotiating initiatives, and had been designed either to prevent a serious dialogue or to ensure that any negotiations would be conducted from a position of strength. Thus the attack on Pebble Island and the bombing of Stanley on 15/16 May were naturally linked in Argentine eyes with British behaviour in the UN negotiations and the return to London of Parsons and Henderson. In military terms it was recognized that these attacks were intended to reduce the air threat to any future landing, which, it was now assumed, could be in *both* Islands.

On 16 May, certain decisions were taken, which might seem surprisingly belated given that an invasion had been considered imminent for a week. Governor Menendez was to establish personal contact with his operational command so as to ensure more fluid communications between the various branches of the Island defences. The Theatre of Operations Command would be moved to Comodoro Rivadavia from Puerto Belgrano so as to avoid delays in determining operational strategy. The Junta resolved that this should be done from 23 May with the presence of the three Operational Commanders, and that the most senior in the military hierarchy would have the decisive voice – General García rather than Brigadier Crespo or Vice-Admiral Lombardo.

The Junta was now preoccupied with the quality of the intelligence information available to Britain. One of the main issues discussed on 16 May, when so much was happening on the diplomatic front and military preparations by both sides were reaching their climax, was a report from the Netherlands of a recent television programme which had shown satellite pictures of the Falklands of such precision that Argentine elements could be identified. This information had apparently come from an American satellite. The Military Committee decided to ask for a video tape of the programme from the Argentine Military Attaché in the Netherlands and if, after analysis, it was established that an American satellite was providing minute military information on the Islands' defences to the British, a formal protest would be handed to the UN and the US.

Operation Sutton

On the morning of 19 May, with the news of Argentina's rejection of Britain's proposal from Parsons, the War Cabinet met at Downing Street with the Chiefs of Staff. A final decision was needed if the landing was to take place in the next few days. Now that the latest effort to achieve a negotiated settlement had failed, Lewin urged that the logic that had informed the sending of the task force in the first place should now be taken to its conclusion, with the repossession of the Islands. Each of the Chiefs then spoke in turn, each arguing in favour of the landing despite concerns that the air battle had yet to be won.

The military answered the inevitable concerns with regard to distance from Stanley, the air threat and the risk to the liner-cum-troopship, *Canberra*, which was to be taken right into the bay. The Cabinet was warned that as the operation took place the task force might well lose a major ship (*Canberra*, *Fearless* or *Intrepid*) with a major unit on board (i.e. 300 crew and 600 troops).[23] The War Cabinet gave its approval.

The original plan required 40 and 45 Commando CDO to land simultaneously by landing craft at night to secure San Carlos settlement and Ajax Bay. Then, using the returned landing craft, 2 and 3 PARA were to take Sussex Mountain and Port San Carlos. From first light the helicopters would start to bring ashore the Rapier air-defence batteries and the guns; the rest of the stores would follow in order of priority. 42 CDO was to stay afloat as a reserve force until it could be seen where they would be most useful.[24] This was later amended, three days before the landing, on receipt of reports that the Argentine strategic reserve was located at Darwin. It was therefore decided to land 2 PARA in the first wave alongside 40 CDO at San Carlos settlement. 2 PARA's task was to establish a block on Sussex Mountain to forestall any attempt at interference at the beachhead by the strategic reserve. 45 CDO and 3 PARA would land in the second wave.

The timing was fixed as a compromise between Thompson's wish to take advantage of the hours of darkness to give his men maximum time to achieve their objectives on shore and the Navy's desire to use the same darkness for its approach through Falkland Sound.

Clapp and Thompson had concluded that it would be best if the men stayed on their troopships such as *Canberra* as they moved close to their landing beaches. Neither the helicopter force, because it was too small, nor the landing craft, because of open-sea conditions, could expect to cope with cross-decking them to other ships. However, there was concern at Northwood that staying on the ships would simply be too risky, if the fleet were spotted by the Argentine Air Force. At least some troops had to be transferred to *Fearless* and *Intrepid*, the two amphibious assault ships. Clapp and Thompson feared that this might cause great delay if the sea conditions were not right, so their staffs prepared, with some apprehension, to transfer the men one at a time by a light jackstay during daylight hours. In the event they were grateful for unusually calm conditions on 19 May which allowed the cross-decking to be achieved using the landing craft and helicopters.*[25]

Because the weather was suitable it was decided to proceed as soon as the political authorization had been obtained. Woodward later explained:

Once transferred, troops would soon lose their edge. We could only poise for a maximum of seven days. The majority of my ships had already been at sea for a month – if they were to last the course and

---

* On the very last helicopter flight, a Sea King transferring SAS men ditched after an encounter with an albatross with the loss of twenty-two men.

provide the necessary support to the land forces, we should not dally – above all, for everyone the impetus had to be maintained. But most important locally was the weather – the passage from the relative safety of the holding position to the landing area entailed running the gauntlet of the Exclusion Zone in daylight. I wanted a good dose of low visibility, or at least overcast weather, to give us a reasonable chance of achieving surprise. Our forecasting expertise, although denied Argentine meteorological data, had developed, and my man promised a good clag on 20 May although the prognosis beyond that was doubtful. The chance to go as soon as we were ready was irresistible.[26]

During daylight on 20 May the amphibious task force moved towards Stanley. Only as it approached East Falkland did it turn west, to move to the entrance of Falkland Sound. A sea mist provided a degree of cover; no Argentine aircraft found the fleet.

The landings went smoothly. They began after midnight. SBS parties were waiting on the beaches, as were naval gunfire spotter teams to call down the fire of the supporting ships. They had been waiting for a week. Helped by cloud and foggy weather the day before, the amphibious group was able to steam in close anti-submarine formation without being spotted and exposed to air attack.

Diversions were organized; an SAS group mounted machine-gun, mortar and Milan missile fire on the Argentine garrison at Darwin, supported by gunfire from *Ardent*; *Glamorgan* bombarded the area north of Berkeley Sound. Every effort had been made to encourage the Argentine commanders to believe that this was a diversion and that the main landing was still to take place nearer Stanley. This effort had some success. At 04.00 on 21 May the first troops landed ashore. By the time Argentine forces had realized what was going on, three separate beachheads had been established and 4,000 men were on land.

The only enemy encountered was in Port San Carlos. On 16 May intelligence had been received that an Argentine company was in position on Fanning Head overlooking the entrance to San Carlos water. The unit made up of sixty-two men from the Goose Green garrison had been moved there, with only two 105mm anti-tank guns and two 81mm mortars, to cover movements in the Falkland Sound. This was a response to *Alacrity*'s passage through the Sound, and the sinking of the *Isla de los Estados*, which had taken place on 12 May.[27]

It was decided to take them out using an SBS team just before the actual landing. The SBS did find twenty of the enemy on Fanning Head, locating them by use of thermal imaging equipment from a helicopter. They had been neutralized during the night of the landing by naval gunfire, which prevented them from employing their 105mm recoilless guns against the landing craft as they passed between Chancho Point and Fanning Head en route to the beaches. After a brief fight, a Spanish-speaking officer suggested surrender. Six Argentines accepted the offer, three were wounded and the rest escaped.

As the SBS had moved to Fanning Head they had passed, without realizing it, half the Argentine company asleep. The Argentine troops awoke to find that the landing had taken place and decided to withdraw, after first reporting back to the garrison at Goose Green that a landing was under way. As the unit withdrew it fired on two Gazelle helicopters, so killing three aircrew – the only British casualties of the day.

Chapter Twenty

FINAL DIPLOMACY

In Buenos Aires the San Carlos landing represented a significant – if not necessarily decisive – change in the strategic position in favour of Britain. The forces unloaded by the British would probably be sufficient to fight off any counter-attack that Menendez would be able to mount. The worst Argentine suspicions of British intentions were thus confirmed: all of the previous week's diplomatic activity had been another exercise in procrastination – to provide cover for the final preparations for the landing.

The diplomatic options had been now reduced to yet another Peruvian initiative, launched as the Secretary-General's mediation was coming to an end, and to a possible referral of the dispute to the Security Council of the UN.

The Second Peruvian Initiative

The new Peruvian initiative was based on the UN Secretary-General's *aide-mémoire*. President Belaunde suggested that the Secretary-General immediately put into effect those items upon which the two sides agreed – a cease-fire, mutual withdrawal of forces, the interim administration – and that he, or the contact group, organize and preside over negotiations to search for a permanent solution and to supervise immediately the withdrawal from the region of both armed forces.

The proposal had been received on 20 May at 18.30 hours, prior to news of the landing, and provoked a positive response from the Junta. When Costa Mendez spoke to Belaunde he encouraged him to pass on the message that 'we support Perez de Cuellar and that we do not want his mission finished tonight and that we are studying alternatives for negotiation'. Belaunde concluded that he had finally 'understood the British position: they want to appear like the good boys and present you like the baddies'.

The initiative was formally accepted by Argentina on 21 May. Not surprisingly the British Government refused to comment; in the circumstances it saw no value in a cease-fire and was to be hostile to all such suggestions from this point on. When Ambassador Wallace went to see President Belaunde on the morning of 21 May he displayed scant interest, insisting on an Argentine withdrawal in line with Resolution 502. The withdrawal could not be mutual as British forces were not going to relinquish their foothold on the Island; even less could they reasonably be expected to return 8,000 miles to Britain. When Belaunde reported this reaction late that night to Galtieri, the Argentine President promised flexibility: 'we are willing to go to the Continent, to Bahia Blanca or even withdraw to Buenos Aires if necessary and they could go to Ascension.' On 23 May Belaunde published a communiqué which announced both his initiative and the Argentine acceptance. The British condition of an immediate Argentine withdrawal, he stated, 'risked human lives unnecessarily by providing a delay in a peaceful solution to the crisis'.

Argentina's Allies

In practice the United States was the focal point for much of the diplomacy of the following week. It was widely recognized that now that its forces had landed there were few incentives for the British Government to do anything other than retake the Islands on its own terms without further negotiation. The only possible source of pressure upon London was the United States, and this (from the American perspective) had the unfortunate consequence of highlighting the already exposed American position.

American anxiety at this exposure was enhanced by the trend of Argentine diplomacy over this period. Mobilization of Latin American support around Argentina had been gathering strength. In the UN debate virtually every member of the Latin American group had supported the Argentine position, with Venezuela and Panama expressing themselves with particular force.

The most obvious way for Argentina to bring this support to bear was through another meeting of the Rio Treaty. With this in mind Costa Mendez had travelled to the United States on the night of 21 May. It should at least be possible to obtain regional support for a cease-fire, mutual withdrawal and negotiations over the future of the Islands.

The prospect of another Rio meeting was more worrisome to the United States than to Britain. The Americans lobbied Latin American governments against such a move. In addition, they sought to mend fences with Argentina, and President Reagan sent a message of congratulations to General Galtieri for Argentine National Day, 25 May. In it he suggested that 'it has never been more important to reaffirm the common interests and values that unite Argentina and the US and to confirm our commitment to hemispheric and world cooperation.' This received a rather dusty reply from Galtieri. It was not 'consistent with the attitude of your government and impossible to understand in the present circumstances'. The Junta did in fact consider breaking formal diplomatic relations with the US because of the military assistance granted Britain; in the event it decided against.

The Junta did achieve a favourable vote at the Rio meeting of 28/29 May. The resolution condemned 'in the most energetic manner the disproportionate and unjustified British armed attack', blamed Britain for everything that had gone wrong in the negotiations and the failure to obtain a cessation of hostilities and demanded that it cease immediately its military actions against the Argentine and 'withdraw its fleet and the totality of armed forces from the Islands'. The US Government should 'immediately lift all coercive measures applied against Argentina and abstain from providing military assistance to the United Kingdom, as per the Rio Treaty clause on continental solidarity', and the EEC and other states supporting Britain should remove all economic and political sanctions. On the other hand 'member states of the Rio Treaty ... should grant the Argentine Republic the support and assistance that they judge convenient in this crisis.'

A second strand of Argentine diplomacy was to start to pave the way for a meeting of the General Assembly later in the year when it would need the vote of the Third World. Clearly the first step was to take a greater interest than normal in the activities of the non-aligned movement and to attend a meeting of its Co-ordination Bureau which was to take place in Cuba in the week beginning 31 May. Costa Mendez travelled to Havana to be present. Obviously meeting with Castro in Cuba had a greater significance in terms of hemispheric politics than the formal business of the non-aligned movement. It caused some unease within the Argentine military, for whom Castro had previously appeared as the source of much continental evil.* The mere fact of an Argentine Foreign Minister in Havana was enough to alarm the Latin American specialists in the State Department. The prospect of Argentina succumbing to this sort of influence was like a nightmare coming true. It was also, however, something of a nightmare for many Argentine officers.

Britain's Allies

All this translated into considerable pressure on Britain to show magnanimity and led to a series of painful exchanges between the Reagan Administration and London. As Perez de Cuellar's efforts had been coming to an end the State Department had raised the possibility of a second Haig initiative, a prospect greeted without enthusiasm in London. Through William Clark, Ambassador Henderson had sought to impress upon the President the 'inappropriateness' of such an initiative.

---

* When he met with Castro, who apparently was not very optimistic on Argentina's behalf, Costa Mendez explained that 'we have not come for military aid', to which the Cuban leader replied that he was glad as 'it would be neither appropriate for me or yourselves'. Castro suggested that the best hope for Argentina was rain and snow. Cardoso *et al., Falklands: The Secret Plot*, p. 269.

After the British landing Haig advised Henderson that Britain should 'seize the first moment of military success to show readiness to negotiate'. He was concerned with the level of long-term bitterness, the threat to the OAS and the American position within it and the possible increase of Soviet influence. Anxiety over the prospect that the United States would be made the scapegoat for a British victory was by no means confined to the Latin American lobby.

As Argentine hints of a rupture of diplomatic relations came through on 22 May Haig stepped up the pressure on Britain, now warning of the position Britain might find itself in after hostilities, with a large garrison to sustain in a hostile environment. British thinking, however, was moving in the opposite direction. On 24 May Henderson told Haig that:

> the establishment of a bridgehead in the Falklands was bound to have a major effect on our diplomatic position. We could not in present circumstances consider the idea of British withdrawal from the Falklands or the establishment of an interim administration. We were determined to bring about Argentine withdrawal with the fewest possible casualties and remained interested in serious negotiations. But the Argentines must demonstrate a real change of position by, for instance, indicating a willingness to withdraw within a fixed time limit.[1]

Haig was not persuaded and with the Rio Treaty meeting imminent he felt a need to make another effort to settle the dispute before further bloodshed. With Brazil, which was emerging as the favoured US interlocutor in Latin America, he had concocted a plan which involved a cease-fire and withdrawal, a US–Brazilian interim administration and negotiations on the future without prior commitment. Henderson intimated immediately that this would be unacceptable in London, and then played the 'Suez card', warning how it would seem if the British position was undercut at the last moment by the United States.

Haig sought to reassure Britain that it enjoyed American support while at the same time promoting his plan. In a letter later that day to

Pym, the plan was reinforced by the inclusion of a US–Brazilian peace-keeping force. London responded coolly. After the traumas of 25 May, when Argentina had achieved some military success, the Americans were told that Britain would only now consider a wider political settlement once British administration had been re-established in the Islands. To Haig's call for a magnanimous gesture, Pym replied with the observation that this would be unrealistic for the moment, but he did not close the door on later negotiations when some of his proposals might find more favour. Haig responded that this would be precisely the point when the Latin Americans would not be interested.[2]

Britain had been finding it more difficult to sustain the political and economic support of its European partners ever since the *Belgrano*, but in the end it succeeded. In mid-April monthly sanctions had been agreed against Argentina and on 16 May they came up for renewal. Sanctions had previously been agreed by ministers unanimously but now a number of countries were expressing doubts about British policy. Britain's position was undermined not only by concerns that the Prime Minister was being too hardline with Buenos Aires, but also by the similarly uncompromising line she was taking in Brussels on questions of Community farm prices and Britain's budgetary contribution. The effort made by the Foreign Secretary in consulting with Europe was weakened by evidence that he lacked the Prime Minister's confidence. In a debate on 12 May in the European Parliament support for continued sanctions was only 137 to 79, as against the 203 to 28 when a similar vote had been taken on 22 April.

In Italy, which has close links with Argentina, opposition parties were insisting that any decision on further sanctions would require parliamentary agreement. The same was true in Denmark, which wanted greater freedom of manoeuvre in the implementation of the sanctions rather than a simple unified measure. West Germany wanted renewal for only a limited period, perhaps until 25 May, when the Ministers of Foreign Affairs could look again at the situation. Ireland was reflecting a domestic consensus that found diplomatic support for Britain in such circumstances almost an affront to a national tradition. Eventually on 17 May at the Council of Ministers, with France and

Germany taking the lead, it was agreed to renew the sanctions for a further seven days, but the decision was not unanimous. The EEC met again on 23 May. This time sanctions were extended without time-limits.[3] Both Ireland and Italy, however, refused to continue with sanctions.

Back to the Security Council

On the day after Perez de Cuellar had reported his failure to the Security Council and on the evening of the landings, the Security Council met in open session. The debate lasted for five days. It opened with a post-mortem on the recent negotiations, led by the Secretary-General and followed by Ros for Argentina and Parsons for Britain. At the end of the debate – on 26 May – Ireland tabled a resolution arguing for a cessation of hostilities and a resumption of negotiations. The first proposals were for an immediate cease-fire to be followed by the application of Resolution 502, now taking into account the fact that both forces were in the area and thus both would have to withdraw. As a minimum, a seventy-two-hour truce in which to negotiate was proposed. All this was watered down under pressure from a number of non-aligned countries who were sympathetic to the sentiment but also anxious to avoid a British veto.

Resolution 505 reaffirmed Resolution 502, and asked the Secretary-General to undertake a renewed mission using his good offices. It urged the two parties to co-operate with him to negotiate acceptable conditions for a cease-fire, including the possible dispatch of UN observers to monitor the cease-fire. The Secretary-General was asked to submit an interim report within seven days (2 June).

This was adopted unanimously. However, the new mission was undertaken without enthusiasm by the Secretary-General. He told the Council: 'You've asked me to do this. I will try, but you should understand that what you are asking is practically impossible. A war is now underway, and it is simply not realistic to think in terms of achieving a cease fire.'[4]

His point was reinforced by Parsons, who emphasized in the

discussions leading to the framing of the resolution as well as in those accompanying the vote that he saw little prospect of success as the British Government's position was that Argentine withdrawal, as requested in Resolution 502, was an essential precondition to any cease-fire agreement.[5] He could support the resolution because it did not actually call for a cease-fire. For its part Argentina saw much to its advantage in the pressure for a cease-fire. If successful it would take the immediate pressure off its forces; even if it failed it could force Britain to use its veto, leaving it diplomatically isolated and exposed as an opponent of peace.

The Cease-Fire Resolution

The Junta considered two possibilities for a cease-fire. Alternative A would involve a simultaneous cease-fire and mutual withdrawal from the region, both with UN supervision, under whatever terms could be agreed in the time available to the Secretary-General. Alternative B would involve the immediate suspension of all land, sea and air operations, with the forces remaining in position until a formal cease-fire had been agreed. As soon as the cease-fire was agreed the UN would send in a mission to supervise it. If necessary separate zones for forces could be established on land or at sea. Neither side would be allowed to reinforce its forces in any way under any circumstances. The UN would be responsible for the conditions on the Islands of both military personnel and the local population for the duration of the negotiations. The Junta decided to propose the first option to Perez de Cuellar with the second being kept in reserve in case it was necessary to compromise – after all, British forces were now back on the Islands and were unlikely to leave voluntarily.

By 31 May it was apparent that Perez de Cuellar's efforts were not going to achieve anything. At an informal meeting of the Security Council that afternoon Panama pressed for an early formal meeting of the Council. However, this was postponed to give the Secretary-General more time. Answers were required from the two sides to proposals from the Secretary-General by the afternoon of 1 June.

349

These proposals involved mutual withdrawal and the substitution of UN forces in the abandoned areas. The British position had not altered from that adopted at the start of the latest exercise. It reported to Perez de Cuellar on 1 June that the total withdrawal of British troops, the presence of UN forces in the Argentine-controlled areas after Argentine withdrawal, and a British renunciation of an extension of its area of control were all unacceptable. The first condition for a cease-fire remained the withdrawal of Argentine troops in a fixed time-scale, with British withdrawal only following repossession of the Islands, restoration of British administration, reconstruction and consultation with the wishes of the inhabitants.

On 2 June the Secretary-General informed the Security Council of his anticipated lack of success. Immediately both Panama and Spain presented a resolution: (1) requesting an immediate cease-fire in the Islands, (2) authorizing the Secretary-General to use any means he judged necessary to put this into effect, and (3) asking the Secretary-General to inform the Council within seventy-two hours of the implementation of this resolution.

It was known that the British would, if necessary, veto the resolution, so for Argentina the key question concerned the American vote. Ros spoke to Thomas Enders at the State Department and warned him that, should the US join with Britain in vetoing the resolution, Argentina would interpret this measure as an extremely serious action that would immediately endanger diplomatic relations between the two countries. Enders explained that a US veto was likely in that his Government did not consider the Spanish resolution to be consistent with Resolution 502. Ros suggested that instead the US should abstain, and Secretary Haig could justify it to Britain on the grounds of the likely impact of a US veto on US–Argentine relations, closing the door to any eventual negotiation with US participation.

Enders agreed to pass the message on directly to Haig, who was in Paris where the seven major Western powers were meeting for a summit. He also indicated that he thought the idea of an abstention reasonable and that he would modify the instructions left for Ambassador Kirkpatrick accordingly.

Further pressure was put on Haig and Reagan through sympathetic members of the Senate, notably Jesse Helms. The Senators got through to Reagan's aides in Paris and obtained a promise from the President to review the vote once he had had a chance to discuss the issue with Mrs Thatcher, who was also attending the summit, on 3 June.

Meanwhile another, informal strand of Argentine diplomacy was developing in New York. This stemmed from a unilateral initiative taken by Lami Dozo. In the days following the San Carlos landing the Air Force chief had met with his pilots, who had shown great gallantry and faced death. They had had neither the time nor the inside information to follow all the diplomatic comings and goings. However, they had noted the Foreign Minister's proposed trip to Cuba. Fears were expressed that the net result of this epic struggle was that Argentina would enter the communist bloc – something that the armed forces had spent previous years trying to prevent.

The Air Force officers demanded of Lami Dozo that Argentina should not be allowed to drift in that direction. They were prepared to continue the fight but only for a reasonable settlement of the Malvinas issue. Convinced as a result of this meeting of the urgent need for diplomatic progress, Lami Dozo sent Miret, his representative on the Malvinas Group, to New York to meet Mrs Kirkpatrick and explore the possibility of refloating US mediation. His move was not discussed with the rest of the Junta, who were still furious with Haig for his past behaviour.

The talks between Miret and Kirkpatrick were very informal, and they did not lead anywhere. Kirkpatrick expressed her desire to reverse the negative trend in relations between the two countries but she could not do this by herself.

It should be noted that there was little disagreement within the US Administration at this time that life would be a lot easier if only the British would show a little more flexibility. At issue was the degree of pressure to be put on London. This question strained relations between the 'Europeanist' and 'Latino' factions within the Administration to breaking point. On 26 May, Miret arranged a meeting between Kirkpatrick and Costa Mendez. The UN Ambassador had taken care to inform Washington of her movements; that did not help when Haig discovered the meeting. As she was objecting strongly to Costa Mendez's plans to visit Havana, Haig got to her by telephone. By the time the acrimonious conversation was over Costa Mendez had left.[6]

Before Reagan had left for Paris Kirkpatrick met with him for forty minutes. The reputation of the United States in Latin American eyes was now threatened by a bloody British victory at Stanley and, she argued, in the first instance, the US being obliged to cast a veto with Britain.[7] In later communications to the President she drew attention to the likely support of the resolution by Japan and Ireland.

At the UN, the US asked for a delay of twenty-four hours before the vote was taken to allow President Reagan time to talk to Mrs Thatcher and to give itself time to sort out a policy for the vote. Britain was content to continue to have the vote delayed. Argentine policy-makers were once again puzzled by these delays. As so often was the case, they overestimated the speed with which Britain could launch its military initiatives. Comments by Haig to a NATO meeting which suggested little doubt that Stanley would soon fall and comments by Mrs Thatcher at the end of May in television interviews to the effect that Argentina only had a 'few days' in which to surrender gracefully implied that an offensive was imminent and that the British, with American connivance, were anxious to get it completed before a UN call for a cease-fire.

Lami Dozo's private initiative had minimal impact on any of this but, when it became known, he was accused of having complicated Argentine diplomatic efforts by providing an excuse for further American procrastination. He did confess his actions to the Junta. In order to maintain unanimity his colleagues decided to endorse his actions retrospectively.

Despite Argentine suspicions Haig was not working closely with London at this point. He was putting pressure on Britain to show magnanimity from the San Carlos landings onwards. Prior to the summit he offered a four-point plan, which took as its starting point a British military victory but then sought to remove the colonial character of a British administration by replacing it with something more international, and offered the prospect of negotiations on the future, although without prejudging the outcome. The basic elements were:

1 With the end of fighting and defeat of the Argentine military forces there would be a British military administration.

2 This military administration would give way to a form of self-government in accordance with the principles of Article 73 of the UN Charter. This system of government would be such as to remove the colonialist tag which a return to the status quo would mean. The establishment of this self-government would be accompanied by some declaration of principles by which the country would be run.

3 This local government would be subject to an international umbrella which would also have a small international force. The umbrella countries would include the United States and probably Brazil. The Argentines would probably have a liaison officer. The terms of reference of the umbrella group would provide for it to ensure that the local government was being carried out in accordance with the principles that had been enunciated and to provide for security.

4 The umbrella group would also have responsibility for considering the ultimate status of the Islands. There would be no cut-off date for this and, if no agreement had been reached, the arrangements of self-government and the umbrella would continue.[8]

This was a much more favourable package than offered by Britain just prior to the landing, and the Foreign Office had been in touch with the State Department on the details. To those looking beyond the conclusion of the current fight, in both the Foreign Office and the Defence Ministry, there was still apprehension over the casualties that might be incurred in the battle for Stanley and little pleasure at the prospect of a non-negotiated settlement which would require subsequent British governments to cling to the Islands at high cost and in the face of unremitting Argentine hostility. The Pope was in Britain and adding his voice to those who now argued the need to avoid further bloodshed: 'The scale and horror of modern warfare make it totally unacceptable as a means of settling differences between nations.'

But the price paid in terms of military effort and lives in getting this

353

far now ensured slight interest in political concessions of any sort.

On 31 May the US President had entered the fray with a phone call to Mrs Thatcher in which he both expressed his concern over the tide of opinion in Latin America and encouraged the idea of a new peace initiative. The Prime Minister saw no reason to respond positively to this idea. Britain had negotiated in good faith for weeks without Argentina demonstrating any interest in a reasonable deal. Now that Britain had returned to the Islands, after a considerable sacrifice, it was not going to step aside again for a multinational contact group.[9]

Despite this pressure the Americans were careful not to waver in their public support for the British position. British diplomats pointed out to the White House that Reagan was to stay with the Queen at Windsor and that it might seem ungracious if there was a major row under way at the time. When Reagan left for Paris he made it clear that he would not impose a negotiated settlement on Britain, while congratulating Britain for responding to 'a threat that all of us must oppose – and that is the idea that armed aggression can succeed in the world today'. At the Paris summit itself the matter of negotiations was not taken much further, although before the UN vote there was a flurry of diplomatic activity in Washington as Stoessel, Haig's deputy, and Enders attempted to cobble something together. As Britain continued to be uninterested in any deal they felt that the United States was justified in making some gesture in the direction of Buenos Aires.

By the evening of 4 June, the vote on the resolution could be postponed no longer. The text stated:

The Security Council, reaffirming its resolutions 502 (1982) and 505 (1982) and in the necessity to have all their parts complied with,

1) Asks the parties in the dispute to have an immediate cease-fire in the region of the Islas Malvinas/Falkland Islands, and to start simultaneously the cease-fire in compliance with resolutions 502 (1982) and 505 (1982) in their entirety.
2) Authorizes the Secretary-General so that he may use the means that he judges necessary to indicate if this resolution has been complied with.

3) Asks the Secretary-General to present a report to the council within the next 72 hours and to keep the council informed on the implementation of this resolution in a period no longer than 72 hours.

Argentina obtained nine favourable votes, forcing Britain to veto, in which it was accompanied by the US. The resolution was supported by Spain, Panama, Poland, Japan, Ireland, China, Zaire, Uganda and the USSR and was opposed by the US and the United Kingdom. Countries abstaining were Togo, Guyana, France and Jordan. This was a disappointment for Britain, for up to the last minute two of the resolution's supporters had appeared more likely to abstain. Zaire and Uganda may have been swayed by sentiment in the non-aligned meeting in Havana, recently addressed by Costa Mendez. Had this not been the case no veto would have been necessary. As it was, consolation was found in the continued unwillingness of three members of the non-aligned bloc to vote for the sort of resolution to which members of the UN are naturally inclined. None the less the Japanese and French votes warned that Britain's friends in the West were placing limits on their support.

The most remarkable aspect of the vote came just after it was completed. An aide entered with a message for the US Ambassador, who then stated:

Mr President, the dilemma continues even in the process of voting this issue. I have been told that it is impossible for a country to change its vote once it has made it known but my Government has asked me to put it on record that if it were possible to change votes, I should change it from a no to an abstention. Thank you.

As Parsons noted later:

Fortunately any odium which might have attached to us for using our veto was diverted by the astonishing statement by Mrs Kirkpatrick ... This revelation left the Council and the media stunned and I was able to escape from the Chamber almost unnoticed by the press, the microphones and the television cameras as they engulfed Mrs. Kirkpatrick.[10]

Haig had left instructions before going to Paris to back the British veto. However, at the last minute, his deputy in Washington, Walter Stoessel, had become convinced that the line being taken by Enders and Kirkpatrick was correct. He contacted Haig, who agreed to shift the vote to an abstention, having by now received a stony response to his most recent ideas from the British Government. However, by the time he had contacted Pym to warn him, and then got back to Stoessel, who in turn had to get back to Kirkpatrick, the veto had been cast.[11] Rather than let matters rest the Ambassador was told to announce the abstention decision, presumably in the hope of salvaging some credibility with Latin America. The result was to satisfy neither side. In Latin America there was still great annoyance over the original veto, while in Britain the gesture itself suggested a slackening of support. Most embarrassed was President Reagan, who when questioned by reporters the next day while standing beside an evidently unimpressed Prime Minister clearly had no idea what had been going on.

Still Perez de Cuellar did not give up. The next day he contacted Arnoldo Listre, the Argentine Chargé d'Affaires at the UN, and asked him to transmit a letter with some further proposals to the Junta. The proposals, which recognized Britain's developing military advantage, involved a truce from 11.00 on 7 June and a cease-fire in place by the end of that week, withdrawal of all Argentine troops over fifteen days while Britain would only need to inform the Secretary-General as to its plan for troop reductions, with the study of possible alternative 'security arrangements under the auspices of the UN'. The Junta saw this as surrender terms and rejected the idea; in all probability so did Britain. The Secretary-General's letter warned that:

The armed conflict in the region of the Falkland Islands is threatening to enter a new and extremely dangerous phase, that will probably result in a great loss of life for both parties – that would gravely compromise for the foreseeable future any prospect of settling the underlying controversy.[12]

Chapter Twenty-One

THE BRIDGEHEAD AND BEYOND

The Argentine High Command was caught out by the British landing, and further confused, as was the intention, by diversionary attacks not only in San Carlos but also in Fox Bay, Darwin and Stanley. The intelligence assessments had been inaccurate and now the decision-making was paralysed.[1]

The landing had been detected by the unit at Fanning Head. At 08.30 it had sent a message warning of the landing to Goose Green, from where it had been sent to General Menendez. Because he had received scant detail, Menendez asked for a reconnaissance flight. An Aeromacchi went off in search of British ships. The pilot was startled to come across twelve in San Carlos Bay. He gallantly attacked a frigate and then returned to Stanley. Menendez contacted Galtieri immediately. The President asked if there were 'many of them'. Menendez said not to worry, 'It was within our expectations. They have landed in an undefended place. And well . . . we are doing what we can.'[2]

The Junta in Buenos Aires met at 21.00 hours on 21 May. It had been delayed until the return to the capital of Lami Dozo, the Commander-in-Chief of the Air Force, who had witnessed the landing from the Air Force Headquarters in the south. He convinced the Junta that whatever effective force was available should be used against the beachhead in San Carlos to prevent it being consolidated.

However, when consulted, Menendez argued that this landing was not the main attack but a secondary action aimed at diverting the attention of the Argentine defences. Studies undertaken at Stanley had concluded that less than a brigade had landed at San Carlos, so that the second brigade (which was in fact still some days away from the Falklands) was still available for a landing elsewhere.[3] He refused to send forces from the Stanley area, in his opinion still the main enemy objective. Only a company could have been sent, which would have made little impression on the British. The only response was to reinforce the Goose Green garrison with 105mm guns which were to be transported from Stanley on the *Rio Iguazu*.

Menendez could think of little else to do to disrupt the British advance. He later told General Garcia:

> We have studied the possibility of sending a contingent of the 12th regiment to the hilly area, and have also moved heavy mortars to increase fire power. Later we are going to try some limited action. We have a plan to climb the hills but there is a risk that the British with their helicopters would trap us there in a sort of sandwich.[4]

His options had not been eased by an attack which caught a Chinook and two Pumas on the ground at Mount Kent. His other Chinook at Stanley was already unserviceable. The British had made the identification of Argentine helicopters a major intelligence task and their removal an early priority. Land transport was extremely difficult across the Falklands, and the trucks and tracked vehicles that the Argentine forces had brought with them were useless outside the capital. The more helicopters denied to the Argentine forces the more they would be pinned down at Stanley.

Bomb Alley

The confusion in the Argentine command over the scale of the British operation at San Carlos led to delays in organizing substantial air attacks against the beachhead. They were only ready to begin after noon on 21 May, although there were a number of smaller raids in the morning.

After the single Aeromacchi came two groups each of three Daggers, flying in at 9.35 and then 9.43 on an armed reconnaissance, one of which was shot down. An hour later two Pucaras based at Goose Green also made an attack. One of these was also shot down. The Skyhawk attacks began at 12.00 prompt by one group of two and another of four. Six more Skyhawks came in at 13.15, to be followed half an hour later by two groups of four Daggers and four skyhawks respectively. The next attack at 14.00 involved two groups each of three Daggers and one group of three Skyhawks. The day's attacks concluded at 14.15 with five Skyhawks.

The sporadic nature of these attacks meant that the British defences were never swamped. Of the thirteen Daggers and nineteen Skyhawks attacking that day, five of each were lost, mainly to Harriers. In the air there was little doubt of the Harriers' supremacy, especially now that they were equipped with the most modern Sidewinder air-to-air missiles. The Harrier lost by Britain that day, along with two helicopters, was caught by ground fire.

The local terrain deprived the ships of warning as the aircraft came in and meant that the air defences had only seconds to acquire targets. Equally the incoming pilots had only a limited amount of time to attack the ships. They managed to penetrate the defences but only so far as the seven warships to the fore in the Falkland Sound and in the entrance to the San Carlos anchorage. As a result the more lucrative targets in terms of the overall war effort, the ships carrying the stores needed for the land campaign, were not touched.

To protect the transports from air attack the frigates and destroyers had placed themselves in a line to meet the incoming aircraft. The cost was one frigate, *Ardent*, sunk and another frigate, *Argonaut*, and destroyer, *Brilliant*, badly damaged.

There were no attacks next morning so an opportunity was missed to strike the British at their most vulnerable.* The delay was the result of an argument that morning between the Air Force and the naval aviators over how airpower should be properly deployed in these circumstances. The argument was a familiar one in the history of

---

* The first engagement of the day was in fact an attack by a Harrier on *Rio Iguazu*, a patrol boat attempting to deliver supplies up Choiseul Sound to the Argentine garrison at Darwin.

airpower. The Air Force wanted to make a decisive strike of their own, by attacking large targets, such as the carriers and major warships, with the hope of success having a commensurate political impact in London. The airmen were also anxious to demonstrate that their older aircraft could take on the same tasks as the Navy's brand-new Super-Etendards. They were not interested in interdiction with the intention of influencing the later land campaign. As a result, and to immense British relief, the supply ships were left alone.

By the time the attack came in the afternoon, the British were better prepared, with anti-air weapons now in place. Over the next few days San Carlos became 'bomb alley' for the British and 'death valley' for Argentine pilots.

On Sunday 23 May, four more Argentine helicopters were lost after meeting a Harrier patrol. During the afternoon, the Argentine pilots attacked again both the beachhead and the task force, often now taking advantage of better intelligence, including information from Argentine units on the Islands (shipping moving to and from San Carlos could be seen from an observer post on the north-east tip of West Falkland). Although British Rapier units were now fully operational they found it difficult to lock on to the Argentine aircraft, who were only momentarily in view, against the background of the hills.

The British ships were saved less by the efficiency of their air defences than by the inefficiency of the Argentine bomb fuses; about half the bombs which struck ships failed to detonate. One of these – lodged in *Antelope* – did eventually explode when an Army bomb-disposal expert was attempting to defuse it. As a result the frigate later sank.[5]

By 24 May the British position on the bridgehead at San Carlos was secure, although the disembarkation of stores and equipment – including helicopters vital to the advance – had still not been completed. A Harrier attack on Stanley airport failed to destroy the airstrip. Four Skyhawks were shot down.

The next day was the worst yet for British forces. As this was Argentina's National Day a major attack had been expected. Woodward intended to use *Coventry* and *Broadsword* to provide radar early warning while the carriers moved in closer to allow the Harriers more sorties. The destroyer had the long-range Sea Dart, while the frigate had the more powerful radar and the point-defence Sea Wolf missile.

In the early morning an Argentine Learjet survey aircraft took an aerial photograph of San Carlos at high altitude and was able to return with a detailed picture of the British positions.[6]

An Argentine attack in the late morning resulted only in the loss of three Skyhawks. However, a second attack, in the early afternoon, inflicted serious damage. *Broadsword* had just repaired a failure in its Sea Wolf system, when its radar picked up the approach of the second threat. Just as it was preparing to fire *Coventry*'s bow moved in front and so the missiles could not be launched.[7] *Coventry* sank after being hit by three bombs.

Argentine naval intelligence had been making a meticulous analysis of Harrier radar contacts in order to identify the location of their launch platforms. As a result a target had been located 100 nautical miles north-east of Stanley.[8] After a journey of four hours, two Super-Etendards took a wide sweep to avoid the Harriers and search for the British carriers. They came within range without detection and each launched an Exocet. At this point operators on the frigate *Ambuscade* realized what was happening and flashed out a warning; chaff rockets were released and Lynx helicopters flew off in an attempt to deflect the Exocets. In this effort they were successful, except that one Exocet locked again on to the container ship *Atlantic Conveyor*, which had neither warning nor defences. It was soon ablaze and had to be abandoned with the loss of an exceptionally valuable cargo. Down went six Wessex, one Lynx and three Chinook helicopters (the fourth was on a mission when the ship was hit and so spared), tents for 5,000 men and the material to build a mobile airstrip for the Harriers as well as a water-distilling plant. These losses required major modifications to the plans.[9] It provided a dramatic example of what might have happened had there been a deliberate Argentine campaign against the British logistics effort.

Buenos Aires

In Buenos Aires the media were still suggesting that the British force was landlocked and surrounded by Argentine forces, sent from Darwin and Stanley. The Joint Chiefs of Staff were obliged on 23 May to try to explain the true nature of events and to warn against taking media accounts too seriously. A second step was to implement previously agreed proposals to reform the command structure which had thus far proved to be wholly inadequate.

At 10.00 the Military Committee met in the Joint Chiefs of Staff building in Buenos Aires to assess the developing military situation. Both Admiral Lombardo and Brigadier Weber were present and both argued the need for improved decision-making at the operational level.

The greatest urgency attached to the establishment of the joint operations centre at Comodoro Rivadavia (Centro de Operaciones Conjuntas – CEOPECON) to take responsibility for both combat and logistics. All the subordinate commands would transmit information and requests through the CEOPECON. It would keep the Military Committee informed of the situation, actions decided upon, its evaluation of the operations under way and those likely to take place in the near future. The Centre was obliged to inform the Military Committee but need not seek its permission to proceed. The Military Committee would be involved only when additional resources or the resolution of major issues were requested by the Centre. General García now became the senior operational commander with, for the first time, a unified command below him. García had commanded the occupying forces on 2 April and was considered to have worked well then as head of a joint command.

On the Islands, General Menendez received an order to provide all necessary information so that the CEOPECON could begin analysis of the possibilities for the employment of the strategic military reserve.

On 24 May the intelligence appreciation by the Joint Chiefs of Staff in Buenos Aires indicated that the enemy had consolidated the beachhead at San Carlos and had established it as a base to act as the centre of future operations on the Island. It was recognized that there was likely to be an immediate attack on Darwin.

However, rather than attack Stanley direct the most likely course was thought to be a blockade, which could provide the military result without endangering the lives of the inhabitants of the Islands. The Air Force therefore argued that the priority targets should be (1) the British aircraft-carriers and (2) the logistic chain between Ascension and the Islands, rather than the beachhead itself or the advancing British forces.

The most appropriate military response was further discussed late the next day when General Galtieri paid a visit to the new command centre at Comodoro Rivadavia. It was decided, for the moment, not to call up the REM (strategic military reserve). Such a major injection of manpower was thought inappropriate to the likely scale of future operations.

As a result of this meeting a cable was sent by the CEOPECON to Menendez in Stanley. It was worded sharply and demanded some action. It began by pointing out that the defensive plan with which he was still working had been designed to deter a British landing against Stanley. In this it had been successful but it had also failed to deter a landing elsewhere and the establishment of a beachhead.

The Navy had 'contributed its quota of blood in this conflict already', while the Air Force tested its 'men and material on a daily basis'. Meanwhile,

the Army seems to have only an attitude of static defence which, should it continue indefinitely, will make the men wilt in their own positions even before being able to engage in combat with the mass of enemy troops.

... In your hands and in your future decisions rests the honour of the Argentine Army.

More British troops were en route to the bridgehead and action should be taken before these reinforcements arrived between 28 and 30 May. The maximum objective would be to expel the bridgehead but at the least, for both 'international and national political consider-ations' as well as the morale of the Argentine Army, action should be taken to contain and even reduce the British presence. Menendez was told that he must 'immediately adopt an offensive attitude' and employ a substantial number of troops.

A significant number of those troops currently defending Stanley, and at Fox and Howard on West Falkland, should be moved to forward defensive positions and then 'advance against San Carlos'. In addition to these forces a task force of the I and IV Air Transport Army Brigade would be placed at Menendez's disposal to be used as he decided. He now had very little time to restructure his plan. It was awaited by the new command at Comodoro Rivadavia for its assessment.[10]

But Menendez was in no position to mount a serious counter-offensive against San Carlos. There were two considerations. First, the distance between Stanley and San Carlos was some 56 miles and given the problems posed by the terrain it would take at least eight days to cover the ground. Movement would be 'under constant enemy fire from the air, in an area without cover, wood, drinking water or means of subsistence'. When his men arrived, worn out by the long trek, they would have to go into immediate action against an enemy well prepared and supported by field artillery.[11] Even if he were to be provided by Buenos Aires with the backpacks necessary for such an operation and he could rely on solid air and naval support, he considered it unnecessarily risky and without much prospect of success. Menendez thus rejected the option which a few days later the British commanders settled upon – in the other direction – as the only way of achieving their objective.

Menendez had another objection to the proposed counter-attack. Even if he could be guaranteed access to air transport, it would require 70 per cent of the forces deployed at Stanley. In providing a critique of the counter-attack plan to the CEOPECON the next day, he noted that as British reinforcements were coming on the QE2, this would provide Britain with an opportunity to seize the capital. So foolish did he think the plan that he claimed, with what conviction it is hard to say, that he was prepared to resign if asked to implement it.[12]

The alternative approach, which was agreed, was to send out more reconnaissance patrols, attempt to infiltrate commando units behind British lines so as to disrupt the rear, move the 12th Infantry Regiment to the perimeter of the beachhead, reinforce the western flank of the Stanley defences and reinforce the Darwin–Goose Green area using airborne troops. This approach foundered on the risks associated with moving forces so close to the San Carlos area, with its high level of enemy air activity.

Breaking Out

Brigadier Julian Thompson, commanding 3 Brigade, had received his orders from General Jeremy Moore, Commander Land Forces, on 12 May:

> You are to secure a bridgehead on East Falkland, into which reinforcements can be landed, in which an airstrip can be established and from which operations to repossess the Falkland Islands can be achieved.
>
> You are to push forward from the bridgehead area so far as the maintenance of its security allows, to gain information, to establish moral and physical domination over the enemy, and to forward the ultimate objective of repossession.

Moore then explained how he expected to arrive from the *QE2* to take command of the land forces within approximately seven days of the landing and with the intention of developing further operations.[13] The absence of the Commander at this critical juncture resulted in considerable tension between London and Brigadier Thompson.

The Chiefs of Staff had promised the War Cabinet before the landing that once forces were ashore they would move quickly forward to seize the initiative as soon as possible. When the War Cabinet met the day after the landing, enthused by its success, they looked forward to an advance from the bridgehead. On the following day the press was briefed from Downing Street, running its own information policy, that an attack on Stanley would come 'in a matter of days'. The Prime Minister's Press Secretary, Bernard Ingham, told reporters: 'We're not going to fiddle around.'[14] John Nott, however, had sought to counter the impression that the military were being hurried by assuring Parliament that there was 'no question of pressing the force commander to move forward prematurely'. Yet that was precisely what happened, for the Chiefs of Staff and Northwood shared the same expectation that the advantage gained by the landing should be exploited immediately. 'We're going to move and move fast!' said Lewin on 22 May.[15]

This enthusiasm was embodied in a signal to Thompson from Northwood on 23 May that his objective was now to 'invest Stanley'. The military meaning of this term is 'to enclose, hem in, besiege, beleaguer, attack', none of which Thompson felt he could then do as all his helicopters and landing craft were engaged in moving logistic supplies ashore and the air battle was still to be won.

As a more modest measure, the obvious target for any attempt to establish 'moral and physical domination' was the enemy positions at Darwin and Goose Green, between 14 and 15 miles' marching distance away on the narrow isthmus connecting the two halves of East Falkland. Goose Green's main tactical relevance was that Pucara aircraft operated from its airstrip. About 120 civilians were being held in the community hall.

On that day, Colonel 'H' Jones, commanding 2 PARA, was told to prepare a plan for a raid on these positions, to eliminate the Pucara aircraft and withdraw. The best information then available came from the diversionary raid which the SAS had undertaken during the night of the landing. However, the information so gathered was patchy.

The next day a plan to approach by sea was ruled out because of navigational problems, as was the use of helicopters because there were simply not enough of them. The continued air attacks meant that it was necessary to land as many stocks as possible before logistics ships withdrew, and these then had to be moved to the relevant units. There were 'insufficient helicopters for tactical as well as this logistic movement'.[16]

The approach to Darwin would therefore be on foot. The first objective would be to secure the area of Camilla Creek House so that three 105mm light guns could be flown in. It was intended to do this that evening but poor visibility meant that the helicopters would be unable to carry the guns, so the operation had to be cancelled.

Thompson's main concern was with Stanley. In order to move in this direction he believed that his first priority must be to establish a strong force on Mount Kent and the surrounding area. He wanted to use his helicopter assets to move SAS units there. An SAS patrol had established that Mount Kent was only lightly held and possibly vulnerable to a *coup de main* by helicopter. This, though, was undoubtedly a risky operation because Mount Kent was more than 30 miles into enemy territory.[17] Thompson had hoped that by the evening of 25 May the *Atlantic Conveyor* would deliver its four Chinook and six Wessex helicopters, which would then start moving men and equipment towards Stanley. Instead he was told that the ship had been sunk and that only one Chinook survived.[18]

His critical path was now dependent upon a fuel installation which would allow the Harriers to be based at the beachhead and keep the remaining helicopters running efficiently. To add to his problems, the store ships carrying the equipment for the installation had been moved away from the beachhead for safety before the equipment was unloaded. The various parts of the installation now had to be located, recovered and then constructed.

With a chronic shortage of helicopters, as yet unable to operate to their full efficiency, and with those available now required to off-load matériel from the ships, Thompson felt inhibited. Until a landing zone on Mount Kent was secured by SAS he dared not risk what helicopters he had by attempting to fly 42 CDO there. The most that might be done was to begin an overland march on foot using helicopters for logistics. Thompson's preference was to wait for the arrival of 5 Brigade and more helicopters.[19]

In London this appeared to be excessively cautious, as if Thompson were unable to think beyond the bridgehead or was following a textbook operation without recognizing the special features of his situation. The Chiefs of Staff and Admiral Fieldhouse saw an early land engagement in the same light as they had seen the recapture of South Georgia – a valuable means of establishing psychological superiority over the enemy. Their assessment was that the enemy was weak and dislocated by the landing and would not put up any serious resistance.

They were also aware of a growing political frustration at the lack of activity, while Argentine pilots took pot-shots at British ships. After the landing, the bridgehead was something of an anti-climax. There was nothing positive to talk about, and the politicians did not know whether this was because of the normal tight secrecy surrounding future operations or because there was nothing to say. Secretary of Defence Nott later observed:

> What Northwood did not understand was that if parliamentary morale goes, then that will take press morale with it. Every politician who has been in Westminster knows that unless you can keep up the morale of your own troops, it will spin right out into the country and it will do so very quickly.[20]

The concern in the War Cabinet was not simply domestic political morale. Pressure was building up internationally for a cease-fire. If Britain was obliged to succumb to this pressure, especially if it was backed by the United States, then the forces would be confined to the beachhead, ships would show wear and tear and aircraft would become unserviceable, while Britain's bargaining position would be poor. Another member of the War Cabinet has explained the concern:

> I think there were many of us who were worried initially that having got a beach head at San Carlos, we were going to get stuck there and not be able to break out of it ... [T]here were memories of the time we took to break out of the beach head in Normandy ... [I]n terms of the whole of the Falklands, it wasn't a big area, but just to be stuck in a very small area and confined there, we'd have had all sorts of troubles. In every way, not least on the diplomatic front because if we didn't get a move on all the proposals for ceasefires would become stronger. And ceasefires, which would have conditions, which would not have been beneficial from our point of view ... So a break out was very important.[21]

After the losses on 25 May the delays started to appear intolerable in London, even though the sinking of the *Atlantic Conveyor*, from Thompson's perspective, made further delay unavoidable. An attack on the Argentine garrison at Darwin and Goose Green would risk valuable assets required for the eventual assault on Stanley. Even if 2 PARA were successful in the attack they would be required to stay back to hold the position they had just captured.

Thompson was beginning to doubt that anybody in London had any conception of the logistical task he faced or the real risks his men were already running. From the standpoint of those facing daily air raids the opposition did not seem quite so weak as it appeared in London. None the less, on 26 May Thompson received a 'clear and unequivocal' order from Northwood: 'The Goose Green operation was to be remounted and more action was required all round.'[22] Jones was now told to use the same plan as before. Meanwhile 45 CDO and 3 PARA were to march out of the beachhead.

There was a short Argentine air raid over San Carlos on 27 May which was one of the most successful conducted by the Argentine Air Force against ground targets. It hit the logistics area and main dressing station at Ajax Bay. Two unexploded bombs lodged in the dressing station and had to be left there for the duration of the campaign. If they had exploded, the resultant deaths of a critical medical team and the casualties they were treating could have been devastating to morale. Bombs elsewhere destroyed the gun, mortar and other ammunition being loaded into helicopter nets ready to be lifted to 2 PARA for their attack on Darwin and Goose Green. All of 45 CDO's anti-tank missiles and launchers were destroyed, and several men were killed and wounded. The ensuing fires and explosions went on all night, just at the time when the logistic base should have been at peak activity, readying loads for the next day's activities.

Yet overall the volume of attacks from the air was now beginning to slacken and so reduce the risks of prolonged and large-scale operations outside the San Carlos air-defence umbrella.

The Battle for Darwin and Goose Green

The argument between Thompson and Northwood, with one feeling that there was no appreciation of the logistical and operational circumstances on the Islands and the other concerned that excessive caution was jeopardizing overall strategy, had important consequences for the conduct of the attack on Darwin and Goose Green.

Although high political stakes were now riding on its success, in 3 Brigade Headquarters the exercise was still seen as a diversion. It was not mounted as a co-ordinated brigade attack, with tactical headquarters co-ordinating air and naval gunfire support. Thompson himself did not take command of the operation. Extra troops were not allocated to 2 PARA. Insufficient artillery was provided. Thompson was advised against sending Scorpion and Scimitar armoured vehicles as requested by Jones. These would have made a considerable difference. Instead of reconnoitring the ground it was assumed – erroneously – that there was a high risk of them getting bogged down en route.

These factors help explain the problems that ensued rather than the factor which has been more often mentioned since – an underestimation of the Argentine strength that would be faced. To understand this aspect of the battle it is necessary to consider the evolution of the intelligence picture.

The intelligence assessment circulated on 12 May mentioned an Argentine detachment of 400–500 troops at Darwin and Goose Green. A four-man SAS patrol had been observing the Argentine garrison for two weeks. The information was unavoidably incomplete and sketchy.[23] None the less it led to an increase in the assessment to 650, which was correct. Thompson described the final estimate prepared just before the attack was launched.

Two companies of 12 Infantry Regiment, one company of 25 Infantry Regiment, a platoon of Infantry Regiment and possibly an amphibious platoon. The guns were assessed as possibly two 105mm howitzers, up to six 35mm anti-aircraft guns or 30mm anti-aircraft guns and up to six 20mm anti-aircraft guns. There was also estimated to be one platoon of engineers and one support helicopter.[24]

On 27 May more information came from a captured Argentine patrol which revealed that the garrison was alert. The intelligence group also got wind of last-minute reinforcements.[25] In fact, after the capture of the Argentine garrison, when casualties were counted with PoWs, the total number was revealed to be 1,007. Of these some 150 were Air Force men who were not involved in the fighting. The initial post-battle estimate suggested numbers of up to 1,500 and this encouraged the view that the discrepancy between the initial estimate and the eventual total was even more marked than it actually was.

There had in fact been three sets of additions. Just prior to the battle some Air Force personnel had arrived from Stanley, which they had left to get away from the aerial and naval bombardment and to be closer to the air base at Goose Green. More relevant were around 100 troops from Stanley who arrived on the morning of 28 May as the battle was under way and another 140 from the Mount Kent area who arrived as it was coming to an end.

It was widely believed in the task force, especially by those engaged in the battle, that the reinforcements arrived because the Argentines had been alerted by the BBC World Service. This view was reinforced in 2 PARA as they watched intensive helicopter activity after the broadcast. At 14.00 GMT on 27 May (10.00 local time) the BBC reported (according to one source, after a tip-off from the Downing Street Press Office) that British troops were some 5 miles from Darwin and about to take Goose Green. It is important to note that although this report was unusually definite, media speculation in Britain with regard to an imminent attack on Goose Green had been rife since 24 May. It was virtually taken for granted by all the defence correspondents.[26]

It had been recognized as likely by General Menendez as soon as he appreciated the substance of the landing at San Carlos. As we have seen, he had been keen to reinforce the garrison at Darwin and Goose Green from then on but had been thwarted by his lack of air transport. By sea some 105mm guns had been sent. Not long after the landing he called for a task force to be ferried from the mainland to Darwin by air. However, the Air Force thought that would be too risky. Instead it offered to fly the troops to Stanley, from where they could be ferried by helicopter to Darwin. Menendez saw little point in this as the troops would take too long to arrive and take up position.[27] He was able to send 80–100 men from Stanley. His only other option was to move men from Mount Kent; two artillery sections arrived using all available helicopters during the afternoon of 28 May.[28] The local Argentine Commander heard the BBC report, but thought it was bluff, designed for intimidation, and took no action as a result.[29] He abandoned plans to mobilize the 12th Infantry Regiment to move out towards San Carlos and also pulled back patrols operating north of Darwin.[30] His forces had been oriented initially to a landing from the sea, but after the landing at San Carlos they now had to redeploy. This widened his defence perimeter considerably.

On 26 May Menendez had ordered General Parada, the Commander of 3 Brigade and also of operations in the Islands, to install his command post at Darwin. The reason given for his non-arrival was that it was too dangerous to move by either sea or air at that time. However, it later emerged that the responsible Air Force and Navy officers would not accept an order from Menendez until it had been ratified by the head of their services. The commander of the Chinook helicopter squadron did not take Parada to his command because his ratified orders did not arrive in time.[31] This left Lieutenant-Colonel I. A. Piaggi in charge, who remained in regular communication with Parada.

Even on the more optimistic assessments of the level of Argentine forces, the attacking force was insufficient to provide the degree of superiority normally deemed necessary for an offensive against fixed defences. 2 PARA was made up of some 600 men with artillery, land and naval, as well as air support. Overnight they walked to Camilla Creek House, in which they were installed by first light on 27 May.[32] That afternoon Jones gave orders for the capture of the settlements. He was limited by his lack of helicopters, which almost obliged a direct attack on foot. The intention was to attack and defeat the enemy during the dark and then take the settlements during the day when the civilians could be identified. He had available three 105mm guns (which had been flown in later), two 81mm mortars, supporting gunfire (until first light) from HMS *Arrow* and detachments with Blowpipe air-defence missiles.

The Argentine forces sensed an attack was imminent. The disappearance of a reconnaissance patrol on 27 April (which had been captured by the paras) was in itself evidence that British forces were close by.

The attack began at 02.30. By first light considerable progress had been made by the paras but directed artillery, mortar and machine-gun fire stopped the advance. Harriers were unable to leave the carriers because of mist at sea but Argentine Pucaras could operate against the battalion and the gun position at Camilla Creek. *Arrow*'s gun jammed. The loss of momentum was marked by an increase of casualties as ammunition ran low.

The Argentine intelligence appreciation of the situation by early morning on 28 May indicated that the Darwin garrison could resist the enemy, which would therefore be obliged to extend the attack southward in an attempt to isolate the garrison from reinforcements. The battle was in the balance.

By 09.00, two of the four companies of 2 PARA were now pinned down. Jones had been attempting to get in a position to observe the two forward companies, only to find his way forward barred by enemy activity. At this point he sought to relieve the pressure by leading an attack on an enemy slit trench. He was killed by fire from another trench.[33] Two Scout helicopters ferrying casualties back were caught in a Pucara attack and one was shot down. The aircraft were less successful in their attack on the gun positions and were seen off by fire from Blowpipes. Slowly the paras extricated themselves and, using artillery and mortar fire, and even a Milan anti-tank weapon, broke down Argentine resistance. By 11.10 Darwin Hill had been taken. The 116 Argentine troops holding the trenches had taken severe punishment – eighteen killed and thirty-nine wounded. The British had suffered six deaths, including the commanding officer, and twelve wounded. Argentine forces withdrew to the next defensive line, around the airfield. They were fortified by the arrival of some extra troops from Stanley.

Major Keeble, now in command, ordered a three-pronged attack against Goose Green. They faced intensive fire. At one point it appeared that a white flag was raised from the Argentine detachment in the schoolhouse. A platoon commander and two NCOs went forward to arrange a surrender, but discovered that this was not the defenders' intention. As they returned, another British position, some distance away, directed machine-gun fire on to the defenders. In response the three British soldiers were fired on in the open, and killed. The rest of the platoon overran the building and killed all the occupants.

In late afternoon Pucaras attacked the British forces, two dropping napalm tanks which only just missed forward troops. One of the Pucaras was hit by a Blowpipe air-defence missile. Two other Pucaras were shot down during the battle, along with an Aeromacchi.

Keeble has described his concern at this time as follows:

we had insufficient ammunition to clear the settlement that evening. I didn't want to fight amongst houses at night. The second problem was that they had at least three 35 mm anti-aircraft guns shooting at us in the direct fire role from the tip of the peninsula. The third problem was that they had an artillery battery somewhere and we had been unable to locate it during the battle. We couldn't be accurate enough with our own artillery in the counter-battery role because we couldn't actually see their guns and we were worried about hitting civilians in the settlement.[34]

An urgent request was sent to the carriers for an air strike. Three Harriers, at last able to leave the carriers and join the battle, attacked Argentine artillery positions to great effect. Meanwhile the airstrip was discovered to have been defended only lightly and was taken without difficulty.

Argentine troops had fought fiercely at first but were now becoming demoralized by their inability to hold on to forward positions and by the arrival of British aircraft. By the evening of 28 May, 2 PARA were in a much better position but still faced a major task to dislodge the Argentine garrison. The paras were tired and depleted through casualties, with supplies that were becoming dangerously low and with a large number of prisoners. There were considerable misgivings with regard to the casualties, from both minefields and Argentine defences, likely to result from a frontal assault on Goose Green. Keeble asked Thompson to send J Company from 42 CDO to move to a position covering the southern approach to Goose Green.[35] Later that night 2 PARA secured a landing zone to enable the commandos to fly in.

Meanwhile, at 12.25 Piaggi was ordered by Parada to organize his forces for a counter-attack. He explained that this was not possible.[36] By the evening he was telling his superiors that he was at the edge of his area, having suffered many casualties. The bulk of his personnel were exhausted and ammunition was running out. The artillery pieces had munitions for only two more hours and, in any event, were of inadequate range. He was holding his position to the north and south but elsewhere the picture was very confusing. Hopefully, he asked his superiors about the operations to be executed that night which would allow this situation to be reversed. On being told that no such operations were being planned, he then suggested that the Puerto Argentino (Stanley) Command be asked whether it was essential that he maintain his position and for how long. 'Not essential' replied the Joint Malvinas Command.[37]

At this time 140 extra troops did arrive by helicopter, to the surprise of Piaggi. This was the reserve that had been based in the Mount Kent area. As they had been about to leave, Parada's HQ tried to stop them, having just heard of the hopelessness of the situation at Goose Green. The communication came too late; the troops and the ten helicopters carrying them were just leaving – to captivity.[38]

The Joint Malvinas Command considered a plan to abandon Darwin by sea to Stanley, but then decided that the appropriate course was to allow the Commander at Darwin and Goose Green to decide if and when to surrender should he judge that continued resistance would only lead to unnecessary loss of life. There is some evidence that Argentine interceptions of British radio communications had encouraged the incorrect view that they were facing a full brigade assault. At approximately 01.00 on 29 May the Commander decided to talk with the British Commander. One of his officers went to the house of the

Goose Green settlement manager and asked him to contact the British with a view to a cease-fire. Keeble sent two Argentine prisoners back to their Commander with a message offering two options – 'unconditional surrender' or the 'inevitable consequence' of a refusal to surrender. He warned the Argentine commanding officer that he was responsible for the fate of any civilians and gave prior notice of his intention to bombard the area.[39] They returned almost immediately and negotiations began.[40] A meeting was arranged for 09.00 and the fighting subsided. Piaggi sent two NCOs to discuss the withdrawal of civilians; they were told that a full surrender was required. By 11.00 a.m. the terms of surrender had been agreed.[41] Later Thompson accepted the surrender of the senior Argentine officer, Air Vice-Commodore Wilson Pedrozo, at the latter's headquarters. Pedrozo, in charge of the 150 Air Force men at Goose Green, had been barely informed of the state of the fighting up to the point where it was necessary to surrender.

On 27 May, Nott told backbenchers to 'expect good news soon'. There had in fact been a premature announcement of success in the battle by the Ministry of Defence on the basis of a phone call from Northwood.[42] After all the premature reports, the confirmation of surrender was a relief to the politicians. 'Goose Green was very important because it made us realise that, if really pushed by first-class troops, probably the Argentines were not as strong soldiers as all that. And that gave us great hopes for the future.'[43]

Chapter Twenty-Two

THE BATTLE FOR STANLEY

As the battle for Goose Green was being fought, 45 CDO and 3 PARA reached their first objectives – Douglas settlement and Teal Inlet – while D Squadron of SAS arrived at the landing site below Mount Kent. On the night of 29/30 May it was intended to fly in the tactical headquarters of 42 CDO, with K Company, the Mortar Troop and three light guns. This was thwarted by atrocious weather conditions, but was achieved the following night. Just as they arrived D Squadron SAS engaged an Argentine patrol which had wandered into the area. This was the only opposition they found. By first light on 31 May the slopes of Mount Kent were reached, made available to British troops by the move of the bulk of the Argentine detachment to Goose Green.

This was a critical piece of ground to seize, the largest hill around Stanley and only 12 miles from the outskirts of the town. However, the forces now holding it were few – around 200 men – and were vulnerable to counter-attack. Five Argentine infantry regiments with considerable artillery support were believed to be somewhere in the vicinity. In the event the troops were mainly placed at risk by the elements. Between 1 and 3 June, Thompson made Teal Inlet the administrative base for his Brigade as planned before D-Day. Soon the build-up of 3 Brigade on the line of Mount Estancia–Mount Kent–Mount Challenger was complete.

There was no counter-attack because General Menendez had now decided that his main priority was to prepare for a battle in the immediate vicinity of Stanley. The possibility of dislodging the British from the beachhead was more remote than ever. Following the battle for Darwin/Goose Green, he ordered the 4th Infantry Regiment to occupy Two Sisters and Mount Harriet – instead of Mount Kent – and take a defensive position to the west, from where the main attack was now expected. News that Mount Kent had been secured helped convince the Argentine command that it must retrench in Stanley for the critical battle, and even that this could begin in forty-eight hours.

On 1 June a number of Argentine patrols were helicoptered in to monitor British movements. They were caught in the areas of Mounts Challenger, Kent and Long Island, and in a series of small encounters lost up to half their strength. Meanwhile the Argentine Air Force claimed that the presence of these patrols inhibited them from conducting strikes against the British position on Mount Kent.[1] This may have been something of a rationalization; the problem may simply have been that the patrols had not identified for them anything worth attacking.

The Argentine Assessment

After Goose Green had fallen, Argentine intelligence and the Joint Chiefs of Staff assumed the final attack to be very close. The Chiefs recommended an increase in offensive air strikes and the maintenance of the air transport link with Stanley. If the Argentine position there was to be defended, additional supplies would be required from either West Falkland or the continent.

The CEOPECON ordered an analysis of all provisions in the Malvinas. This study confirmed that there was enough food and fuel to deal with all Argentine needs until 15 June. In order to allow the garrison to hold out longer, the CEOPECON decided to prepare two naval auxiliary ships to sail on 30 May with food and ammunition, as soon as a third ship (which was already on its way to the Islands) had deposited its cargo in the harbour.

As it turned out the two additional ships never left San Juan de Salvamento (Staten Island). This was because Admiral Lombardo thought that the provisions taken by the first ship would allow the defendants sufficient margin to resist until 31 July: the other ships should be sent only if required in the near future. Nevertheless they were to remain ready, loaded and waiting for the signal to sail.

The air strikes that had been ordered were executed on 30 May, notable as the first occasion on which the Air Force and Naval Aviation had acted jointly. The Air Force had asked to join the raid after the Navy had completed its initial planning. The Navy were worried that taking along four Skyhawks, while increasing the ordnance that could be delivered, risked compromising secrecy. The Air Force pilots, who had to rely on the superior navigation equipment of the Super-Etendard, were told to follow exactly the same flight profile and accept the same restrictions on radar emissions as the two Navy aircraft, which had to refuel in flight twice from a plane that accompanied them most of the way. One of the Super-Etendards carried the fifth of Argentina's total of six Exocets. Their objective was to attack a naval group that was sailing 180 miles south-east of Stanley. At the centre of this group was believed to be *Invincible*.[2]

Taking a long route by the south enabled the aircraft to catch the task force by surprise. The Exocet was launched and the Skyhawks followed up with an attack, during which two were shot down. The Argentine pilots were convinced that *Invincible* had been hit. When this was denied by Britain it was assumed that the loss was too great to be acknowledged publicly. However, the aircraft had been attacking not *Invincible* but the destroyer *Exeter* and the frigate *Avenger*. Both ships had picked up the incoming attack and had decoyed the Exocet with chaff. It exploded some distance away. The two Skyhawks were hit by Sea Dart missiles from *Exeter*. *Avenger* was mistaken for *Invincible*; visibility was poor and the 'thick black column of smoke' observed by a Skyhawk pilot was from the frigate's funnel as she manoeuvred at high speed.[3]

The Argentine assessment on 31 May in the aftermath of the attack certainly did not rely on *Invincible* having been put out of action. Some damage was supposed but the extent was uncertain. There had been a decrease in enemy air activity compared with the previous day; on the other hand there had been use of MARTEL (sea to land) missiles.

There should be no slackening of Argentine operations – the attack on Stanley was now expected within two days.

On 3 June Argentine intelligence, once again overestimating the British position, judged that all that was restraining British forces from the final assault were political limitations and the need for reinforcements to improve firepower. The Joint Chiefs of Staff recommended that both submarines and aircraft should be used to interdict the enemy's supply lines while at the same time, and contrary to Lombardo's judgement, Argentine supplies at Stanley should be increased.

On 4 June the Army reported more British artillery and air attacks. Particularly damaging had been an anti-radar missile fired from a Vulcan that had destroyed the radar of the Argentine air-defence system. Subsequent reliance on a smaller mobile radar diminished its service. It was believed that the Argentine air attacks against British positions on Mount Kent and Mount Challenger had led to a slackening of British activity, although in practice any slowing down of operations during this period was due to the fact that the main priorities were logistics – most helicopter lifts from 1 to 11 June were devoted to moving ammunition forward, mainly gun ammunition – and further reconnaissance.

Argentine reconnaissance reported many bivouacs to the west of Mount Kent and logistic installations at Estancia House (where Thompson had established his forward logistic base). Less reliable were reports of 'numerous troops marching towards the north-west, especially in Green Patch and towards Mount Long Island'. There were no British troops at either location other than a few patrols keeping watch on 3 Brigade's left flank.

The Argentine commanders were still considering whether to attempt to mount some sort of operation beyond their defensive positions around Stanley. Studies had been ordered by CEOPECON of a possible operation against the rear of the advancing British forces. On 6 June an officer from General Menendez's staff left Stanley to meet with Galtieri to discuss a plan. By the time he arrived Argentine hopes had been briefly raised by a reverse suffered by British troops.

Reinforcements

Since the initial landings the British forces had been reinforced. On 26 May a group of escorts had arrived – the Type 82 destroyer, HMS *Bristol*, and the Type 42, HMS *Cardiff*, along with the frigates, HMS *Active*, HMS *Andromeda*, HMS *Avenger*, HMS *Minerva* and HMS *Penelope*. HMS *Exeter* had also come from the Caribbean. This meant that Woodward now had replacements for his area defence ships as well as more offensive naval capability. Three more submarines had also arrived – the nuclear-powered HMS *Courageous* and HMS *Valiant* and the conventional HMS *Onyx*.[4]

On 27 May the three battalions of 5 Brigade arrived at South Georgia on board the prestige liner, *Queen Elizabeth II*. It was even larger than the *Canberra*, which had been risked in San Carlos, a risk that the War Cabinet were unwilling to take again. At South Georgia the Scots and Welsh Guards were transferred to *Canberra* and the Gurkhas to *Norland*. The liner had also brought valuable helicopter reinforcements of Sea Kings and Wessex, as had the *Atlantic Causeway*, a sister to the *Atlantic Conveyor*.

On 5 June the base for the Harriers was eventually established at San Carlos, so allowing the carriers to keep at a safer distance.

On 30 May, General Jeremy Moore arrived to command the land forces. The new command structure had Moore reporting directly to Admiral Fieldhouse at Northwood, with Thompson commanding 3 Brigade and Brigadier Tony Wilson in charge of 5 Infantry Brigade, which now once again included 2 PARA (although it was later to be returned to 3 Brigade).

Moore had good reason to be pleased with the situation awaiting him on arrival. The landings had been successfully completed, psychological superiority had been established at Darwin and Goose Green, while a critical piece of ground was in the process of being taken at Mount Kent. In addition, these operations provided important intelligence on Argentine forces.

This latter factor was crucial. Thompson notes the problems he had faced just after the landing:

Although reports from Special Forces patrols indicated a militarily inept enemy, sloppy, disinterested and dozy, only contact between the British and Argentine main bodies of ground troops would show how good, or bad, the enemy really was. Special Forces patrols, by their very nature and given the short time for reconnaissance, could only 'sample' parts of the Argentine positions and it would be a foolish commander who based his assessment of 11,000 men and their likely reactions on a few patrol reports. Furthermore without air photographs, it was not possible to locate the enemy positions with the sort of accuracy required by soldiers fighting a land battle ... Until patrols could 'eyeball' the enemy positions, prisoners be taken and interrogated, captured documents and maps be scrutinized and observations posts (OPs) be established to keep a continuous watch on the enemy, the positions that regiments and batteries might occupy had to be arrived at by an educated guess.[5]

From diaries captured at Goose Green a picture emerged of low morale and the impact of gunfire and air attacks. The main prize from Mount Kent was an Argentine map together with the original operation order from 2 April. The map showed the location of every unit and the boundaries within which it was expected to operate. It contained a number of little circles, designating areas of counter-attack and defence, confirming the Argentine presumption that the British attack would come from the south. From this point on, the intelligence operation became much easier, despite the continuing, chronic lack of aerial photography.[6] The main interest was the extent to which Argentine forces had moved from those positions set out in the map: patrols and the capture of further documents and maps[7] gradually established that they had moved very little.

The more the Argentine forces stayed where they were – and this was forced on them by the lack of helicopter capability – the easier the intelligence task became. By the time Stanley was taken, the Argentine capabilities and positions were known to within 5 per cent accuracy.

The knowledge that Argentine forces were still deployed facing southwards encouraged Moore to have his forces attack from the north. The British commanders had calculated that because the

Argentine forces had been trained by the American marines they would expect the British to adopt the American approach and land as close as possible to Stanley and then attempt to overcome Argentine defences by means of intense firepower. If this was the case the obvious approach was from the south. By landing at Port San Carlos and then moving forces laboriously across East Falkland a measure of surprise had therefore been obained.

What Moore found difficult to understand was the lack of a firm response by the Argentine garrison at Stanley even after his line of approach had become evident.* His objective now was to get men and equipment into position around Stanley for the final assault. 3 PARA and 45 CDO were already walking overland in that direction. Until full supplies were available any major engagement was to be avoided, and in this sense the passivity of Argentine forces was a relief.

British patrols were stepped up during this period. They went out every night between 1 and 10 June. Strictly, reconnaissance patrols (by about four men) kept as low a profile as possible. Patrols of up to about twenty men were sent out to harass the Argentine positions on Mounts Harriet, Longdon and Two Sisters to draw fire in order to pinpoint machine-guns and other weapons, as well as to kill as many men as possible in the process in order to cause demoralization. They succeeded in doing both. One patrol noted Argentine helicopters land seventeen men at Top Malo House and this led to a group of marines moving off from San Carlos and taking the house.

---

* Following the example of Montgomery during the Second World War campaign in North Africa, he had obtained not only a full briefing on General Menendez but a picture of him which he studied while travelling to the South Atlantic. This was a paratrooper who could be expected to attempt an aggressive battle rather than the reactive defensive battle that was actually fought. It was only after he had met General Menendez at the surrender negotiations that it became apparent that he had been given information on the wrong General Menendez (there were five in the Argentine Army in all!).

5 Brigade

A far more difficult problem was what to do with 5 Brigade. Its dispatch to the South Atlantic had been belated. In April Wilson had seen the two parachute battalions taken from him. He had been left with the Gurkhas, but then the Foreign Office suggested that they should not be sent because it was feared that this would offend Third World countries. The Army disagreed, as this would involve deliberately removing the Gurkhas, who seemed likely to be suitable for cold and miserable conditions, from their assigned brigade. The Army was supported by John Nott, formerly an officer with the Gurkhas, and also by the Nepalese Government. In the event the Gurkhas saw little fighting, although their fearsome reputation had a psychological impact on some Argentine defenders.[8] After some consideration, the 2nd Battalion Scots Guards and 1st Battalion Welsh Guards were chosen. Both were on public duties in London (although the Welsh Guards had recently returned from a tour in Northern Ireland) and intensive training was deemed necessary. The headquarters staff of 5 Brigade needed to forge a brigade out of these various units.

Accordingly the re-formed 5 Brigade was sent off for intensive training in Wales. Wilson concentrated the exercises at the platoon and company level; the Brigade staff would naturally get their exercise from co-ordinating all this activity. None the less there was concern in the Army that not enough had been done at the Brigade level and, as a result, the exercises were not considered a great success, leading to doubts about Wilson's suitability.[9] It was decided that it would be unwise to change the Brigade Commander at this stage, but Brigadier John Waters was sent with him to the Falklands, to serve both as Moore's deputy and as a possible replacement for Wilson should this become necessary.

Wilson's role as a commander depended on what 5 Brigade was actually going to do, and this was uncertain. According to the circumstances when it arrived it could be used to take over the defence of the bridgehead from 3 Brigade, or act as a garrison if repossession had already successfully taken place or, possibly, take part in a two-brigade assault on Stanley. If 3 Brigade had got bogged down outside Stanley, then it was envisaged that 5 Brigade could take over while *Canberra* was used as a barracks in which 3 Brigade could recover.

The Brigade was given a powerful impression that its role was seen largely as a reserve and that early combat was not expected. Wilson, on the other hand, was anxious to get involved. For his part, Moore had always been inclined to the view that he would need two brigades for the final battle. As he travelled with Wilson on the *QE2*, it was agreed that 5 Brigade would join in the attack on Stanley by coming from the south, and that it would be allocated equivalent support and resources to 3 Brigade for this purpose.[10] Moore not only believed that he would need its extra strength to overcome the Argentine garrison of six battalions, but he also hoped to keep Menendez looking to the south and south-west.

However, the helicopter shortage which faced Moore on arrival and the actions already taken by 3 Brigade made allocation of transport to 5 Brigade impossible. In particular, looking after the troops which had seized Mount Kent was greedy of helicopter time.

Wilson therefore at first decided to get his men to walk to Fitzroy settlement, from where he intended to launch his attack on Stanley. They needed to take their equipment with them, as there were no obvious points of call, such as settlements or harbours, where they could rendezvous with supply helicopters or ships. Even without the added burden there were doubts whether the Guards' battalions could manage a 35-mile trek. There was also a risk that when they arrived Fitzroy would be properly defended. In this case attack would be difficult – especially if conducted by weary men, lacking sufficient supplies of food and ammunition.

Bluff Cove and Fitzroy[11]

One answer was to carry the men round to Fitzroy settlement by sea. This move had logical advantages but it depended on the route being clear. To this end the Divisional Headquarters on board *Fearless* had requested aerial reconnaissance on 2 June. However, before this had been carried out 2 PARA had taken matters into their own hands, making use of some Scout helicopters and the Chinook that was helping move stores that day from San Carlos. A group of paras went to Swan Inlet House on a Scout and, on the advice of settlers from Goose Green, phoned a resident at Fitzroy who told them that the few Argentines who had been there had departed. To Wilson this seemed a marvellous opportunity to take a critical position without a fight.

He did not know when the aerial photographs would come, if at all, so he decided to check the position with a Scout helicopter. On confirmation that the coast appeared clear, the Chinook helicopter was quickly commandeered to take the paras to Bluff Cove and the neighbouring Port Fitzroy. Wilson was confident that the first group of paras had enough men and equipment to cope with any likely attack from Argentine forces should they be discovered.

News of this move was greeted with less than enthusiasm at Divisional Headquarters. Instead of waiting for the aerial reconnaissance a gamble had been taken with the only Chinook on the basis of information from someone whose knowledge of Argentine movements might have been limited. There was now no obvious means to support or supply the paras if they were discovered by Argentine forces. The enterprise did not endear Wilson to either 3 Brigade or Moore's staff. Moore himself, however, was pleased with the move: it helped ensure that Menendez kept on looking to the south.

Although some Sea King helicopters were able to lift the rest of the paras to Fitzroy settlement and Bluff Cove, the rest of 5 Brigade would need to be taken by sea. It was three days before the first shipments could be organized.

The move could have been managed relatively quickly if *Fearless* with her greater speed and superior off-loading capacity in open waters had been used. Fieldhouse, however, contacted Moore and told him that, while he realized the military logic, Moore should be aware of London's preference, with the diplomatic position still uncertain, that neither *Fearless*, with the Divisional Headquarters on board, nor her sister ship *Intrepid* should be used. They were too important to risk in an area such as this. One reason for this caution was the knowledge that an Exocet had been prepared for operations by Argentine forces on land. The Royal Navy wanted to keep their more valuable ships, for which escorts could not be provided, out of its potential range. The need of the carriers to keep their distance because of the fear of the ground-launched Exocet also meant that fewer air patrols could operate at the time. (It was questioned on land whether the Navy had given themselves an unnecessary margin of safety.)

Unable to make a few journeys on small ships, 5 Brigade were obliged to make a large number on small ships. Over the next few nights landing ships and the recently captured coaster *Monsoonen* brought the rest of 5 Brigade around from Port San Carlos, concluding with the Welsh Guards.

Problems with loading meant that the departure of one of the landing ships on 7 June, *Sir Galahad*, was delayed. The Captain intended to wait until the next night but was ordered to go to Fitzroy, which could be reached before dawn. However, no signal was received by 5 Brigade Headquarters at Fitzroy warning them of this and so when *Sir Galahad* arrived, joining *Sir Tristram* which had arrived the previous day, there were insufficient landing craft to facilitate a quick unloading. In general, communications between the ships and the Divisional Headquarters were inadequate. 5 Brigade's command structure was scattered between San Carlos, Darwin and Bluff Cove.

The landing-craft officer attempted to persuade the Guards to get off before the equipment was unloaded. The Welsh Guards company commanders preferred to wait on board until they could be delivered to Bluff Cove. This was their ultimate destination and they saw no need to accept an unnecessary 16-mile march. Nor did they wish to be separated from their own equipment. They intended to wait until a landing craft could ferry them to Bluff Cove.[12] When, eventually, a landing craft arrived the first priority was then to get off the field ambulance. Meanwhile, a defective ramp made transfer of troops difficult.

On 7 June Argentine Army observers had reported sighting British vessels sailing towards the west in the area of Fitzroy and requested Air Force intervention. The next day, in the early hours, the observation posts at Mount Harriet reported a small naval force sailing for Fitzroy. As the Joint Command at Stanley could do little about the

British convoy, for it no longer had any serviceable aircraft at its disposal, an urgent message was sent to the CEOPECON in Comodoro Rivadavia asking for an air strike against the ships.

The weather was clear for air operations and the Air Force were planning a major effort for 8 June, with a first wave involving six Daggers and eight Skyhawks along with two Mirages in a diversionary role to draw away any Harriers.

The Daggers came across *Plymouth* in Falkland Sound and attacked. Four bombs hit the ship; none exploded and the damage was manageable. The only Harrier patrol up at the time went off in pursuit. Meanwhile the Skyhawks, now down to five as a result of technical problems, went off in search of the landing ships, which were only seen as the aircraft were about to return to base. The anchorage itself was not yet protected by air defences; one Rapier group was set up but pointing in the wrong direction when the attack came. *Sir Tristram* and *Sir Galahad* were both hit, leaving fifty men dead and fifty-seven injured. As a major rescue operation got under way, further waves of Argentine aircraft attacked targets. In the ensuing engagements a number of aircraft were shot down and a landing craft was hit.*

The British radio-intercept service with Thompson at Teal Inlet had intercepted the message from the observation post on Mount Harriet and passed it back to Divisional HQ. By the time it was translated and passed to someone who could act upon it there was nothing that could be done.

Moore spoke that evening direct to Fieldhouse, to inform him personally of the bad news and to discuss its consequences. He warned that it might delay the final assault by four days; in the event it was two. Moore requested that no information be sent out about the extent of the casualties. He hoped that the Argentines would *under*estimate the impact of British losses, because he still wanted them to think that an attack was coming from the south – i.e. from the Bluff Cove area – in

---

* According to British sources three A–4s and four Mirages were certainly shot down and probably two more Mirages during the day but Argentine sources put this at considerably less. See House of Commmons, Fourth Report of the Defence Committee, *Implementing the Lessons of the Falklands Campaign*, Vol. II, pp. 370–8, and Ethell and Price, *Air War: South Atlantic*, pp. 243–7.

order to preserve the element of surprise for his forces north and west of Stanley. Within MoD the presumption was that the idea was to encourage *over*estimation so that the Argentines would be off their guard when the attack came. Certainly little was done to discourage greatly inflated casualty estimates until 11 June. Then the Prime Minister's Press Secretary brought an end to the speculation, which was beginning to damage domestic morale, and released an almost correct figure.[13] The War Cabinet, which by now had become hardened to casualty reports, was relieved that the casualties had not been worse and that the consequent delay to the attack on Stanley would not be great.

Argentina Reviews Its Options

The Argentine assessment erred on the side of exaggeration. In the press there were claims that 500–900 men had been lost. Menendez was aware straightaway that the attacks had hit home, for signals intercepts soon became available requesting emergency assistance during the early evening and night. He ordered an assessment of whether it was feasible to exploit the situation by an attack with his ground forces. He decided against this. His own forces lacked sufficient transport and it was impossible to move heavy artillery pieces. The enemy had air and naval superiority, and it had been even more active following the Fitzroy attack; its line at Mounts Kent and Challenger would have to be broken before such an attack could take place.[14]

The CEOPECON and the Joint Chiefs of Staff made their own interpretation of the possibilities for offensive operations following the attack on Fitzroy. They correctly noted that the successful strike had been made possible by the absence at the time of enemy air patrols. If there were deficiencies in British air defences, then, suggested CEOPECON, it might be possible to execute an operation using air transport. CEOPECON requested from the Military Committee in Buenos Aires an increase in both transport and combat capacity for the Air Force.

However, although Britain had undertaken no air operations on 8 June, the next day the air attacks on Stanley and other targets intensified once again. It became difficult to explain the lull the previous day and revived the previous caution with regard to further air operations.

On 9 June General Daher, Menendez's Chief of Staff, arrived in Buenos Aires to explain the situation in the Islands. There is some debate about this meeting. According to Büsser, Daher did not make clear the true picture, but reported that despite the weather, the prolonged stay in static positions and some problems of provision the 'physical state of the troops is good and the morale is excellent thanks to the hard work of the officer corps'. He described problems in obtaining both tactical and strategic intelligence. As for logistics, there was enough ammunition and food to last until 23 June. The main requests were for infra-red visors and 155mm artillery ammunition.

All this provided a somewhat rosier picture than the actual situation of Argentine troops on the ground justified. Galtieri later claimed that all that was asked for was 'ten thousand pairs of bootees and long underpants as a change of clothes'.[15]

Cardoso and his colleagues, however, reflecting Menendez's view, suggest that Galtieri was unrealistic throughout, still preoccupied with the possibility of an advance from Stanley against the beachhead at San Carlos, despite Daher explaining the lack of fuel and transport for such an operation. 'For God's sake, Daher,' Galtieri is said to have exclaimed, 'with a little will and imagination you can do anything.' They further suggest that at this point Daher decided to abandon the plan for a counter-attack he had brought with him.[16] However, it would seem that the plan was put forward and that it suggested a lack of realism as acute as that exhibited by Galtieri.

In terms of future operations two possible courses of action were outlined: a campaign of attrition and/or counter-attack. The second option could be attempted alone or by drawing in other friendly countries on Argentina's side. Whatever was done had to be done quickly because of the build-up of British pressure. General Daher proposed a counter-attack first to CEOPECON and then to Galtieri. Menendez argued later that at least action along the lines proposed would have disrupted British preparations and provided some extra time; at most it might have changed the course of the war.[17]

The plan – Operation Buzon (Mailbox) – had three objectives: (1) the beachhead at San Carlos, to be attacked by the 5th Regiment at Port Howard reinforced by a parachute force flown over from the continent; (2) the British position at Darwin, to be taken by the 8th Regiment from Fox Bay; (3) the British troops encircling Stanley, to be attacked from Stanley.

To achieve this the Navy was asked to seize control of the San Carlos Strait, bombard enemy forces in both San Carlos and Darwin, and provide transport for the 5th and 8th Regiments in the *Monsoonen* and *Bahia Buen Suceso*. For its part the Air Force was required to achieve local air superiority for the duration of the operation, as well as transport, escorts and air support at close range for the parachutists who had to disembark near San Carlos.[18]

The plan got a cool reception. The possible landing points near San Carlos and Darwin were ill-defined. Wherever the regiments were to be taken, this would be across the San Carlos Strait, which varied between 20 to 60 miles, by a ship with a speed of 8 to 12 knots. Büsser elaborates on some decisive flaws in the plan:

> Because of the capacity of the ARA *Bahia Buen Suceso* it was possible to transport the 8 regiment complete but the ARA *Monsoonen* did not have the capacity to transport the whole of the 5 regiment, so that ship would have had to make a number of crossings. There was an additional problem: neither of these ships was made for beach landings, and therefore the situation would demand that the troops be transported to the land via small boats which would make the entire operation very tiring and slow. All this required a prolonged period of naval and air control of the area. In any case all this discussion was otiose since the ARA *Bahia Buen Suceso* was at the time detained at Fox Bay with damage and the *Monsoonen* was no longer in Argentine hands since it had been captured by the British forces a few days back.[19]

Büsser describes the possibility of obtaining naval control of the San Carlos Strait as 'at best utopic'.[20] The Argentine fleet would need to get through the invisible line of five British nuclear-powered submarines and a conventional submarine patrolling the Islands with, it was believed, satellite information. Then they would need to take on British warships, 'supported by their own aircraft that already had control of the air and that moreover had superiority in numbers, technology and information'.

Even then the requisite naval bombardment of San Carlos and Darwin would have been at best inefficient, as suitable targets were not known with any precision. It was noted that the British naval bombardment had been intense, sophisticated and prolonged against the Stanley defences and this had not managed to prevent the airstrip from being used.

Nor was the Air Force in any better condition to help. It had never obtained air control in the war, even when it was gaining its greatest successes. Also it lacked the capability for very close land support for the parachute forces. The credibility of an offensive against the troops encircling Stanley was undermined by Menendez's reluctance, the previous day, to launch a ground attack against the forces at Fitzroy and Bluff Cove.*

What is remarkable about this plan was not only the unreality which surrounded it, which says a lot about the general grasp of events in the Argentine HQ, but also the fact that while all these grand plans were being put together the vulnerable British position on Mount Kent had been left well alone, even though an early attack by Argentine forces from Stanley might have dislodged it.

On 10 June the CEOPECON analysed Menendez's proposed offensive and discarded it. According to Daher, Galtieri told him that there were enough troops in the Falklands to deal with the British without risking the fleet and the remnants of the Air Force. 'I was told to tell Menendez that he must be prepared to fight to the end, even if we had to die. We were not to surrender.'[21] In the event he was not

---

* Some indications that these plans were being considered had been picked up by General Moore, and as a precaution he kept back 40 CDO at San Carlos. However, as the British assessment was that the weather and terrain were wholly unsuitable for parachute landings it was doubted that Argentina would try, though it did have a notional capability.

able to deliver his message in person. British artillery fire against the airfield prevented him landing at Stanley and he had to return to the mainland.

In all probability the most important consequence of Daher's presentation to the President was that whatever the former thought he was saying the latter did not appreciate that the Argentine position on the Islands was critical or that the situation was deteriorating.[22] While Daher had been on his trip to Buenos Aires, Menendez's confidence declined further. On 10 June there had been further naval bombardment, which for the first time led to civilian casualties.

Yet when the full Argentine Cabinet met later that day they had no reason to believe that the fall of the Stanley garrison was imminent or that there was any reason why it would not be possible to continue to prosecute the war. In fact there was, if anything, a modest optimism in Buenos Aires. The British had been obliged to veto the cease-fire resolution in the UN while at the same time taking considerable casualties in Fitzroy. Galtieri believed that the attack now would only come on 20 June.[23]

The Joint Chiefs of Staff's assessment of the Fitzroy attack, where their targets had been unprotected, was that this movement of troops had been a gamble that had failed and this must have an effect on future operations. The British media were presenting the episode as a tragedy. This ought to mean that more time would lapse before new operations could be mounted: the onset of winter could be expected to slow the British down further. Problems resulting from low temperatures and the lack of adequate logistic support would lead to attrition of war matériel. International pressures would meanwhile reduce the political space available for a military resolution of the conflict.

All this would add urgency to British preparations for the assault on Stanley: a military result was required as early as possible. Yet to achieve this Britain would need to reorganize its forces, drawing on the material and personnel rescued from the landing area of Fitzroy, and also on those more recently sent south from Great Britain, which would not arrive until 15 June at the earliest.

Although Defence Minister Nott had acknowledged the problems resulting from Fitzroy, his refusal to release detailed casualty figures indicated a tendency to minimize losses out of sensitivity to public opinion. So in the belief that demoralization was setting in, plans of attack being slowed and international pressure growing, there still appeared to be some hope of forcing Britain into a political compromise.

This political logic suggested a military approach based on attrition rather than counter-attack. It depended on getting reinforcements into the Islands and then inserting combat units behind enemy lines. Planning for this had begun on 4 June and planning directives for the action were approved on 9 June (Operational Plan No. SZE–21) and agreed by the High Command on 11 June. It was co-ordinated with Lombardo through Captain Cufre, who travelled to the Islands on 10 June and back to Comodoro Rivadavia the next day to report that it was ready to be implemented.

Under the impression that Argentine troops would be able to sustain a defence for at least eight to ten more days (which were seen as politically crucial), Argentine diplomacy began to prepare for a last effort in the international arena, with the main objective now one of convening a session of the General Assembly of the United Nations in order to bring maximum pressure to bear on Britain.

Argentine diplomacy was not to be allowed its breathing space nor was the Argentine military plan ever implemented. On the night of 11 June the battles for Mount Harriet, Two Sisters and Mount Longdon began in earnest. The drive for the capture of Stanley had begun. The only significant Argentine success of the following two days was with the ground-launched Exocet missile. This struck the *Glamorgan*, which had supported the attacks on the night of 11/12 June but had overstayed its time in the fire-support area. In an attempt to get away from air-attack range before daylight it cut across the 'no go' circle and was hit by the missile; thirteen men were lost, although the damage to the ship was not in itself serious.

The Final Assault

In the Stanley area, Argentine forces totalled up to 9,000 men, although only some 5,000 were fighting troops. They had three 155mm and forty-two 105mm guns. There were virtually no ground-support aircraft left and anti-aircraft cover did not extend much beyond Stanley and the airfield.[24]

By this time it was evident to the Argentine command in Stanley that the British attack would come from the west. This was contrary to previous expectation that a large landing effort might be expected from the south or east of the Argentine positions, in which direction the defences were still pointing.[25] The failure to reorient defences meant that very wide fronts were being covered with few troops, while there were units in the rear that would not be used in combat at all. Those ordered to move towards the west either never arrived at the arranged place or else arrived too late, and then into positions inadequately prepared for the conduct of the defence. Although six units of infantry, equivalent to a regiment, were available to Menendez, not one had been assigned to a reserve. Far too much reliance was placed on minefields to inhibit a British advance, and there was still, despite the evidence of Goose Green, far too little appreciation of the British preference for night-attacks.

During 11 June British forces completed preparations for the attack that would take place that night. 3 Brigade had been strengthened at 5 Brigade's expense and now consisted of 42 and 45 CDO, 2 PARA and 3 PARA as well as the 1st Battalion Welsh Guards (1WG) with two companies of 40 CDO replacing the two Welsh Guards companies who had lost men and weapons at Fitzroy. Although Moore had initially been pleased by Wilson's performance, he had gradually lost confidence in the organization of 5 Brigade. Wilson, in turn, had become frustrated by the apparent priority given to 3 Brigade and the extra burdens he therefore had to carry, especially the lack of helicopters. Now he saw Thompson's Brigade strengthened at the expense of his own.

Despite some discussion of a narrow line of advance, the British command decided that the operations over the coming nights must leave Stanley surrounded, with British forces enjoying freedom of movement to carry supplies forward and casualties back.[26] The plan was therefore for a developing series of attacks on the three key areas of high ground on the outer perimeter of the Àrgentine defences – Mount Longdon, Two Sisters and Mount Harriet. They would be attacked by 3 PARA, 45 CDO and 42 CDO respectively, with some 600 men each, and 2 PARA and 1 WG in reserve. The Argentine defence consisted of one company on Mount Longdon, and two each on Two Sisters and Mount Harriet.

Only on Longdon was the attacking strength the 3:1 ratio required by the classics on infantry offensives. Elsewhere the attacking strengths were 3:2, well below the optimum for such operations. If the Argentine forces around Stanley had been properly redeployed these attacks could have faced severe difficulties.

The battle for Mount Longdon was fierce, even though the force ratio was the most favourable. Because of the layout of the defence,[27] 3 PARA were fighting along the spine of the ridge and only had enough elbow-room to deploy one company at a time, an experience likened to advancing down a bowling alley in the dark being fired on from both sides. If troops moving forward unintentionally bypassed Argentine positions in the darkness they could be shot in the back. As a result 3 PARA took the highest casualties of any British unit in the land battles. The battle started just after 21.00 and was not over until around 07.00 the next day. It went slowly at first, with mortar and artillery fire being used to soften up the defences, which eventually gave way.

Although Two Sisters should have provided ideal defensive opportunities, Argentine forces had moved there belatedly, and so their positions were makeshift, manned by companies from two different regiments and with a divided command. In the face of heavy artillery fire, they did not put up very stern resistance to 45 CDO. A number of platoons were withdrawn when the battle started going badly. By dawn the British were in control.

The defenders on Mount Harriet were better prepared, but still caught by an attack that came from the rear, after two companies moved through areas which had been mined, avoiding the main defences. As the Argentine rear was overwhelmed, the other forces were pinned down by artillery and mortar and prevented from either counter-attacking or escaping. They had little option but to surrender.

In Stanley, there was an attempt to organize reinforcements which came to little. As it became apparent that all three positions were falling, artillery bombardments were ordered to pin the British down but this could now have little impact on the outcome of the campaign. Of the 850 Argentine defenders that night, 50 had died and 420 were captured. British losses were twenty-five dead and sixty-five wounded.[28]

Now British forces had conquered the heights that ran in the north–south direction and were situated some 6 to 7 miles from Stanley. The next evening was relatively quiet, as British forces completed their preparations for the final assault. It had been hoped to mount this assault on 12 June, but it was postponed because of logistical problems: the gun lines had to be restocked with ammunition and 5 Brigade also needed to conduct a quick reconnaissance which they had been unable to do before. Argentine forces knew of the original plan and so spent an anxious night waiting for an attack which never materialized.

On Sunday 13 June little happened by day on land, although there were two Argentine air attacks, one of which, possibly guided by radio intercepts, was against Thompson's HQ near Mount Kent and almost caught Moore and Thompson, with a number of other senior staff while they were in conference discussing the imminent attack.

Menendez warned Galtieri: 'judging by the activity that the British have displayed during the day, this very night they will launch the final attack and consequently between today and tomorrow the fate of Port Stanley will be in the balance.' 'Very well,' replied Galtieri '. . . Put everything you have around the capital. We shall make the stand there.'[29]

The Last Stand

The final assault on 13 June involved both brigades. 3 Brigade now consisted of 2nd Battalion Scots Guards (2SG), 1st Battalion Welsh

Guards (1WG) and 1st Battalion 7th Gurkha Rifles (1/7GR). As the Guards attacked Tumbledown, 2 PARA was to attack Wireless Ridge and the Gurkhas Mount William.

The marines at Tumbledown were among the more effective Argentine troops and were well prepared for an assault. Reinforcements had been brought in. The defenders were on full alert. At 16.00 hours, as the sun began to set and snow began to fall, the attack began.

The British opened the battle with a diversionary move using light tanks (for the first time in the campaign) which had a brief exchange of fire before withdrawing. The main body of 2SG pushed forward up Tumbledown in three groups. Initially they were forced back with serious casualties by fierce resistance and heavy artillery fire, but they persisted and in the early hours of the morning started a slow but firm advance.

Although some ground had been conceded the Argentine marines still held on to the critical high ground. When the officer commanding the marines informed Menendez of this at around 07.00 he also anticipated a renewed British offensive to his rear and so requested more ammunition. Instead he was ordered to withdraw. According to the officer's own account:

> I was convinced that we could still resist, and that is why I ordered the O Company – which was ready – to begin a counter-attack together with the M Company. I planned to direct this attack personally.
>
> As the time went by, the situation became critical, since we had practically finished our ammunition on the supporting firearms (105mm batteries, mortars and anti-tank guns). We had not received the reinforcement of ammunition that we had requested and we only received from the rearguard some ammunition for the 81mm mortar. The transport vehicles only reached the barracks of the engineer group (9 kilometres away from the front line). The enemy artillery fire was overwhelming.[30]

By 08.00 the Argentine position at Tumbledown was at risk. When at 09.00 the High Command was informed of this it repeated its original order to withdraw. The marines moved back to Sapper Hill.

Wireless Ridge was attacked by 2 PARA, who faced companies of the 5th Marine Infantry Battalion, veterans of Mount Longdon, and the 7th Infantry Regiment of the Argentine Army. Wireless Ridge had never been given a high priority and was now manned by tired and demoralized conscripts, who had been suffering from Harrier attacks. They were no match for the paras, who employed light tanks and were able to call on artillery and naval gunfire. Argentine resistance began to deteriorate and became confused around 02.00 as 2 PARA reached their objective. Before the first light of day the defending forces had withdrawn and by 05.00 2 PARA were occupying the ridge. There they stopped and waited, while SAS forces conducted an independent and ineffectual operation of their own against Cortley Hill ridge to the north.

The Argentine command belatedly ordered whatever small units were available to engage in rearguard counter-attacks, to block the enemy advance and cause whatever attrition was possible. But such operations are difficult to co-ordinate at night and in the confusion of battle. They were unsuccessful. At Mount William the Gurkhas, after being held back until Tumbledown was secured, were allowed to go forward. The advantage of using the Gurkhas in a daytime attack was that they would be seen, and their ferocious reputation would unnerve the opposition. To the Gurkhas' disappointment, they found the enemy melting away in front of them.

By now British forces were on the outskirts of Stanley. They had overrun the main Argentine gun positions. The three batteries of guns with 3 Brigade and the two batteries with 5 Brigade were, or were almost, in range of the whole of the territory remaining in the hands of the Argentine forces. The only credible defence left was on Sapper Hill. The Welsh Guards, who, Wilson felt, had not recovered sufficiently from Bluff Cove to be involved in the initial attacks, began to prepare to take this final position. Argentine marines in occupation of the hill were joined by troops who had been told to withdraw from Tumbledown. By the time that both sides were ready for the fight, a cease-fire had been ordered.

Chapter Twenty-three

SURRENDER

Although the Junta was not prepared for the sudden collapse in Stanley, there had been a growing sense that things were moving to an uncomfortable climax and this was accompanied by heightened political tension.

As the armed services faced defeat, traditional inter- and intra-service rivalries had come to the fore. The Army hierarchy in particular was beginning to divide. It was only five months since Galtieri had come to power. Even without the trauma of possible defeat over the Falklands there were many who were hostile to the President, especially men in the officer corps who had suffered a loss of influence and position. Many senior officers felt that they had been kept in the dark as to the state of the negotiations and had not really understood how the war had come about in the first place.

Now there was growing anxiety that the war was taking Argentina out of the Western sphere and into the communist, despite the intensity of the previous 'war' against Marxism and subversion. This was highlighted by the meeting between Costa Mendez and Castro on 31 May. It was true that the West appeared to have deserted Argentina – but the communist bloc had little to offer in its place.* Political parties of the centre and right shared this anxiety, and there is evidence that this was encouraged by the US Embassy in Buenos Aires.

* The Soviet Union had offered arms after the landings and then more decisively after the US 'tilt', with the idea that they would be delivered through a third party such as Libya. However, the conditions for this – including diplomatic support in the UN on

In Buenos Aires suspicions centred on General Walters. Although he had been put into Haig's negotiating team because of his supposedly good relations with Latin American generals, he was warily received as an expert in indirect American intervention. Anaya for one was convinced that Walters had been involved in an effort to install a pro-American government in Bolivia during the previous year. On 11 May, when relations between the two countries were particularly low, he had visited Buenos Aires. This was ostensibly to reassure the Junta that US satellites were not being used to support Britain. However, he had arrived without being invited and so the Junta interpreted his presence in terms of Haig's warning, issued as the US tilted to Britain at the end of April, that they would be 'wiped off the face of the earth'.

As a result of this warning and Walters's visit, precautionary measures had been taken to get intelligence from the US Embassy. On 15 May Ambassador Schlaudeman was noted having discussions with Galtieri's opponents in the military. There were a number of meetings of senior politicians and retired military officers to the point where the Junta feared a conspiracy.

Meanwhile popular discontent over the conduct of the war grew. During the Pope's visit to Argentina on 12–13 June (to maintain his own 'balance' after carrying on with his scheduled visit to Britain), the first expressions were heard of a desire for the war to be ended.

Climax

When the Argentine High Command heard at 09.00 on 14 June that the position at Tumbledown could no longer be sustained this confirmed its growing suspicion that the battle was lost and it began to prepare for surrender. There had been a vague plan to evacuate the

---

such issues as American withdrawal from Central America – were considered too high. In practice the only equipment actually delivered from the Soviet Union was a scrambling device which Costa Mendez requested in early April to make possible secure communications while he was in the United States. It was widely assumed that the Soviet Union was providing intelligence to Argentina (it was certainly collecting it for itself) but this was not the case.

city and continue the fight around the airfields, perhaps in conjunction with a last, desperate political initiative, but this was now wholly impractical.

In the early morning of that day the Commander-in-Chief of the Air Force, Lami Dozo, flew to Comodoro Rivadavia to follow the events in the Islands and then on to the San Julian air base in Patagonia. At 09.50 he was called by Brigadier Castellano, in the Islands, informing him of an order from Menendez to group all the personnel of the Argentine Air Force in the Islands by Stanley airport.

The Commander-in-Chief of the Navy, Anaya, discovered what was happening when, at 09.15, he received a call from the naval units on the Islands notifying him that they were already destroying archives and codebooks. Meanwhile the Joint Chiefs of Staff in Buenos Aires received a cable from General Menendez informing them that the principal positions west of Tumbledown, William and Wireless Ridge were now in British hands, and that there had been intense fighting with numerous casualties. Artillery and support weapons had been destroyed. The defence was being restructured around the 3rd and 25th Infantry Regiments but little could be expected of them. Menendez concluded that he saw no possibility of maintaining his position any longer.

Galtieri and Anaya, together with Lami Dozo's Chief of Staff, were meeting when, at 10.55, Menendez phoned Iglesias. Menendez was blunt: 'This is finished. We have no means left. We fought strongly until the last hours. The artillery group has been pulverized. General Jofre has been able to restructure a very precarious line of defence. I do not know if he will be able to hold it later than midnight today.' He suggested that the options were to accept Resolution 502 and withdraw the Argentine flag, 'a killing', or else to disband the troops, who now were both exhausted and running short of ammunition. He warned that the matter must soon be decided. 'If you need time to consider this, we do not have such time here. They tell me that the English are four or five blocks away from here ... For the decision we only have minutes.'

As Iglesias was reporting this to the President a second call came through from Menendez. This time he spoke directly to the President.

Surrender

GALTIERI: Here, General Galtieri, whatever day it is, General Menendez – good or bad – is a day that shall always be remembered in Argentine history. Go ahead, over.

MENENDEZ: I share with you the feeling, I send you an embrace and would like to know if General Iglesias has explained the situation to you, as I tried to make it known to him. Over.

GALTIERI: Received, Menendez, received. General Iglesias explained to me the situation that you described. Over.

MENENDEZ: My General, I don't know if I can go into details but the truth that I tried to convey coincides with professional judgement, though it is very painful. This defence has no future; it makes no sense as it is now. There is a precarious defence, of which we have no high hopes, but there are still people remaining in their combat positions. There is a little left of the artillery; other groups are fighting or, at least, still have their two feet on the earth to do something.

But in this situation, if the British, as I believe, continue with their attacks with the means that they have displayed in air, sea and land during the night and with insistent fire, I do not know if I can hold out until tonight. That is why I explained my doubts to Iglesias and to you. This means that right now there are still men in their positions but there are many that are returning to the rear without ammunition and disorganized, though we still do not convey that impression.

. . . this can also result in losing a lot of people in a little time and this is worse than having to surrender the flag. This is what I am saying to you personally and as Commander of the Malvinas. Over.

GALTIERI: Understood, Menendez, received. You are living the situation in full detail. That is something, that I, here in the Plaza de Mayo – no matter how hard you try to describe the situation – cannot capture in its entirety. In any case, though this is true, I think that if there have been sectors of the Argentine position broken by the English attack, there must also be other sectors of the Argentine Army and the Navy Marines that must organically still exist, still resist in the rear of the first English units. I believe that perhaps these should be used. The English are also in a critical situation, as much as we are, as much as we. And we should impel our men to fight, make them get out of their foxholes and move forward – not backwards or to abandon their positions; to attack the flanks of the enemy penetration force even if it is done with few units and some fire. Perhaps we can prevent the English penetration.

Use all the means at your disposal, especially Regiments 3 and 25, and counter-attack. Use all the means at your disposal and continue fighting with all the intensity with which you are capable, move the personnel out of the foxholes. Over.

MENENDEZ: My General, really, I must say that then I have not been able to give you the whole picture of what we have been living through all night, in the morning and for the last couple of days, my General, oh well, for the last three days even. Really, my General, at this moment there are no pieces of artillery left here, no possibilities of air support, and the physical surrender of the troops, my General. The Navy Marines of the 5 Battalion have counter-attacked a number of times through the night and three, four times they have been rebutted. The Infantry Regiment 25 has already been moved forward and one of its companies has practically disappeared and what is left . . . you cannot ask such a measure of this remnant in the circumstances that we are living. Excuse me, I am giving you wrong information, Infantry Regiment 3 has moved with a company of the 25. That company has disappeared. The elements of Regiment 6 that were moved forward have also disappeared.

My General, there is practically no ammunition left in many of the places where there has been a total battle, as is the case of the Navy Marines after resisting all attacks and recovering their territory. On the other hand, General, the troops cannot stand this any more, they are fighting in hand to hand combat in many of the trenches, I have seen it. Look, my General, what you are suggesting, the troops cannot accomplish. That is my obligation as Commander of the Malvinas. I hate not being able to accede to your request and I beg you to decide immediately. Over.

GALTIERI: You know, of course, better than I do, the situation, Menendez. I told you that from the Plaza de Mayo I cannot know what you are telling me but I accept your expressions and your reflections. In any case you are the commanding officer, you are the commandant. You have norms to follow, rules to obey and a mission to accomplish. You have your personnel, you have the military code* and you have the authority to resolve and decide. From up here, I can do nothing but suggest modes of action, but the responsibility today is with you, the Commander of the Islas Malvinas. Over.

MENENDEZ: My General, precisely because I feel such a responsibility for all those around me, despite this current moment in which I feel the need to describe to you what I said, and suggest the possibilities of action that I consider feasible, I must tell you that before this conversation I have been talking to the troops. I have seen them returning from the front; I have seen the wounded helping each other back; I also know some have come back to town because they have no ammunition left; many, many people have been overcome for lack of ammunition.

My General, I cannot ask more of these troops, after what they have been through. I told you already that last night and the night before, and all through the day that today is a crucial day and we shall see what I predict.

We have not been able to hold on to the heights. We have no room, we have no means, we have no support as would be necessary and I believe, my General, that we have a responsibility towards our soldiers, soldiers that will die fighting a fight that has no prospects, for a few more hours and that will be very

---

* The implication of Galtieri's remark here is that under the military code of conduct Menendez would not be expected to surrender until he had lost half his men and three-quarters of his ammunition, otherwise he should expect to be court-martialled. Galtieri is in effect saying that if Menendez wants to surrender he can only assume that he has lost 4,000 men and has no munitions left. This was far from the case: the Army's losses for the whole conflict were less than 800 men. As the Air Force, with all that it had been through, was still managing to break the air blockade, Galtieri could not understand how it was that Menendez found himself in such dire circumstances.

costly in lives. This is what I tell you as Commander of the Malvinas. Over.

GALTIERI: Understood and received, Menendez, I will think over what you told me. I think this conversation is finished. Have you got anything else to tell me? Over.

MENENDEZ: No, but can I wait for your answer? Over.

GALTIERI: I will come back to you, Menendez. Over.

MENENDEZ: Perhaps there will be nothing left tonight of the Malvinas garrison. I repeat, I am ready to take on all the responsibility that afterwards I will have to face. Over and out.

Just after this conversation, Menendez was informed of a British message offering talks following a cease-fire. Menendez had until 13.00 to answer. To give him time British troops were being held back and had been told not to enter Stanley. Menendez spoke with General García, who authorized negotiations.

García reported what he had done to Galtieri, who agreed, but only so long as Menendez did not commit the Government politically, nor sign any document, or discuss surrender or capitulation except in terms of evacuation and withdrawal of troops. It was not a limitation that would be easy to enforce.

At 12.45 García spoke again with Galtieri, reporting a further conversation with Menendez. Menendez had outlined to him the terms for the eventual surrender received over the radio. He also reported British concern with the possibility of an Argentine air attack from the continent during the evacuation process.* García reported the instructions given to Menendez:

I told him that the commitment of surrender only applies to the forces in my command in the Islands. I have not requested nor will request as of now any air mission from the continent which can

---

* The British were anxious that the very independence of, and lack of co-ordination between, elements of the Argentine services, which had undermined their joint operations, might now result in a last-minute tragedy. They were worried that the Argentine Air Force would continue the fight, and Rapier missiles were therefore moved forward at the first opportunity.

hazard the situation. I cannot sign a political commitment that is beyond my responsibilities as commander. Please have this point discussed and decided upon at 19.00 hours at the latest.

Although the first contact with the British had been around midday it took a few hours before an actual meeting could be arranged. At 16.00 Menendez eventually met with Lt Colonel Rose and Captain Bell of the British forces at the Secretariat Building which had been used by the Argentine civilian administration.

At 19.45 García transmitted the surrender terms to Buenos Aires for Galtieri's information. The Junta met until the early morning of 15 June,[1] shocked not only at the surrender itself but at the speed with which it had come about. They had believed that it would take at least a further eight days for Menendez's troops to be overcome – time which might have made a critical difference in terms of diplomatic activity.

Surrender

Rose and Bell had been preparing the ground for the surrender ever since Goose Green. Rose, of the SAS, had become convinced that Argentine forces were so dispirited that they could be persuaded to capitulate rather than fight a final battle. As the key positions around Stanley, which had been surprisingly lightly defended, were taken, a psychological as well as physical superiority was established. British firepower could pick out any Argentine position; Argentine artillery was blind. Rose, who had been closely involved in the dramatic rescue of hostages from the Iranian Embassy in London the previous year, saw the similarities to a classic terrorist situation in which the opposition faced overwhelming force and only had hostages – in this case the civilian residents in Stanley – with which to bargain.

Bell, as a Spanish-speaker, had been involved in the battle for Darwin and Goose Green and the subsequent surrender negotiations. He too was convinced that the Argentine command could be persuaded to capitulate. The two men gained the agreement of Moore to develop a psychological approach to the Argentine command. It was based on the assumption that Menendez had no desire to see major casualties among his own forces or the civilians. On the other hand he was under pressure to fight. The stratagem was to establish a line of contact, initially on humanitarian issues, and then use this when the time came to argue that:

> as both countries had to live together after the war, we, the British, did not wish to bring about the complete destruction of the Argentine forces in the Falkland Islands. Such an outcome would not be in the long-term interests of either side. Argentina, long a close friend of Britain, was still regarded by the British as an important bastion against Soviet expansionism in the region.

Later the futility of a continued Argentine struggle would be indicated while taking care to give due regard to 'Argentine professionalism and bravery'. It would also be suggested that those on the mainland did not appreciate the problems faced on the Islands.

To implement this approach it was first necessary to establish contact with the local Argentine command. An opportunity to do this had come on 5 June. On the assumption that the civilian medical radio net was being monitored Bell interrupted it, introduced himself as a British officer and asked to speak to an Argentine officer. By this means he established contact with a naval officer, Captain Barry Melbourne Hussey, who was senior administrator in Stanley. Although Hussey would not enter into conversation with the British he listened to Bell's daily call and reported back to Menendez. As the ground around Stanley was taken on 11–13 June, Bell sent a forceful message, expressing concern over the civilians in Stanley and warning of the risk of destruction of Argentine forces.*

From 09.00 on 14 June, as it became apparent that the Argentine situation was hopeless, Bell sought to contact the Argentine command. He achieved no response, as Menendez was then engaged in his

---

* On 13 June three civilians were killed by a British shell. Dr Alison Bleaney, who had listened in on the broadcasts, went to Hussey on the morning of 14 June to persuade him to talk.

frantic conversations with Galtieri and Garcia. At 11.00 Argentine forces were told to abandon their positions and began to move back into the town. This was observed by the British forces, who were ordered by Moore to hold fire. Almost at once a call came on the radio net from Hussey asking to speak to a British staff officer to arrange a cease-fire. It was then agreed that Bell and Rose would meet Menendez at 15.45. (In fact they were late because of a confusion over the precise location.)

Moore sent Bell and Rose to do the initial talking because it would strengthen their hand if they could refer to a higher authority when being pressed on a difficult point. They took with them a surrender document which had been prepared on *Fearless* in consultation with London. It contained the phrase 'unconditional surrender', which Moore thought excessive: he was seeking surrender, and he did not want to have to resume fighting for the sake of the word 'unconditional'. If that had become necessary then the fighting could well have been in Stanley itself. His mission was to 'repossess the Islands' and that is what he had done. Having brought the enemy to the point of surrender it seemed unnecessary to offend his dignity. But when he asked for the word to be removed he was told that London insisted on its inclusion. Moore had little choice but to forward the document so drafted to Menendez, but he decided to remove the offending word if it started to cause problems. He took exactly the same view on the question of having the ceremony photographed.

Menendez welcomed British recognition of the honour of Argentine forces, and, despite Galtieri's expectation, had little choice but to discuss the surrender of the troops at Stanley. Initially he would not discuss surrendering troops not directly under his command, such as those on West Falkland. He eventually agreed, after a lengthy argument, that the same logic which had persuaded him to surrender would apply to other forces. His main concern, as he discussed the mechanisms of surrender and the transfer of administration, was to avoid humiliation.[2]

The British agreed to allow Argentine units to keep their banners and flags, and to be administered by their own commanders. Mixed working groups would be formed to resolve the problems of personnel and logistics. Argentine personnel would return to the continent on ships of the Argentine flag. They would abandon Stanley by moving to the airport the next day. Any ceremony to sign the agreement would be private, without the presence of journalists.

Moore came in to confirm the final details. As he had anticipated, Menendez had balked at the phrase 'unconditional surrender', and insisted instead that it was a 'surrender with conditions'. Moore agreed to delete the word 'unconditional'. The surrender would cover all Argentine forces in the archipelago. At 19.45, after Menendez had spoken again with García, he met again with Moore.[3] The surrender document was actually signed at 21.15 14 June local time and 00.15 15 June GMT. To avoid having to put two dates on the document, it was decided to keep matters simple and time the formal surrender at 20.59 and 23.59 14 June.

In London the War Cabinet had few decisions to take. Its members had been following the news of events on the Falklands closely and had received encouraging reports of the campaign's progress, along with details of Argentine demoralization. They expected the war to conclude on 14 June. In the evening they sat in the Prime Minister's room at the House of Commons, waiting for news of the surrender, while officials drafted a statement for the Commons, which the Prime Minister hoped to be able to deliver before the session closed that evening. Lewin was receiving reports which came via the SAS net to its base at Hereford, on to Northwood and then on to Westminster. At 21.30 he received news that Menendez was negotiating terms. Although the actual surrender document had yet to be signed, the news was sufficient for the champagne to be opened and for Thatcher to go to the chamber to announce to the House that Argentine soldiers 'are reported to be flying white flags over Port Stanley', and that talks were under way about the surrender of Argentine forces.

Not only were the reports of white flags incorrect, but she incorrectly described Moore's deputy, Brigadier Waters, as the negotiator. None the less the talks were under way and they were soon concluded. Much of the next day in London was spent attempting to get hold of a copy of the surrender document before the Prime Minister made her formal statement to the House in the afternoon of 15 June.

Surrender

In Buenos Aires the mood was dejected. After the Junta had finished discussing the situation, early in the morning of 15 June, Galtieri met with the divisional generals, who now were the main source of effective power. At 04.00 the meeting broke up after discussing possible future developments, including the formal cessation of hostilities with Britain and the position of the President himself. During the morning of 16 June the generals met again without reaching definite conclusions. Their discussions continued the following day. By this time it was evident that the failure of Buenos Aires to announce a full cessation of hostilities was complicating the whole situation, especially with regard to the repatriation of prisoners of war. After yet another meeting, it was decided that Galtieri would have to resign his posts as Commander-in-Chief of the Army and as President of the Nation. General Nicolaides took his place in the Army.[4]

Some of the generals wished to internationalize the conflict by drawing in other Latin American countries that had offered practical military assistance to Argentina. It was recognized that this would have totally unpredictable consequences, and could lead to uncomfortable results for an officer corps imbued with a professional anti-communism. On the other hand, the mood within the military and in public opinion would not allow a formal declaration of a cessation of hostilities.

As the evacuation procedures were worked out, the bulk of the Argentine troops were sent back to the mainland (using British ships) with a number of officers retained, essentially as hostages in the event of an air attack. It was also thought wise to separate the officers from their troops, in case the former decided to incite trouble. The British were anxious to get the bulk of Argentine prisoners off the Islands as soon as possible. There were major problems with providing food, shelter and sanitation for so many. Before they could be moved out of Stanley mines had to be cleared from the harbour area so that troopships could be brought round. It then proved difficult to agree a destination for the prisoners. They were eventually returned to an isolated spot where there were few spectators to mark their arrival. When it was decided that the risk of air attack was slight, the officers were also returned, although there had been no formal cessation of hostilities.

On 17 June *Endurance* occupied the Corbeta Uruguay station that

Argentina had kept in the South Sandwich Island of Thule since 1977. The same day, at 13.35 hours, President Galtieri spoke with Admiral Moya to ask him to inform the Commanders-in-Chief of the Navy and Air Force that he had just been asked by the Generals of the Nation to resign as Commander-in-Chief of the Army and as President of the Argentine Republic. This was accomplished by 15.00 on 17 June 1982.

CONCLUSION

On 4 November 1982 the UN General Assembly voted on a resolution based on an original Latin American draft. It began by 'realizing that the maintenance of a colonial situation is incompatible with the United Nations ideal of universal peace', before noting all the old General Assembly resolutions, the more recent Security Council resolutions and the existence of a *de facto* cessation of hostilities (which Argentina would not make *de jure*). It said nothing about the principle of self-determination and in talking about the views of the islanders used the words 'interests' rather than 'wishes'. It reaffirmed the principle of the non-use of force and then requested the governments of Argentina and the United Kingdom 'to resume negotiations in order to find as soon as possible a peaceful solution to the sovereignty dispute relating to the question of the Falkland Islands (Malvinas)'. Finally it asked the Secretary-General 'to undertake a renewed mission of good offices in order to assist the parties in complying with the request'.

The resolution was adopted by 90 votes to 12, with 52 abstentions. A number of Commonwealth countries, some with large neighbours, voted with Britain. Other Commonwealth countries and members of the European Community abstained. Latin American and non-aligned countries voted in favour, and so did the United States.

In one sense Argentina's strategy had succeeded. The war had enabled it to attract international attention to the Falklands issue, convince the General Assembly that this was a dispute requiring a long-term settlement and put pressure on the United Kingdom to negotiate seriously. It even gained American support for this stance: Washington was desperate to mend fences with Latin America.

However, the resolution had no binding force. The British Ambassador, Sir John Thomson, explained that it was 'impossible to accept a call for negotiations as if the Argentine invasion had never occurred'. The British Government now saw no reason to discuss the future of the Falklands with anyone but the islanders. It refused to forgive Buenos Aires for seeking to take by force what it had not achieved by negotiation. Unlike the pre-war period, Britain's uncompromising position was now to be backed by a full garrison, supported by formidable air and sea power.

The political pressure which Argentina had sought to impose on London only made sense when London itself was uncertain as to its long-term intentions towards the Islands. At the start of the year it had been torn between intransigence and compromise, between its sentimental support for the Falkland islanders and its unwillingness to spend resources on practical support, between its sense of obligation to people who identified with Britain and its own economic and political interests in Latin America. The objective of the Junta had been to force Britain to tilt in favour of compromise. Unfortunately by its own actions it had encouraged a firm move in the other direction.

It is difficult to speculate on the consequences of an Argentine victory in the war. It is by no means clear, even with a new British Prime Minister, that it would have been easy to obtain long-term recognition of Argentine sovereignty. On the other hand, serious negotiations, if not a guaranteed outcome, along with an agreed Argentine presence on the Islands, could have been obtained as the fruits of its seizure of the Islands at the start of April. This was on offer during all the various mediation attempts. But the Junta could not bring itself to accept any solution to the conflict which did not enforce a transfer of sovereignty.

If Britain had not been able to mobilize so quickly, the Junta's maximum political objective might have been achieved. But once the task force had been dispatched the Junta faced a wholly different strategic situation from the one that it had expected to face and its objectives should have been moderated accordingly. This inability to relate its available military means closely to the developing political situation characterized the Junta's overall conduct of the campaign.

It was caught by surprise not only by the strength of the British response but also by the lack of international support for its own action. Questions of legitimacy (i.e. aggression shall not be rewarded) are more important than politicians nurturing a long-standing grievance often recognize. If Britain's response had depended only on the asset value of the Islands then Argentina would have had little difficulty. But if this had been the case then there would have been a peaceful transfer of sovereignty many years earlier. Even the influence of the Falkland Islands lobby might not by itself have turned British opinion in favour of a costly and dangerous mission to repossess the Islands. The key factor was a sense of national humiliation compounded by confidence that Britain would be seen to be upholding norms of international behaviour.

The Islands were occupied by Argentina in the belief that this was part of a subtle bargaining process rather than *force majeure*, but the Junta was then only prepared to bargain about second- and third-order issues. Its own freedom of manoeuvre was undermined from the start by popular delight at the fulfilment of a deeply cherished national goal. Thereafter it was unable to relate the military and the diplomatic aspects of its campaign.

Britain's failure to match diplomacy with military capability was more pronounced before the conflict than it was afterwards. It adopted a negotiating stance that was wholly at variance with every other aspect of policy connected with the Falklands. When the Islands were then seized by Argentina the negotiating stance was not much altered but this could now only be sustained by promoting the issue from the lowest level of priority to the highest. Even then it only just managed a credible military response to the situation. Having done so, and having rallied popular opinion behind the task force, it too was only prepared to compromise on second-order issues.

Diplomacy was offered an opportunity to remove Argentine forces from the Islands: if that failed, the Islands would be repossessed by force. Military action unfolded at its own pace but this gave time for the 'crisis managers' to get to work. Problems of distance and logistics ensured that after the April occupation another three weeks would pass before the next engagement (South Georgia), a further week before the naval battle (*Belgrano*) and another three weeks before the landing at San Carlos. It was a full two months after Operation Rosario before British forces reached the outskirts of Stanley. As far as British policy-makers were concerned this provided ample time for negotiations: the imposition of further delay would be to the detriment of British forces and, in consequence, their ability to back diplomatic action as well as achieve a military solution. During the Haig mediation military action was contained by diplomatic considerations, but these constraints were gradually weakened and soon diplomacy had to fit in with the military time-table.

During all the attempts at a peaceful settlement the gap on the first-order issue of sovereignty was never bridged. This made it inevitable that the matter would be decided by force of arms. The result was not inevitable. Britain's armed forces were more professional in every respect and had some advantages in equipment. However, Argentina had the advantage of surprise and a much shorter supply line. It failed to exploit to the full either advantage.

The secrecy required by the operation meant that Argentine forces were as surprised by the situation as the British forces. No thought had been given to possible events after the occupation and so no preparations had been made for a prolonged defence. The rush to occupy meant that the conflict began when the Argentine re-equipment programme was not yet complete and when Britain was in an unusually good position to respond. If there had been any additional delay in triggering British mobilization, the balance would have been even more favourable to Argentina.

Not only did Argentina fail to use its initial period of occupation to prepare fully for the British, once the fighting began it did not fully use its opportunities to disrupt Britain's supply lines. After the landing at San Carlos the Air Force went for the high-prestige warships rather than the supply ships the warships were defending. As the marines trecked from San Carlos towards Stanley they were relatively unhindered by either air strikes or Argentine patrols. There is a sense throughout the conflict of a lack of appreciation in Argentina of the importance of logistics, leading at times to an overestimation of the ease with which Britain was conducting its operations.

This was part of a larger failing in command. Here the problem was not only in the lack of appropriate tactics but in a tendency to act as if its own military operations could be calibrated to the requirements of diplomacy, almost as if it was applying some strategic studies theory. British moves were constantly interpreted for their deeper political meaning, for what they revealed about British preparations for the decisive negotiations rather than preparations for the decisive battle. This exaggerated the possibility of *any* state manipulating armed conflict in this manner. Military action has its own logic, especially in conflicts where superiority cannot be taken for granted by either side and so defeat remains a real possibility. It cannot be turned on or off, or completely redirected, as diplomatic circumstances require.

The signals of war are often partial, confused and contradictory. Warnings of imminent conflict can be lost in the general noise of international affairs, explicit threats dismissed as bluster while intelligence assessments are caught in traditional patterns of thought, limited by inadequate information and contained by sheer disbelief that the adversary could possibly resort to violence. Once war begins the signals of war become explicit and brutal, tending to drown the subtleties of the original dispute and confound mediators. Britain failed because it did not recognize the coming signals of war; Argentina failed because it believed that these signals could be controlled.

ORDER OF BATTLE

Argentina

Navy

Aircraft Carrier:
25 de Mayo

Amphibious Landing Ship:
Cabo San Antonio

Destroyers:
Comodoro Py
Hercules
Hipolito Bouchard
Piedra Buena
Santisma Trinidad
Segui

Corvettes:
Drummond
Granville
Guerrico

Cruiser:
General Belgrano

Patrol Boats:
Alférez Sobral
Comodoro Somellera
Francisco de Gurruchaga

Polar Vessels:
Almirante Irizar
Bahia Paraiso

Submarines:
San Luis
Santa Fé

Tanker:
Punta Medanos

Transports:
Bahia Buen Suceso
Isla de los Estados

Naval Air Units:
1st Attack Squadron
(six Aeromacchi 339As)
2nd Fighter and Attack Squadron
(four Super-Etendards)
3rd Fighter and Attack Squadron*
(ten Skyhawk A–4Bs)
4th Attack Squadron
(four Turbo-Mentor T–34c–1s)
Anti-Submarine Squadron
(Grumman Tracker S–2Es)
Reconnaissance Squadron
(four Neptune SP–2Hs)
1st and 2nd Transport Squadrons
(three F–28 Fellowships, three
Electras)

---

* This was on carrier 25 de Mayo. The aircraft were later transferred to land base.

Order of Battle

1st and 2nd Helicopter Squadrons
(Lynx, Alouette and Sea King)

Coast Guard

Patrol Boats:
Islas Malvinas
Rio Iguazu

Merchant Ships

Cargo Ships:
Formosa
Lago Argentino
Rio Carcaraña
Rio Cincel
Rio de la Plata

Coasters:*
Forrest
Monsoonen

Oil-Rig Tender:
Yehuin

Tanker:
Puerto Rosales

Trawler:
Narwal

Marines

Amphibious Vehicles Battalion
2nd Marine Infantry Battalion
5th Marine Infantry Battalion
Field Artillery
(six 105mm guns)
Anti-Aircraft Unit
Machine-Gun Company
(twenty-seven 12.7mm machine-guns)
Amphibious Commando Company
Amphibious Engineer Company
Tactical Divers

Army

3rd Brigade:
4th Infantry Regiment
5th Infantry Regiment
12th Infantry Regiment
4th Air Mobile Artillery Regiment
(eighteen 105mm guns)

9th Brigade:
8th Infantry Regiment
25th Infantry Regiment

10th Brigade:
3rd Infantry Regiment
6th Infantry Regiment
7th Infantry Regiment
3rd Artillery Regiment
(eighteen 105mm field guns, four
155mm guns)
101st Anti-Aircraft Regiment
(eight 30mm guns, ten 12.7mm heavy
machine-guns)
601st Anti-Aircraft Regiment
(twelve twin 35mm guns, three 20mm
guns, one Roland and three Tiger Cat
surface-to-air-missile (SAM)
launchers)
601st Combat Aviation Battalion
(helicopters – nine Hueys, three
Augustas, two Chinooks)
9th Engineer Company
10th Engineer Company
601st Engineer Company
601st Commando Company
602nd Commando Company
601st National Guard Special Forces
Company
10th Armoured Car Squadron
181st Military Police Company

Air Force

1st Air Transport Group
(seven Hercules C–130s, two Hercules
KC–130s, three Boeing 707s)

---

* These were owned by the Falkland Islands Company but were seized by Argentina.

1st Aerial Photographic Group
  (four Learjets)
2nd Bomber Group
  (seven Canberra B–62s)
3rd Attack Group
  (twenty-four Pucara ground-attack
  aircraft)
4th Fighter Group
  (twelve to fifteen Skyhawk A–4Cs)
5th Fighter Group
  (twelve Skyhawk A–4Bs)
6th Fighter Group
  (twenty-four Daggers)*
8th Fighter Group
  (eleven mirage IIE As)
Helicopters
  (two Chinooks, two Bell 212s)

United Kingdom

Royal Navy

Aircraft-Carriers:
  Hermes
  Invincible

Destroyers:
Type 82
  Bristol
County Class
  Antrim
  Glamorgan
Type 42
  Cardiff
  Coventry
  Exeter
  Glasgow
  Sheffield

Frigates:
Type 22
  Brilliant
  Broadsword
Type 21
  Active

  Alacrity
  Ambuscade
  Antelope
  Ardent
  Arrow
  Avenger
Leander Class
  Andromeda
  Argonaut
  Minerva
  Penelope
Rothesay Class
  Plymouth
  Yarmouth

Ice Patrol Ship:
  Endurance

Submarines:
Nuclear
  Conqueror
  Courageous
  Spartan
  Splendid
  Valiant
Diesel
  Onyx

Amphibious Warfare Vessels:
Landing Platform Dock (LPD)
  Fearless
  Intrepid
Landing Ship Logistic (LSL)
  Sir Bedivere
  Sir Galahad
  Sir Geraint
  Sir Lancelot
  Sir Percivale
  Sir Tristram

Royal Fleet Auxiliary:
Fleet Replenishment Ships
  Fort Austin
  Fort Grange
  Regent
  Resource
  Stromness

* Israeli versions of Mirage Vs.

Order of Battle

Casualty Ferry
  Hecla
  Herald
  Hydra
Helicopter Support Ship
  Engadine
Tankers
  Appleleaf
  Bayleaf
  Blue Rover
  Brambleleaf
  Olmeda
  Olna
  Pearleaf
  Plumleaf
  Tidespring
  Tidepool

Royal Maritime Auxiliary Service:
Tug
  Typhoon
Mooring Vessel
  Goosander

Ships Taken up from Trade:
Liners
  Canberra
  QE2
  Uganda
Ferries
  Baltic Ferry
  Elk
  Europic
  Nordic ferry
  Norland
  St Edmunds
  Tor Caledonia
Container Ships
  Atlantic Causeway
  Atlantic Conveyor
Freighters
  Geestport
  Lycaon
  Saxonia
Oil-rig Support Ships
  British Enterprise
  Stena Inspector

  Stena Seaspread
Trawlers
  Cordella
  Farnella
  Junella
  Northella
  Pict
Ocean Tug
  Irishman
  Salvageman
  Wimpey Seahorse
  Yorkshireman
Islands Supply Ship
  St Helena
Cable Ship
  Iris
Tankers
  Alvega
  Anco Charger
  Avon
  Balder London
  Dart
  Eburna
  Esk
  Fort Toronto
  G. A. Walker
  Scottish Eagle
  Tay
  Test
  Trent
  Wye

Land Forces

3 Commando Brigade:
40 Commando, Royal Marines
42 Commando, Royal Marines
45 Commando, Royal Marines
2nd Battalion Parachute Regiment
3rd Battalion Parachute Regiment
29 Commando Regiment, Royal Artillery
  (eighteen 105mm guns)
59 Independent Commando Squadron,
  Royal Engineers
Commando Logistics Regiment, Royal
  Marines

HQ and Signals Squadron, Royal
  Marines
Air Squadron
  (eleven Gazelle, six Scout helicopters)
B Squadron, the Blues and Royals
  (four Scorpion, four Scimitar Combat
  Tracked Reconnaissance Vehicles, one
  Samson Field Recovery Tractor)
T Battery 12 Air Defence Regiment
  (twelve Rapier)
Air Defence Troop
  (twelve Blowpipe)
Raiding Squadron, Royal Marines
  (seventeen craft)
Mountain and Arctic Warfare Cadre,
  Royal Marines
2, 3 and 6 Sections, Special Boat
  Squadron, Royal Marines
D and G Squadrons, 22nd SAS Regiment
Further units for air maintenance, satellite
  and high-frequency communications,
  postal courier communications, air
  dispatch, bomb disposal, Mexefloat,
  landing ship logistics, surgical support
  and stretcher bearers.

5 Infantry Brigade:
2nd Battalion Scots Guards
1st Battalion Welsh Guards
1st/7th Duke of Edinburgh Own Gurkha
  Rifles

97 Battery Royal Artillery
  (six 105mm guns)
HQ 4 Field Regiment, Royal Artillery
656 Squadron Army Air Corps
  (six Gazelle, three Scout helicopters)
16 Field Ambulance
81 Ordnance Company
Forward Air Control Party

Royal Air Force

1 Squadron (Harriers GR3s)
55, 57 Squadrons (Victor Tankers)
44, 50, 101 Squadrons (Vulcan bombers)
42, 120, 201, 206 Squadrons (Nimrod
  maritime reconnaissance)
24, 30, 47, 70 Squadrons (Hercules
  C–130 transport aircraft)
10 Squadron (VC–10 transport aircraft)
63 Squadron RAF Regiment (Blindfire
  Rapier)
18 Squadron (Chinook helicopters)

Sources: Max Hastings and Simon Jenkins,
The Battle for the Falklands (London:
Michael Joseph, 1983); David Brown, *The
Royal Navy and the Falklands War*
(London: Leo Cooper, 1987); Martin
Middlebrook, *The Fight for the 'Malvinas'*
(London: Viking, 1989).

NOTES

Introduction

1. For two recent contributions *see* Peter Beck, *The Falkland Islands as an International Problem*, London, Routledge, 1988, and Lowell S. Gustafson, *The Sovereignty Dispute over the Falkland (Malvinas) Islands*, New York, Oxford University Press, 1988. For an extremely valuable collection of key documents *see* Ralph Perl (ed.), *The Falkland Islands Dispute in International Law and Politics: A Documentary Sourcebook*, London, Oceana Publications, 1983.

2. Lawrence Freedman, *Britain and the Falklands War*, London, Blackwell, 1988; Virginia Gamba, *The Falkland/Malvinas War: A Model for North–South Crisis Prevention*, Boston, Allen & Unwin, 1987.

3. Good surveys are found in the works cited in note 1. An earlier work by Peter Beck, 'Cooperative Confrontation in the Falkland Islands Dispute: The Anglo-Argentine Search for a Way Forward 1968–81', *Journal of Interamerican Studies and World Affairs*, Vol. 24, No. 1, February 1982. *See also* Adrian Hope, 'Sovereignty and Decolonization of the Falklands Islands', *Boston Comparative Law Review*, December 1983. In addition, for the British perspective *see:* V. F. Boyson, *The Falkland Islands*, Oxford, Clarendon Press, 1924; J. C. J. Metford's introduction to Julius Goebel's book, *The Struggle for the Falklands*, New Haven, Yale University Press, edition of 1982; M. B. R. Cawkell, D. H. Malling and E. M. Cawkell, *The Falkland Islands*, London, St Martin's Press, 1960; and Ian C. Strange, *The Falkland Islands*, Harisburg, Pa, 1972. *See also* House of Commons, *Minutes of the Proceedings of the Foreign Affairs Committee, Session 1982–3*, 11 May 1983. Support for the Argentine position is found in Ricardo Caillet-Bois, *Una Tierra Argentina: Las Islas Malvinas*, Buenos Aires, Peuser, 1948; Enrique Ruiz Guinazu, *Proas de Espana en el Mar Magallanico*, Buenos Aires, Peuser, 1947; Ricardo Zorraquin Becu, *Inglaterra Prometio Abandonar las Islas: Estudio Historico-Juridico del Conflicto Anglo-Espanol*, Buenos Aires, Libreria Editorial Platero, 1975; Paul Groussac, *Las Islas Malvinas*, Buenos Aires, Editorial del Congreso, 1936; Manuel Hidalgo Nieto, *La cuestion de las Malvinas, contribucion al estudio de la relacion hispano inglesa en el siglo XVIII*, Madrid, Instituto Gonzalo Fernandez de Ouiedo, 1947; Octavio Gil Munilla, *El conflicto anglo espanol de 1770*, Sevilla, Escuela de Estudio Hispano-Americanos, 1948; Camilo Barcia

423

Notes

Trelles, *El Problema de las Islas Malvinas*, Madrid, Editora Nacional, 1968. *See also* Julius Goebel, *The Struggle for the Falkland Islands*, first published in 1927.

Chapter One

1. 'Informe Final de la Comision Rattenbach (II parte)', *Siete Dias*, Buenos Aires, XV, No. 859, 30 November to 12 December 1983, p. 68.

2. Carlos Büsser, *Malvinas: La Guerra Inconclusa*, Ediciones Fernandez Reguera, Buenos Aires, pp. 336–8.

3. *See* J. Child, *Geopolitics and Conflict in South America: Quarrels among Neighbours*, New York, Praeger, 1985, p. 43. On this type of thinking and its implications *see also* L. R. Einaudi, *Beyond Cuba: Latin America Takes Charge of its Future*, New York, 1974; *The Andean Report*, Lima, Peru, September 1980; and V. Gamba, 'The Pacific Issue in Bolivian, Latin American and World Politics,' MSc thesis, 1981, UC Wales, Aberystwyth.

4. Marshall Van Sant Hall, *Argentine Policy in the Falklands War: The Political Results*, US Navy War College, 25 June 1983.

5. This thesis is developed in M. Morris and V. Millan (eds), *Controlling Latin American Conflicts*, Boulder, Colo, Westview, 1983.

6. *See* S. W. Simon, *The Military and Security in the Third World: Domestic and International Impacts*, Boulder, Colo, Westview, 1978; Carlos Moneta, 'The Malvinas Conflict: Analyzing the Argentine Military Regime's Decision Making Process', in Munoz and Tulchin (eds), *Latin American Nations in World Politics*, Colo, 1984, pp. 122–4.

7. *See* J. Child, *Antarctica and South American Geopolitics: Frozen Lebensraum*, Washington DC, 1987, and Jorge A. Fraga, *La Argentina y el Atlantico Sur*, Buenos Aires, Pleamar, 1983.

8. *See* Moneta, *op. cit.*, p. 126.

9. This is thoroughly discussed in Martin Walker, 'The Give-Away Years', *Guardian*, 19 June 1982.

10. Virginia Gamba, *El Peon de la Reina*, Buenos Aires, Editorial Sudamericana, 1984, p. 59.

11. Roberto Etchepareborda, 'La Cuestion Malvinas en Perspectiva Historica', paper prepared for seminar on 'The Use of Force in the Solution of International Controversies: The Conflict of the Malvinas Islands, Turin, May 1983.

12. Gamba, *The Falkland/Malvinas War*, p. 114.

13. *See Official Report*, House of Commons, 14 December 1981; House of Lords, 16 December 1981.

14. *See* interview with Oscar Camilion, Costa Mendez's predecessor, in Michael Charlton, *The Little Platoon*, London, Blackwell, 1989, p. 108.

15. General Galtieri, *La Nueva Provincia*, Bahia Blanca, 28 November 1985 (Personal Discharge of Accusations by the Armed Forces Supreme Council).

16. Moneta, *op. cit.*, p. 126.

17. Nicanor Costa Mendez, 'La situacion al 2 de abril de 1982', *La Nacion*, Buenos Aires, 1 September 1983; Galtieri, *op. cit.* For an interesting view on how the foreign perception of Argentine determination on the Falklands issue was enhanced by the military decision to intervene in the Islands, *see* J. T. Goyret, 'El Ejercito argentino en la

Notes

guerra de las Malvinas', *Armas y Geoestrategia*, Buenos Aires, May 1983, Vol. 2, No. 6, p. 20.

18. *Operacion Rosario* (Argentine Navy's account of the military intervention on 2 April 1982), preface by Admiral Carlos Büsser, Buenos Aires, Editorial Atlantida, 1984, p. 7.

Chapter Two

1. Lord Carrington, *Reflect on Things Past: The Memoirs of Lord Carrington*, London, Collins, 1988, pp. 349–50.
2. On the complex character of Island politics and public opinion *see* G. M. Dillon, *The Falklands, Politics and War*, London, Macmillan, 1989, ch. 3; *Minutes of the Proceedings of the Foreign Affairs Committee, Session 1982–83.*
3. *Official Report*, House of Commons, 2 December 1980, cols 195–204.
4. Carrington, *op. cit.*, p. 352.
5. Quoted in Charlton, *op. cit.*, p. 74. On the limited Prime Ministerial interest *see ibid.*, p. 69.
6. Simon Jenkins, 'Britain's Pearl Harbor', *Sunday Times*, 22 March 1987, p. 45.
7. *Falkland Islands Review: Report of a Committee of Privy Counsellors*, Chairman, The Rt Hon. The Lord Franks, Cmnd 8787, London, HMSO, 1983, para. 83. Hereinafter referred to as *Franks*.
8. S. De Martini, 'Ultimo acto de un drama', *La Prensa*, Buenos Aires, 20 October 1988.
9. Sir Michael Palliser, quoted in Charlton, *op. cit.*, p. 138.
10. *Franks*, para. 99.
11. *Ibid.*, para. 90.
12. *Ibid.*, paras 94–5.
13. *Ibid.*, paras 99, 100.
14. *Ibid.*, paras 108–12.
15. Quoted in Charlton, *op. cit.*, p. 155. Emphasis in the original. The Navy agreed with this choice.
16. *Franks*, paras 114–17.
17. *Ibid.*, paras 122–5.

Chapter Three

1. Costa Mendez, 'La situacion al 2 de abril de 1982'.
2. Oscar Cardoso, Ricardo Kirschbaum and Eduardo van der Kooy, *Falklands: The Secret Plot*, London, Preston Editions, 1983, p. 35.
3. Costa Mendez, 'La situacion al 2 de abril de 1982'.
4. 'Informe Final de la Comision Rattenbach (II parte)', *Siete Dias*, para. 187.
5. Cited in Cardoso *et al.*, *op. cit.*; *Franks*, para. 126, says 'without warning'.
6. Gamba, *The Falkland/Malvinas War*.
7. Walker, *op. cit.*
8. *Franks*, para. 133.
9. Charlton, *op. cit.*, pp. 182–3.

10. Walker, *op. cit.*

11. Max Hastings and Simon Jenkins, *The Battle for the Falklands*, London, Michael Joseph, 1983, p. 51.

12. *Franks*, para. 138; Cardoso *et al.*, *op. cit.*, pp. 42–3.

13. *Franks*, para. 139.

14. *Ibid.*, paras 149–51, 158–9.

15. *Ibid.*, paras 140–1.

16. *Ibid.*, paras 147, 152.

17. Richard Haass quoted in Gregory Treverton and Don Lippincott, *Falklands/Malvinas*, Pittsburgh, Pa, Pew Program in Case Teaching and Writing in International Affairs, 1988, p. B.3.

18. Charlton, *op. cit.*, p. 165. Emphasis in the original.

19. Nicanor Costa Mendez, 'El papel de los EEUU en la fase inicial del conflicto del Atlantico Sur', part I, *Revista Argentina de Estudios Estrategicos*, No. 6, October–December 1985.

20. Cardoso *et al.*, *op. cit.*, pp. 46–50.

21. Hastings and Jenkins, *op. cit.*, p. 51.

22. *Franks*, para. 157.

23. *Ibid.*, paras 154–6, 187–8.

24. *Ibid.*, para. 188.

Chapter Four

1. S. Ceron, *Malvinas: Gesta Heroica o Derrota Vergonzoza*, Buenos Aires, Sudamericana, 1985.

2. 'Informe Final de la Comision Rattenbach (II parte)', *Siete Dias*, para. 175; and *Franks*, para. 161.

3. *Franks*, paras 52–4; Michael P. Socarras, 'The Argentine Invasion of the Falklands and International Norms of Signalling', *Yale Journal of International Law*, Vol. 10:356, 1985, pp. 368–9.

4. Jimmy Burns, *The Land That Lost Its Heroes: The Falklands, The Post-War and Alfonsin*, London, Bloomsbury Publishing, 1987, p. 43; Jenkins, 'Britain's Pearl Harbor', *Sunday Times*, 22 March 1987, p. 45.

5. 'Informe Final de la Comision Rattenbach (II parte)', paras 175–80; *see also* Walker, *op. cit.*

6. R. Perkins, *Operation Paraquat: The Battle for South Georgia*, Chippenham, Picton Publishing, 1986, p. 32. According to Burns it was on the recommendation of the Navy that Davidoff timed his formal notification so that it would not arrive until after the boat's departure. Burns, *op. cit.*, p. 44.

7. *Franks*, para. 163.

8. *Ibid.*, para. 164.

9. *Ibid.*, para. 165.

10. 'Caso Malvinas, Acusacion, Defensa y Alegato Personal', *Boletin Del Centro Naval*, Supplement 751–D–5, Vol. 105, year 106, Buenos Aires, 1987, p. 37.

11. Cardoso *et. al.*, *op. cit.*, pp. 62–6; Jenkins, 'Britain's Pearl Harbor', *Sunday Times*, 22 March 1987, p. 46.

Notes

12. Costa Mendez, 'La situacion al 2 de abril de 1982'. The summer months between November and March tend to see an increase in activity among all countries with an interest in the Sub-Antarctic region.

13. 'Informe Final de la Comision Rattenbach (II parte)', *Siete Dias*, para. 187.

14. For further confirmation of the cancellation and the desire to avoid speculation on any link between the negotiations with Britain and Chile and military moves, *see Boletin Del Centro Naval*, pp. 33–4.

15. Jenkins, 'Britain's Pearl Harbor', *Sunday Times*, 22 March 1987, p. 46.

16. After the war Anaya denied this and also another suggestion, to the effect that ten Navy personnel, all of whom had been originally picked to take part in the project, were among the Davidoff party that set off in March to South Georgia. See Jorge Isaac Anaya, 'La Crisis Argentino-Britanica en 1982', *La Nueva Provincia*, Bahia Blanca, 8 September 1988, and his view as reported by Train, in Charlton, *op. cit.*, p. 118. The allegation on the military involvement is made in Cardoso *et al.*, *op. cit.*, pp. 68–9. According to Haig, Galtieri told him that the Argentines who came ashore on 19 March 'were in fact Argentinian military personnel in civilian clothes'. Alexander Haig, *Caveat*, London, Weidenfeld & Nicolson, 1984, p. 263. Galtieri later denied having said this. It has also been claimed that the *Bahia Paraiso*, a new fleet auxiliary under the command of Captain Trombetta, left the port of Ushuaia in January with commandos on board. However we have seen the log for the *Bahia Paraiso* and it does not support this allegation. It did not leave Ushuaia for its critical voyage until 18 March. Antarctic Joint Command for Joint Chiefs of Staff, Argentina, *Final Report of the Summer Antarctic Campaign 81/82*.

17. *Franks*, para. 166. Trombetta told Barker he was going to the Belgrano base, but Barker was able to track his actual route.

18. 'Informe Final de la Comision Rattenbach (II parte)', *Siete Dias*, paras 188–93.

19. *Franks*, paras 167–8; Perkins, *op. cit.*, p. 35.

20. According to the Sunday Times Insight team, 'To the scrapmen's surprise, the *Bahia Buen Suceso* had maintained strict radio silence from the moment she left port.' *The Falklands War: The Full Story*, London, Sphere Books, 1982, pp. 67–8.

21. Simon Jenkins notes that in the original Project Alpha, the plan was that 'nothing should arouse British suspicions' until HMS *Endurance* had left the South Atlantic for good. 'Britain's Pearl Harbor: Part II', *Sunday Times*, 29 March 1987, p. 29.

22. Davidoff has claimed that it was not the case that his group had planted a flag, but that when they arrived a flag was already *in situ*. Their own flag was still on a container in the ship. However, the BAS had visited the site just a couple of days before and had found nothing untoward. 'Informe Final de la Comision Rattenbach (II parte)', *Siete Dias*, paras 192–214. Robert Headland, 'Hostilities in the Falkland Islands Dependencies March–June 1982', *Polar Record*, 21(135): 549–58, 1983, p. 551.

23. Headland, *op. cit.*, pp. 551–2.

Chapter Five

1. Buxton gave his account initially to the British Embassy in Buenos Aires, but later during the height of the crisis on 26 March he sent a full account to Richard Luce in the Foreign Office. *Franks*, para. 133.

2. *Ibid.*, para. 166; Perkins, *op. cit.*, p. 43.

3. Perkins, *op. cit.*, p. 120.

4. *Ibid.*, pp. 47–8.

5. *Franks*, para. 169.

6. Charlton, *op. cit.*, p. 184; *Franks*, para. 169.

7. Hastings and Jenkins, *op. cit.*, p. 55; Luce in Charlton, *op. cit.*, p. 185.

8. *Franks*, para. 169.

9. *Ibid.*

10. 'Informe Final de la Comision Rattenbach (II parte)', *Siete Dias*, paras 192–214. Ambassador Williams reported the lack of apology but also the 'hope that the significance of the affair would not be exaggerated'. *Franks*, para. 169.

11. *Franks*, para. 173.

12. 'Informe Final de la Comision Rattenbach (II parte)', *Siete Dias*, paras 192–214.

13. Headland, *op. cit.*, pp. 552–3.

14. An entry in the KEP diary of the BAS base for 21 March notes: 'Quite a few people on base feel the incident has been blown up out of all proportion, although it is irrefutable that the Argies have broken the law on several counts.'

15. *Franks*, para. 170.

16. Perkins, *op. cit.*, p. 111.

17. *Franks*, paras 171, 175; Headland, *op. cit.*, p. 553.

18. *Franks*, para. 176; 'Informe Final de la Comision Rattenbach (II parte)', *Siete Dias*, paras 192–214.

19. *Franks*, paras 172, 175, 177.

20. *Ibid.*, paras 177, 178.

21. *Official Report*, House of Commons, 23 March 1982, cols 798–801.

22. *Franks*, para. 183.

23. This is taken from the Rattenbach Commission, 'Informe Final de la Comision Rattenbach (II parte)', *Siete Dias*, paras 192–214. The Franks Report mentions the letter but does not quote its contents.

24. His account of the days previous to 2 April 1982 was published in the book *Operacion Rosario*, Buenos Aires, Editorial Atlantida, 1984, pp. 310–30.

25. *Franks*, para. 181.

26. News arrived in London of the incident on 22 March from the Governor. *Franks*, para. 174. That evening there was another incident when 'UK OK' was written on the external windows of the LADE office.

27. Anaya, 'La Crisis Argentino–Britanica en 1982', p. 2.

28. Martin Middlebrook, *The Fight for the 'Malvinas': The Argentine Forces in the Falklands War*, London, Viking, 1989, p. 14.

29. Cardoso *et al.* (*op. cit.*, pp. 73, 75) argue that their orders were to prevent HMS *Endurance* returning to Stanley if it succeeded in getting to Leith first or else to try to prevent it getting to Leith. This is certainly what the British believed, *see* next chapter p. 65. However, the Junta order was that there should be no interception.

Chapter Six

1. *Franks*, paras 193–4, 199.

2. *Ibid.*, paras 182, 184, 185, 186, 191, 198.

Notes

3. Costa Mendez, Testimony to the Rattenbach Commission, *Gente*, Buenos Aires, 8 December 1983, p. 70.

4. Cardoso *et al.*, *op. cit.*, p. 75.

5. For example from the 1988 trials. *See La Nacion*, 3 and 5 September 1988.

6. Cardoso *et al.*, *op. cit.*, p. 70.

7. Moro notes the 'arbitrary and exaggerated manner in which the British had used the South Georgia incident'. Comodoro R. O. Moro, *Historia del Conflicto del Atlantico Sur: La Guerra Inaudita*, Buenos Aires, Escuela superior de guerra aerea de la fuerza aerea Argentine, 1985, pp. 37–8.

8. Costa Mendez, 'La situacion al 2 de abril de 1982'.

9. Galtieri, *La Nueva Provincia*, 28 November 1985.

10. *Ibid.*

11. It is mentioned, for example, by Costa Mendez, in 'La situacion al 2 de abril de 1982'.

12. Costa Mendez, Testimony to the Rattenbach Commission, *Gente*, p. 32.

13. Anaya, *La Nueva Provincia*, 28 November 1985. After the war Galtieri claimed that not to land on 2 April 'would have meant a passive acceptance of the British military reinforcement of the islands. Today, we would still have a "Fortress Falkland" facing the Argentine coast with the difference that Great Britain would have paid no price for it.' Declaration of General Galtieri, *La Nueva Provincia*, 28 November 1985. Costa Mendez has also claimed that Britain 'knew that Buenos Aires only had one bargaining chip left: to occupy the islands peacefully', and that it had therefore decided 'to militarize the islands so as to deter Argentina from this course of action' and was using the South Georgia incidents for this purpose. 'La situacion al 2 de abril de 1982'.

14. Perkins, *op. cit.*, pp. 54–6. Observation was abandoned the next day as the Argentines now realized that they were being watched.

15. *Franks*, para. 59.

16. *Ibid.*, para. 58.

17. *Ibid.*, para. 204.

18. Testimony to the Rattenbach Commission, *Gente*, p. 70.

19. '[T]he British response had been equally calculated and programmed: to put into effect minutely detailed plans, of which the fact that she put one hundred warships to sea in less than three days is only but the first phase.' Galtieri, *La Nueva Provincia*, 28 November 1985.

20. Perkins, *op. cit.*, pp. 52, 92.

21. *See* Admiral Carlos Büsser as quoted in Charlton, *op. cit.*, p. 114.

22. Gamba, *The Falkland/Malvinas War*, p. 120.

23. David Brown, *The Royal Navy and the Falklands War*, London, Leo Cooper, 1987, p. 145.

24. *Franks*, para. 213.

25. Carrington, *op. cit.*, p. 366.

26. *Official Report*, House of Commons, 30 March 1982, cols 163–70; House of Lords, cols 1276–81.

27. Galtieri, *La Nueva Provincia*, 28 November 1985; Costa Mendez, 'La situacion al 2 de abril de 1982'; Moro, *op. cit.*, pp. 37–8, 61; Gamba, *El Peon de la Reina*.

28. Brown, *op. cit.*, p. 67.

29. Derrick Mercer, Geoff Mungham and Kevin Williams, *The Fog of War*, London,

Heinemann, 1987, p. 199; Jenkins, 'Britain's Pearl Harbor: Part II', *Sunday Times*, 29 March 1987, p. 29.

30. *Daily Telegraph*, 31 March 1982.

31. House of Commons, First Report from the Defence Committee, Session 1982–3, *The Handling of Press and Public Information During the Falklands Conflict*, Vol. II, December 1982, p. 23.

32. Charlton, *op. cit.*, pp. 186–7; *Franks*, para. 229. *See below*, p. 93.

33. Anaya, 'La Crisis Argentino-Britanica en 1982', p. 2.

34. Train, reporting Anaya's views in Charlton, *op. cit.*, p. 116. Care should be taken with this second-hand account as it is clearly muddled in some areas. However, this assessment has been corroborated by other sources.

35. Gamba, *The Falkland/Malvinas War*, pp. 134–6; Moro, *op. cit.*

36. Costa Mendez, 'La situacion al 2 de abril de 1982'.

37. *Ibid.*

38. Gamba, *The Falkland/Malvinas War*, pp. 139–40; Moro, *op. cit.*, testimony of Galtieri, Anaya and Costa Mendez before Rattenbach Commission, *Gente*.

39. Costa Mendez, 'La situacion al 2 de abril de 1982'.

40. Declaration of Admiral Anaya, *La Nueva Provincia*, 28 November 1985.

41. Cardoso *et al.*, *op. cit.*, p. 76.

42. Admiral Büsser, *Operacion Rosario*, pp. 13–15.

43. *Ibid.*, pp. 14–15.

Chapter Seven

1. *Franks*, paras 233, 239. House of Commons, *The Falklands Campaign: A Digest of Debates in the House of Commons 2 April to 15 June 1982*, London, HMSO, 1982, p. 25. (See also debate on 2 April, *ibid.*, p. 6.)

2. *Franks*, para. 304.

3. George Brock, *The Times*, 1 July 1982; Jenkins, 'Britain's Pearl Harbor', *Sunday Times*, 22 March 1987, p. 45.

4. However, one of the most prescient analyses of Argentine military options, including the character of a possible operation, against the Falklands was made by the Defence Attaché in Buenos Aires. This was on the basis of a private visit to the Falklands in January 1982, paid for out of his own resources. *Franks*, para. 150.

5. Hastings and Jenkins, *op. cit.*, p. 58.

6. *Franks*, para. 312.

7. Jenkins, 'Britain's Pearl Harbor', *Sunday Times*, 22 March 1987; Jeffrey Richelson and Desmond Ball, *The Ties That Bind: Intelligence Cooperation Between the UKUSA Countries*, London, Allen & Unwin, 1986, pp. 77, 304. For an extremely exaggerated account of Britain's capabilities *see* Duncan Campbell, 'How We Spy on Argentina', *New Statesman*, 30 April 1983.

8. Jenkins, 'Britain's Pearl Harbor', *Sunday Times*, 22 March 1987, p. 46. For details of the satellite trajectories *see* Bhupendra Jasani, 'The Military Uses of Outer Space', *SIPRI Yearbook 1983*, London, Taylor & Francis, 1983, p. 429. For a claim that one of these satellites observed the invasion and that another is 'understood to have monitored

Notes

the follow-up force', *see* Christopher Lee, *War in Space*, London, Hamish Hamilton, 1986, p. 143. He states: 'This information was passed to the British authorities.'

9. *Franks*, Annex A; Hastings and Jenkins agree with this (*op. cit.*, p. 58).

10. After a visit from the British Ambassador, Secretary of State Haig asked the US intelligence community to check the British information. It was confirmed. Haig, *op. cit.*, p. 263.

11. *Franks*, para. 50.

12. *Ibid.*, para. 192.

13. *Ibid.*, para. 208.

14. Jenkins, 'Britain's Pearl Harbor, Part II', *Sunday Times*, 29 March 1987, p. 29.

15. *Franks*, para. 200.

16. Martin Middlebrook, *Operation Corporate: The Story of the Falklands War 1982*, London, Viking, 1985, p. 43.

17. The reconnoitring was being undertaken by the submarine *Sante Fé*, whose signals had been intercepted. Sunday Times Insight Team, *op. cit.*, p. 78. Middlebrook suggests that this signal was not picked up until 31 March (*op. cit.*, p. 43).

18. *Franks*, para. 223.

19. *Ibid.*, paras 224, 225.

20. *Ibid.*, para. 233.

21. Hastings and Jenkins, *op. cit.*, p. 60; Sunday Times Insight Team, *op. cit.*, p. 80.

22. This appears to have been the evidence picked up by the US. Another report notes: 'NSA [US National Security Agency] had early warning of Argentina's mobilization for the Falklands invasion simply by the increased volume of radio traffic, and changes in the transmitting points made it possible to determine not only which units were involved but to plot their movements.' 'Exit Smiley, Enter IBM', *Sunday Times*, 31 October 1982.

23. *Franks*, para. 241.

24. Testimony to the Rattenbach Commission, *Gente*, pp. 74–5. Costa Mendez, 'La situacion al 2 de abril de 1982'.

25. *Franks*, para. 209. The Franks report failed to appreciate the significance of this message because it assumed that the Argentine decision to invade was not taken until 31 March.

26. *Ibid.*, paras 214, 217.

27. *Ibid.*, paras 219, 226, 227; Carrington, *op. cit*, p. 366.

28. *Franks*, para. 229.

29. *Ibid.*, paras 237–8, 244. Costa Mendez's reminiscence is not wholly accurate: 'Later, when Carrington offered to send an envoy to talk about the issue, we also told him that we would accept his representative as long as he came to talk about the underlying dispute rather than the incidents.' The response was phrased much more negatively. Testimony to the Rattenbach Commission, *Gente*, p. 70.

30. *Franks*, para. 211. Ambassador Williams doubted whether the United States could persuade Argentina to climb down (*ibid.*, para. 215).

31. Carrington, *op. cit.*, p. 366.

32. *Franks*, para. 216.

33. Haig, *op. cit.*, p. 262.

34. Costa Mendez, 'La situacion al 2 de abril de 1982'.

35. *Franks*, para. 243.

36. Cardoso *et al.*, *op. cit.*, pp. 83–6.

Notes

Chapter Eight

1. Anaya, 'La Crisis Argentino-Britanica en 1982', p. 1.
2. Cardoso *et al.*, *op. cit.*, pp. 1–6; Jenkins, 'Britain's Pearl Harbor', *Sunday Times*, 22 March 1987, pp. 45, 46. In these two accounts – both of which are clearly based on interviews with Lombardo – it is reported that Anaya contacted Lombardo as early as 15 December 1981, and ordered him to put together a small team to plan for an occupation of the Falklands. It is not impossible that Anaya spoke to Lombardo informally prior to 23 December, although unlikely that it was before 18 December. It is important to note here as elsewhere that all retrospective accounts by key players are coloured by the desire to salvage reputations, especially when dealing with events central to the débâcle that followed.
3. Admiral Büsser, *Operacion Rosario*, pp. 14–15. This account has been drawn on extensively in this section.
4. *Ibid.*, p. 16.
5. Jenkins, 'Britain's Pearl Harbor', *Sunday Times*, 22 March 1987, p. 46.
6. Cardoso *et al.*, *op. cit.*, p. 52.
7. *Ibid.*, pp. 17–18.
8. *Ibid.*, pp. 26–7.
9. Major Michael Norman, interview in Max Arthur, *Above All, Courage. The Falklands Front Line: First Hand Accounts*, London, Sidgwick & Jackson, 1985, p. 8.
10. Perkins, *op. cit.*, p. 64.
11. Major Michael Norman, interview in Arthur, *op. cit.*, p. 9.
12. *Ibid.*, pp. 29–31.
13. *Ibid.*, p. 73.
14. Thus Perkins describes it as a 'murderous attack intended to kill each and every British serviceman on the island in a single blow'. *Op. cit.*, p. 66; Middlebrook is more cautious but describes the attack as 'a test of the Argentine claim that minimum force was used'. *Operation Corporate*, p. 47.
15. Norman in Arthur, *op. cit.*, p. 13.
16. Norman in *ibid.*, p. 19.
17. Büsser, quoted in Middlebrook, *The Fight for the 'Malvinas'*, pp. 38–9.
18. *Ibid.*, p. 42.
19. This account of the occupation of South Georgia is largely based on Moro, *op. cit.*, pp. 62–5; Perkins, *op. cit.*, pp. 69–87; Brown, *op. cit.*, pp. 61–4.
20. It is probable that Trombetta was not actually trying to mislead as he would have been more explicit if trying to convey the news that Governor Hunt had already surrendered on their behalf. As likely an explanation is that this was the normal form of words in which Argentinians spoke about the disputed territories and Trombetta did not think to refine it for this occasion.
21. In the event all that *Endurance* could do was to send one of its Wasp helicopters to observe the battle. The distance was too far for the helicopter to carry any armaments.

Chapter Nine

1. *See Official Report*, 30 March 1982; *see also* Keith Speed, *Sea Change: The Battle for the*

Notes

Falklands and the Future of Britain's Navy, Ashgrove, Bath, 1982. Speed resigned as Navy Minister in 1981 in protest against the impending cuts to the Royal Navy.

2. House of Commons, *The Falklands Campaign*, p. 8.

3. *Ibid.*, pp. 5, 7–8.

4. *Franks*, para. 234.

5. Charlton, *op. cit.*, pp. 188–9.

6. Hastings and Jenkins, *op. cit.*, pp. 67–8; *Franks*, paras 234, 235.

7. Hugo Young, *One of Us*, London, Macmillan, 1989, p. 268.

8. Hastings and Jenkins, *op. cit.*, pp. 68–71, 77; *Franks*, paras 242, 251, 258; Charlton, *op. cit.*, p. 190.

9. Charlton, *op. cit.*, pp. 193–4.

10. Carrington, *op. cit.*, pp. 370–1.

11. Young, *op. cit.*, p. 266.

12. Hastings and Jenkins, *op. cit.*, p. 81.

13. Much of the following draws on the authoritative account in David Brown, *op. cit.*, chs 4–7.

14. The allegations were based on reports that a deep-diving vessel had been sent to recover equipment from the sunken wreck of HMS *Coventry*, a Type 42 destroyer. Earlier reports had spoken of attempts to find nuclear weapons in the wreck of HMS *Sheffield*, another Type 42 destroyer. However, it is now believed that the deep-diving vessel was attempting to recover top-secret cryptographic equipment and codebooks. At any rate Type 42 destroyers do not normally carry nuclear weapons. *New York Times*, 1 July 1988. Duncan Campbell, 'Too Few Bombs to Go Round', *New Statesman*, 29 November 1985.

15. Lieutenant David Tinker reports on 5 June 1982: 'One of our jobs out here is to transfer stores around and between ships and yesterday I walked into the hangar and found a nuclear bomb there ... Of course, it turned out to be a drill round, full of concrete, that *Fort Austin*, now eventually going home, was taking back to England.' David Tinker, *A Message from the Falklands*, London, Junction Books, 1982, p. 198.

16. It has also been suggested that after this discovery there was great reluctance to let nuclear weapons go to sea again for some time. Campbell, 'Too Few Bombs to Go Round'. For a speculative analysis based on the assumption that nuclear weapons were taken to the South Atlantic *see* George Quester, 'The Nuclear Implications of the South Atlantic War', in R. B. Byers (ed.), *The Denuclearization of the Oceans*, London, Croom Helm, 1986.

17. Writing home on 14 April, Lieutenant Tinker on HMS *Glamorgan* mocked a newspaper reference to the 'best naval intelligence': 'Our intelligence consists of the "schoolie", who knew where the Falklands were because he had an Atlas, the Jane's Fighting Ships, to tell us what the Argentines had in their Navy.' Tinker, *op. cit.*, p. 163. He did note that since the task force had set sail intelligence had done a 'good job'. 'From knowing nothing a fortnight ago we now know quite a lot' (*ibid.*, p. 164). For a discussion of sources such as this in connection with the Falklands campaign *see* Valerie Adams, *The Media and the Falklands Campaign*, London, Macmillan, 1986.

18. *The British Army in the Falklands*, London, HMSO, 1982, p. 29. Some thirty officers and NCOs were sent south with the task force, with another forty officers and NCOs found for work in Whitehall and in HQ Commander-in-Chief Fleet at Northwood.

19. *The Times*, 8 May 1984.

433

20. *The Economist*, 3 March 1984.

21. Hastings and Jenkins suggest that NSA was helping right from the start: 'SIGINT was very copious, pouring out of the NSA in Washington and from GCHQ.' *Op. cit.*, p. 88.

22. Lieutenant Sethia, the diarist of HMS *Conqueror*, observed: 'We are evidently able to intercept much, if not all, of the enemy's signal traffic. The boys in Cheltenham know their stuff.' *Guardian*, 9 January 1985.

23. *Guardian*, 2 October 1984; *Sunday Telegraph*, 8 April 1984.

24. *New Statesman*, 3 May 1985.

25. *The Economist*, 3 March 1984. For corroboration *see International Herald Tribune*, 8 March 1984. The move was said to be unpopular in the Pentagon because it used up scarce fuel and so shortened the satellite's life.

26. Haig, *op. cit.*, p. 301.

27. Jeffrey Ethel and Alfred Price, *Air War: South Atlantic*, London, Sidgwick & Jackson, 1983, p. 26.

28. Commander Jorge Luis Colombo, '"Super-Etendard" Naval Aircraft Operations During the Malvinas War', *Naval War College Review*, May–June 1984. On the state of intelligence in mid-April *see* the briefing on HMS *Fearless* of mid-April reported by Robert Fox, *Eyewitness Falklands*, London, Methuen, 1982, p. 22. Fox reports the degree of concern over Argentine submarines, the lack of mention of Exocet and the sketchy knowledge on how Argentine ground forces were faring on the Falklands.

29. Major-General Sir Jeremy Moore and Rear Admiral Sir John Woodward, 'The Falklands Experience', *Journal of the Royal United Services Institute for Defence Studies*, March 1983, p. 25.

Chapter Ten

1. Charlton, *op. cit.*, p. 200.

2. Sir Anthony Parsons, 'The Falklands Crisis in the United Nations, 31 March– 14 June 1982', *International Affairs*, Vol. 59, No. 2, Spring 1983, p. 170. *See also* his description of the diplomacy surrounding the resolution in Michael Bilton and Peter Kosminsky, *Speaking Out: Untold Stories from the Falklands War*, London, André Deutsch, 1989, pp. 31–4.

3. This point was also noted favourably in Argentina where it was believed that the original British draft had been softened on advice from the American delegation. However, to describe Argentina as an aggressor would have raised questions about the UN's obligations as a collective security organization which were best not posed.

4. This has been described as the sole result of intensive Panamanian lobbying on behalf of Argentina. Hastings and Jenkins, however, suggest that Parsons was happy for the slight delay caused by the insertion of these words to give time for Mrs Thatcher to contact King Hussein of Jordan to persuade him to change his country's vote. Hastings and Jenkins, *op. cit.*, p. 100.

5. According to *ibid.*, p. 100.

6. Cardoso *et al.*, *op. cit.*, p. 111.

7. For an elaboration of this argument *see* Inis L. Claude Jr, 'UN Efforts at a Settlement', in Albert R. Coll and Anthony C. Arend (eds), *The Falklands War: Lessons for*

Strategy, Diplomacy and International Law, Boston, Allen & Unwin, 1985.
8. Cardoso *et al.*, *op. cit.*, p. 113.

Chapter Eleven

1. Middlebrook, *The Fight for the 'Malvinas'*, p. 54.
2. *Ibid.*, p. 55.
3. Galtieri was severely criticized for this decision after the war and it was raised during the 1988 trials. *See La Nacion*, 3, 19 and 21 September 1988.
4. Middlebrook, *The Fight for the 'Malvinas'*, pp. 68–71. He reports the irritated reaction of the Captain of one of the merchant ships on discovering that one of the containers was full of television sets for the kelpers – part of the effort to win their 'hearts and minds'.
5. Carlos H. Turolo, *Malvinas: Testimonio de su Gobernador*, Buenos Aires, Sudamericana, 1983, p. 44.
6. *Ibid.*, p. 46.
7. Auguiar, Cervo, Machinandiarena, Balza and Dalton, *Operacions Terrestres en Las Islas Malvinas*, Buenos Aires, Circulo Militar, 1985.
8. *La Nacion*, 13 September 1988.
9. He adds 'the same happened in England'. Nicanor Costa Mendez, 'El papel de los EEUU en le fase inicial del conflicto del Atlantico Sur', Part II, *Revista Argentina de Estudios Estrategicos*, No. 8, October–December 1986, p. 28.

Chapter Twelve

1. *See* Geoffrey Edwards, 'Europe and the Falkland Islands Crisis of 1982', *Journal of Common Market Studies*, Vol. XXII, No. 4, June 1984.
2. Quoted in Chaim Kaufman, *U.S. Mediation in the Falklands/Malvinas Crisis: Shuttle Diplomacy in the 1980s*, Pittsburgh, Pa, Pew Program in Case Teaching and Writing in International Affairs, 1988, p. 13.
3. Kaufmann quotes Eagleburger's experience with a Latin American delegation which came to express solidarity with Argentina. The leader stayed behind as the others left and said: 'Don't you let those admirals and generals win in the Falklands; we have our own admirals and generals, and I don't want them to get the wrong ideas.' Cited in *ibid.*, p. 14.
4. CBS News, *Face the Nation*, 11 April 1982. She prefaced this remark by noting that the US had 'no position' on who owned the islands.
5. Haig in Charlton, *op. cit.*, pp. 159, 160.
6. According to Haig, Henderson wanted the US to take the issue of Argentine aggression to the Organization of American States. This is the opposite of the case. *Op. cit.*, p. 266. Henderson's memoir makes no mention of such a suggestion and for 6 April he records considerable hostility to the idea. 'America and the Falklands', *The Economist*, 12 November 1983, p. 53.
7. Haig, *op. cit.*, p. 270.
8. *Ibid.*, p. 266.
9. She had gained notoriety before taking office by arguing that the United States should distinguish between totalitarian and authoritarian regimes. This was not because

human rights were unimportant but because authoritarian regimes were easier to reform. Argentina was seen as an example of that. Unfortunately her article also suggested that authoritarian regimes did not have territorial ambitions. 'Dictatorship and Double Standards', *Commentary*, November 1979.

10. Bilton and Kosminsky, *op. cit.*, pp. 27–8.

11. Ricard Haass, quoted in Treverton and Lippincott, *op. cit.*

12. Costa Mendez, 'El papel de los EEUU en le fase inicial del conflicto del Atlantico Sur', Part II, p. 19.

13. Jim Rentschler, NSC staff member on the team, quoted in Treverton and Lippincott, *op. cit.*, p. 11.

14. Quoted in *ibid.*, p. 12.

Chapter Thirteen

1. David Gompert, 'US Shuttle Mediation', in Diane B. Bendahame and John W. McDonald Jr (eds), *Perspectives on Negotiation: Four Case Studies and Interpretations*, Washington DC, Center for the Study of Foreign Affairs, Foreign Service Institute, US Department of State, 1986, p. 75.

2. David Gompert, 'American Diplomacy and the Haig Mission', in Coll and Arend, *op. cit.*, p. 111.

3. The two countries were probably Colombia and Brazil.

4. Haig, *op. cit.*, p. 271.

5. Henderson, *op. cit.*, p. 53.

6. Costa Mendez, 'El papel de los EEUU en la fase inicial del conflicto del Atlantico Sur', Part I.

7. Henderson, *op. cit.*, p. 50.

8. Haig, *op. cit.*, p. 272. In addition to private sources, the following account draws on this memoir plus that of Henderson, *op. cit.*; Hastings and Jenkins, *op. cit.*, p. 109; Sunday Times Insight Team, *op. cit.*, pp. 131–2.

9. Haig, *op. cit.*, p. 273.

10. *Ibid.*, p. 273. Pym describes this as a 'nonsensical passage', presumably in its implications, for he does not deny the exchange. Charlton, *op. cit.*, p. 192.

11. Charlton, *op. cit.*, p. 177.

12. Record of American participant, cited in Treverton and Lippincott, *op. cit.*, p. B.15.

13. Gompert, 'American Diplomacy and the Haig Mission', p. 108.

14. The reference to hunger strikers was to IRA prisoners. Charlton, *op. cit.*, p. 173. For other descriptions of this meeting *see* Haig, *op. cit.*, pp. 279–80; Cardoso *et al.*, *op. cit.*, pp. 151–2.

15. Haig, *op. cit.*, pp. 280–1. The Argentine record does not differ greatly except for the significant addition of Argentine and British members on the consortium.

16. This conversation is reported in Arthur Gavshon and Desmond Rice, *The Sinking of the Belgrano*, London, Secker & Warburg, 1984, pp. 60–1.

17. On 10 April the European Community agreed in principle on a package of economic sanctions, including a trade embargo, although they did not come into force until 16 April.

18. Haig, *op. cit.*, p. 282.

19. At various times Haig says the concession came between 'midnight and one', that he had parted from Costa Mendez at 'one o'clock' and that the new draft took 'less than an hour'. The account by Hastings and Jenkins, based on interviews, also suggests that Haig was working on an inference rather than a concession. Hastings and Jenkins, *op. cit.*, p. 108.

20. Haig, *op. cit.*, pp. 282–3.

21. *Ibid.*, p. 283.

22. Charlton, *op. cit.*, p. 172.

23. Hastings and Jenkins, *op. cit.*, p. 109.

24. Haig says that the call was placed by Costa Mendez (Haig, *op. cit.*, p. 283).

25. *Ibid.* Haig has Costa Mendez concluding, 'I will do my homework now.' Haig describes Costa Mendez's suggestion of finding new language as 'disingenuous'.

26. *Ibid.*, p. 284.

27. US Press Release 126 of 14 April 1982. Kenneth Adelman, *The Great Universal Embrace*, New York, Simon & Schuster, 1989, p. 68.

28. House of Commons, *The Falklands Campaign*, pp. 73–7.

Chapter Fourteen

1. For a full description of American support *see* 'America's Falklands War', *The Economist*, 3 March 1984. *See also* BBC Television, *An Ocean Apart: Programme Seven, Turning Up the Volume*, transmitted 1 June 1988.

2. *The Economist*, 3 March 1984, p. 24.

3. In *An Ocean Apart*, Walters suggests, apparently as a *post hoc* rationalization, that the assistance might have helped the diplomatic process by encouraging Britain to be more flexible.

4. Haig, *op. cit.*, p. 285.

5. A transcript is found in Cardoso *et al.*, *op. cit.*, pp. 165–8.

6. For text *see ibid.*, pp. 172–4.

7. Quoted in *ibid.*, p. 171.

8. Haig, *op. cit.*, pp. 286–7. There is some confusion in Haig's account in that he mentions no negotiations between the meeting with Galtieri in the morning and the meeting with the Junta the next day, including this meeting with Costa Mendez. However, his description of a meeting with Costa Mendez on the night of 15 April bears a considerable resemblance to that of 16 April and certainly fits in better with the circumstantial evidence.

9. Hastings and Jenkins, *op. cit.*, p. 111; Cardoso *et al.*, *op. cit.*, p. 176.

10. Haig, *op. cit.*, p. 288.

11. Transcript of recording of Haig's meeting with Galtieri obtained by BBC for *Panorama*, 16 April 1984.

12. Haig, *op. cit.*, p. 288.

13. Costa Mendez, 'El papel de los EEUU en la fase inicial del conflicto del Atlantico Sur', Part II, p. 39. Cardoso *et al.*, *op. cit.*, p. 179, suggest that some of the negotiators themselves realized the damage that this would do to the extent that it was nicknamed the 'mad clause'.

14. Jim Rentschler, cited by Treverton and Lippincot, *op. cit.*, pp. 29–30.

15. Press Release 139 of 20 April 1982.
16. Haig, *op. cit.*, pp. 289–90.
17. *Ibid.*, p. 289.
18. *See* for example his report to Henderson of the 'irrationality and chaotic nature of the Argentine leadership'. Henderson, *op. cit.*, p. 54. According to one well-informed account, Haig's team was receiving 'increasingly shabby treatment': 'forced to linger with no food – or even chairs – for hours at a time in the presidential palace'. Treverton and Lippincott, *op. cit.*, p. B.29.
19. Hastings and Jenkins, *op. cit.*, p. 112.
20. Cardoso *et al.*, *op. cit.*, pp. 185–6.
21. Hastings and Jenkins, *op. cit.*, p. 138.
22. House of Commons, *The Falklands Campaign*, pp. 118, 120–1.

Chapter Fifteen

1. Ethell and Price, *op. cit.*, p. 34; *see Aviation Week and Space Technology*, 26 July 1982.
2. According to Middlebrook, this report came from London. It led to some anxiety on *Endurance* when taken in conjunction with a report from members of the British Antarctic Survey, still on South Georgia, to the effect that two Argentine warships were also in the area (they were in fact British ships which had been spotted). Middlebrook, *Operation Corporate*, p. 108.
3. Srilal Perera, 'The Oas and the Inter-American System: History, Law and Diplomacy', in Coll and Arend, *op. cit.*, p. 146.
4. Later Haig was to recount to Ambassador Henderson that the twenty-minute standing ovation was the worst pressure he had ever encountered in his diplomatic career. See Henderson, *op. cit.*
5. The full list is: 'The recall of chiefs of missions; breaking of diplomatic relations; breaking of Consular relations; partial or complete interruption of economic relations or rail, sea, air, postal, telegraphic, telephonic, radio-telephonic or radio-telegraphic, or other means of communication; and use of armed force.'
6. Cardoso *et al.* suggest that there was a possibility of the two Foreign Ministers being brought together by Haig in Washington but that the idea was vetoed by both the Junta and Thatcher. *Op. cit.*, p. 193.
7. Haig, *op. cit.*, p. 290. Haig puts this on 23 April but the actual date was 22 April.
8. *Ibid.*
9. According to Haig: 'Although I did not disclose the thought to Costa Mendez, I believed that the British would not carry out further attacks if the American Secretary of State was in Argentina or en route.' *Ibid.*, p. 291.
10. Hastings and Jenkins, *op. cit.*, p. 138.
11. Young, *op. cit.*, pp. 271–2.
12. Haig, *op. cit.*, p. 292.
13. House of Commons, *The Falklands Campaign*, pp. 147, 180.
14. He gave more than sixty interviews and briefings during the course of the conflict, of which more than thirty were for television or radio stations. House of Commons, First Report from the Defence Committee, *The Handling of Press and Public Information During the Falklands Conflict*, Vol. I, p. xix.

15. For an account of the moves in the Senate based on the perceptions of Jesse Helms, *see* Gavshon and Rice, *op. cit.*, pp. 65–6, 69, 71, 72.

Chapter Sixteen

1. Evidence of Lord Lewin, in House of Commons, Third Report of the Foreign Affairs Committee Session 1984–5, *Events Surrounding the Weekend of 1–2 May 1982*, London, HMSO, 1982, hereinafter referred to as *Foreign Affairs Committee Report*, pp. 77, 78. (Lord Lewin had been Vice-Chief of Naval Staff during the 'Cod War' with Iceland in the 1970s.) See also R. P. Bartson and P. W. Birnie, 'The Falkland Islands/ Islas Malvinas Conflict: A Question of Zones', *Marine Policy*, January 1983.
2. Lewin evidence, *Foreign Affairs Committee Report*, 1–2 May, pp. 79–80.
3. House of Commons, *The Falklands Campaign*, p. 117.
4. Prime Minister's letter to George Foulkes MP, reproduced in *Hansard*, 22 October 1984, cols 469–72, hereinafter referred to as *Foulkes letter*.
5. Lewin, *Foreign Affairs Committee Report*, p. 84.
6. Peter Greig, 'Revelations', *Granta*, No. 15, Spring 1985, pp. 257–8. This article contains a full account of the 'crown jewels' on the sinking of the *Belgrano* which were prepared by civil servant Clive Ponting in 1984 as a result of persistent allegations from Labour MPs, and in particular Tam Dalyell (*see* Tam Dalyell MP, *Thatcher's Torpedo: The Sinking of the 'Belgrano'*, London, Cecil Woolf, 1983). Ponting argued that full answers to parliamentary inquiries should be made on the basis of the 'crown jewels'. When this was refused he leaked draft answers and an internal memo to Dalyell. He was arrested on a charge under the Official Secrets Act but later acquitted. Richard Norton-Taylor, *The Ponting Affair*, London, Cecil Woolf, 1985; Clive Ponting, *The Right to Know: The Inside Story of the Belgrano Affair*, London, Sphere Books, 1985.
7. David Brown, *op. cit.*, pp. 111–12.
8. Moore and Woodward, *op. cit.*, p. 28.
9. For a full description of the day's operations see Brown, *op. cit.*, pp. 119–28.
10. *See* Julian Thompson, *No Picnic: 3 Commando Brigade in the South Atlantic: 1982*, London, Leo Cooper for Secker & Warburg, 1985.
11. On the effort involved to get the Vulcan to its target *see* Ethell and Price, *op. cit.*, ch. 3. On the problems of post-attack reconnaissance *see* Lawrence Freedman, 'Intelligence Operations in the Falklands', *Intelligence and National Security*, Vol. 1, No. 3, September 1986, p. 324.
12. Eric Grove, *Vanguard to Trident: British Naval Policy Since World War II*, London, Bodley Head, 1987, p. 366.
13. Moore and Woodward, *op. cit.*, p. 28.
14. Argentine Army source reports that one Sea Harrier was brought down by a Roland air-defence missile at 07.40 and another at 08.25 by an Oerlikon 35mm cannon. Both were reported to have fallen into the sea. Informe Oficial Ejencito Argentino, *Conflicto Malvinas*, 1983, Vol. II, Annex 69, Art. 8009 d.2. At around 08.25 one Sea Harrier was hit by ground fire but was able to return safely to *Hermes*. The earlier claim probably refers to the Sea Harriers attempting to assess the damage caused by the Vulcan attack on Stanley airfield. Reports from British sources suggest that effective reconnaissance could not be carried out because of considerable anti-aircraft fire, the result of the

air-defence forces already having been alerted by the Vulcan raid. Middlebrook, *Operation Corporate*, pp. 127–8; Ethell and Price, *op. cit.*, pp. 57–9. Visual observation of the damage to *Arrow* may account for the Argentine confidence. Ethell and Price describe the damage as 'spectacular rather than serious'. Ethell and Price, *op. cit.*, p. 68.

15. Robert Scheina, 'Where Were Those Argentine Subs?', *Proceedings of the US Naval Institute*, March 1984.

16. Most accounts put the attempted flight of the Super-Etendards on 2 May. Robert Scheina, 'The Malvinas Campaign', *Proceedings of the US Naval Institute: Naval Review*, 1983, p. 107. Ethell and Price, *op. cit.*, pp. 75–6. However, private sources indicate that this was another one of the operations attempted on 1 May.

17. Moro, *op. cit.*, pp. 192–4; Busser, *op. cit.*, pp. 261, 236.

18. A number of sources have been used here, some of which have been able to draw on Argentine materials: Scheina, 'The Malvinas Campaign'; Gavshon and Rice, *op. cit.*; Moro, *op. cit.* The material is contradictory on questions of timing, which is unfortunate given the importance of these questions to the later controversy. The following account has been supplemented by information provided by a senior and reliable Argentine figure which has been corroborated by other material as well as being supported by circumstantial evidence.

19. Scheina, 'The Malvinas Campaign', p. 105.

20. *Panorama* transcript, 16 April 1984, p. 6.

21. Moro, *op. cit.*, p. 181.

22. Anaya testimony to Rattenbach Commission, *Gente*, 8 December 1983, p. 90.

23. Anaya, *ibid.*, suggests that the 20.07 order was to withdraw. This was mistaken and appears to represent a confusion between an order to attack and one to withdraw. It would have been a curious time to order a withdrawal, given the reports of British activity at that time, and would also have left an unexplained gap of four to five hours before the order was 'confirmed'. This would appear to be the source of a similar mistake in Gavshon and Rice, *op. cit.*, which has the effect of skewing much of their analysis of what the British Government could and should have known.

24. According to Brown, the last naval gun was fired at Argentine positions around Stanley at 22.35. Brown, *op. cit.*, p. 127.

25. Moro, *op. cit.*, p. 205.

26. Brown, *op. cit.*, p. 127.

27. Cited in Gavshon and Rice, *op. cit.*, p. 81.

28. *Panorama* transcript, p. 11. Some accounts of this set of events have put the withdrawal later by suggesting that it was only after a failed attempt to launch the Skyhawks at dawn on the 2 May that the *25 de Mayo* withdrew. (For example, Scheina, 'The Malvinas Campaign'; Ethell and Price, *op. cit.*) As can be seen it was a plan to mount an air raid at dawn from the carrier that was aborted, not the raid itself.

29. Scheina, 'The Malvinas Campaign', p. 106.

30. Moro, *op. cit.*, pp. 206–7. Some confusion has resulted from a series of leading questions put to Admiral Lombardo on *Panorama*, in which he agreed that *Belgrano*'s orders were to move eastward and then afterwards northwards in order to intercept British ships in what he agreed could be described as a 'pincer movement', and that it was going to enter the TEZ. This interview was seized upon by the British Government as confirming their fears of 1 and 2 May. However, Lombardo complained that his remarks had been quoted out of context. *Tiempo Argentino*, 26 August 1984.

31. *Clarin*, 18 April 1984.

32. Fox, *op. cit.*, p. 326.

33. On the signals between *Conqueror* and Northwood *see Foreign Affairs Committee Report*, pp. 183–4. A diary kept by an officer on *Conqueror*, Lieutenant Sethia, has been widely quoted. A full text appeared in the *Observer*, 25 November 1984.

34. Grove, *op. cit.*, p. 367; Clive Ponting in the Belgrano Action Group, *The Unnecessary War*, Nottingham, Spokesman Books, 1988, p. 55; *Foulkes letter*. Other sources seem to be twelve hours out and put the order as early as 16.10 on 1 May. Granada Television, *World in Action*, 10 June 1985; *Guardian*, 11 June 1985.

35. *Foreign Affairs Committee Report*, p. 184.

36. Grove, *op. cit.*, p. 367.

37. Moore and Woodward, *op. cit.*, p. 28. This was in an October 1982 lecture, so it is interesting to note the hint that the *Conqueror* was already following the *Belgrano* on 1 May, contrary to the official version of events at this time.

38. Brown, *op. cit.*, pp. 134–5; Grove, *op. cit.*, p. 367.

39. Greig, *op. cit.*, pp. 258–9. *Guardian*, 5 January 1985; *Observer*, 6 January 1985.

40. Interviews in *Sunday Times*, 8 April 1984, and *Guardian*, 2 October 1984.

41. Brown, *op. cit.*, pp. 130–1. *Foreign Affairs Committee Report*, p. 182. Gavshon and Rice assume that the Nimrod surveillance planes based on Ascension Island would have picked up all Argentine signals traffic and therefore been able to provide the critical information on Argentine ship movements. However, the Nimrods did not begin to operate in this manner, which required in-flight refuelling, until 15 May. The range of radars on the task-force ships was insufficient.

42. Apparently when the existence of a signal to this effect was disclosed in the book by Gavshon and Rice an inquiry was ordered which was conducted by Sir Brian Tovey, Director of GCHQ at Cheltenham. No trace of a deciphered text was found. Greig, *op. cit.*, pp. 260–1; *New Statesman*, 3 May 1985.

43. *Foreign Affairs Committee Report*, p. xxii. A number of reports of what British intelligence *really* intercepted appear to be based entirely on what might have been suggested from a reading of Gavshon and Rice *could* have been picked up. Thus the reports cited above in Greig, *op. cit.*, *Guardian*, 5 January 1985, and *Observer*, 6 January 1985, all state confidently that Lombardo's signal of 01.19 was intercepted though no record was actually found. Meanwhile all report that the signal of 20.07 was picked up. This they assume, along with Gavshon and Rice, ordered a withdrawal. As we have seen (above note 23) this assumption was based on muddled evidence from Admiral Anaya and in fact this signal ordered offensive action. So if it had been picked up the British perception was reinforced. Nevertheless Greig speculates: 'Perhaps the Northwood analysts, erring on the side of prudence, interpreted the signal as being of uncertain meaning; perhaps the attack was only temporarily suspended; perhaps, indeed, Argentina knew its codes were being broken, and was sending deliberately misleading signals' (*op. cit.*, p. 259). Furthermore, as we have seen, there were many communications between the Argentine task groups and their headquarters. As the House of Commons Foreign Affairs Committee has noted:

While it is clear from many recent ministerial statements that some intelligence intercepts were made, it is by no means clear that all the Argentine signals mentioned in journalistic accounts were in fact intercepted by GCHQ or other intelligence-gathering organizations. Nor is it clear that the signals referred to in the media were the only orders issued to the various Argentine naval task groups between 30 April and 2 May, nor that other signals, with quite different purport, were not themselves intercepted and decoded by the UK authorities.

Foreign Affairs Committee Report, p. xxii.

44. *Foreign Affairs Committee Report*, p. 184.

45. Lord Lewin, *The Times*, 2 October 1984.

46. *Foreign Affairs Committee Report*, p. 88.

47. *The Times*, 2 October 1984.

48. Charlton, *op. cit.*, p. 212.

49. Hastings and Jenkins, *op. cit.*, p. 148.

The cabinet discussion wound back over many previous debates about the rules of engagement (though significantly without Pym's presence on this occasion). What was the extent of the threat to the task force? Was it feasible to follow the cruiser into the total exclusion zone? Might conventional rather than wire-guided Tigerfish torpedoes be used to cripple rather than sink her? Should the escorts be left unattacked so they could pick up survivors? It was acknowledged that, of the two big Argentine ships, the aircraft carrier would have made a preferable victim. But Lewin left ministers in no doubt of Northwood's collective view that the *Belgrano* should be put out of action at once. No minister demurred. The order was issued before lunch.

50. In Bilton and Kosminsky, *op. cit.*, p. 299.

51. *Foulkes letter.*

52. Charlton, *op. cit.*, pp. 212, 214.

53. Grove, *op. cit.*, p. 366.

54. *Foreign Affairs Committee Report*, p. 184; Greig, *op. cit.*, p. 261; *Observer*, 23 September 1984.

55. Speculation immediately after the attack suggested that the more modern Tigerfish missile might have been used. In addition to the positive operational reasons, it has also been suggested that the Captain wished to retain Tigerfish for its primary anti-submarine warfare role. It may also, of course, have been a simple lack of confidence that Tigerfish would work. *See* House of Commons, Fourth Report from the Defence Committee, Session 1986–7, *Implementing the Lessons of the Falklands Campaign*, Vol. II, Minutes of Evidence and Appendices, London, HMSO, 1987, pp. 149–50.

56. For discussion of the media's initial coverage of the episode, *see* Adams, *op. cit.*; Glasgow University Media Group, *War and Peace News*, Milton Keynes, Open University Press, 1985; Robert Harris, *Gotcha: The Media, the Government and the Falklands Crisis*, London, Faber, 1983. The title of the last of these books was inspired by one of the more distasteful headlines of the whole campaign in the *Sun* on 4 May.

57. After the war controversy soon turned on the degree to which this statement was incorrect, which it was in two respects: the suggestions that the *Belgrano* was only detected on 2 May, and that at the time it was attacked it was closing in on the task force. Elsewhere in his statement, Mr Nott said that the two destroyers had not been attacked in order to allow them to pick up survivors (in fact at least one was hit with a torpedo). There was early suspicion that the submarine Commander had been acting on his own

initiative. The initial statements to the House of Commons by the Prime Minister and the Secretary of State for Defence stressed that the task force was 'under full political control' but this was widely interpreted to mean that the actual decision to attack the *Belgrano* was taken by the submarine Commander. House of Commons, *The Falklands Campaign*; Glasgow University Media Group, *op. cit.*, pp. 59–61.

58. Brown, *op. cit.*, p. 135.

59. Anaya testimony, *Gente*, pp. 90–1. See also evidence from 1988 trial (Annex 10, pp. 7, 14, 19).

60. *Boletin Del Centro Naval*, p. 70.

61. Christopher Craig, 'Fighting by the Rules', *Naval War College Review*, May–June 1984, p. 25; Brown, *op. cit.*, pp. 152–3, 156.

62. Scheina, 'Where Were Those Argentine Subs?', p. 119; Brown, *op. cit.*, pp. 156–7.

63. Defence Committee, *Implementing the Lessons of the Falklands Campaign*, pp. xliii–xliv; Scheina, 'Where Were Those Argentine Subs?'; US Department of the Navy, *Lessons of the Falklands*, February 1983.

Chapter Seventeen

1. Henderson, *op. cit.*, p. 55.

2. According to Gavshon and Rice, on the afternoon of 1 May between fifteen and twenty divisional and brigade commanders and field commanders met informally to discuss the situation at the Campo de Mayo military base. The recommendation was to negotiate and avoid all-out war. Some then went on to a higher-level meeting at Army HQ presided over by the Chief of the Army's General Staff, who later went on to meet with Galtieri and Air Force chief Lami Dozo. Their recommendation was no open war. (Gavshon and Rice, *op. cit.*, pp. 79, 81). Mr Rice told the Foreign Affairs Committee that the information came from 'somebody near to Galtieri' (*Foreign Affairs Committee Report*, p. 55) but there was no other proof. These Army commanders would not have had the same perspective on the day's events as those who had been assessing the day's reports of the fighting, so even if these meetings did take place the impact of the recommendation may have been limited.

3. Busser, *op. cit.*, pp. 236–7; Moro, *op. cit.*, p. 195.

4. Evidence to Foreign Affairs Committee. *Foreign Affairs Committee Report*, Qs 305, 306.

5. Nicanor Costa Mendez, 'The Peruvian Mediation', *La Nueva Provincia*, 2 April 1985.

6. Gavshon and Rice, *op. cit.*, pp. 82–3. Haig's account is muddled. In an erratum to his book (and in a later interview with the BBC Television programme *Panorama* of 16 April 1984) he admits that he got the date wrong. He does, however, suggest that Belaunde took the initiative in ringing him. He also says: 'Speaking over an open line, we worked all day on a new draft.' Haig, *op. cit.*, p. 293.

7. Charlton, *op. cit.*, p. 175. Ambassador Kirkpatrick is said to have described it as 'a new Haig mission in disguise'. Costa Mendez's initial assessment was that the plan 'reflected US thinking'. Pym's first reaction when the plan was presented to him by Haig was to observe the similarities with Haig's own plan, which had just been rejected by Argentina. Cardoso *et al.*, *op. cit.*; Costa Mendez, 'The Peruvian Mediation'; Henderson, *op. cit.*, p. 55.

8. Charlton, *op. cit.*, p. 178.
9. Haig, *op. cit.*, p. 293. He described the proposals to BBC Television as a 'simplified version of the earlier negotiations' (*Panorama*, 16 April 1984).
10. Costa Mendez, 'The Peruvian Mediation'.
11. Henderson, *op. cit.*, p. 56.
12. Costa Mendez, 'The Peruvian Mediation'.
13. *Ibid.*
14. Gavshon and Rice, *op. cit.*, pp. 86, 87.
15. *Ibid.*, p. 86.
16. Büsser, *op. cit.*, p. 237.
17. *Foreign Affairs Committee Report*, p. 84. There are other versions which essentially take the same form. The most authoritative British version (Henderson, *op. cit.*, p. 55) makes reference in clause 4 to a 'dispute over sovereignty' and in 5 and 7 to a 'definitive settlement' rather than a 'final solution'.
18. Costa Mendez, 'The Peruvian Mediation'.
19. Ambassador Wallace confirms that the version of the plan that he received that evening contained the word 'aspirations'. *Foreign Affairs Committee Report*, p. 66.
20. The Argentine Foreign Minister's response to the Haig memorandum is contained in Gavshon and Rice, *op. cit.*, pp. 192–4. Costa Mendez's reaction to the Peruvian plan is in Costa Mendez, 'The Peruvian Mediation'.
21. Gavshon and Rice, *op. cit.*, pp. 85, 87.
22. German Sopena, 'Historia de una mediacion frustrada', *Siete Dias*, 26 January 1983.
23. Henderson, *op. cit.*, p. 55.
24. *Panorama* transcript, p. 15; *Foreign Affairs Committee Report*, pp. 384–5; Charlton, *op. cit.*, p. 208.
25. Sopena, *op. cit.* Cited by Gavshon and Rice, *op. cit.*, p. 91.
26. *Foreign Affairs Committee Report*, p. 120.
27. Gavshon and Rice, *op. cit.*, p. 116.
28. *Panorama* recognizes the importance of the Belaunde–Galtieri conversation but has got the timing slightly wrong in relation to the Haig–Pym conversation.
29. *Panorama* transcript, p. 14; Henderson, *op. cit.*, p. 56. In another account Pym suggests a greater irritation with Haig: 'Well, not only had I had a couple of *hours* with Al Haig in the morning, he had come to lunch. We talked over the whole thing. The gravamen of Al Haig's telephone message, when I was just getting into the car, was to stress the importance of this. Well, do you think I *needed* to be told that.' Charlton, *op. cit.*, p. 207.
30. Gavshon and Rice, *op. cit.*, p. 96.
31. *Foreign Affairs Committee Report*, pp. 52–3, 61, 181.
32. Labour MP Tam Dalyell argued as early as late 1982 that the Government knowingly acted in such a way as to preclude a diplomatic solution in preference to a military solution. He alleged that the Prime Minister 'coldly and deliberately gave the orders to sink the *Belgrano*, in the knowledge that an honourable peace was on offer and in the expectation – all too justified – that the *Conqueror*'s torpedoes would torpedo the peace negotiations.' Speech to House of Commons, 21 December 1982, reprinted along with other speeches on the issue in Tam Dalyell MP, *Thatcher's Torpedo*, pp. 22–3. *See also* Tam Dalyell MP, *One Man's Falklands*, London, Cecil Woolf, 1982, pp. 81–3. A full but not wholly accurate account of the Peruvian initiative based on interviews in Lima by

Notes

Paul Foot ('How the Peace Was Torpedoed', *New Statesman*, 13 May 1983) reinforced the allegations made by Dalyell. A more recent summation of the arguments is found in the Belgrano Action Group, *op. cit.*

33. Costa Mendez, 'The Puruvian Mediation'.
34. *Ibid.*
35. Cited in Gavshon and Rice, *op. cit.*, p. 176.
36. *Ibid.*, p. 118.
37. Charlton, *op. cit.*, p. 175.
38. Henderson, *op. cit.*, pp. 56–7.
39. *Foreign Affairs Committee Report*, p. 65.
40. Transcript of conversation cited in *ibid.*, p. 175. Interestingly both agree that this is the first direct communication from Britain.
41. Brown, *op. cit.*, p. 141.
42. Colombo, *op. cit.*, pp. 16–17.
43. BBC Television, *Horizon: In the Wake of HMS Sheffield*, transmitted 17 March 1986. Colombo, *op. cit.*, pp. 18–19.
44. Brown, *op. cit.*, pp. 142–3.
45. Hastings and Jenkins, *op. cit.*, pp. 167–8. Another source suggests that this over-states the level of anxiety.
46. Young, *op. cit.*, p. 271.
47. Henderson, *op. cit.*, p. 27.
48. *Hansard*, 7 May 1982, vol. 23, col. 394.
49. Gavshon and Rice, *op. cit.*, pp. 123–5.

Chapter Eighteen

1. Gunnar Nielsson, *Mediation under Crisis Management Conditions: The United Nations Secretary General and the Falkland/Malvinas Islands Crisis, April 1–June 14, 1982*, Pittsburgh, Pa, Pew Program in Case Teaching and Writing in International Affairs, 1988.
2. James S. Sutterlin, 'The Good Offices of the Secretary-General', in Bendahame and McDonald, *op. cit.*, p. 84.
3. In Charlton, *op. cit.*, p. 209. He adds, 'There was no coordination between the efforts of the Peruvian government, the Peruvian president himself, and my own efforts.'
4. In UN jargon 'provisional measures' refer to measures without prejudice to the position of either party as to the ultimate resolution of the problem.
5. Henderson, *op. cit.*, p. 57.
6. House of Commons, *The Falklands Campaign*, pp. 224–5, 226.
7. Cardoso *et al.*, *op. cit.*, p. 255. (CBS, *Face the Nation*.)
8. Parsons, *op. cit.*, p. 173. In the Commons on 13 May, Pym noted: 'There have been some indications – actually the first since the crisis began – of genuine Argentine willingness to negotiate on some of the important points.' House of Commons, *The Falklands Campaign*, p. 242.
9. Bilton and Kosminsky, *op. cit.*, p. 37.
10. *Ibid.*, p. 231.
11. *Ibid.*, p. 241.

12. House of Commons, *The Falklands Campaign*, p. 278.

13. *See* Government of the United Kingdom, *Falkland Islands: Negotiations for a Peaceful Settlement*, London, 21 May 1982.

14. Costa Mendez, at Ros's request, had been prepared to travel to New York on 14 May to participate in the final stages of the negotiation. However, when news came of Parsons's return to London he stayed in Buenos Aires to review the situation with the Junta.

15. Charlton, *op. cit.*, p. 219.

16. Cardoso *et al.*, *op. cit.*, pp. 260–2.

17. *See* Bilton and Kosminsky, *op. cit.*, p. 40.

18. House of Commons, *The Falklands Campaign*, p. 304.

19. *Ibid.*, pp. 280–1.

20. *Ibid.*, p. 305.

21. Parsons, *op. cit.*, p. 174.

22. Sutterlin, *op. cit.*, pp. 85–6.

23. Charlton, *op. cit.*, p. 219: He observed 'From Argentina's point of view, perhaps they thought, while they were playing on the United Nations "board", "Why should we accept this idea when perhaps we can achieve a better outcome through the Peruvians?"'

Chapter Nineteen

1. Hastings and Jenkins, *op. cit.*, p. 125.

2. *Ibid.*, pp. 122–3.

3. This title has tended to become simplified to 3 Brigade and will be in the following narrative. It should, however, be noted that 3 Brigade proper is a regular infantry brigade of the British Army based in Germany.

4. Sunday Times Insight Team, *op. cit.*, p. 180.

5. Ethell and Price, *op. cit.*, p. 26.

6. Scheina, 'The Malvinas Campaign', p. 109.

7. *Aerospacio*, XLII, No. 42, September–October 1982, p. 26.

8. Middlebrook, *Operation Corporate*, pp. 127–8. It may also have been the case that the Harrier pilots would have been reluctant to venture too close to the area when Argentine air defences had been alerted by the Vulcan raid.

9. *See* Defence Committee, *Handling of Press and Public Information During the Falklands Conflict*, Vol. II, pp. 292–3, 411, 458, 462; *Aviation Week and Space Technology*, 26 July 1982. The lack of formal acknowledgement of this, even after the showing of film on Argentine television that could only have been brought back to the mainland by plane in late May, was one reason for a growing questioning of British claims in the media on the course of the war.

10. Hastings and Jenkins, *op. cit.*, p. 121; Sunday Times Insight Team, *op. cit.*, pp. 178–9.

11. Sunday Times Insight Team, *op. cit.*, pp. 179–80.

12. It had been identified by Southby-Tailyour as a likely possibility from the start, and Thompson had been convinced of its potential as early as 17 April. *Ibid.*, pp. 180–1.

13. Moore and Woodward, *op. cit.*, p. 27.

14. Thompson, *op. cit.*, p. 22.

15. Thompson, *op. cit.*, p. 32; Middlebrook confirms that two weeks had been the 'working assumption' (*Operation Corporate*, p. 126). However, this assumption did not last long, and 19–20 May was pencilled in early on as the most likely date. On the patrols *see The British Army in the Falklands*, p. 21. None of these patrols was discovered before the landings.

16. Thompson, *op. cit.*, p. 31.

17. *The Economist*, 3 March 1984.

18. Ethell and Price, *op. cit.*, p. 32.

19. Thompson, *op. cit.*, p. 19.

20. According to Middlebrook, some idea of the numbers and dispositions were provided by those islanders remaining reporting on their radios to HMS *Endurance*. *Operation Corporate*, pp. 76, 86. However, Hastings and Jenkins note: 'Contrary to popular mythology, the British gained no intelligence of value from the Falklands population during the weeks of the Argentine occupation.' *Op. cit.*, p. 177. Special forces were forbidden to contact islanders: they might get punished for collusion if caught, and they might gossip on the radio net and give away information to the Argentine forces. For the same reason any information sent out to *Endurance* would have been regarded by British intelligence as suspect.

21. Middlebrook, *The Fight for the 'Malvinas'*, p. 55.

22. Thus it was suggested by the Argentine Army after the war that the British had been forced to follow the indirect route via San Carlos after the failure of the direct approach near Stanley. 'El Ejercito Argentino en la Guerra de las Malvinas', *Armas y Geostrategica*, Vol. 2, No. 6, May 1983.

23. It was judged that *Canberra* would be safer in San Carlos Water than out of it and that it was needed close by because of the importance of the stores it was carrying and the need to leave movement on to the assault ships until the last possible moment because of the cramped conditions on board.

24. Thompson, *op. cit.*, p. 42.

25. *Ibid.*, p. 52.

26. Moore and Woodward, op. cit., p. 30.

27. Middlebrook, *The Fight for the 'Malvinas'*, p. 143.

Chapter Twenty

1. Henderson, *op. cit.*, p. 58.

2. *Ibid.*, p. 59. The Prime Minister observed publicly that in the circumstances 'magnanimity' was not part of her vocabulary.

3. Edwards, *op. cit.*, pp. 304–11.

4. Sutterlin, *op. cit.*, p. 86.

5. Parsons, *op. cit.*, p. 176.

6. Cardoso *et al.*, *op. cit.*, p. 266. *Newsweek* quoted the contents of the telephone row between the UN Ambassador and the Secretary of State, in which Mrs Kirkpatrick described the State Department under Haig as being 'Brits in American clothes', and suggested that it could simply allow 'the British Foreign Office to make our policy'. For his part Mr Haig remarked that Mrs Kirkpatrick was 'mentally and emotionally incapable of thinking clear on this issue because of her close links with the Latins'.

7. Hastings and Jenkins, *op. cit.*, p. 258.
8. Henderson, *op. cit.*, p. 59.
9. *Ibid.*
10. Parsons, *op. cit.*, p. 176.
11. Hastings and Jenkins, *op. cit.*, p. 259.
12. Cardoso *et al.*, *op. cit.*, pp. 302–3.

Chapter Twenty-One

1. Büsser, *op. cit.*, chs X and XI, pp. 244–331.
2. Cardoso *et al.*, *op. cit.*, p. 285.
3. Middlebrook, *The Fight for the 'Malvinas'*, p. 166.
4. *Ibid.*, p. 286.
5. Ethell and Price, *op. cit.*, p. 135. As early as 14 May there had been a briefing in London that a ship (HMS *Glasgow*) had been hit by a bomb which passed right through without exploding and there had been some speculation as to why this had happened. That evening the BBC reported: 'Following the Argentine air attacks on 21 May two unexploded bombs on one warship have been successfully defused and a further one dealt with on another warship. Repairs are being carried out on the other warships, which sustained minor damage in the raid.' The next day American reporters were briefed on possible explanations for the failure of the bombs to explode, including the lack of correct fuses. By 23 May the Chiefs of Staff were anxious that no more publicity should be given to this issue. However, the initial remarks were now encouraging speculation in the press. This was further fuelled by reports from Argentina indicating that its pilots were fully aware of the problem. There was no improvement in the proportion of detonations. *Ibid.*, p. 135; Defence Committee, *The Handling of Press and Public Information During the Falklands Conflict*, Vol. II, pp. 420–3.
6. Ethell and Price, *op. cit.*, p. 144.
7. BBC Television, *Horizon: In the Wake of HMS Sheffield*.
8. Colombo, *op. cit.*, pp. 19–20.
9. Murguizur argues that Argentine intelligence had discovered the contents of the *Atlantic Conveyor* and designed the attack accordingly. Juan Carlos Murguizur, 'The South Atlantic Conflict: An Argentinian Point of View', *International Defence Review*, 2/1983, p. 140. Other sources suggest that it was not known precisely what was being attacked.
10. For another account of this communication *see* Cardoso *et al.*, *op. cit.*, p. 287.
11. 'El Ejercito Argentino en la Guerra de Las Malvinas'.
12. *Ibid.*; Cardoso *et al.*, *op. cit.*, p. 288.
13. Thompson, *op. cit.*, pp. 73–4.
14. Harris, p. 117.
15. Hastings and Jenkins, *op. cit.*, pp. 254–5.
16. Nick Vaux, *March to the South Atlantic*, London, Buchan & Enright, 1986, p. 97.
17. *Ibid.*
18. Thompson, *op. cit.*, pp. 77–8.
19. *Ibid.*, p. 80.
20. Quoted in Mercer *et al.*, *op. cit.*, p. 58. The statement refers to the need to keep backbench MPs briefed.

21. Lord Whitelaw in Bilton and Kosminsky, *op. cit.*, p. 301. Also broadcast in *The Falklands War – The Untold Story*, Yorkshire Television, transmitted 2 April 1987.

22. Thompson, *op. cit.*, p. 81.

23. Middlebrook, *Operation Corporate*, pp. 252–3.

24. Thompson, *op. cit.*, p. 81. This contradicts Middlebrook's claim that the 105mm guns took the British forces by surprise (*Operation Corporate*, p. 255). Captured equipment included four 105mm pack howitzers, two 35mm anti-aircraft guns, six 120mm mortars and two Pucara aircraft. *See also* Fox, *op. cit.*, pp. 158, 161, who suggests that the estimate had not been updated.

25. Fox claims that a message from General Menendez in Stanley to General Galtieri in Buenos Aires had been intercepted 'earlier', in which Menendez had provided an appreciation of his military position and the disposition of the main Argentine forces, including the statement that his second-strongest force was in Goose Green, apparently indicating that this was already in the region of 1,500. According to Fox: 'General Menendez's appreciation of his position was circulated amongst Intelligence Officers in London, but security clearance was not given for it to be transmitted to either Brigade Commander with the Task Force.' Fox, *op. cit.*, pp. 205–6. Apart from the fact that the figure of 1,500 would have been incorrect, there seems little evidence to support this claim. The intelligence group on *Fearless* was receiving all raw, unsanitized information from all sources by this time, having complained earlier about getting sanitized versions prepared for Whitehall briefing purposes and possibly excluding critical tactical intelligence.

26. Adams, *op. cit.*, pp. 119–21.

27. Cardoso *et al.*, *op. cit.*, p. 286.

28. 'El Ejercito Argentino en la Guerra de Las Malvinas'.

29. Middlebrook, *The Fight for the 'Malvinas'*, p. 180.

30. 'El Ejercito Argentino en la Guerra de Las Malvinas'.

31. *La Nacion*, 26 September 1988.

32. The battle is described in detail in Fox, *op. cit.*, and John Frost, *2 Para Falklands: The Battalion at War*, London, Sphere Books, 1983.

33. It has been suggested that one of the reasons why Colonel Jones put himself at risk is that without good intelligence it was necessary to command from the front so as to be able to react to the disposition and strength of the enemy as discovered in battle. *See* Patrick Bishop and John Witherow, *The Winter War*, London, Quartet, 1982, p. 92. However, in these sorts of operations this was the natural place for the commanding officer to be.

34. Quoted in Ethell and Price, *op. cit.*, p. 164.

35. Hastings and Jenkins, *op. cit.*, pp. 248–9.

36. Middlebrook, *The Fight for the 'Malvinas'*, p. 192.

37. 'Informe Oficial Ejercito Argentino', tomo I, pp. 89–90.

38. Middlebrook, *The Fight for the 'Malvinas'*, p. 193.

39. The full text is in Frost, *op. cit.*, pp. 170–1.

40. Sunday Times Insight Team, *op. cit.*, pp. 218–30.

41. 'Informe Oficial Ejercito Argentino', tomo I, p. 91, mentions a surrender document but none appears to have been drawn up.

42. Defence Committee, *The Handling of Press and Public Information During the Falklands Conflict*, Vol. II, p. 424–7.

43. Whitelaw in Bilton and Kosminsky, *op. cit.*, p. 301.

Notes

Chapter Twenty-Two

1. 'Informe Oficial del Ejercito Argentino', tomo I, pp. 97–8.
2. Colombo, *op. cit.*, pp. 20–1.
3. Ethell and Price, *op. cit.*, pp. 169–70.
4. Groves, *op. cit.*, pp. 378–9.
5. Thompson, *op. cit.*, p.38.
6. According to Fox:

> Units moving up to the last battles around Stanley had frequently to use intelligence photographs weeks old ... I remember the Intelligence Officer of 45 Commando receiving his latest batch of pictures of the Argentinians on the Mount Kent and Two Sisters features the day after Two Sisters had been taken by Royal Marines.

Op. cit., p. 314.
7. Fox reports the Intelligence Officer of 45 Commando on 12 June finding a bundle of maps and notes in a prisoner's briefcase. 'His maps had all the defensive fire zones marked for the Argentine artillery and on one piece of greased paper he had the positions of all major infantry units marked in black crayon.' *Ibid.*, p. 257.
8. For some fanciful stories *see* D. Kon, *Los Chicos de la Guerra*, Buenos Aires, Editorial Galerina, 1982.
9. Hastings and Jenkins, *op. cit.*, pp. 268–9.
10. Middlebrook, *Operation Corporate*, p. 295, claims that Wilson persuaded Moore of this. This is not the case.
11. A number of private sources have been used for this account. However, *see* Brown, *op. cit.*, pp. 293–306; Hastings and Jenkins, *op. cit.*, pp. 276–7; and Jenny Rathbone, 'A Clear Day and a Sitting Target', *The Times*, 8 June 1983.
12. For a description of these heated exchanges *see* the interview with Ewan South-Tailyour, the landing-craft officer, in Bilton and Kosminsky, *op. cit.*, pp. 156–9.
13. Adams, *op. cit.*, p. 131.
14. 'Informe Oficial del Ejercito Argentino', tomo I, pp. 100–1. Menendez's overall attitude at this point is indicated by his suggestion on 8 June to CEOPECON at Comodoro Rivadavia that a communication line should be opened with the enemy at once. This message was answered on 9 June through the Joint Military Communiqué No. 184 of the CEOPECON informing Menendez that there was a channel via the hospital ships of both sides.
15. Interview with Juan Bautista Jofre, *Clarin*.
16. Cardoso *et al.*, *op. cit.*, p. 290.
17. Turolo, *op. cit.*, pp. 256–8.
18. Büsser, *op. cit.*, p. 310.
19. Büsser notes that by a curious coincidence on 9 June, the same day of this exposition, news of the capture of the *Monsoonen* hit the press in Argentina.
20. Cardoso *et al.* report that this element had been prepared by Admiral Otero, who did consider it feasible. *Op. cit.*, p. 291.
21. Quoted in Middlebrook, *The Fight for the 'Malvinas'*, p. 219.
22. Büsser, *op. cit.*, pp. 309–10.
23. *La Nacion*, 26 August 1988.
24. Middlebrook, *The Fight for the 'Malvinas'*, p. 217.

25. As late as 13 June Galtieri was still enjoining Menendez to 'watch out for them coming from the south' without being contradicted. Cardoso *et al.*, *op. cit.*, p. 292.
26. Hastings and Jenkins, *op. cit.*, pp. 290–1.
27. *See* Annex 49 of Volume II of the Argentine Army official report.
28. Middlebrook, *The Fight for the 'Malvinas'*, p. 244.
29. Cardoso *et al.*, *op. cit.*, p. 293.
30. 'El BIM 5 en las Malvinas', *Boletin Del Centro Naval*, No. 735, quoted by Busser, *op. cit.*, pp. 318–19.

Chapter Twenty-Three

1. *See* Moro, *op. cit.*, pp. 500–4, for details of the capitulation.
2. This account is taken from H. M. Rose, 'Towards an Ending of the Falklands War', *Conflict*, Vol. 7, No. 1, 1987. *See also* Hastings and Jenkins, *op. cit.*, pp. 288, 308–10.
3. Busser, *op. cit.*, pp. 319–21.
4. There were considerable suspicions within Buenos Aires at this time of an indirect US intervention in the internal affairs of the country. *Ibid.*, pp. 327–30.

BIBLIOGRAPHY

Official Documents

(i) Argentina

Antarctic Joint Command for Joint Chiefs of Staff, Argentina, *Final Report of the Summer Antarctic Campaign 81/82*

'El Ejercito Argentino en la Guerra de Las Malvinas', *Armas y Geostrategia*, Vol. 2, No. 6, May 1983

'Informe Final de la Comision Rattenbach (II parte)', *Siete Dias*, Buenos Aires, XV, No. 859, 30 November to 12 December 1983

Testimony by Admiral Anaya, Dr Costa Mendez and General Galtieri to the Rattenbach Commission, *Gente*, Buenos Aires, 8 December 1983.

Informe Oficial Ejercito Argentino, *Conflicto Malvinas*, 1983, Vol. 11

Operacion Rosario (Argentine Navy's account of the military intervention on 2 April 1982), preface by Admiral Carlos Busser, Buenos Aires, 1984, Editorial Atlantida

Admiral Anaya and General Galtieri, *La Nueva Provincia*, Bahia Blanca, 28 November 1985 (Personal Discharge of Accusations by the Armed Forces Supreme Council)

'Caso Malvinas, Acusacion, Defensa y Alegato Personal', *Boletin Del Centro Naval*, Supplement 751–D–5, Vol. 105, year 106, Buenos Aires, 1987

(ii) United Kingdom

House of Commons, *The Falklands Campaign: A Digest of Debates in the House of Commons 2 April to 15 June 1982*, London, HMSO, 1982

House of Commons, First Report of the Defence Committee, Session 1982–3, *Handling of Press and Public Information During the Falklands Conflict*, two volumes, London, HMSO, 1982

Government of the United Kingdom, *Falkland Islands: Negotiations for a Peaceful Settlement*, London, 21 May 1982

Supplement to the *London Gazette*, London, HMSO, 8 October 1982

Secretary of State for Defence, *The Falklands Campaign: The Lessons*, Cmnd 8758, London, HMSO, 1982

The British Army in the Falklands, London, HMSO, 1982

House of Commons, *Minutes of the Proceedings of the Foreign Affairs Committee, Session 1982–3* (including 'Chairman's Draft Report on a Policy for the Falkland Islands'), London, HMSO, 11 May 1983

Falkland Islands Review: Report of a Committee of Privy Counsellors, Chairman, The Rt Hon. The Lord Franks, Cmnd 8787, London, HMSO, 1983

Prime Minister's letter to George Foulkes MP, reproduced in *Hansard*, 22 October 1984, cols 469–72

House of Commons, Third Report of the Foreign Affairs Committee, Session 1984–5, *Events of the Weekend of 1st and 2nd May 1982*, London, HMSO, 1985

House of Commons, Fourth Report from the Defence Committee, Session 1986–7, *Implementing the Lessons of the Falklands Campaign*, two volumes, London, HMSO, 1987

(iii) United States

Thomas O. Enders, Assistant Secretary of State for Inter-American Affairs: *Prepared Statement before the Subcommittee on Inter-American Affairs, US House of Representatives*, Washington DC, 5 August 1982

US Department of the Navy, *Lessons of the Falklands*, February 1983

Bibliography

Books

Adams, Valerie, *The Media and the Falklands Campaign*, London, Macmillan, 1986

Aguiar, Cervo, Machinandiarena, Balza and Dalton, *Operacions Terrestres en Las Islas Malvinas*, Buenos Aires, Circulo Militar, 1985

The Andean Report, Lima, Peru, September 1980

Armitage, Michael and Mason, Tony, *Air Power in the Nuclear Age*, London, Macmillan, 1984

Arthur, Max, *Above All, Courage. The Falklands Front Line: First Hand Accounts*, London, Sidgwick & Jackson, 1985

Barcia Trelles, Camilo, *El Problema de las Islas Malvinas*, Madrid, Editora Nacional, 1968

Beck, Peter, *The Falkland Islands as an International Problem*, London, Routledge, 1988

The Belgrano Action Group, *The Unnecessary War*, Nottingham, Spokesman Books, 1988

Bilton, Michael and Kosminsky, Peter, *Speaking Out: Untold Stories from the Falklands War*, London, André Deutsch, 1989

Bishop, Patrick and Witherow, John, *The Winter War*, London, Quartet, 1982

Boyson, V. F., *The Falkland Islands*, Oxford, Clarendon Press, 1924

Brown, David, *The Royal Navy and the Falklands War*, London, Leo Cooper, 1987

Burden, Rodney, Draper, Michael, Rough, Douglas, Smith, Colin, Wilton, David, *Falklands: The Air War*, London, Arms and Armour Press, 1986

Burns, Jimmy, *The Land That Lost Its Heroes: The Falklands, The Post-War and Alfonsin*, London, Bloomsbury Publishing, 1987

Burns, Robert Andrews, *Diplomacy, War, and Parliamentary Democracy: Further Lessons from the Falklands or Advice from Academe*, New York, University Press of America, 1985

Büsser, Carlos, *Malvinas: La Guerra Inconclusa*, Buenos Aires, Ediciones Fernandez Reguera, 1987

Caillet-Bois, Ricardo, *Una Tierra Argentina: Las Islas Malvinas*, Buenos Aires, Peuser, 1948

Bibliography

Calvert, Peter, *The Falklands Crisis: The Rights and the Wrongs*, London, Frances Pinter, 1982

Cardoso, Oscar, Kirschbaum, Ricardo and van der Kooy, Eduardo, *Falkands: The Secret Plot*, London, Preston Editions, 1983

Carrington, Lord (Peter), *Reflect on Things Past: The Memoirs of Lord Carrington*, London, Collins, 1988

Cawkell, M. B. R., Malling, D. H. and Cawkell, E. M., *The Falkland Islands*, London, St Martin's Press, 1960

Ceron, S., *Malvinas: Gesta Heroica o Derrota Vergonzoza*, Buenos Aires, Sudamericana, 1985

Charlton, Michael, *The Little Platoon*, London, Blackwell, 1989

Child, J., *Geopolitics and Conflict in South America: Quarrels among Neighbours*, New York, Praeger, 1985

Child, J., *Antarctica and South American Geopolitics: Frozen Lebensraum*, Washington DC, Praeger, 1987

Coll, Albert R. and Arend, Anthony C. (eds), *The Falklands War: Lessons for Strategy, Diplomacy and International Law*, Boston, Allen & Unwin, 1985

Curteis, Ian, *The Falklands Play*, London, Hutchinson, 1987

Dalyell MP, Tam, *One Man's Falklands*, London, Cecil Woolf, 1982

Dalyell MP, Tam, *Thatcher's Torpedo: The Sinking of the 'Belgrano'*, London, Cecil Woolf, 1983

Dillon, G. M., *The Falklands, Politics and War*, London, Macmillan, 1989

Einaudi, L. R., *Beyond Cuba: Latin America Takes Charge of Its Future*, New York, 1974

Ethell, Jeffrey and Price, Alfred, *Air War: South Atlantic*, London, Sidgwick & Jackson, 1983

Fox, Robert, *Eyewitness Falklands*, London, Methuen, 1982

Fraga, Jorge A., *La Argentina y el Atlantico Sur*, Buenos Aires, Pleamar, 1983

Freedman, Lawrence, *Britain and the Falklands War*, London, Blackwell, 1988

Frost, John, *2 Para Falklands: The Battalion at War*, London, Sphere Books, 1983

Gamba, Virginia, *El Peon de la Reina*, Buenos Aires, Editorial Sudamericana, 1984

Bibliography

Gamba, Virginia, *The Falklands/Malvinas War: A Model for North–South Crisis Prevention*, Boston, Allen & Unwin, 1987

Gavshon, Arthur and Rice, Desmond, *The Sinking of the Belgrano*, London, Secker & Warburg, 1984

Gil Munilla, Octavio, *El conflicto anglo espanol de 1770*, Sevilla, Escuela de Estudio Hispano-Americanos, 1948

Glasgow University Media Group, *War and Peace News*, Milton Keynes, Open University Press, 1985

Goebel, Julius, with introductory chapter by J. C. J. Metford, *The Struggle for the Falklands*, New Haven, Yale University Press, 1982 edition; first edition, 1927

Groussac, Paul, *Las Islas Malvinas*, Buenos Aires, Editorial del Congreso, 1936

Grove, Eric, *Vanguard to Trident: British Naval Policy Since World War Two*, London, Bodley Head, 1987

Gustafson, Lowell S., *The Sovereignty Dispute over the Falkland (Malvinas) Islands*, New York, Oxford University Press, 1988

Haig, Alexander, *Caveat*, London, Weidenfeld & Nicolson, 1984

Harris, Robert, *Gotcha: The Media, the Government and the Falklands Crisis*, London, Faber, 1983

Hastings, Max and Jenkins, Simon, *The Battle for the Falklands*, London, Michael Joseph, 1983

Hidalgo Nieto, Manuel, *La cuestion de las Malvinas, contribucion al estudio de la relacion hispano inglesa en el siglo XVIII*, Madrid, Instituto Gonzalo Fernandez de Ouiedo, 1947

Jolly, Rick, *The Red and Green Life Machine: A Diary of the Falklands Field Hospital*, London, Century Publishing, 1983

Kaufman, Chaim, *U.S. Mediation in the Falklands/Malvinas Crisis: Shuttle Diplomacy in the 1980s*, Pittsburgh, Pa, Pew Program in Case Teaching and Writing in International Affairs, 1988

Kon, D., *Los Chicos de la Guerra*, Buenos Aires, Editorial Galerina, 1982

Lee, Christopher, *War in Space*, London, Hamish Hamilton, 1986

McManners, Hugh, *Falklands Commando*, London, William Kimber, 1984

Mercer, Derrick, Mungham, Geoff and Williams, Kevin, *The Fog of War*, London, Heinemann, 1987

Bibliography

Middlebrook, Martin, *Operation Corporate: The Story of the Falklands War 1982*, London, Viking, 1985

Middlebrook, Martin, *The Fight for the 'Malvinas': The Argentine Forces in the Falklands War*, London, Viking, 1989

Moro, Comodoro R. O., *Historia Del Conflicto Del Atlantico Sur: La Guerra Inaudita*, Buenos Aires, Escuela superior de guerra aerea de la fuerza aerea Argentine, 1985

Morris, Michael and Millan, V. (eds), *Controlling Latin American Conflicts*, Boulder, Colo, Westview, 1983

Nielsson, Gunnar, *Mediation under Crisis Management Conditions: The United Nations Secretary General and the Falkland/Malvinas Islands Crisis, April 1 – June 14, 1982*, Pittsburgh, Pa, Pew Program in Case Teaching and Writing in International Affairs, 1988

Norton-Taylor, Richard, *The Ponting Affair*, London, Cecil Woolf, 1985

Perkins, Roger, *Operation Paraquat: The Battle for South Georgia*, Chippenham, Picton Publishing, 1986

Perl, Ralph (ed.), *The Falkland Islands Dispute in International Law and Politics: A Documentary Sourcebook*, London, Oceana Publications, 1983

Ponting, Clive, *The Right to Know: The Inside Story of the Belgrano Affair*, London, Sphere Books, 1985

Richelson, Jeffrey and Ball, Desmond, *The Ties That Bind: Intelligence Cooperation Between the UKUSA Countries*, London, Allen & Unwin, 1986

Ruiz Guinazu, Enrique, *Proas de Espana en el Mar Magallanico*, Buenos Aires, Peuser, 1947

Simon, S. W., *The Military and Security in the Third World: Domestic and International Impacts*, Boulder, Colo, Westview, 1978

Smith, John, *74 Days: An Islander's Diary of the Falklands Occupation*, London, Century Publishing, 1984

Speed, Keith, *Sea Change: The Battle for the Falklands and the Future of Britain's Navy*, Ashgrove, Bath, 1982

Stewart, Norma Kinzer, *South Atlantic Conflict of 1982: A Case Study in Military Cohesion*, Research Report 1469, Washington DC, US Army, Research Institute for the Behavioral and Social Sciences, April 1988

Strange, Ian C., *The Falkland Islands*, Harisburg, Pa, 1972

Bibliography

The Sunday Times Insight Team, *The Falklands War: The Full Story*, London, Sphere Books, 1982

Thompson, Julian, *No Picnic: 3 Commando Brigade in the South Atlantic: 1982*, London, Leo Cooper for Secker & Warburg, 1985

Tinker, David, *A Message from the Falklands*, London, Junction Books, 1982

Treverton, Gregory and Lippincott, Don, *Falklands/Malvinas*, Pittsburgh, Pa, Pew Program in Case Teaching and Writing in International Affairs, 1988

Turolo, Carlos H., *Malvinas: Testimonio de su Gobernador*, Buenos Aires, Sudamericana, 1983

Van Sant Hall, Marshall, *Argentine Policy in the Falklands War: The Political Results*, Newport, Rhode Island, US Navy War College, 25 June 1983

Vaux, Nick, *March to the South Atlantic*, London, Buchan & Enright, 1986

Young, Hugo, *One of Us*, London, Macmillan, 1989

Zorraquin Becu, Ricardo, *Inglaterra Prometiro Abandonar las Islas: Estudio Historico-Juridico del Conflicto Anglo-Espanol*, Buenos Aires, Libreria Editorial Platero, 1975

Articles

'America's Falklands War', *The Economist*, 3 March 1984

Anaya, Jorge Isaac, 'La Crisis Argentino-Britanica en 1982', *La Nueva Provincia*, Bahia Blanca, 8 September 1988

Bartson, R. P. and Birnie, P. W., 'The Falkland Islands/Islas Malvinas Conflict: A Question of Zones', *Marine Policy*, January 1983

Beck, Peter, 'Cooperative Confrontation in the Falkland Islands Dispute: The Anglo-Argentine Search for a Way Forward 1968–81', *Journal of Interamerican Studies and World Affairs*, Vol. 24, No. 1, February 1982

Beck, Peter, 'The Anglo-Argentine Dispute Over Title to the Falkland Islands: Changing British Perceptions on Sovereignty Since 1910', *Millennium: Journal of International Studies*, Vol. 12, No. 1, Spring 1983

Bologna, Alfredo Bruno, 'Argentinian Claims to the Malvinas Under

International Law', *Millennium: Journal of International Studies*, Vol. 12, No. 1, Spring 1983

Calvert, Peter, 'Latin America and the United States During and After the Falklands Crisis', *Millennium: Journal of International Studies*, Vol. 12, No. 1, Spring 1983

Campbell, Duncan, 'How We Spy on Argentina', *New Statesman*, 30 April 1983

Campbell, Duncan, 'The Belgrano Cover-Up', *New Statesman*, 31 August 1984

Campbell, Duncan, 'Too Few Bombs to Go Round', *New Statesman*, 29 November 1985

Campbell, Duncan and Rentoul, John, 'All-Out War', *New Statesman*, 24 August 1984

Claude Jr, Inis L., 'UN Efforts at a Settlement', in Albert R. Coll and Anthony C. Arend (eds), *The Falklands War: Lessons for Strategy, Diplomacy and International Law*, Boston, Allen & Unwin, 1985

Colombo, Jorge Luis, '"Super-Etendard" Naval Aircraft Operations During the Malvinas War', *Naval War College Review*, May–June 1984

Costa Mendez, Nicanor, 'La situacion al 2 de abril de 1982', *La Nacion*, Buenos Aires, 1 September 1983

Costa Mendez, Nicanor, 'The Peruvian Mediation', *La Nueva Provincia*, 2 April 1985

Costa Mendez, Nicanor, 'El papel de los EEUU en la fase inicial del conflicto del Atlantico Sur', Part I, *Revista Argentina de Estudios Estrategicos*, No. 6, October–December 1985

Costa Mendez, Nicanor, 'El papel de los EEUU en le fase inicial del conflicto del Atlantico Sur', Part II, *Revista Argentina de Estudios Estrategicos*, No. 8, October–December 1986

Craig, Christopher, 'Fighting by the Rules', *Naval War College Review*, May–June 1984

De Martini, S., 'Ultimo acto de un drama', *La Prensa*, Buenos Aires, 20 October 1988

Edwards, Geoffrey, 'Europe and the Falkland Islands Crisis of 1982', *Journal of Common Market Studies*, Vol. XXII, No. 4, June 1984

Foot, Paul, 'How the Peace Was Torpedoed', *New Statesman*, 13 May 1983

Freedman, Lawrence, 'Intelligence Operations in the Falklands', *Intelligence and National Security*, Vol. 1, No. 3, September 1986

Gompert, David, 'American Diplomacy and the Haig Mission', in Alberto R. Coll and Anthony C. Arend (eds), *The Falklands War: Lessons for Strategy, Diplomacy and International Law*, London, Allen & Unwin, 1985

Gompert, David, 'US Shuttle Mediation', in Diane B. Bendahame and John W. McDonald Jr (eds), *Perspectives on Negotiation: Four Case Studies and Interpretations*, Washington DC, Center for the Study of Foreign Affairs, Foreign Service Institute, US Department of State, 1986

Goyret, J. T., 'El Ejercito argentino en la guerra de las Malvinas', *Armas y Geoestrategia*, Buenos Aires, May 1983, Vol. 2, No. 6

Greig, Peter, 'Revelations', *Granta*, No. 15, Spring 1985

Headland, Robert, 'Hostilities in the Falkland Islands Dependencies March–June 1982', *Polar Record*, 21(135): 549–58, 1983

Henderson, Sir Nicholas, 'America and the Falklands', *The Economist*, 12 November 1983

Hope, Adrian, 'Sovereignty and Decolonization of the Falklands Islands', *Boston Comparative Law Review*, December 1983

Hopple, G. W., 'Intelligence and Warning: Implications and Lessons of the Falklands Islands War', *World Politics*, 1984

Jasani, Bhupendra, 'The Military Uses of Outer Space', *SIPRI Yearbook 1983*, London, Taylor & Francis, 1983

Jenkins, Simon, 'Britain's Pearl Harbor', *Sunday Times*, 22 March 1987

Jenkins, Simon, 'Britain's Pearl Harbor: Part II', *Sunday Times*, 29 March 1987

Kirkpatrick, Jeane, 'Dictatorship and Double Standards', *Commentary*, November 1979

Lebow, Richard Ned, 'Miscalculation in the South Atlantic: The Origins of the Falkland War', *Journal of Strategic Studies*, Vol. 6, No. 1, March 1983

Makin, Guillermo, 'The Military in Argentine Politics, 1880–1982', *Millennium: Journal of International Studies*, Vol. 12, No. 1, Spring 1983

Bibliography

Moneta, Carlos, 'The Malvinas Conflict: Analyzing the Argentine Military Regime's Decision Making Process', in Munoz and Tulchin (eds), *Latin American Nations in World Politics*, Boulder, Colo, Westview, 1984

Moore, Major-General Sir Jeremy and Rear Admiral Sir John Woodward, 'The Falklands Experience', *Journal of the Royal United Services Institute for Defence Studies*, March 1983

Murguizur, Juan Carlos, 'The South Atlantic Conflict: An Argentinian Point of View', *International Defence Review*, 2/1983

Myhre, Jeffrey D., 'Title to the Falklands–Malvinas under International Law', *Millennium: Journal of International Studies*, Vol. 12, No. 1, Spring 1983

Parsons, Sir Anthony, 'The Falklands Crisis in the United Nations, 31 March–14 June 1982', *International Affairs*, Vol. 59, No. 2, Spring 1983

Perera, Srilal, 'The Oas and the Inter-American System: History, Law and Diplomacy', in Albert R. Coll and Anthony C. Arend (eds), *The Falklands War: Lessons for Strategy, Diplomacy and International Law*, Boston, Allen & Unwin, 1985

Quester, George, 'The Nuclear Implications of the South Atlantic War', in R. B. Byers (ed.), *The Denuclearization of the Oceans*, London, Croom Helm, 1986

Rathbone, Jenny, 'A Clear Day and a Sitting Target', *The Times*, 8 June 1983

Rose, H. M., 'Towards an Ending of the Falklands War', *Conflict*, Vol. 7, No. 1, 1987

Scheina, Robert, 'The Malvinas Campaign', *Proceedings of the US Naval Institute: Naval Review*, 1983

Scheina, Robert, 'Where Were Those Argentine Subs?', *Proceedings of the US Naval Institute: Naval Review*, March 1984

Socarras, Michael P., 'The Argentine Invasion of the Falklands and International Norms of Signalling', *Yale Journal of International Law*, Vol. 10:356, 1985

Sopena, German, 'Historia de una mediacion frustrada', *Siete Dias*, 26 January 1983

Spence, J. E., 'The UN and the Falklands Crisis', in G. R. Berridge and A. Jenning (eds), *Diplomacy at the UN*, London, Macmillan, 1984

Sutterlin, James S., 'The Good Offices of the Secretary-General', in Diane B. Bendahame and John W. McDonald Jr (eds), *Perspectives on Negotiation: Four Case Studies and Interpretations*, Washington DC, Center for the Study of Foreign Affairs, Foreign Service Institute, US Department of State, 1986

Walker, Martin, 'The Give-Away Years', *Guardian*, 19 June 1982

Williams, Phil, 'Miscalculation, Crisis Management and the Falklands Conflict', *The World Today*, 39, 1983

Windsor, Philip, 'Diplomatic Dimensions of the Falklands Crisis', *Millennium: Journal of International Studies*, Vol. 12, No. 1, Spring 1983

Television Documentaries

BBC Television, *Panorama* transcript, transmitted 16 April 1984

BBC Television, *Horizon: In the Wake of HMS Sheffield*, transmitted 17 March 1986

BBC Television, *An Ocean Apart: Programme Seven, Turning Up the Volume*, transmitted 1 June 1988

Granada Television, *World in Action*, transmitted 10 June 1985

Yorkshire Television, *The Falklands War – The Untold Story*, transmitted 2 April 1987

Unpublished Material

Gamba, Virginia, 'The Pacific Issue in Bolivian, Latin American and World Politics', MSc thesis 1981, UC Wales, Aberystwyth

Etchepareborda, Robert, 'La Cuestion Malvinas en Perspectiva Historica', paper prepared for seminar on 'The Use of Force in the Solution of International Controversies: The Conflict of the Malvinas Islands', Turin, May 1983

INDEX

Index

Index

Index

Inman, Robert, 162
Intelligence Corps, 130
Interamerican Juridical Committee, 9
Inter-American Treaty of Reciprocal Aid
 (IATRA), 32, 158, 225–9, 232, *see also*
 Rio Treaty
Intrepid, HMS, 127, 129, 338–9, 386
Invincible, HMS, 127, 129–30, 143, 379
Iran, 160, 196n
Ireland, 137, 140, 293, 300, 347–8, 352,
 355
Irrangu Station, HMNZS, 86
Isla de los Estados, 270, 341
Israel, 89, 92, 138, 240
Italy, 150, 152, 347–8

Japan, 137, 140, 300, 352, 355
Jenkins, Simon, 52, 183
Jofre, Brigadier General Oscar, 145, 335,
 402
John Biscoe, RSS, 74, 110
Joint Intelligence Committee, 18, 84n, 85
Jones, Colonel 'H', 366, 369, 370, 372–3
Jordan, 137–8, 140, 355
Junta:
  attitude to UN negotiations, 313
  attitude to US negotiations, 192–5
  British landing report, 357
  cease-fire options, 349, 356
  comes to power, 3–4, 104
  Communications Agreement, 31
  conduct of Falklands campaign, 414–15
  Costa Mendez' approach, 24, 28
  decision-making process, 214, 239
  emissary proposal, 93
  Falklands defence plans, 337–8
  Falklands invasion, 116
  Falklands surrender, 407, 411
  Haig meeting, 201–3
  Lombardo instructions, 109
  military option, 12–13, 23–4, 62, 98,
   104–6
  negotiations, 10–11, 23–4, 70–1, 87,
   104
  perception of British position, 69–71,
   73–4, 142
  Peruvian plan, 281

popular standing, 62
Project Alpha, 44–6
Rio Treaty, 225–6
South Georgia crisis, 62, 64, 67–71,
 73–4, 82–3, 219
task force information, 76–8
UN mediation, 286
US relations, 344, 401

Kamanda Wa Kamanda, Ambassador,
 135
KC-130 aircraft, 223, 224
Keeble, Major Chris, 374–6
Kirkpatrick, Jeane:
  Latin American sympathies, 155, 157,
   159–62, 168, 311
  Perez de Cuellar rumour, 307n
  Reagan's offer of assistance, 97
  Ros and Roca meeting, 311
  South Georgia crisis, 134–5
  UN cease-fire resolution, 350–2,
   355–6
Kissinger, Henry, 160, 161, 162, 238, 240

LADE (Argentine Air Force airline), 63
Lami Dozo, General Basilio:
  British landing report, 357
  Falklands defence, 402
  Haig discussions, 178, 201
  mediation initiative, 351–2
  new Junta, 3
  Peruvian initiative, 286n
LANDSAT, 132
Leach, Admiral Sir Henry, 123
Learjet aircraft, 361
Legislative Council, *see* Falkland Islands
Lehman, John, 190
Leith, South Georgia:
  Argentine marine landing, 64, 73
  Argentine presence, 72–3, 221
  Caiman trip, 45
  Davidoff's landings, 43, 47–8, 49,
   54–61, 63, 67
  whaling station scrap, 40
Lewin, Admiral Sir Terence:
  Argentine surrender reports, 410
  Belgrano, 262, 263, 265–7

Index

Index

Index